W9-BCC-538

DATE DUE

DEC 22 99	
NOV 23 2004	

PRINTED IN U.S.A.

401.9
L269

Language and Learning

Language and Learning
The Debate between Jean Piaget and Noam Chomsky

Edited by
MASSIMO PIATTELLI-PALMARINI

HARVARD UNIVERSITY PRESS
Cambridge, Massachusetts
1980

This book is published by arrangement with Editions du Seuil, publishers of the French edition, *Théories du langage, théories de l'apprentissage* © Editions du Seuil, 1979

Copyright © 1980 by the President and Fellows of Harvard College and Routledge & Kegan Paul Ltd
Printed in the United States of America

LIBRARY OF CONGRESS CATALOGING IN PUBLICATION DATA

Main entry under title:

Language and learning.

Translation of Théories du langage/théories de l'apprentissage.
Based on the transcription of the debate held in Oct. 1975 at Abbaye de Royaumont near Paris; also includes 2 papers written for the participants and distributed before the colloquium.

Includes index.
1. Psycholinguistics—Congresses.   2. Cognition—Congresses.
3. Piaget, Jean, 1896–   —Congresses.   4. Chomsky, Noam—
Congresses.   I. Piaget, Jean, 1896–   II. Chomsky, Noam.   III.
Piattelli-Palmarini, Massimo.
P37.L34   401′.9   80–10588
ISBN 0–674–50940–4

CONTRIBUTORS

SCOTT ATRAN	*Department of Anthropology, Columbia University, New York*
GREGORY BATESON	*Kresge College, University of California, Santa Cruz*
NORBERT BISCHOF	*Institute of Psychology, University of Zurich*
GUY CELLÉRIER	*International Center for Genetic Epistemology, University of Geneva*
JEAN-PIERRE CHANGEUX	*Chair of Cellular Communications, Collège de France; Director, Laboratory of Neurobiology, Institut Pasteur, Paris*
NOAM CHOMSKY	*Department of Linguistics and Philosophy, Massachusetts Institute of Technology*
ANTOINE DANCHIN	*Institute of Physicochemical Biology and Institut Pasteur, Paris*
DIETER DÜTTING	*Department of Molecular Biology, Max-Planck Institute, Tübingen*
JERRY FODOR	*Department of Psychology and Department of Linguistics and Philosophy, Massachusetts Institute of Technology*
MAURICE GODELIER	*Laboratory of Social Anthropology, Collège de France and Ecole des Hautes Etudes en Sciences Sociales, Paris*
BÄRBEL INHELDER	*Faculty of Psychology and Educational Sciences, University of Geneva*

401.9
£269

v

FRANÇOIS JACOB	Chair of Cellular Genetics, Collège de France; Director of the Department of Molecular Biology, Institut Pasteur
JACQUES MEHLER	Center for the Study of Cognitive Processes and Language, Ecole des Hautes Etudes en Sciences Sociales, Paris
JACQUES MONOD	Former director of the Institut Pasteur, Paris; former chairman of the board of directors of the Royaumont Center for a Science of Man
SEYMOUR PAPERT	Division for Study and Research in Education, Department of Mathematics, Massachusetts Institute of Technology
JEAN PETITOT	Center of Mathematics as Applied to the Social Sciences, Maison des Sciences de l'Homme, Paris; University of Paris-VIII, Vincennes
JEAN PIAGET	Director of the International Center for Genetic Epistemology, University of Geneva
MASSIMO PIATTELLI-PALMARINI	Center for Transdisciplinary Studies, Ecole des Hautes Etudes en Sciences Sociales, Paris; Director of the Royaumont Center for a Science of Man
DAVID PREMACK	Department of Psychology, University of Pennsylvania, Philadelphia
HILARY PUTNAM	Department of Philosophy, Harvard University
DAN SPERBER	Laboratory of Ethnology and Comparative Sociology, University of Paris-X, Nanterre
RENÉ THOM	Institut des Hautes Etudes Scientifiques, Bures-sur-Yvette

STEPHEN TOULMIN — *The Committee on Social Thought, University of Chicago*

ANTHONY WILDEN — *Department of Communication Studies, Simon Fraser University, British Columbia*

THOMAS DE ZENGOTITA — *Department of Anthropology, Columbia University*

CONTENTS

PREFACE

IN OCTOBER 1975 the participants in the debate between Jean Piaget and Noam Chomsky met at the Abbaye de Royaumont near Paris. This book, a rare testimony, emerged from that debate, the first, and to this date the only, personal encounter between the founders of genetic epistemology and of generative linguistics, two conceptual systems that from their beginnings have inspired innumerable scientific works throughout the world. In essence the debate is between two still-developing programs, defined by some as two of the major scientific revolutions of our time. The light shed by the meeting at Royaumont is bound to extend far beyond the circle of what I would call the natural readers of this book—linguists, psychologists, and epistemologists. Pioneers in the fields of neurobiology, ethology, animal psychology, cognitive anthropology, artificial intelligence, and philosophy of mental processes took an active part in the debate between Piagetian constructivism and Chomskian innatism, widening its scope and allowing for an unprecedented synthesis. Philosophers of science and every person attuned to the development of scientific theories will discover in this book an eyewitness account of the processes of scientific consensus.

Piaget's and Chomsky's theories have created an intense and growing fascination in a number of fields of research. Often relying on scanty information or even a "principle of authority," people talk about the two systems as scientific paradigms. The theoretical positions and the data on which they are founded are discussed here in the light of objections raised by specialists from other areas. *Language and Learning*, in short, is intended to be a vast, critical inventory of the research strategies that in the future will give us new insights into the problem of human nature. Reading such a book may constitute a turning point for anyone interested in the foundations of language and the development of cognitive structures. In order to make the book accessible to a wider public, I have endeavored to remove unnecessary technical jargon and to clarify any references that might prove an obstacle to the lay reader.

Before giving an overview of the book's structure, I would like to explain the origins of the meeting and the special circumstances that allowed for its realization. The observation that convinced the Centre Royaumont pour une Science de l'Homme to organize the debate was this: the well-known theory of cognitive development elaborated by Piaget and the equally famous theory of generative grammars elaborated by Chomsky were being compared more and more frequently—sometimes in terms of oppositions, sometimes in terms of complementarity—in courses, lectures, epistemological discussions, and specialized reviews. However, an examination of the works of these two authors reveals that cross-references were few and unsystematic. The analyses of Piaget's theses in Chomskian terms and of Chomsky's theses in Piagetian terms were sketchy at best, and a reader could draw the most disparate conclusions. Taking into account the paradigmatic status assigned to the two theories in examinations of the relationships between what is innate and acquired and between biological and cognitive structures, we at the Centre thought it would be a service to the scientific community to arrange a direct confrontation between Piaget and Chomsky. Beyond the intrinsic interest of such an encounter, we hoped to produce as complete and detailed a document as possible, to arrive at a transdisciplinary synthesis so that in the future all discussion on the oppositions or "compromises" between Chomsky and Piaget would have a firmer base.

Scott Atran, at that time a permanent associate at the Centre, became the main proponent of this idea, and his enthusiasm was contagious. Piaget declared himself willing to meet Chomsky and discuss the foundations of their systems of thought in the presence of scientists working in related fields. Jacques Monod, president of the Centre Royaumont, did not let the opportunity go by, for he had been pondering such a project for quite a long time. This meeting, moreover, was an ideal step toward the Centre's goal of widening communication between the life sciences and the social sciences. Monod enthusiastically supported the project, helped us to finance it, participated in the discussions, and presided over one of the sessions with the mixture of open-mindedness and ruthless criticism that was such a salient feature of his personality. Because of his premature death, his own comments and questions during the meeting unfortunately could not be corrected or amplified, but they have been transcribed here, testimony to his positions on contructivism and innatism.

The book is based on a transcription of the debate as well as on two papers written for the participants and distributed before the colloquium. Nevertheless, in its present format the book is more than a mere proceedings. Chapter 1 consists of Piaget's brief, programmatic "invitational" text and Chomsky's reply, which together identified the crucial points of the debate. The rest of Part I presents the stages of the debate in their original sequence. However, to emphasize the most important passages and the problems to which the debate brought new solutions, I found it necessary to make selections, develop certain arguments and counterarguments, and omit digressions. The exchanges are respected nearly word for word for entire pages; I did, however, seek a compromise between literal fidelity and free recreation, making a special effort to preserve the "convivial" character of the colloquium.

After carefully rereading the transcriptions, the authors were given the opportunity to amplify their comments, in some cases quite extensively. Any new or newly formulated arguments were then communicated to their challengers, sometimes provoking fresh or more detailed responses. As a result of these additions, the transcriptions gained in clarity and rigor. I felt that it was unnecessary to indicate in the text the transitions between the original debate and later additions, because the spirit of the discussion has been respected everywhere. The result, deemed acceptable by the authors, is therefore an enlarged, enriched, and at the same time more concise debate.

Because of the numerous and important changes and this "epigenetic" growth of the transcriptions, Piaget reread the entire manuscript and offered his responses in "Afterthoughts," which concludes Part I.

Part II is a debate on the debate. Hilary Putnam, a logician and philosopher, was not able to participate in the colloquium, but he studied the transcriptions carefully and drew up a rigorous, thought-provoking text. Indeed, his "What Is Innate and Why?"

calls into question some fundamental points made by Piaget, Chomsky, and Jerry Fodor. Piaget responds briefly to Putnam in "Afterthoughts." Chomsky and Fodor each develop detailed and polemical counterarguments, and a short reply by Putnam follows. The four texts of the Putnam-Chomsky-Fodor "quarrel" have been unofficially circulated in some academic circles as a kind of philosophical *samizdat;* we cannot help being delighted that the second part of this book has become a "classic" even before its publication.

In his comments at the end of Part II, Jacques Mehler, a psycholinguist and former colleague of both Chomsky and Piaget (and as such a bridge between the Geneva and MIT groups), draws up a synthetic picture of the actual and potential points of convergence between their scientific programs. Mehler also sketches lines of future research in cognitive psychology and psycholinguistics.

The three appendixes clarify particular aspects of the debate. The idea of phenocopy, introduced in Piaget's opening remarks, rekindled by François Jacob's and Jean-Pierre Changeux's critical comments, and taken up again by Piaget in his "Afterthoughts," still needed a precise definition. In Appendix A, Antoine Danchin analyzes this apparently technical issue, upon which Piaget's biology and the biologists' split. His "critical note," written from a neo-Darwinian standpoint, highlights the sharp divergence between the "instructivist" and "selectivist" theories of the appearance of new forms of life or of new cognitive structures.

Appendix B presents mathematician René Thom's criticism of the Geneva school's theories of the genesis of space, together with Piaget's response to Thom, once again a debate on the debate. It was not possible to make this unhoped-for insight into the problems of mathematical foundations a genuine Part III, solely because of the physical limitations of the book. I hope that this appendix, along with Jean Petitot's very interesting text on the "catastrophic" approach to linguistics, will one day become the point of departure for another debate and another book.

At the beginning and end of chapters, I have inserted some introductory remarks, comments, and reminders of crucial points in the debate. These editorial comments are given in italics to distinguish them from the text proper and to help the reader who wishes to follow a particular problematic axis.

I would like to stress that all credit for this achievement must be given to the competence, generosity, and dedication of the participants. The colloquium and the book would not have been possible without the financial assistance of the Volkswagen Foundation and Editions du Seuil. During the editing phase, the Centre Royaumont benefited from the aid of the Ford Foundation and the Délégation Générale à la Recherche Scientifique et Technique.

I wish to pay my respects to the memory of the late Henri Gouïn and to thank Isabelle Gouïn for generously offering part of their living quarters at the Abbaye de Royaumont at the time of the colloquium. Constantin Jelenski and Sylvia Duchacek lent us their valuable and efficient assistance during the colloquium itself. The high quality of the bilingual translation is attributable to the remarkable competence of Christopher Thiery. Marilu Mehler transcribed the debates and assisted me in preparing the book. I would also like to thank Joseph Garreau, who did the English translations of Piaget's papers and of many of the other presentations that were originally written in French.

Although most of the debate and the original manuscript were in English, the American edition is being published a few months later than the French edition. This interval has been full of rewards, because the French-speaking public and the press have manifested a keen interest in the book. Some European psychologists and linguists have gone as far as to call it *"the* book of the year." However, it has become evident that the great interest in the book is accompanied by some frustration among nonprofessionals. Some questions have recurred, such as: "In the end, where does all this lead?" "What is really at stake here?" and "How does that relate to problems in my field?" Quite often, this "field" is simply the human condition.

In the meantime I discovered that the American psychologist Howard Gardner's brilliant, crystal-clear review of the book, originally published in *Psychology Today*, then made available to the French public in *Psychologie*, was a very good "primer." I was glad, therefore, that the director of Harvard University Press had the idea of asking Gardner to write an additional, less technical foreword. It is a pleasure to acknowledge the quality and appeal of Gardner's synopsis, and many readers will find it useful to have the plot and the backgrounds of the main characters presented before they enter the opera house. They will be as grateful as I am both to Professor Gardner for accomplishing a very difficult task and to Harvard University Press for having commissioned it. If cognition, as Gardner contends, has come of age because of the debate and this book, he must definitely be credited for having made this somewhat elusive event a public fact.

December 1979   *Massimo Piattelli-Palmarini*

Cognition Comes of Age

Howard Gardner

A FUTURE HISTORIAN of the cognitive sciences—that recently formed amalgam of disciplines which probes the operations of the human mind—might select any of a number of episodes as the initial milestone in the emergence of this field. If struck by the earliest manifestations of interest in mental phenomena, he might revert to the questions posed by classical philosophers—for example, Socrates seeking the nature of knowledge. Searching for less remote antecedents, he might alight on certain dramatic moments in the history of modern thought— Descartes arguing that his existence could be inferred from his capacity to doubt, or Locke responding to Molyneux's questions about the experiences of a blind man restored to sight. If our mythical historian discerned the origins of the cognition movement in the earliest days of experimental psychology, he might describe Wilhelm Wundt's opening of the first laboratory in Leipzig in 1879, or the microscopic investigation by researchers in Würzburg around 1900 of humans engaged in solving problems. If on the alert for seminal publications that have inspired the current cadre of scholars, he might well cite Jean Piaget's *Origins of Intelligence in Children* (French edition, 1936), or Noam Chomsky's *Syntactic Structures* (1957).

Although the time of origin of the cognitive sciences may be a matter of dispute, the time when they came of age seems reasonably clear. Only in the last decade or so have cognitive studies seized the limelight of psychology and pointed toward a significant integration among such diverse fields as philosophy, neurology, and anthropology. Journals have proliferated, many hundreds of books have been published, foundations and government agencies have virtually swarmed to support such research. Were it necessary to select a set of dates to mark the official coming-of-age of this field, there might still be dispute.* But certainly a strong contender would be October 10–13, 1975, when Jean Piaget and Noam Chomsky engaged in the debate on language and learning chronicled in these pages.

The encounter at the Abbaye de Royaumont was historically important for several reasons. To begin with, Chomsky and Piaget were recognized leaders of two of the most influential (possibly *the* most influential) schools of contemporary cognitive studies. Taken seriously by all scientists in their respective fields of linguistics and developmental psychology, they had achieved international reputations that far transcended their areas of specialization. Accompanied by colleagues who were associated to varying degrees with their own programs of research, Piaget and Chomsky presented their ideas to an illustrious gathering of scholars: Nobel laureates in biology, leading figures in philosophy and mathematics, and several of the most prominent behavioral scientists in the world today. Those in attendance listened critically to the arguments and joined vigorously in the ensuing discussion, seldom hesitating to make pronouncements and take sides. It was almost as if two of the great figures of the seventeenth century—Descartes and Locke, say, could have defied time and space to engage in discussion at a joint meeting of the Royal Society and the Académie Française.

This meeting may well have had additional significance. Possibly for the first time figures at the forefront of relatively "tender-minded" disciplines like psychology and linguistics succeeded in involving a broad and distinguished collection of "tough-minded" scholars in debates formulated by the behavioral scientists themselves—with scarcely a hint of condescension by the representatives of such firmly entrenched disciplines as biology and mathematics. Equally noteworthy, the protagonists represented the cognitive sciences—a field hardly known (and not even christened) two decades ago, and one far less familiar to both the general public and the scholarly community than many other pockets of the behavioral sciences.

* In a recent unpublished essay on the history of cognitive sciences, George Miller singled out a symposium held at MIT in September 1956. At this meeting, attended by Claude Shannon, Jerome Wiesner, Noam Chomsky, Herbert Simon, and Miller, various approaches in information theory, computer simulation, experimental psychology, and theoretical linguistics were first brought together.

The gathering at Royaumont raised numerous questions for observers of the contemporary intellectual and scientific scene. Many questions dealing with the "core" theoretical assumptions of the major participants at the conference are considered in detail in the Introduction and section notes by Massimo Piattelli-Palmarini, one of the conveners of the conference and the individual who undertook the arduous task of preparing both the French and the English versions of this book. Therefore I will discuss here several more general issues about the nature and significance of the events at Royaumont. In particular, questions arise about the backgrounds and orientations of the two men at the center of these debates; the reasons for an encounter at this time; and the factors in recent years that have given rise to the cognition movement they exemplify. Finally, publication of the conference transcripts spurs reflection on the outcome of this encounter, both for the participants themselves and for the larger public for whom the debates have been recreated. For even if a verdict on the importance of the cognitive sciences is already congealing within the scientific community, the significance of this movement remains mysterious to the world at large.

It is instructive that neither Piaget nor Chomsky is a psychologist by training, nor would either answer readily to the label of cognitive psychologist. Having had an interest since childhood in the behavior of mollusks, Piaget began his professional career as a biologist. By a circuitous route, so often recounted that it barely requires fresh summary, Piaget was stimulated to investigate the origins of knowledge in infancy and the stages through which children pass en route to acquiring an adult level of logical thought. Although at one time he considered his days with children merely a detour in his effort to devise a biological account of the nature of knowledge, Piaget remained a student of children's thought for nearly sixty years and eventually founded a new field—genetic epistemology—which probes the origins of intellectual structures in children, the evolution of knowledge within specific scientific disciplines, and the parallels that may obtain between these two developmental trajectories. Nearing eighty at the time of the conference, Piaget had seen his once-marginal views about children become enormously influential in academic developmental psychology and increasingly cited by educators. Moreover, even as he had swayed many skeptical psychologists to join his pursuit of the developing structures of knowledge, Piaget had achieved surprising success in integrating his views with those of other leading figures in the social, biological, and physical sciences.

Noam Chomsky began his academic career as a student of language whose approach was rooted in rigorous philosophical analysis and in formal logical-mathematical methods. Convinced early on of the inadequacy of previous attempts to explain the nature of language, Chomsky introduced into linguistics a set of revolutionary concerns. He formulated an agenda for scientific linguistics: to find a set of grammatical rules that would generate syntactic descriptions for all of the permissible and none of the nonpermissible sentences in any given language. His hypothesis was that such a grammar would constitute a valid description of the knowledge that a language user employs when producing and understanding the sentences of his language. Chomsky then put forth a specific set of proposals articulating the formal nature of the grammatical system that could fulfill these goals. In a series of influential writings, he posited a set of extremely abstract linguistic structures to which the human mind was deemed sensitive, structures that do not have to be taught because they are part of the child's innate knowledge system.

Chomsky's break with the linguistic past was perhaps more radical than Piaget's rupture with earlier psychology, and his influence on the next generation of researchers spread even more quickly. Not content to rest on his achievements in linguistics, Chomsky soon became a spokesman for a variety of causes. To the general public he has been known chiefly as an unsparing critic of American foreign policy, but within the scholarly community what has gained the most attention is his vision of how behavioral science should be pursued.

These impressive intellectual biographies were perhaps the chief stimulus for the encounter at Royaumont. Both men had developed programs for cognitive science, and because so many observers were struck by various parallels and various conflicts, it became important that they have the opportunity to meet and confront each other. At the conference both made statements that were true to form in their examples, style of argument, and vision of science. Piaget characteristically focused on the arresting behavioral phenomena of children that he and his collaborators have discovered—the understanding of the permanence of objects, which does not occur until the end of infancy; the general capacity to symbolize, which is said to underlie both linguistic and "pretend" play activities; the ability to appreciate the conservation of matter, which arises only during the early school years. Although Piaget criticized his old nemeses, the behaviorists and the nativists, for the most part he remained eager to convert others to his general picture of universal human development—a portrait attractive and convincing in its overall outlines but difficult to formulate in terms sufficiently precise for ready confirmation or disconfirmation.

Chomsky also offered a number of intriguing specific examples to support his point of view, but his overall approach was markedly different. Unlike Piaget's, his examples were not of dramatic behavioral phenomena; rather he pointed to abstract internal rules, such as the specified subject condition described in his opening remarks, that seem necessary to account for certain regularities of linguistic output. These rules are discovered by examining the features of correct linguistic utterances and of certain incorrect but "possible" syntactic constructions that seem never to appear. Once pointed out, such regularities (though not necessarily Chomsky's specific explanations) are evident, and further experimentation to demonstrate their validity seems superfluous. Accordingly, Chomsky relied heavily on such examples and on artful *reductiones ad absurdum* to discount alternative rules and rival points of view. Disenchanted with empiricist accounts, he displayed little patience with the version of genetic-environmental contact that stands at the core of Piaget's interactionism. Impelling Chomsky's stance was a vivid image of what scientific practice should be like: metaphoric or impressionistic accounts must be avoided in favor of more precise statements phrased in a sufficiently formal manner to allow testing and, in good Popperian time, disconfirmation. Here, too, was a markedly different view of human nature: where Piaget saw the human child—and his mind—as an active, constructive agent that slowly inches forward in a perpetual bootstrap operation, Chomsky viewed the mind as a set of essentially preprogrammed units, each equipped from the first to realize its full complement of rules and needing only the most modest environmental trigger to exhibit its intellectual wares.

Although the main lines of the debate were familiar to those within the cognitive sciences, they were not common coin among those in the "hard sciences" and even less familiar to the intelligent lay public. At least in the United States, discussions by those outside psychology have centered on two areas remote from the halls of Royaumont. On the one hand there is psychoanalysis, the study of unconscious mechanisms of mind opened up by Freud's brilliant investigations. This discipline began in clinical medicine, has long since been absorbed by large segments of the helping professions, and now constitutes an integral part of humanistic studies in history, literature, and the analysis of culture. Equally renowned but standing in sharp contrast is behaviorism, the study of the overt actions of organisms and the search for a small set of principles to account for all learning. This discipline was launched through provocative studies of animal behavior by investigators like Pavlov and Skinner, soon proved itself an effective means of training animals and certain human populations, and has now become a widely used principle of human engineering, one not altogether free (as Chomsky would remind us) from political overtones.

As any instructor of college freshmen can confirm, both psychoanalysis and behaviorism exert an instant and notably seductive appeal among those with an incipient interest in psychology. And this is true not just because the interpretation of dreams and the reinforcement of pigeons have long since worked their way into public consciousness. Rather, the appeal of these fields comes primarily from their confrontation of certain aspects of human nature that command immediate interest: the baser human emotions, our irrational "animal" self, the experiences of pleasure and pain, the possibility of free will, the drives of aggression and sexuality. To be sure, psychoanalysis and behaviorism do not treat each of these issues in equal measure— nor do they concur in their interpretations! But these two approaches—both sympathetic to an evolutionary analysis, both focused on issues of affect, both largely ignoring the varieties of logical reasoning and the computing powers of the mind— attack from an allegedly scientific vantage point issues of human existence that have long formed the core of stories, dramas, and personal crises. The absence of psychoanalysts and behaviorists from Royaumont testifies to the nearly unbridgeable chasm between those interested primarily in human emotional and motivational existence and those intrigued by human reason.

A third field of psychology—scarcely known to the general public and also absent from Royaumont, but one that has almost totally dominated the university scene—is academic psychology. Dating from the opening of Wundt's laboratory and culminating in the professional monolith of the American Psychological Association, this discipline has focused on discovering the general laws governing such often-invisible but nonetheless crucial activities as perception, learning, and memory. Working largely in artificial experimental settings and relying excessively on findings obtained with laboratory rats and college sophomores, researchers in this field have methodically constructed, brick by brick, an edifice that includes chambers on how people see three-dimensional forms, how they learn to type, how they remember lists of words, and how electrical shocks can influence their behavior, as well as an assortment of other issues that lend themselves to experimental manipulation. Forming the mainstay of teaching in colleges and having a virtual stranglehold on the awarding of doctoral degrees, academic psychology has had little effect on the wider public, which (despite the deluge of popularized psychology) remains almost wholly ignorant of the substance of its findings. Moreover, this neglect may be justified. If traditional academic psychology has first raised and then solved many little puzzles, it has failed to convince many critical observers (including, most probably, Piaget and Chomsky) that its studies are central to an understanding of the mind.

The field of cognitive sciences as represented at Royaumont seldom tackles issues of affect and motivation and is dubious about the laboratory tinkerings of standard academic psychologists. In their proudest and boldest moments, cognitive scientists address directly the nature of the human mind: how does it work when performing the most complex forms of reasoning —playing chess, solving differential equations, composing a story, a sonnet, or a sonata? Standing at the elbow of the modern computer, whose simulation powers they do not hesitate to employ, monitoring the latest findings from the neuropsychological and biological domains, the cognitive sciences do not flinch from anticipating a synthesis in which the basic forms of the human mind will be laid bare.

The willingness to examine mental life in all its complexity is not, of course, wholly an inspiration of cognitivists during the past ten years: early intimations could be discerned in a number of locales even in the first years of psychology.* But the exorcism of three obstacles—the fascination of psychoanalysis with nonrational thought, the refusal of behaviorism to countenance mental entities and introspective accounts, and the idolatry within academic psychology of atomistic methods and units

---

* Indeed, the preceding portrait unavoidably minimizes the importance in the history of psychology of several individuals—for example, James Gibson, Karl Lashley, Frederic Bartlett—and several schools— such as Gestalt psychology and Soviet developmental psychology—that have confronted more molar issues and have, perhaps as a result, secured more public attention.

of analysis—only began in the United States during the 1950s and 1960s. The chief stimulants were the computer's increased capacity to simulate complex thought processes, a reawakened interest in the strategies people use to solve difficult problems, a demonstration of certain reasoning and communicative powers in animals that defied explanation in terms of stimulus-response models, the publication of Ulric Neisser's enormously influential *Cognitive Psychology* (1967), and, in no small measure, Piaget's pioneering explorations of the thought processes of children and Chomsky's convincing demonstrations of certain linguistic principles. Where Piaget and Chomsky concur is in their aversion to the earlier approaches to psychology and in their (relative) sympathy with the more recent practitioners of cognitive science, such as Roger Brown, Jerome Bruner, George Miller, and Herbert Simon, and with recent nonatomistic "top-down" approaches, such as schema theory. But although they are linked by certain common opponents and broad historical influences, there surfaced repeatedly during the debate at Royaumont profound differences in analytic style, models of human cognition, and basic scientific themata.

Piaget and Chomsky can be viewed within a psychological tradition rooted in the recent past, but much more important, they are heirs to the venerable tradition of classical philosophy. Dating back to the Greco-Roman era, but with a more direct antecedent in the philosophy of the post-Renaissance period, the concerns of both men can be seen as contemporary efforts to engage, sharpen, and provide answers to issues that preoccupied such philosophers as Berkeley, Descartes, Hobbes, Hume, Leibniz, Locke, Rousseau, and, most especially, Kant. And even as the efforts at Royaumont can be seen as a contemporary attempt to tackle entrenched philosophical issues, the ultimate success of the cognition movement may well be evaluated in terms of its progress in resolving these questions. Having proposed Royaumont as a modern incarnation of a debate between classical philosophers, one might ask as one measure of its significance whether, if these philosophers had been witnesses, they would have understood the debate, felt it responsive to the agenda they had initially formulated, and believed that some progress had been made toward fulfilling that agenda.

Which issues, formulated in classical philosophy, reverberated through the Abbaye de Royaumont? Among the themes that surfaced in discussions were the relation of the child's understanding to the adult's; the connections between animal intellect and the minds of humans; the nature of various vehicles of knowledge, such as primary and secondary qualities, words, images, schemas, and signs; the nature of language and its relation to thought. Perhaps the most dominant issue at Royaumont was one that took its original formulation from the pages of Shakespeare and has constituted a continuing source of contention between philosophers on opposite sides of the English Channel: whether (as Chomsky held) knowledge is largely inborn, part of the individual's birthright, a form of innate ideas existing in the realm of "nature"; whether (as traditional empiricists have contended) knowledge is better conceived of as a product of living in an environment, a series of messages of "nurture" transmitted by other individuals and one's surrounding culture, which become etched onto a *tabula rasa*; or whether (as Piaget insisted) knowledge can be constructed only through interaction between certain inborn modes of processing available to the young child and the actual characteristics of physical objects and events. This issue of genetic versus cultural contributions to mind was pointedly phrased by the chief convener of the conference, Jacques Monod: "In asking myself the vast question, 'What makes man man?' it is clear that it is partially his genome and partially his culture. But what are the genetic limits of culture? What is its genetic component?"

To be sure, though all these issues were touched upon, they were not equally prominent. Whether by design or happenstance, considerable time was spent discussing Chomskian nativism versus Piagetian "interactionism," a conflict that at Royaumont centered particularly on questions pertaining to the origins of language. At issue was whether human linguistic capacities can in any interesting sense be considered a product of general "constructed" intellectual development (as Piaget contended), or whether they are a highly specialized part of human genetic inheritance, largely separate from other human faculties and more plausibly viewed as a kind of innate knowledge that has only to unfold (as Chomsky insisted).

To be sure, whether language is interestingly dependent on certain nonlinguistic capacities is crucial, and this question was discussed at a sophisticated level during the conference. Yet the specific debate between nativism and interactionism strikes many observers as unnecessary and sterile. Within the biological sciences, many feel it is no longer fruitful to attempt to sort out hereditary from environmental influences, and within the behavioral sciences, even those seduced by this question often have difficulty agreeing on just what counts as evidence in favor of one side or the other. That Chomsky and Piaget could draw such different conclusions from equally pertinent bodies of data about early cognitive and linguistic milestones and that they occasionally shifted positions on what might count as evidence for their positions indicates to me that the reason why this issue was so extensively reworked was that the two spokesmen had strong views on it, rather than that either of them was likely to convince the other or skeptical "others."

More substantive and soluble topics were also addressed at Royaumont. In particular, three related and recurring issues are worth citing, for they underline pivotal differences between the two protagonists and, unlike the nature/nurture miasma, may well be resolved in the coming years. A first argument centers on the Rousseauean dilemma of the relationships between child and adult thought: whereas Piaget and his followers believe in the utility of stages, with children as they become older attaining qualitatively different (and increasingly more powerful) modes of reasoning, Chomsky's colleague Jerry Fodor argued strongly that such an account of stages of thought is logically indefensible. According to Fodor, it is in principle impossible to generate more powerful forms of thought from less powerful ones; essentially, all forms of reasoning that an individual will eventually be capable of are specified at birth and emerge via a maturational process during development.

A second enduring discussion concerned the nature of the mental representations by which we conceive of our experiences, including the objects and persons of the world. In the Piagetian view, the ability to represent knowledge to oneself and to others is a constructive process that presupposes a lengthy series of actions upon the environment, which awaits the completion of sensorimotor development at age two and which, in turn, makes possible symbolic play, dreams, mental images, language, in fact the whole gamut of symbolic capacities. Chomsky and his colleagues, on the other hand, expressed doubts about the legitimacy of grouping together a family of representations, of referring to a symbolic function that is supposed to emerge at a certain point in development: in Dan Sperber's view, language as a symbol system must be radically dissociated from other symbolic forms; in Jerry Fodor's formulation, the child is *born* with a form of representation, a language of thought upon which all others are simply grafted.

The final issue, intimately related to the first two, involves the generality of thought and of thought processes. According to Piaget, thought is an extremely broad set of capacities: identical mental operations underlie one's encounters with a wide range of cognitive materials and topics (space, time, morality, causality), and the roots of later forms of thought (for example, reasoning in language) can be located in earlier forms (such as sensorimotor problem solving by the one-year-old). From Chomsky's radically different point of view, language is divorced from other (and earlier) forms of thinking. Moreover, each intellectual faculty is sui generis—a separate domain of mentation, possibly located in a separate region of the brain, exhibiting many of its own processes and maturing at its own rate. Indeed, Chomsky repeatedly invokes the striking, if somewhat bizarre metaphor of the mind as a collection of organs, rather like the liver or the heart. We do not speak of the heart as learning to beat but rather as maturing according to its genetic timetable. So, too, we should conceive of language (and other "organs of the mind" like those that account for the structure of mathematics or music) as mental entities that are programmed to unfold over time. Just as the physiologist dissects the heart in order to unravel its anatomy and its mechanisms, the linguist must perform analogous surgery on the human faculty of language.

The positions taken by the protagonists on these issues convey their general intellectual styles and substance, facets of their intellectual bequest that came across with increasing clarity and finality as the discussions progressed. Although both Piaget and Chomsky pay homage to models provided by biology and logic, they are fundamentally interested in quite different kinds of examples and explanations. Piaget is fascinated by the behaviors children emit and, more specifically, the errors they make when solving the challenging puzzles he poses. He has developed an elaborate technical vocabulary, rooted in biology, to describe these phenomena, a rich description of the stages through which children pass in each of these realms of achievement, and his own logical formalism to describe the affinities underlying structually related behaviors and the differences that obtain across discrete mental stages. The phenomena he discerns offer a convincing series of snapshots of how development proceeds, but the specific terms he has devised and the models he has formulated have fared less well in the face of rigorous criticism. At most, Piaget's adventures into technical vocabulary and formal models offer a convenient way of synthesizing the enormous amount of data he has accumulated. In the end, it is his overall *vision* of how capacities relate and of how knowledge in its varied forms develops that inspires workers in the field.

Though similar in certain respects, Chomsky's achievement

is of a fundamentally different order. Rather than being struck by behavioral phenomena that he feels compelled to describe, Chomsky is driven by a powerful vision of how linguistic science should be pursued and by a belief about how this analytic approach can be extended across the social sciences. In his view the student of linguistics should construct models of human linguistic competence and thereby specify the "universals" of language. Stating the rules, steps, and principles with utmost (mathematical) precision becomes a prerequisite for work in this area. And so, even as Chomsky has high regard for models stated in such a way that they can be definitively tested, he dismisses more general and more allusive "positions," "rules," and "strategies." Those domains of thought that are susceptible to study (and Chomsky has deep reservations about which domains can in fact be studied in this formalistic way) must be investigated as the linguist does *à la* Chomsky: he must propose a formal system of rules that will either generate just the acceptable behaviors in that domain or will be shown in principle to fail (because, for example, they generate too many, too few, or the wrong behaviors), and he must strive to discover just those rules that the human mind actually follows.

Building on this rigorous notion of how linguistics should operate, Chomsky has gone on to other domains of knowledge and has reached extremely strong (and controversial) conclusions about the operations of the mind. He is convinced that language is represented in the mind in an extremely abstract fashion and that individuals acquire language despite scanty tutelage and impoverished examples. He voices a number of bold claims: that the essential knowledge about language is specified by one's genome, that nearly all possible hypotheses about the rules of syntax that the child might conceivably invent are precluded by the human genetic inheritance, and that languages the world over are in all critical respects the same. By extension, other domains of knowledge are also fixed by one's genetic inheritance —the environment plays at most a triggering role, and the role of cultural and social factors in the elaboration of fundamental knowledge is minimal. Chomsky is of course aware that such claims, like those of all empirical science, can never be proved: it is impossible to demonstrate, as logicians and mathematicians demonstrate their conclusions, that something is *not* learned or that the environment is *not* contributing; nor can one ever deductively conclude that some element is a universal property of language—the next language studied may disprove your claim. But to Chomsky these vulnerabilities are actually virtues, for unless a theory can be subjected to disconfirmation (and Chomsky doubts that Piaget's theory can be disconfirmed), then it is not worth propounding.

By borrowing some terminology from Piaget we may obtain insight into an impasse reached at the conference. Piaget's approach was that of an *assimilator*—one willing to widen his system to embrace potential critics—while Chomsky's tack required *accommodation*—he expected others to accommodate to his scheme—so it is not surprising that their minds did not converge. Piaget did not succeed in assimilating Chomsky to the tenets of genetic epistemology, and Chomsky did not persuade Piaget to renounce his system and accommodate totally to the assumptions of generative linguistics. In a way, each protagonist presupposed the body of knowledge that interested the other: Chomsky, displaying little interest in the ways in which knowledge happens to unfold, directed his formidable powers to specifying the forms of knowledge that are part of the adult repertoire. Piaget conceded that some forms of knowledge may be present at the beginning but insisted that that still left unanswered the fundamental question of how what is latent comes to be expressed (or suppressed). The most that could be said for rapprochement, then, was that these two "structuralist" approaches may be complementary.

As for the reactions of others at Royaumont, a somewhat more complex score card is necessary. Not surprisingly, those already attuned to Piaget or Chomsky remained committed to their perspectives—sometimes even more uncompromisingly so than the protagonists themselves! The biologists, having little or no professional connection to either "school," seemed closer to Chomsky than to Piaget. Some reasons why this was so are suggested in the editor's Introduction; in addition, it may be that some of Piaget's anti-Darwinian ideas rankled the biological scientists, that Chomsky's skillful style and powerful arguments persuaded even normally skeptical observers, or that a number of the "hard" scientists happened to be more in sympathy with a nativist view to begin with.

A few participants did attempt a reconciliation between the two stances, notably the neurobiologist Jean-Pierre Changeux, with his theory of neuronal plasticity. On occasion, however, this was done by damning with faint praise: in his trenchant comments framed after the debate, the philosopher Hilary Putnam identified valuable ideas in each of the major essays but accused both Piaget and Chomsky of proffering illegitimate and unconvincing arguments. The comparative psychologist David Premack endorsed many of Chomsky's methodological strictures but embraced Piaget's notion of a central representational capacity. And Guy Cellérier, affiliated with the Geneva circle, furnished a metaphor of cognitive growth that seemed responsive to both Piaget's and Chomsky's concerns: he portrayed mental development as a variety of hill climbing, a directed but still open ascent to greater intellectual heights. Personally I found this figure appealing, but it failed to impress Chomsky.

Clearly the meeting at Royaumont was an exploration rather than a conclusion of the weighty issues under discussion there. Such lack of closure is hardly surprising—it would be difficult to envisage any meeting at which scientists who had devoted their lives to the development of independent and somewhat antagonistic systems could arrive at a consensus in less than a week.

Yet to my mind an event of equal importance occurred at Royaumont. The cognitive sciences, a latent interest of scholars over many centuries and freshly invigorated over the past few decades, were finally integrated into the current intellectual scene. Moreover, this milestone occurred at a meeting that to my mind ranks with such memorable colloquia as the Hixon Symposium of 1951 and the *Discussions in Child Development* in the middle 1950s. With greater clarity than before, cognitive science was linked to pivotal scientific and philosophical issues of the past and shown to be relevant to their clarification, even where the ultimate solutions remain obscure.

Risky though it is to be a historian, it is even riskier to pose as a prophet. I hesitate to forecast the ultimate outcome of the specific debates at Royaumont. It is possible that a genuine intellectual paradigm shift may be at work here: within a few years, the Chomskian approach, rigorous and formal, and the Chomskian assumptions, bold and programmatic, may envelop Piaget's, retaining the phenomena that genetic epistemology has uncovered but not the theory that purports to explain them. It is equally possible that Chomsky's point of view, while indubitably a brilliant tour de force, may prove somewhat irrelevant to the mainstream of modern developmental psychology and may even be dismissed as a Cartesian anachronism. It is possible (indeed likely) that future scientists will glean from the works of both men those treasures most worthy of preservation: intriguing phenomena (Piaget's conservations, Chomsky's specified subject condition), useful methodologies (Piaget's clinical interviews, Chomsky's linguistic formalism), pregnant theoretical orientations (Piaget's search for structures underlying diverse cognitive achievements and his desire for a logic founded on action that can also model mental performances, Chomsky's search for linguistic universals and his passion for explanatory models of language processes). With the passage of time, the differences that strike us—and Chomsky—as vast may recede, and what surfaces will be the structuralist affinities of the two men, their allegiances to biology and logic, their visions of a unified cognitive science in the spirit of Descartes and Kant. If so, their efforts may be seen more legitimately (to use Cellérier's own words) as a division of labor: Chomsky focusing on what is special about language, Piaget focusing on the commonalities among various intellectual faculties; Chomsky defining humanity's common innate endowment, Piaget describing its universal path of development. In any case, many fields being vigorously pursued at the present time can ill afford to ignore the lessons learned by the Piaget *and* the Chomsky schools.

Yet even if the cognitive sciences should thrive, even if Royaumont launched an Augustan age of cognition, in which workers from various fields will begin to collaborate with one another and a synthesis will ultimately emerge, a question remains—one that no one concerned about the cognitive sciences can afford to ignore. Will this field remain a bead game among intellectuals, an interesting and exciting exercise for those involved but remote from the concerns of those outside the academy? Or will it ultimately connect to those issues of mind and those aspects of human experience that in the past have engaged nonspecialists, and that have long since integrated psychoanalysis and behaviorism into the intellectual firmament of the twentieth century?

If the Cartesian biases of both Chomsky and Piaget were on target, if the employment of reason were central to the human enterprise and the human experience, there would be little need to explain and justify cognitive science. The issues discussed at Royaumont would immediately find their audience, this volume would quickly become a best seller, and Piaget's and Chomsky's intellectual contributions (as opposed to their names) would be assimilated in short order into all educated minds. Yet I submit that this is not very likely to happen. The dismal popular fate of other academic psychologies, the still-forbidding nature of the philosophy of centuries past, and the technical knowledge sometimes required to follow modern cognitive science—all militate against a ready recognition of the relevance and importance of the issues that engage Piaget, Chomsky, and the other contributors to the debate.

If these debates do not as yet speak directly to those outside academic circles, the possibility that they may someday do so rests, I believe, on three prerequisites. There is first of all the possibility that Chomsky and Piaget or others of equal or even greater eloquence may succeed (as did Freud) in convincing a public that the issues which concern scholars are worthy of keen attention. They might convince us, for example, that the operations of our mind which we take for granted—such as language or reasoning—are as interesting as those aspects of our soul—such as guilt or free will—which have an immediately compelling and dramatic flavor. They may convince us that what makes humans special is the way we think more than the fact that we exhibit unconscious motivations or that our "freedom" can be dissolved by trained manipulators. Indeed, one reason why the study of cognition has failed to capture the public imagination is not that the issues under examination are intrinsically uninteresting—many ordinary people also find them fascinating—but rather that professional cognitivists themselves have often been delinquent in pointing up, in an understandable and appealing way, the centrality of these issues.

A second means for highlighting the study of cognition is through its application to issues that are central to people's lives. In this regard it is worth noting that the two protagonists adopt divergent views about the relation of their scientific contributions to broader public concerns. Piaget has always disavowed a connection between his research and issues of the larger society, even those of an educational tenor. He has for the most part shied away from questions about affect or will. For him the human mind is best treated as a domain apart.

While admitting that the connections may be tenuous, Chomsky has been more willing in the past to suggest certain political and sociological implications of his research. For instance, he discerns a tie between his notions of the nature of mind and the social institutions in which he believes. By the same token, he views his intellectual contributions as an argument against behaviorist-style manipulation of individuals—basically an antitotalitarian and libertarian stance. And he said at Royaumont, more clearly than in earlier writings, that the goal of his scientific efforts is to define human nature: thus his work may be viewed as a contribution to humanistic study, albeit one framed in rigorous scientific terms. If Chomsky is right, if his (or Piaget's) science does in fact have implications for how we conceive of ourselves and how we lead our lives, then certainly this body of work will eventually have to be pondered by every reflective individual.

To my mind, the greatest challenge confronting any science of cognition is the task of explaining superior and revolutionary intellectual achievements—the plays of Shakespeare, the symphonies of Beethoven, the scientific system devised by Einstein, and, yes, the achievements, almost equivalent, of investigators like Chomsky and Piaget. The height of creativity, as exemplified by the scientist or the artist, remains one of the most enigmatic issues facing any student of human psychology. Until now, neither academic psychology (with its embarrassing tests of creativity), nor psychoanalysis nor behaviorism have had much of importance to say about the substance of individual contributions; as Freud was candid enough to admit, "The nature of artistic attainment is psychoanalytically inaccessible to us." Indeed those who seek some explanation for the cognitive processes involved in the creation of a major work would still be better advised to read Thomas Mann's *Doktor Faustus* or to examine Beethoven's sketchbooks than to sequester themselves in a psychology library.

Neither Chomsky nor Piaget has directly addressed the issue of human creativity. It has not been a central interest in the research program of either individual, though both have written and said enough on the subject (including some passages in this debate) to indicate that it is on their minds. Nor have their students pointed out implications in their works relevant to understanding individual creative achievement or creative activity in general.* Yet in Piaget's model of the child as a constantly constructive individual and in Chomsky's notion of infinite creativity in language following mastery of a rule system, I find intimations of what might be central in an eventual theory of human creative activity. My own guess—and, I should confess, my hope—is that the branch of knowledge launched publicly at Royaumont can before too long make seminal contributions to our understanding of how the human mind works,

---

* An exception deserving mention is Howard Gruber, a student of Piaget's who has studied Darwin's discoveries from the point of view of genetic epistemology; see his *Darwin on Man* (New York: Dutton, 1974). Gruber is now carrying out an analogous investigation of Piaget's own scientific development. An additional source is David Feldman's *Beyond Universals in Cognitive Development* (Norwood, N.J.: Ablex, forthcoming).

how it works well, and how it is capable, under certain circumstances, of creative breakthroughs. When that happens, the field will have done more than come of age—it will have become part of the intellectual landscape of our time, featured in public discussions and affecting the ways individuals think about themselves, interact with others, initiate changes in their society, and create significant products of mind.

When I find myself asking the vast question: how does it come about that Man is Man? I ascertain that there is, on the one hand, his culture, and on the other hand, his genome. This is all clear. But then, what are the genetic limits of culture? What is culture's genetic component? We know nothing at all about these matters—most regrettably, because there is no deeper or more fascinating problem than this one.

—Jacques Monod, from a 1970 interview (*De Homine*, 1975)

How Hard Is the "Hard Core" of a Scientific Program?

Massimo Piattelli-Palmarini

It is legitimate to regard this debate as a representative cross section of a scientific domain in full growth, right at the opening of the last quarter of the twentieth century. Though focused on language and learning, the debate presents, in fact, a number of compelling arguments on a wide range of topics, challenging current patterns of explanation both in the natural and in the social sciences. Piaget's constructivism and Chomsky's innatism are to be framed within a long-standing tradition of rational inquiry into the nature and structure of the human mind, and it is against the background of such tradition that theories, facts, and standards of intelligibility can adequately be evaluated. Reflecting most of the methodological options that now lie open for assent before the scientific community, but whose different degrees of cogency are yet to be fully appreciated, the present volume constitutes an exploration more into alternative research programs as a whole than into locally opposing psychological or linguistic theories.

I have attempted in this introduction to draw an outline of the "archeology" of Piaget's and Chomsky's programs, stressing the continuity between each program and their respective analogues in the natural sciences. Jacques Mehler, in his paper, delves into the present structure of scientific programs in psychology, linguistics, and psycholinguistics, charting their actual or possible lines of convergence in an attempt to give a long-term evaluation of the impact of Piaget's and Chomsky's theories. The reader can, however, according to his personal preference, invert the order and read Mehler's comments first

1

and then the debate, leaving the introduction for the end. Mehler and I have anticipated such an alternative itinerary and have written each section accordingly. The natural scientist and all those who find the genealogical approach to problems particularly congenial may well appreciate the existing sequence. The more analytically oriented reader and the professional linguist or psychologist, on the other hand, may want to enter the debate straight away and jump to Piaget's and Chomsky's own introductory papers. Since this volume has an open structure, it will, we hope, prove to be a rewarding and enjoyable journey no matter which pathway the reader selects.

THE PIAGETIAN HARD CORE

Ontological commitments that are liable to steer a scientific research program must usually satisfy two requirements: to be a priori plausible enough to safeguard the program against destabilization and readjustment (what responsible scientist is willing to accommodate too many ad hoc hypotheses?); and to be at the same time bold enough to lock a vast domain of empirical evidence into nontrivial sets of relations. Programs of systematic inquiry often fail because of inherent inadequacy of the embedded ontological commitments, going too far in one direction or the other. Locke's program and its manifold reenactments, from Condillac's statue to Skinner's pigeon boxes, have foundered on the shoals of a Spartan ontology, committed to the "empty bucket theory of mind," as Popper rightly calls it. Jerry Fodor provides in this volume (see Chapter 6 of Part I and his reply to Putnam in Part II) a vivid account of this momentous wreckage and argues for a much richer ontology of "what is in the mind." The Kantian program has run aground on the opposite bank. This is in part because of the reformation of programs in mathematics and logic that yielded, for instance, non-Euclidian geometries, Bourbakian set theory, logical types, and many-valued logics; and in part because of a progressive "problemshift" (to quote Lakatos) in cognitive psychology, due to Piaget more than to anyone else. Kant's assumptions bearing on the universal built-in limitations of human cognitive ability proved to be too restrictive or, to adopt a modern terminology, chronocentric (parochial to the science of his own time) and adultocentric (*static,* as Piaget correctly specifies in his reply to Bischof). The Piagetian program is, in his own words, "anti-empiricist" and inspired by a "dynamic Kantism." Correspondingly, his ontological commitments are halfway between the empty bucket of the empiricist tradition and the a priori perceptual forms postulated by Kant and the neo-innatists such as Chomsky and Fodor. But where precisely do these commitments stand?

From its inception, every scientific program develops out of "themata" extremely general strategies of ordering reality expressed through "quasi-aesthetic judgments . . . with deep psychological roots."[1] Gerald Holton suggests a discipline, called "thematic analysis of science," which adds a third dimension or a "Z-axis" to the empirical and the heuristic-analytical axes heretofore established by historians and philosophers of science. "This third dimension is the dimension of fundamental presuppositions, notions, terms, methodological judgments and decisions—in short, of themata or themes—which are themselves neither directly evolved from, nor resolvable into, objective observation on the one hand, or logical, mathematical, and other formal analytical ratiocination on the other hand."[2] Interestingly enough, Holton appeals to a Piagetian genetic epistemological analysis of such themes: "It is likely that the origin of themata will be best approached through studies concerned with the nature of perception, and particularly of the psychological development of concepts in young children."[3]

Let us try to apply a thematic analysis, almost in a self-referential context, to Piaget and to the foundations of his genetic epistemology. It has not escaped the attention of many commentators that Piaget's program in developmental psychology relies heavily on the theme of *equilibrium*.[4] Subservient to this dominant theme is Piaget's constant emphasis on adaptation, assimilation, homeostasis, and autoregulation. His complex and tightly argued essay on biology and knowledge is, ideally and admittedly, a kind of self-oriented epistemology.[5] The guiding ontological commitment (*hypothèse directrice*), perhaps a bit acritically justified on the grounds of its "banality" and its "simplicity," (*très simple et d'une banalité complète*)[6] is the following: "Life is essentially autoregulation." The essay as a whole purports to be a sequential unfolding of the innumerable implications of this assertion. Anticipating what Piaget also states in the present volume, we are told that self-regulation is a *third* way, avoiding both Darwinism and Lamarckism. Cybernetic feedback loops and information flows are the cornerstone of self-regulation, to which cognition belongs as a subdomain proper. The focal problem is "describing those organs that bring about regulations," entailing a search for the mechanisms through which organic regulations include "as a fundamental element of ever-increasing importance, exchanges with the environment. These exchanges are subject to their own progressive adjustments." These presuppositions lead to a core hypothesis, out of which the entire program of genetic epistemology has been developed. We read the following, italicized in the original text: "Cognitive processes seem, then, to be at one and the same time the outcome of organic autoregulation, reflecting its essential mechanisms, and the most highly differentiated organs of this regulation at the core of interactions with the environment." Piaget adds that "in the case of man, these processes are being extended to the universe itself."[7] This I take to be the "hard core" of the Piagetian program, around which a protective belt of strictly psychogenetic hypotheses has been fastened.

There are two interpretations of what Piaget commits us to believing. The weaker interpretation is "simple" and "banal," exactly as he claims; the stronger one is not trivial, but is susceptible to refutation. The weaker interpretation is that the process we call life rests on a process of a more general kind, detectable also in inorganic and artificial systems, called regulation. No biologist since Claude Bernard would contend with that. The stronger interpretation is that regulation patterns and the structures on which they are based get "swallowed" *(englobées)* by the organism by means of a sequence of operations called *assimilation, reorganization,* and *accommodation.* The ideal metaphor for describing this stronger interpretation is "transfer of order" or even "transfer of structure." Although Piaget does not himself use these words in exactly these combinations, he nonetheless speaks of *structures of order, nested structures (emboîtements),* and *epigenotype*[8] in a dynamic framework that encourages us to relabel the hypothesis in question in a somewhat more provocative, almost blunt statement. Can there be a "transfer of structure" from the milieu to the organism? Piaget's answer seems to be yes. The present volume amply testifies that this is indeed what his evolutionary "third way" boils down to. What Guy Cellérier calls "Piaget's gentleman's disagreement with Darwin" (see Chapter 2) recurs in Piaget's contributions here. His reliance on the notion of "phenocopy" goes toward a transfer of structure, that is, toward what molecular biologists such as Jacob, Danchin, and Changeux purport to exclude categorically. Jacob states squarely: *"There is regulation only on structures and with structures that exist and that are there to regulate"* (see Chapter 2), which must be understood as having an implicit presupposition and an unspoken consequence: the presupposition is that both structures (the regulating and the regulated) already preexist when regulation takes place; the consequence is that the total range of regulatory mechanisms available to an organism is constrained from the start by the blueprint of that organism. One cannot pierce what Changeux calls the "genetic envelope" of a given species except through random mutations occurring from the inside, unrelated to any "structure" the outside world may offer. Thus Piaget and contemporary molecular biology appear to uphold very different— even antithetical—ontological presuppositions. It seems to me that this debate shows clearly and for the first time that (1) Piaget's "hard core" is to be interpreted according to the stronger version, accommodating the concept of transfer of structures within its constitutive hypotheses, and (2) this assumption openly clashes with the ontological commitments of molecular biologists.

Piaget's hard core corresponds more closely to that of a distinct scientific research program which, although a few biologists like C. H. Waddington and Ludwig von Bertalanffy have adhered to it, shares very little with what is now "classical" molecular biology. This program can be thought of as the "self-organizing systems" approach. In his "Afterthoughts" (Chapter 13), Piaget says that he had, subsequent to the meeting, an "aha-experience" while reading Heinz von Foerster's statement of the "order from noise" principle. We will now turn our attention to this principle in order to get a clearer picture of the inner logic of Piaget's hard core.

THE "ORDER FROM NOISE" PRINCIPLE VERSUS THE "CRYSTAL" PARADIGM

A universal tendency of all systems toward their state of equilibrium has been the focal ontological commitment of classical mechanics, later refined and generalized by analytical mechanics in terms of the principles of "least action" and of "shortest path," and in such sophisticated disguise, this principle has trespassed into contemporary quantum physics. In classical thermodynamics, a complementary and parallel commitment was endorsed and translated into the macroscopic (that is, purely phenomenological) principle of energy conservation and of constant increase of entropy (that is, increasing disorder) in isolated systems. The progressive "problemshift" promoted by Boltzmann's scientific research program of statistical thermodynamics, started somewhere between 1865 and 1870,[9] became gradually capable of translating these different but related principles one into the other and of making of classical thermodynamics an average approximation of ideally precise molecular interactions. Mechanical reversibility and thermodynamic irreversibility were reconciled by treating the latter as an average gross approximation of the former. The "law of large numbers" was there to guarantee that microscopic shocks, spreading out uniformly in time and space the distribution of local dynamic variables associated with single molecules, inevitably ended up with less ordered (and therefore more "probable") macroscopic states.

These bridging laws, however welcome they were to the physicist and the chemist, seemed to baffle the hope of reducing the principles of biological organization to a mere appendage of "ordinary" physicochemical principles. If the spontaneous trend of inanimate matter points toward increasing uniformity and the intimate mixing of everything with everything else, how can one account for the progressive complexity and finer differentiation shown by biological evolution? The entropy law of spontaneous increasing disorder seems to fly in the face of the laws of evolution as ascertained by the biologist. Each living system is, however, an "open" system from the thermodynamic point of view. It is, moreover, a system that is "far from equilibrium," as recent works by Ilya Prigogine and Manfred Eigen have emphasized. Biological order is maintained at the expense of a constant incoming flow of matter and energy. Even though Helmholtz had declared in his momentous paper of 1847, "On the Conservation of Energy," that "the question . . . whether the combustion and metamorphosis of the substances which serve as nutriment generate a quantity of heat equal to that given out by animals . . . can be approximately answered in the affirmative,"[10] the mutual compatibility between thermodynamic laws and biological phenomena has remained an open problem for a long time. Two opposing ontological commitments face each other and keep offering their mutually incompatible credentials to provide *the* explanation of how life is possible. These opposing themes are best visualized by the *crystal* on the one side (invariance of specific structures) and the *flame* on the other (constancy of external forms in spite of relentless internal agitation). The search for a *third* way out of this dilemma (structure *or* process, inborn patterns *or* self-reorganization) has constituted for more than a century the common trait of otherwise distinct and sometimes contrasting research programs. For the sake of simplicity, let us confine our archeology to the research programs extending uninterruptedly until today, in fact until this very debate between Piaget and Chomsky.

The "crystal" theme, first raised to the level of a plausible scientific world model or archetype by René-Just Haüy in 1784,[11] entails at least two far-reaching assumptions, namely: (1) that specific visible patterns are always, at least in principle, traceable to the microscopic world, where they correspond to specific molecular patterns, and (2) that the crystalline (or molecular) underworld can only change according to its own rules. There is no symmetry of determinism between the two worlds; the microscopic dictates its laws to the macroscopic. August Weismann, the father of the germ-plasm theory, was already categorical on this point: "As in the growing crystal the single molecules cannot become joined together at pleasure, but only in a fixed manner, so are the parts of an organism governed in their respective distribution . . . In the case of a crystal it has not occurred to anybody to ascribe the harmonious disposition of the parts to a teleological power; why then should we assume such a force in the organism, and thus discontinue the attempt, which has already been commenced, to refer to its natural causes that harmony of parts which is here certainly present and equally conformable to law?"[12] Weismann's discovery of chromosomes and the subsequent identification of these microstructures as the material carriers of hereditary traits are the main stepping-stones toward contemporary molecular genetics. Another far-reaching assumption, to which we will return in some detail when examining the Chomskian hard core, is the dichotomy first established by Johannsen between *genotype* and *phenotype*, thereby separating physically, logically, and operationally the ideal stock of potentialities relative to a species (genetic competence) from its multifarious, context-dependent expression in terms of individual patterns (actual performance).

In 1943 Erwin Schroedinger, with almost prophetic insight, advanced the hypothesis that genes are "aperiodic crystals," and in ten years, thanks to Watson and Crick, the structure of such aperiodic crystals was decoded. This is, in rough summary, the scientific research program of molecular biology, whose hard core forms the background of Jacob's remarks (see Chapter 2) and of Danchin's "critical note" concerning phenocopy (see Appendix A).

Schroedinger's lectures of 1943 are, however, in retrospect, the Y-junction from which a quite different research program also developed.[13] Crystals are fine, but, so this new story goes, there is much more, physically speaking, to life than crystal structures alone can account for. There is statistical disorder, which constantly surrounds the crystal patterns, and vibrational, rotational, and twisting random motions, which are revealed by closer inspection at the atomic level. After all, it had long been recognized that mutations arising from within the genetic structure are part and parcel of the evolution of living beings. Schroedinger was thus compelled to make the important consideration that life "feeds on" both order (the aperiodic crystals and other regular molecular patterns) and disorder (random atomic vibrations and collisions). This apparently untendentious remark was to be grafted, within the space of a few years, onto the freshly developed hard core of Shannon's information theory, and especially to the notion of messages flowing through a channel perturbed by parasitic noise. In 1959 Léon Brillouin added to the research program of information theory a new ontological commitment: the identity between information and entropy, as previously defined by thermodynamics (with a minus algebraic sign, hence the term "neg-entropy"). The dispersed elements then click together, and the ontological framework is reassessed under the guidance of the following assumption: living systems are, basically, informational devices, their genes being a *source* of messages, their different processing mechanisms a *channel,* and the mature individual the *receiver*. The bio-informational hard core and the Piagetian guiding commitment *(hypothèse directrice)* are based on the belief that life is a gigantic information flow mediating (or regulating) the transition of the "entire universe" from a less organized initial state to increasingly more organized steady states. Cognitive acts (human cognitive acts in particular) are the most efficient mediators of such information flow, the privileged catalysts of a cascade of transfers of order from one portion of the universe to the next.

There is a major puzzle to be solved, however, if this ontological commitment is to be protected from the devious assaults of rational criticism and carefully collected evidence. How can order *increase* other than by execution of a predetermined ad hoc program? How can the notion of spontaneity and strict autonomy of development be matched with that of an increase in degree of complexity? Molecular biology (that is, the contemporary edition of the crystal outlook) can accommodate these conflicting injunctions thanks to the concept of genetic programs or genomes. Order can increase and structure can become more and more complex because the organism is equipped with a constructive plan, distinct from its material expressions and containing from the very start the "envelope" of its possible realizations. Noise (that is, random fluctuations) can hinder or facilitate the process of growth, divert or block the possible pathways of development, but it can never dictate their geometry. There is no transfer of structure from the macro-environment to the micro-archive.

Heinz von Foerster, whose ideas are now enthusiastically endorsed by Piaget, makes a different assumption, of which the manifold implications have not yet been fully examined.[14] He contends that random fluctuations can indeed *create* order and not only reveal (as in a photographic processing) the underlying constructive plan. When a highly complex system is submitted to all sorts of indignities, such as shaking, twisting, and scrambling, its component parts are amenable to interlocking with one another and materializing into a new system instantiating unprecedented ordered patterns. The order that thus arises from noise is "potentially encoded" in the local organization of the component parts, but *nowhere else,* that is, in no global blueprint applying to the system *as a whole.* Coherence and order at a global level arise from local interactions only.

A rigorous treatment of the "order from fluctuations" principle has been developed, albeit from a different standpoint and at the physicochemical level, by Prigogine through his theory of dissipative structures. Both approaches fit very well into Piaget's more general conception of "autoregulation" and seem to provide even harder physicomathematical justifications for his cognitive-psychological hard core. It is reasonable to anticipate that any assailant of the Piagetian hard core (leaving aside local incursions into the protective belts of his "psychology" proper) will have to take arms simultaneously against a host of related conceptions. Ontological commitments tend to form clusters, and although some may be more resistant than others, or bear on separate domains of reality, the history of science proves that local wounds heal quickly when the surrounding tissue is unaffected. In my opinion von Foerster's principle is far from being flawless, and Prigogine's theory may well also support a "selectivist" explanation of cognitive processes, as opposed to an "instructivist" or a "constructivist" one. But it would be out of place to delve any deeper into these technical questions here. Before moving on to the main topic of this debate, we must analyze the Chomskian hard core.

THE CHOMSKIAN HARD CORE

The overpowering "theme," in Holton's terms, of the Chomskian scientific research program in linguistics is undoubtedly the classical notion of *rationalism.* An allegiance to Descartes and Leibniz is recurrent throughout all of Chomsky's major writings. Its affinities for what I have labeled the "crystal" program are manifold, as I will attempt to show.[15] The focal assumption of the rationalist program, as will be made clear in the present debate, can be expressed as follows: the environment per se has no structure, or at least none that is *directly* assimilable by the organism. All laws of order, whether they are biological, cognitive, or linguistic, come from inside, and order is *imposed* upon the perceptual world, not *derived* from it. These laws of order are assumed to be species-specific, invariant over time and across individuals and cultures. The positive heuristics of all such programs, Kant's included, is to characterize in depth and in detail the internal structure of a universal subject (the "ideal speaker" of Chomsky) through adequate abstractions from empirical givens.

Abstraction is *not*, however, generalization through progressive extension, and data are *not* brute facts observed by an "innocent eye" (in Gombrich's terms). The rationalist positive heuristic is grounded on an awareness that theory is involved from the outset in the sorting out of *relevant* observation from sheer noise (from which no order is expected to arise). In the present debate, Chomsky and Fodor frequently emphasize the notion of relevance within their rationalist approach (see Chapters 3, 5, 15, 16). There is no denial, in Chomsky's and Fodor's sometimes extreme positions, that there is much more to language and cognition (for example, culture, social interactions, affectivity) than the nativist approach alone can account for, but the demarcation is still very sharp between what in all these contexts is *pertinent to the problem at hand* (the structure of the universal subject) and what is irretrievably *alien* to it.

In addition to the commitment to universal inborn structures and to theory-determined abstractions, rationalism is also committed to a "compartment theory" of the human mind. The internal structure of the ideal speaker, or of the universal cognitive-perceptive subject, not only has to be specific in its totality, but also has to be decomposable into equally specific substructures, amenable to separate investigations. The rationalist commitment entails a kind of lumping strategy through which domains are demarcated and rendered as little as possible "conversant" with one another. Such abstract models, to be of any scientific value, have to be general enough to give a grasp of a truly universal subject, but detailed enough to become informative and falsifiable by experiment. They can, moreover, afford to be local (that is, relative to a well-defined subdomain) and very exacting in terms of the innate properties that one is led to attribute to the organism. It is one thing to allow for some rudimentary, poorly articulated *inborn potentialities* (not even the extreme behaviorists have rejected that), and quite another to postulate very complex and highly *specific* innate structures that are *actually available* to the organism. This is what Putnam calls the "messy miracle" of human nature (see Chapter 14)— to which Chomsky and Fodor respond with a characteristic "rationalist" statement, revealing their underlying negative heuristic: "Why should it be otherwise?" Since beavers show highly specific inborn patterns of behavior to build dams, and spiders to build webs, why should not humans, who are by evidence endowed with much more complex brains, not have inborn linguistic structures as complicated as the "specified subject condition" or "bound anaphora?" (See Chapters 1 and 15.) The rationalist ontological commitment is very transparent here.

Is it out of mere coincidence—or worse, just through free association of words—that the "crystal" theme was turned into a scientific research program by Haüy's "law of rational indexes?" Do the two notions of "rationality" have anything in common? I think they do, and I will proceed to explain why. This will not be an idle exercise in scientific archeology; on the contrary, I see no better and quicker way to attune the reader to the far-reaching resonances of this debate. We have seen above, in broad outline, why the Piagetian program departs from the molecular biological one. It is useful to see now why the Chomskian program comes so close to it.

Haüy is committed to "the idea, so satisfying and so true, that in general nature tends to uniformity and simplicity."[16] This is the crystal theme in its pure and lofty form. It becomes a more sanguine commitment, however, when it descends to earth, to the mineral world: "The ratios between the dimensions of the limiting forms possess this last property [simplicity] in a remarkable way."[17] But the crystal conception of orderly forms, the living ones included, had more compelling hypotheses in its conceptual tool kit than just "simplicity"; it had *specificity* (of patterns), *directiveness* (of forces), *stability* (of local structures), *numerability* (of a finite set of combinatorial build-ups), and, finally, the all-important notion of pattern *revelation* (as opposed to infinite creation of forms by the environment). We will see in the debate that today, using more technologically sophisticated terms, this concept is visualized by "photographic development" (see Chapter 4) or, to borrow from molecular biology, by the concept of "template." The German botanist

Schleiden, with the less sophisticated language available to him in 1850, wrote that "the matter of the crystal exists in the liquid, already formed, and it suffices to withdraw the solvent in order to force its appearance in fixed form."[18] The chemical statement is directly translatable into Chomsky's photographic concepts of "exposure" (to linguistic data) and of "development." After all, photographic development is literally a process of light-induced crystallization. The hard core of both crystallographic "rationality" and generative linguistics is that "all structure comes from within." Environment *reveals* this structure; it does not *imprint* its own patterns on the system. It should by now be evident why the confrontation between constructivism and innatism runs, all through this book, precisely on this crucial dividing line.

Positive Heuristic and Protective Belts

The continuum connecting the "crystal" program in the natural sciences and the Chomskian program in linguistics subsists also at the level of the *positive heuristic.* According to Lakatos, "the negative heuristic specifies the 'hard core' of the program which is 'irrefutable' by the methodological decision of its protagonists; the positive heuristic consists of a partially articulated set of suggestions or hints on how to change, develop the 'refutable variants' of the research program, how to modify, sophisticate the 'refutable protective belt.' "[19] Ontological commitments pertaining to the negative heuristic consist of *negative expectations* (there is no structure in the environment per se, there is no transfer of structure from the outside to the inside, and so on); those pertaining to a positive heuristic consist of *selective conditional expectations.* Assuming, as all tenants of the "crystal" negative heuristic do, that no laws of order are supplemented by the environment, the positive heuristic entails the consequential assumption that structures (1) are internal to the organism, (2) are species-specific, (3) are contingent (logic *alone,* unaided by experiment, cannot account for what they are), and (4) preexist to any orderly interaction with the outer world.

This is, however, a rather approximative set of statements, which need to be amended and spelled out more precisely. What Chomsky (or a "crystal theorist" in general) will say is rather that the structure of the environment is *not* the intrinsic structure of the organism, nor can the former be incorporated *as such* into the latter. The intrinsic structure of the organism determines what structured features of the environment will be transferred within. ("Transfer" has to be understood here in terms of a decoding or mapping function, and not as literally an incorporation or a direct embodiment.) Thus if one is interested in the nature of the organism rather than in the order in the environment, one will focus attention on *intrinsic determinants*, such as the built-in properties of the visual cortex (which permit certain structures from the environment to affect the steady state attained in a certain way), the genotype, or universal grammar (see my remarks at the beginning of Chapter 4).

The "protective belt" of the "crystal" program is made up of precise hypotheses on how patterns are selected, by the varying parameters of the environment, out of a finite numberable *set of possible configurations*. In structural chemistry (and biochemistry), the sets of possible conformations are generated through groups of transformations (symmetry groups, translational groups, rotational groups, and so forth) applying to ideal elementary units or "cells." Each observed pattern instantiates a *specific ordered string* of such transformations. The chemical nature of the atoms and the specification of environmental parameters (temperature, pressure, ionic force of the solvent) determine which string is selected in each case out of the set of all possible ones. Forms, in Schleiden's terms, "preexist" in the liquid and are "forced to materialize" under appropriate conditions. The positive heuristic of the Chomskian program is expressed through commitments that resemble very closely those of Schleiden. Chomsky specifies that a "rationalist" account of language acquisition is based on "the assumption that various formal and substantive universals are intrinsic properties of the language acquisition system, these providing a schema that is applied to data and that determines in a highly restricted way the general form and, in part, even the substantive features of the grammar that may emerge upon presentation of appropriate data."[20] Data exert no "formative" action on the ideal speaker-listener. There is, according to Chomsky, no assimilation or interiorization by the subject of structures subsisting independently outside. Data have, in the rationalist approach, a sort of "triggering" action. Chomsky is explicit on this point: "In part [primary linguistic] data determine to which of the possible languages the language learner is being exposed . . . but such data may play an entirely different role as well; namely, certain kinds of data and experience may be required in order to set the language-acquisition device into operation, although they may not affect the manner of its functioning in the least."[21] In the present volume, Chomsky and Fodor call this the "ignition key" hypothesis (see Chapter 7): the engine is switched on by the ignition key, but the structure of the ignition device bears no resemblance to the structure of the combustion engine. Their positive heuristic is dominated by this assumption.

Every rationalist program, at least since Leibniz, is committed to a search for the set of formal rules governing the world of possible structures. Access to this hidden world can only be secured by theoretical insight and steel-hard reasoning, not by simple enumeration of actually observed patterns. Catalogues are of no use unless they are collected, *from the start,* under the guidance of a nontrivial falsifiable and theoretical model. Information only informs if there is a theory behind it. "There is, first of all, the question of how one is to obtain information about the speaker-hearer's competence, about his knowledge of the language. Like most facts of interest and importance, this is neither presented for direct observation nor extractable from data by inductive procedures of any known sort."[22]

Chomsky's linguistic program, in contrast to the classical rationalist program in philosophy, is a scientific research program and is thus committed to painstaking work on relevant data that can provide tests for the conjectures embedded in the protective belt. But even though facts are irretrievably enmeshed with theory, linguistics and cognitive psychology are not pure mathematics, as Chomsky points out in the present debate (Chapter 2), nor should there continue to be endless brooding on the consequences of a theoretical assumption (see Chapter 12). Observation must have its say, and observation is sometimes messy, perturbed by noise, and not rigorously reproducible, especially in the human sciences. From this comes the need to separate, on logical and operational grounds, the universe of possible organizations from actually observable organized patterns. The latter *have to be seen* (in a rationalist positive heuristic) as *instantiations* of the former. The partition of the scientific "object" into two related but distinct realms is cardinal to the rationalist program (and in particular to its naturalistic version that we have called the "crystal" program). Such a partition has ontological consequences, since the sets of possible forms and the laws governing them are conceived as objectively *inherent to* the domains under study, and not just as useful figments of imagination existing solely in the heads of scientists. Part II of this volume delves deeply into this question. (Are grammars properties of the brain of the speaker or properties of the language?)

Crystallographers introduced concepts such as crystal force (von Leonhard), formative processes and formative powers

(Ungar), and valence and coordination power, ending up, after Schroedinger, with the notion of informational content associated to the aperiodicity of biological crystals (proteins and nucleic acids). Cytologists produced the working hypothesis of a functional distinction between germen and soma (Weismann), and geneticists endorsed the subtler distinction between genotype and phenotype (Johanssen), the inner logic of which dictates the remarks made at this meeting by Jacob, Changeux, and Danchin (see Chapters 2 and 8 and Appendix A). Chomsky introduces a similar distinction between *competence* and *performance,* respectively defined as "the speaker-hearer's knowledge of his language" and "the actual use of language in concrete situations."[23] How closely the competence/performance and the genotype/phenotype distinctions relate to each other will appear in the course of this debate.[24] It is worth noting, however, that Premack (see Chapter 7) opens a crucial problem when he asks whether the concept of competence should include the actual propensity to *use* the competence—a problem that, as Monod reminds us (Chapter 7), was already present in Descartes.[25] The ongoing refinement of models in generative linguistics has led to important reassessments within this partition and to movable frontiers between "linguistic levels" (syntactic, semantic, pragmatic) since Chomsky first stated their constitutive principles.[26] These are, however, the typical refinements of a "protective belt," and they need not concern us here. Reverting back to the unchanged (and, as Lakatos anticipates, intrinsically irrefutable) hard core, we see that there are immediate consequences of the competence/performance dichotomy. Universal grammar is, by definition, invariant across individuals and across languages; it is ultimately to be accounted for in terms of species-specific neuronal circuits. Chomsky often reminds us that this biological "reduction" is possible *in principle,* though not as yet accomplished in fact (see Chapters 2 and 4). More precisely, what Chomsky suggests is that it is a very satisfying first approximation to make the assumption that the initial state of the language faculty is invariant or species-specific (that is, to abstract away from such individual or cultural differences as may exist). Of course, in a more complete analysis the real competence attained in the steady state will show differences; there is *a* competence for *a* given language (French, English, Japanese, and so on). There are also individual differences within a given language. Nor is it claimed that such a characterization of the initial stage of the language faculty (presumably genetically coded) is literally invariant, but rather that one can properly abstract away from variation to determine the basic species character of the organism, just as one abstracts away from individual differences when one tries to find out what it is that makes humans grow arms instead of wings (see Chapter 2). Competence is an abstract property ascribed to the "steady state" attained by the ideal speaker-listener in the course of time, as a result of neurological development and of a suitable schedule of exposure to "relevant" linguistic data. Apart from gross neurological insults or extreme deprivations of sensory input (such as the *enfants sauvages* severed from all contacts with a community of speakers), the steady state is invariably attained. Constructing a plausible (though specific, informationally rich, and refutable) model of this steady state is the central task of the "universal grammar." Since the concept of a steady state is a substantial part of the Chomskian hard core, it requires a bit of "thematic" analysis.

The heuristic power of the steady state is equal to that of Piaget's "autoregulation," but it points toward a different chain of ontological commitments. Once again I assume there are two possible levels of commitment, a weaker one, certainly sound but of no momentum, and a stronger one, relevant but subject to questioning. Every physical system can be characterized as "being in" a state of some sort, specifiable if need be by a set of values attached to its constitutive parameters. The first concept of state presupposes no more (but no less) than the accessibility of the system to measurement (even approximative) and sufficient identification through descriptive statements (a state has to be different from another state). This is the weaker commitment. Chomsky specifies that linguistic analysis must aim at gaining insight into "the tacit knowledge of the native speaker" through "introspective evidence." The steady state implies, therefore, accessibility to measurement (of a particular kind) and identification in terms of describable properties of *that* state. We will, moreover, read in this volume (Chapter 4) that a hypothetical alternative model of the idealized speaker that allows the system to draw inferences of a different kind from those demonstrably drawn by real human speakers when exposed to a given set of data (for instance, inferring structure-independent rules as "good" rules for forming the interrogative) is a "bad" model; it cannot work because it presupposes a different and *incompatible* underlying steady state.

States are, therefore, attributed to systems that are accessible to "measurement" (rules of transformation imply quantitative assessments) and are describable through statements identifying state A as distinct from state B. But Chomsky goes further than that, for he assumes that some computations or "inferences" are, as we will see, incompatible with the supposed structure of the system. Thus, states are not only distinguishable and susceptible to being ordered (hierarchically, sequentially, chronologically) but also are subject to eliminative induction, in terms of compatibility and incompatibility. The stronger commitment, as indeed was to be expected, is the one that Chomsky endorses. States are conceived as deterministic "regimes" of functioning, susceptible to factorial analysis. Steady states, in the conjectural ascription that Chomsky makes of them to the ideal speaker-listener, are, characteristically, *computational abilities* of a specific kind.

Such an ontological commitment entails the identity between linguistic representations (in the mind of the speaker-listener) and computations in a suitable "medium." The far-reaching consequences of an a priori identification between mental states and computations are exhaustively analyzed by Jerry Fodor in his book *The Language of Thought*[27] (see also his presentation in Chapter 6 and his "Reply to Putnam" in Part II of this volume). The "theme" of computation appears to be deeply entrenched in the hard core of generative linguistics and cognitive psychology. Fodor is categorical on this point: "The only psychological models of cognitive processes that seem even remotely plausible represent such processes as computational." Such a commitment, in turn, entails the assumption that mental states (and in particular those that are involved in the processing of linguistic data) are orderly sequences of microstates characterized by finite differences between local parameters. In principle, at least, neurobiologists in the twenty-first century will make it their business to specify in terms of neuronal switches what these microstates consist of. The steady state can therefore be assimilated to a multipurpose master program endowed with vast arrays of optional subroutines running in sequence or in parallel, whose different stages of accomplishment correspond to specific microstates of the brain machinery. But here the positive heuristic faces some serious problems. Microstates of this kind are ideal states, on precisely the same unsafe footing that made Boltzmann's program of statistical mechanics crumble under the brunt of quantum mechanics. The microstates of statistical mechanics turned out to be *illegitimate* idealizations of macroscopic dynamic states. Quantum laws *in principle* forbid extrapolating to the ideal case of microscopic systems the measurements that can be carried out at a macroscopic level. The notion of state is *not* an invariant across physical orders of magnitude. Therefore, some ontological assumptions that are constitutive of the Chomskian hard core may, in the long run, prove untenable. To dispel all immediate concerns, it is safe to assume that linguists and psychologists will not have to grapple with these niceties for a long time to come, if ever. Nonetheless, a thematic analysis is forced to contemplate such prospective predicaments. The notion of state is, after all, less innocent than it appears at first sight.

STEADY STATES, FLAMES, AND CRYSTALS

The adjective *steady*, unassuming as it may appear at first sight, actually opens a thematic bridge toward the tenets of the "other" school of thought, that is, the "order-from-noise" conception of life and cognition. This shift is probably unintentional on the Chomskian side and is certainly, at the present macroscopic stage, noncommittal. Steady states are typical of *dynamic equilibria*, whereas stable states are typical of *static equilibria*. Chomsky is right in describing the standard computational "regime" of his ideal subjects as steady rather than stable. A billiard ball coming to rest at the bottom of a basin, or crystals being formed under progressive saturation of a solution, constitute canonical examples of stable equilibrium states. In dynamic processes, whenever a constant turnover of matter is geared to a uniform flow of transformable energy, steady states may appear. The canonical example is the flame of a candle in an environment devoid of turbulence.

Historically and epistemologically, the archetype of the crystal and the archetype of the flame as "models" of life have always been opposed to each other. Modern biology has successfully avoided the horns of that dilemma by committing itself to the model of a "tape-recorded program." Biomolecular crystals are tightly packed containers of information (the DNA template, the messenger RNA, the catalytic site of enzymes, and so on) whereby dynamic equilibria are produced and controlled in the living organism. The concept of *information* and the ensuing concept of *processing* (that is, computing) fill the gap, in biology as well as in cognitive psychology, between the hard core of the "orthodox" crystal program and the more dynamically oriented requirements that have to be met if new fields of inquiry are to bend under its dictum. The "bound information" program is, essentially, a more sophisticated makeup of the crystal program, having appointed Schroedinger and Crick-Watson as chief cosmeticians.

Flows of information are processed in the brain by standard programs whose compiler is, in ultimate analysis, the genetic program itself. It is precisely at this delicate joint that constructivists and proponents of order-from-noise drive their wedge. In fact, they assume it to be an integral part of their job to find adequate explanations of how any program whatsoever can be assembled in the first place. Following this line of argumentation, if an innatist explanation holds for man, it must on the same grounds hold for bacteria and viruses (see Piaget's remarks in Chapters 1 and 2 and my editorial notes at the end of Chapters 1 and 6). One therefore invariably comes to the point where a program must have materialized out of something that was *not* a program. But this, Chomsky and Fodor retort, is none of their concern—linguists and psychologists already have a difficult enough time explaining the gross properties of a particular species without getting involved in the parochial *biochemical* problem of how life originated. Up to this point, the quibble is about "what interests me" or "what is an integral part of my job as psychologist or linguist." No philosophical argument will ever be of help in matters of taste. Innatists retort, rather cogently, that to try to determine the characteristics of, say, the visual cortex of the cat or for some future biologist to try to find out in some detail how the genetic program for humans gives rise to brain lateralization and how it shapes brain connectivity is by no means sweeping the dust under the rug. They contend that the study of the nature and unfolding of the genetic program is a study *on a very different level* from the investigation of how this genetic endowment reached its present state in the species. They cannot see any contradiction inherent in this methodological stand. The tenants of the order-from-noise principle purport, however, to demonstrate that no explanation in terms of preset programs is *logically* sound unless one gives at least a hint of how programs are assembled at their source. Sweeping the dust under the rug (that is, pretending not to bother with the origins of programs) does not improve, in the long run, the cleanliness of the innatist clubroom. The problem will have to be met head on one day or another. Self-organization, so their story goes, has to precede, logically and factually, program-directed regulation. The "self" prefix stands for "out of non-organization" or, in von Foerster's terms, "from noise." There is no program dictating the shape and the constancy of the flame, but nonetheless, whenever the external conditions are fulfilled, a flame will materialize and will go on burning with always exactly the same pattern of bright, dark, and dimly luminous zones. A steady state can fathom its inner necessity nowhere else than in the disordered shocks of particles, governed by their *local* microscopic structures. Piaget's positive heuristic is dominated by the assumption that there can be "necessity without innateness"; in other words, that structures can form, reproduce, and subsist without a program dictating all their possible assemblies *as a whole* and *from the very beginning.* Global order can arise from local "myopic" orders. The steady state is the cornerstone of such a conception.

Is the notion of steady state a sort of "traffic circle" where Piaget's constructivism and Chomsky's rationalist innatism, at least momentarily, converge? It is for the reader to answer this question. The debate supplies ample food for thought. Piaget and Changeux, as well as Papert, Cellérier, and Inhelder, opt for a possible compromise. Chomsky and Fodor insist that their conceptions diverge from those of the Geneva school on practically all assumptions of some methodological importance. In my editorial remarks I will draw the reader's attention to these problems in more detail. For the time being, I will close by mentioning that the themes "local versus global" or "centered versus acentered" or "structure versus process" are as yet the "soft" core of future biological programs. The destiny of the "bound information" program of contemporary molecular biology will depend on the ultimate success of these themes in explaining vast bodies of experimental data. For the moment, this program is in all respects by far the best that has been envisaged by science to account for man's own constitutive principles as a living being. As to language and learning, about which this introduction has intentionally said very little, the programs are stated by Piaget and Chomsky themselves. After all, that is precisely what the book is about.

PART I

The Debate

CHAPTER ONE

Opening the Debate

The Psychogenesis of Knowledge and Its Epistemological Significance

Jean Piaget

Fifty years of experience have taught us that knowledge does not result from a mere recording of observations without a structuring activity on the part of the subject. Nor do any a priori or innate cognitive structures exist in man; the functioning of intelligence alone is hereditary and creates structures only through an organization of successive actions performed on objects. Consequently, an epistemology conforming to the data of psychogenesis could be neither empiricist nor preformationist, but could consist only of a constructivism, with a continual elaboration of new operations and structures. The central problem, then, is to understand how such operations come about, and why, even though they result from nonpredetermined constructions, they eventually become logically necessary.

EMPIRICISM

The critique of empiricism is not tantamount to negating the role of experimentation, but the "empirical" study of the genesis of knowledge shows from the onset the insufficiency of an "empiricist" interpretation of experience. In fact, no knowledge is based on perceptions alone, for these are always directed and

23

accompanied by schemes of action. Knowledge, therefore, proceeds from action, and all action that is repeated or generalized through application to new objects engenders by this very fact a "scheme," that is, a kind of practical concept. The fundamental relationship that constitutes all knowledge is not, therefore, a mere "association" between objects, for this notion neglects the active role of the subject, but rather the "assimilation" of objects to the schemes of that subject. This process, moreover, prolongs the various forms of biological "assimilations," of which cognitive association is a particular case as a functional process of integration. Conversely, when objects are assimilated to schemes of action, there is a necessary "adaptation" to the particularities of these objects (compare the phenotypic "adaptations" in biology), and this adaptation results from external data, hence from experience. It is thus this exogenous mechanism that converges with what is valid in the empiricist thesis, but (and this reservation is essential) adaptation does not exist in a "pure" or isolated state, since it is always the adaptation of an assimilatory scheme; therefore this assimilation remains the driving force of cognitive action.

These mechanisms, which are visible from birth, are completely general and are found in the various levels of scientific thought. The role of assimilation is recognized in the fact that an "observable" or a "fact" is always interpreted from the moment of its observation, for this observation always and from the beginning requires the utilization of logico-mathematical frameworks such as the setting up of a relationship or a correspondence, proximities or separations, positive or negative quantifications leading to the concept of measure—in short, a whole conceptualization on the part of the subject that excludes the existence of pure "facts" as completely external to the activities of this subject, all the more as the subject must make the phenomena vary in order to assimilate them.

As for the learning processes invoked by the behaviorist empiricists on behalf of their theses, Inhelder, Sinclair, and Bovet have shown that these processes do not explain cognitive development but are subject to its laws, for a stimulus acts as such only at a certain level of "competence" (another biological notion akin to assimilation). Briefly, the action of a stimulus presupposes the presence of a scheme, which is the true source of the response (which reverses the SR schema or makes it symmetrical [$S \leftrightarrows R$]). Besides, Pribram has demonstrated a selection of inputs existing even at the neurological level.

PREFORMATION

Is it necessary, then, to turn in the direction of the preformation of knowledge? I will return later to the problem of innateness and will limit myself for the moment to the discussion of the hypothesis of determination. If one considers the facts of psychogenesis, one notes first the existence of stages that seem to bear witness to a continual construction. In the first place, in the sensorimotor period preceding language one sees the establishment of a logic of actions (relations of order, interlocking of schemes, intersections, establishment of relationships, and so on), rich in discoveries and even in inventions (recognition of permanent objects, organization of space, of causality). From the ages of 2 to 7, there is a conceptualization of actions, and therefore representations, with discovery of functions between covariations of phenomena, identities, and so forth, but without yet any concept of reversible operations or of conservation. These last two concepts are formed at the level of concrete operations (ages 7 to 10), with the advent of logically structured "groupings," but they are still bound to the manipulation of objects. Finally, around the age of 11 to 12, a hypothetico-deductive propositional logic is formed, with a combinatorial lattice, "sums of parts," algebraic four-groups, and so on.

However, these beautiful successive and sequential constructions (where each one is necessary to the following one) could be interpreted as the progressive actualization (related to factors such as neurological maturity) of a set of preformations, similar to the way in which genetic programming regulates organic "epigenesis" even though the latter continues to interact with the environment and its objects. The problem is therefore to choose between two hypotheses: authentic constructions with stepwise disclosures to new possibilities, or successive actualization of a set of possibilities *existing from the beginning*. First, let us note that the problem is similar in the history of science: are the clearly distinct periods in the history of mathematics the result of the successive creations of mathematicians, or are they only the achievement through progressive thematizations of the set of all possibilities corresponding to a universe of Platonic ideas? Now, the set of all possibilities is an antinomic notion like the set of all sets, because the set is itself only a possibility. In addition, today's research shows that, beyond the transfinite number "kappa zero" (which is the limit of predicativity), some openings into new possibilities are still taking place, but are in fact unpredictable since they cannot be founded on a combinatorial lattice. Thus, either mathematics is a part of nature, and then it stems from human constructions, creative of new concepts; or mathematics originates in a Platonic and suprasensible universe, and in this case, one would have to show through what psychological means we acquire knowledge of it, something about which there has never been any indication.

This brings us back to the child, since within the space of a few years he spontaneously reconstructs operations and basic structures of a logico-mathematical nature, without which he would understand nothing of what he will be taught in school. Thus, after a lengthy preoperative period during which he still lacks these cognitive instruments, he reinvents for himself, around his seventh year, the concepts of reversibility, transitivity, recursion, reciprocity of relations, class inclusion, conservation of numerical sets, measurements, organization of spatial references (coordinates), morphisms, some connectives, and so on—in other words, all the foundations of logic and mathematics. If mathematics were preformed, this would mean that a baby at birth would already possess virtually everything that Galois, Cantor, Hilbert, Bourbaki, or MacLane have since been able to realize. And since the child is himself a consequence, one would have to go back as far as protozoa and viruses to locate the seat of "the set of all possibilities."

In a word, the theories of preformation of knowledge appear, for me, as devoid of concrete truth as empiricist interpretations, for the origin of logico-mathematical structures in their infinity cannot be localized either in objects or in the subject. Therefore, only constructivism is acceptable, but its weighty task is to explain both the mechanisms of the formation of new concepts and the characteristics these concepts acquire in the process of becoming logically necessary.

REFLECTIVE ABSTRACTION

If logico-mathematical structures are not preformed, one must, in contrast, go far back to discover their roots, that is, the elementary functioning permitting their elaboration; and as early as the sensorimotor stages, that is to say, much before language, one finds such points of departure (though without any absolute beginning, since one must then go back as far as the organism itself; see the section on the biological roots of knowledge). What are the mechanisms, then, that provide the constructions from one stage to the other? The first such mechanism I will call "reflective abstraction."

It is, in fact, possible to distinguish three different kinds of abstraction. (1) Let us call "empirical abstraction" the kind that bears on physical objects external to the subject. (2) Logico-mathematical abstraction, in contrast, will be called "reflective"* because it proceeds from the subject's actions and operations. This is even true in a double sense; thus we have two interdependent but distinct processes: that of a projection onto a higher plane of what is taken from the lower level, hence a "reflecting," and that of a "reflection" as a reorganization on the new plane—this reorganization first utilizing, only instrumentally, the operations taken from the preceding level but aiming eventually (even if this remains partially unconscious) at co-ordinating them into a new totality. (3) We will speak finally of "reflected abstraction" or "reflected thought" as the thematization of that which remained operational or instrumental in (2); phase (3) thus constitutes the natural outcome of (2) but presupposes in addition a set of explicit comparisons at a level above the "reflections" at work in the instrumental utilizations and the constructions in process of (2). It is essential, therefore, to distinguish the phases of reflective abstractions, which occur in any construction at the time of the solution of new problems, from reflected abstraction, which adds a system of explicit correspondences among the operations thus thematized.

Reflective and reflected abstractions, then, are sources of structural novelties for the following reasons: In the first place, the "reflecting" on a higher plane of an element taken from a lower level (for example, the interiorization of an action into a conceptualized representation) constitutes an establishment of correspondences, which is itself already a new concept, and this then opens the way to other possible correspondences, which represents a new "opening." The element transferred onto the new level is then constituted from those that were already there or those that are going to be added, which is now the work of the "reflection" and no longer of the "reflecting" (although initially elicited by the latter). New combinations thus result which can lead to the construction of new operations operating "on" the preceding ones, which is the usual course of mathematical progress (an example in the child: a set of additions creating multiplication).[1] As a rule, all reflecting on a new

* Translator's note: Piaget distinguishes two types of abstractions: *abstraction réfléchissante* and *abstraction réfléchie*. We have translated these two terms as "reflective" and "reflected" abstraction, respectively. Reflective abstraction is the result of "reflectings" (*réfléchissements*) and reflected abstraction is the result of "reflections" (*réflexions*).

plane leads to and necessitates a *reorganization*, and it is this reconstruction, productive of new concepts, that we call "reflection"; yet well before its general thematization, reflection comes into action through a set of still instrumental assimilations and coordinations without any conceptual awareness of structures as such (this is to be found all through the history of mathematics). Finally reflected abstraction or retrospective thematization become possible, and although they are found only on preconstructed elements, they naturally constitute a new construction in that their transversal correspondences render simultaneous that which was until now elaborated by successive longitudinal linkings (compare, in scientific thought, the thematization of "structures" by Bourbaki).

Constructive Generalization

Abstraction and generalization are obviously interdependent, each founded on the other. It results from this that only inductive generalization, proceeding from "some" to "all" by simple extension, will correspond to empirical abstraction, whereas constructive and "completive" generalizations in particular will correspond to reflective and reflected abstractions.

The first problem to be solved, then, is that of the construction of successive steps that have been established in the preceding paragraphs. Now, each one of them results from a new assimilation or operation aimed at correcting an insufficiency in the previous level and actualizing a possibility that is opened by the new assimilation. A good example is the passage of action to representation due to the formation of the semiotic function. Sensorimotor assimilation consists only of assimilating objects to schemes of action, whereas representative assimilation assimilates objects to each other, hence the construction of conceptual schemes. Now, this new form of assimilation already was virtual in sensorimotor form since it bore on multiple but successive objects; it was then sufficient to complete these successive assimilations by a simultaneous act of setting into transversal correspondence before passing to the next level. But such an action implies the evocation of objects not presently perceived, and this evocation requires the formation of a specific instrument, which is the semiotic function (deferred imitations, symbolic play, mental image which is an interiorized imitation, sign language, and so on, in addition to vocal and learned language). Now, sensorimotor signifiers already exist in the form of cues or signals, but they constitute only one aspect or a part of the signified objects; on the contrary, the semiotic function commences when signifiers are differentiated from what is thereby signified and when signifiers can correspond to a multiplicity of things signified. It is clear, then, that between the conceptual assimilation of objects between themselves and semiotization, there is a mutual dependence and that both proceed from a completive generalization of sensorimotor assimilation. This generalization embeds a reflective abstraction bearing on elements directly borrowed from sensorimotor assimilation.

Likewise, it would be easy to show that the new concepts inherent in the levels of initially concrete, then hypothetico-deductive operations proceed from completive generalizations as well. It is thus that concrete operations owe their new abilities to the acquisition of reversibility, which has already been prepared by preoperative reversibility; but the reversibility, in addition, requires a systematic adjustment of affirmations and negations, that is to say, an autoregulation which, by the way, is always working within the constructive generalizations (I will return to the subject of autoregulation in the section on necessity and equilibration). As for the hypothetico-deductive operations, these are made possible by the transition from the structures of "groupings" devoid of a combinatorial lattice (the elements of which are disjoint), to the structures of the "set of components" embedding a combinatorial lattice and full generalization of partitions.[2]

These last advances are due to a particularly important form of constructive generalizations, which consist of raising an operation to its own square or a higher power: thus, combinations are classifications of classifications, permutations are seriations of seriations, the sets of components are partitions of partitions, and so on.

Finally, let us call attention to a simpler but equally important form which consists of generalizations by synthesis of analogous structures, such as the coordination of two systems of references, internal and external to a spatial or cinematic process (the 11- to 12-year-old level).

THE BIOLOGICAL ROOTS OF KNOWLEDGE

What we have seen so far speaks in favor of a systematic constructivism. It is nonetheless true that its sources are to be sought at the level of the organism, since a succession of constructions could not admit of an absolute beginning. But before offering a solution, we should first ask ourselves what a preformationist solution would mean biologically; in other words, what *a priorism* would look like after having been rephrased in terms of innateness.

A famous author has demonstrated this quite clearly: it is Konrad Lorenz, who considers himself a Kantian who maintains a belief in a hereditary origin of the great structures of reason as a precondition to any acquisition drawn from experience. But as a biologist, Lorenz is well aware that, except for "general" heredity common to all living beings or major groups, specific heredity varies from one species to another: that of man, for instance, remains special to our own particular species. As a consequence, Lorenz, while believing as a precondition that our major categories of thought are basically inborn, cannot, for that very reason, assert their generality: hence his very enlightening formula according to which the *a prioris* of reason consist simply of "innate working hypotheses." In other words, Lorenz, while retaining the point of departure of the *a priori* (which precedes the constructions of the subject), sets aside necessity which is more important, whereas we are doing exactly the opposite, that is, insisting on necessity (see the next section), but placing it at the end of constructions, without any prerequisite hereditary programming.*

Lorenz's position is therefore revealing: if reason is innate, either it is general and one must have it go back as far as the protozoa, or it is specific (species-specific or genus-specific, for instance) and one must explain (even if it is deprived of its essential character of necessity) through which mutations and under the influence of which natural selections it developed. Now, as research stands at present, current explanations would be reduced for this particular problem to a pure and simple verbalism; in fact, they would consist of making reason the product of a random mutation, hence of mere chance.

But what innatists surprisingly seem to forget is that there exists a mechanism which is as general as heredity and which even, in a sense, controls it: this mechanism is autoregulation, which plays a role at every level, as early as the genome, and a more and more important role as one gets closer to higher levels and to behavior. Autoregulation, whose roots are obviously organic, is thus common to biological and mental processes, and its actions have, in addition, the great advantage of being di-

---

* Editor's note: Lorenz's theses are presented by Bischof and commented on by Piaget in Chapter 10. Piaget also analyzes them in his "Afterthoughts" at the end of Part I.

rectly controllable. It is therefore in this direction, and not in mere heredity, that one has to seek the biological explanation of cognitive constructions, notwithstanding the fact that by the interplay of regulations of regulations, autoregulation is eminently constructivist (and dialectic) by its very nature.[3]

It is understandable, therefore, that while fully sympathizing with the transformational aspects of Chomsky's doctrine, I cannot accept the hypothesis of his "innate fixed nucleus." There are two reasons for this. The first one is that this mutation particular to the human species would be biologically inexplicable; it is already very difficult to see why the randomness of mutations renders a human being able to "learn" an articulate language, and if in addition one had to attribute to it the innateness of a rational linguistic structure, then this structure would itself be subject to a random origin and would make of reason a collection of mere "working hypotheses," in the sense of Lorenz. My second reason is that the "innate fixed nucleus" would retain all its properties of a "fixed nucleus" if it were not innate but constituted the "necessary" result of the constructions of sensorimotor intelligence, which is prior to language and results from those joint organic and behavioral autoregulations that determine this epigenesis. It is indeed this explanation of a non-innate fixed nucleus, produced by sensorimotor intelligence, that has been finally admitted by authors such as Brown, Lenneberg, and McNeill. This is enough to indicate that the hypothesis of innateness is not mandatory in order to secure the coherence of Chomsky's beautiful system.

NECESSITY AND EQUILIBRATION

We still have to look for the reason why the constructions required by the formation of reason become progressively necessary when each one begins by various trials that are partly episodic and that contain, until rather late, an important component of irrational thought (non-conservations, errors of reversibility, insufficient control over negations, and so on). The hypothesis naturally will be that this increasing necessity arises from autoregulation and has a counterpart with the increasing, parallel equilibration of cognitive structures. Necessity then proceeds from their "interlocking."

Three forms of equilibration can be distinguished in this respect. The most simple, and therefore the most precocious, is that of assimilation and accommodation. Already at the sensorimotor level, it is obvious that in order to apply a scheme of actions to new objects, this scheme must be differentiated according to the properties of these objects; therefore one obtains an equilibrium aimed at both preserving the scheme and taking into account the properties of the object. If however, these properties turn out to be unexpected and interesting, the formation of a subscheme or even of a new scheme has to prove feasible. Such new schemes will then necessitate an equilibration of their own. But these functional mechanisms are found at all levels. Even in science, the assimilation between linear and angular speeds involves two joint operations: common space-time relationships are assimilated while one accommodates for these nonetheless distinct solutions; similarly, the incorporation of open systems to general thermodynamic systems requires differentiating accommodation as well as assimilations.

A second form of equilibrium imposes itself between the subsystems, whether it is a question of subschemes in a scheme of action, subclasses in a general class, or subsystems of the totality of operations that a subject has at his disposal, as for example, the equilibration between spatial numbers and measurement during calculations in which both can intervene. Now, since subsystems normally evolve at different speeds, there can be conflicts between them. Their equilibration presupposes in this case a distinction between their common parts and their different properties, and consequently a compensatory adjustment between partial affirmations and negations as well as between direct or inverted operations, or even the utilization of reciprocities. One can see, then, how equilibration leads to logical necessity: the progressive coherence, sought and finally attained by the subject, first comes from a mere causal regulation of actions of which the results are revealed, after the fact, to be compatible or contradictory; this progressive coherence then achieves a comprehension of linkings or implications that have become deductible and thereby necessary.

The third form of equilibration relies upon the previous one but distinguishes itself by the construction of a new global system: it is the form of equilibration required by the very process of differentiation of new systems, which requires then a compensatory step of integration into a new totality. Apparently, there is here a simple balance of opposing forces, the differentiation threatening the unity of the whole and the integration jeopardizing the necessary distinctions. In fact, the originality of the cognitive equilibrium (and, by the way, further down in the hierarchy, also of organic systems) is to ensure, against expectations, the enrichment of the whole as a function of the importance of these differentiations and to ensure their multiplication (and not only their consistency) as a function of intrinsic (or having become such) variations of the totality of its own characteristics. Here again one clearly sees the relationship between equilibration and progressive logical necessity, that is, the necessity of the *terminus ad quem* resulting from the final integration or "interlocking" of the systems.

In summary, cognitive equilibration is consequently "accretive" *(majorante)*; that is to say, the disequilibria do not lead back to the previous form of equilibrium, but to a better form, characterized by the increase of mutual dependencies or necessary implications.

As for experimental knowledge, its equilibration admits, in addition to the previous laws, of a progressive transfer *(passage)* from the exogenous to the endogenous, in the sense that perturbations (falsifications of expectations) are first nullified or neutralized, then progressively integrated (with displacement of equilibrium), and finally incorporated into the system as deducible intrinsic variations reconstructing the exogenous by way of the endogenous. The biological equivalent of this process (compare "from noise to order" in von Foerster)[4] is to be sought in the "phenocopy," as I have endeavored to interpret and to generalize this notion in a recent paper.[5]

PSYCHOGENESIS AND HISTORY OF SCIENCE

As Holton said, one can recognize certain convergences between psychogenesis and the historical development of cognitive structures;[6] this is what I will attempt to define in an upcoming work with the physicist Rolando Garcia.

In some cases, before seventeenth-century science, one can even observe a stage-by-stage parallelism. For instance, in regard to the relationship between force and movement, one can distinguish four periods: (1) the Aristotelian theory of the two motors with, as a consequence, the model of *antiperistasis*; (2) an overall explanation in which force, movement, and impetus remain undifferentiated; (3) the theory of impetus (or *élan*), conceived by Buridan as a necessary intermediary between force and movement; and (4) a final and pre-Newtonian period in which impetus tends to conflate with acceleration. Now, one notes a succession of four very similar stages in the child. The first one is that one in which the two motors remain rather systematic as residues of animism, but with a large number of spontaneous examples of *antiperistasis* (and this often occurs in very unexpected situations, and not only for the movement of projectiles). During a second stage, an overall notion comparable to "action" intervenes and can be symbolized by *mve*, in which *m* represents the weight, *v* the speed, and *e* the distance covered. During a third period (ages 7 to 10), the "impetus" in the sense of Buridan's middle term spontaneously appears, but with, in addition, the power of "passing through" motionless intermediaries by passing through their "interior" when a movement is transmitted through their mediation. Finally, in a fourth phase, (around the age of 11 to 12), the first inklings of the notion of acceleration appear.

For larger periods of history, obviously one does not find any stage-by-stage parallelism, but one can search for common mechanisms. For instance, the history of Western geometry bears witness to a process of structuration whose steps are those of a centration on an emphasis by Euclid on simply intrafigural relationships, then a construction of interfigural relationships with Cartesian coordinate systems, and then finally a progressive algebrization by Klein.* Now one finds, on a small scale, a similar process in children, who naturally begin with the "intrafigural," but who discover around their seventh year that in order to determinate a point on a plane, one measurement is not sufficient, but two are necessary, and they must be orthogonally arranged. After this "interfigural" stage (which is necessary also for the construction of horizontal lines) follows that which we can call the "transfigural" stage, in which the properties to be discovered cannot be read on a single diagram, but necessitate a deduction or a calculation (for example, mechanical curves, relative motions, and so on).

Now, these analogies with the history of science assuredly speak in favor of my constructivism. *Antiperistasis* was not transmitted hereditarily from Aristotle to the little Genevans, but Aristotle began by being a child; for childhood precedes adulthood in all men, including cavemen. As for what the scientist keeps from his younger years, it is not a collection of innate ideas, since there are tentative procedures in both cases, but a constructive ability; and one of us went so far as to say that a physicist of genius is a man who has retained the creativity inherent to childhood instead of losing it in school.

---

* Editor's note: On the parallelism between the history of geometry and the development of cognitive structures in the child, see the Piaget-Thom debate in Appendix B.

On Cognitive Structures and Their Development: A Reply to Piaget

Noam Chomsky

In his interesting remarks on the psychogenesis of knowledge and its epistemological significance, Jean Piaget formulates three general points of view as to how knowledge is acquired: empiricism, "preformation" ("innatism"), and his own "constructivism." He correctly characterizes my views as, in his terms, a variety of "innatism." Specifically, investigation of human language has led me to believe that a genetically determined language faculty, one component of the human mind, specifies a certain class of "humanly accessible grammars." The child acquires one of the grammars (actually, a system of such grammars, but I will abstract to the simplest, ideal case) on the basis of the limited evidence available to him. Within a given speech-community, children with varying experience acquire comparable grammars, vastly underdetermined by the available evidence. We may think of a grammar, represented somehow in the mind, as a system that specifies the phonetic, syntactic, and semantic properties of an infinite class of potential sentences. The child knows the language so determined by the grammar he has acquired. This grammar is a representation of his "intrinsic competence." In acquiring language, the child also develops "performance systems" for putting this knowledge to use (for example, production and perception strategies). So little is known about the general properties of performance systems that one can only speculate as to the basis for their development. My guess would be that, as in the case of grammars, a fixed, genetically determined system of some sort narrowly constrains the forms that they can assume. I would also speculate that other cognitive structures developed by humans might profitably be analyzed along similar lines.

Against this conception Piaget offers two basic arguments: (1) the mutations, specific to humans, that might have given rise to the postulated innate structures are "biologically inexplicable"; (2) what can be explained on the assumption of fixed innate structures can be explained as well as "the 'necessary' result of constructions of sensorimotor intelligence."

Neither argument seems to me compelling. As for the first,

35

I agree only in part. The evolutionary development is, no doubt, "biologically unexplained." However, I know of no reason to believe the stronger contention that it is "biologically inexplicable." Exactly the same can be said with regard to the physical organs of the body. Their evolutionary development is "biologically unexplained," in exactly the same sense. We can, *post hoc*, offer an account as to how this development might have taken place, but we cannot provide a theory to select the actual line of development, rejecting others that appear to be no less consistent with the principles that have been advanced concerning the evolution of organisms. Although it is quite true that we have no idea how or why random mutations have endowed humans with the specific capacity to learn a human language, it is also true that we have no better idea how or why random mutations have led to the development of the particular structures of the mammalian eye or the cerebral cortex. We do not therefore conclude that the basic nature of these structures in the mature individual is determined through interaction with the environment (though such interaction is no doubt required to set genetically determined processes into motion and of course influences the character of the mature organs). Little is known concerning evolutionary development, but from ignorance, it is impossible to draw any conclusions. In particular, it is rash to conclude either (A) that known physical laws do not suffice in principle to account for the development of particular structures, or (B) that physical laws, known or unknown, do not suffice in principle. Either (A) or (B) would seem to be entailed by the contention that evolutionary development is literally "inexplicable" on biological grounds. But there seems to be no present justification for taking (B) seriously, and (A), though conceivably true, is mere speculation. In any event, the crucial point in the present connection is that cognitive structures and physical organs seem to be comparable, as far as the possibility of "biological explanation" is concerned.

The second argument seems to me a more important one. However, I see no basis for Piaget's conclusion. There are, to my knowledge, no substantive proposals involving "constructions of sensorimotor intelligence" that offer any hope of accounting for the phenomena of language that demand explanation. Nor is there any initial plausibility to the suggestion, as far as I can see. I might add that although some have argued that the assumption of a genetically determined language faculty is "begging the question," this contention is certainly unwarranted. The assumption is no more "question-begging" in the case of mental structures than is the analogous assumption in the case of growth of physical organs. Substantive proposals regarding the character of this language faculty are refutable if false, confirmable if true. Particular hypotheses have repeatedly been challenged and modified in the light of later research, and I have no doubt that this will continue to be the case.

It is a curiosity of our intellectual history that cognitive structures developed by the mind are generally regarded and studied very differently from physical structures developed by the body. There is no reason why a neutral scientist, unencumbered by traditional doctrine, should adopt this view. Rather, he would, or should, approach cognitive structures such as human language more or less as he would investigate an organ such as the eye or heart, seeking to determine: (1) its character in a particular individual; (2) its general properties, invariant across the species apart from gross defect; (3) its place in a system of such structures; (4) the course of its development in the individual; (5) the genetically determined basis for this development; (6) the factors that gave rise to this mental organ in the course of evolution. The expectation that constructions of sensorimotor intelligence determine the character of a mental organ such as language seems to me hardly more plausible than a proposal that the fundamental properties of the eye or the visual cortex or the heart develop on this basis. Furthermore, when we turn to specific properties of this mental organ, we find little justification for any such belief, so far as I can see.

I will not attempt a detailed argument here, but will merely sketch the kind of reasoning that leads me to the conclusions just expressed.

Suppose that we set ourselves the task of studying the cognitive growth of a person in a natural environment. We may begin by attempting to delimit certain cognitive domains, each governed by an integrated system of principles of some sort. It is, surely, a legitimate move to take language to be one such domain, though its exact boundaries and relations to other domains remain to be determined. In just the same way, we might proceed to study the nature and development of some organ of the body. Under this quite legitimate assumption, we observe that a person proceeds from a genetically determined initial state S_0 through a sequence of states $S_1, S_2, \ldots$, finally reaching a "steady state" S_s which then seems to change only marginally (say, by the addition of new vocabulary). The steady state is attained at a relatively fixed age, apparently by puberty or somewhat earlier. Investigating this steady state, we can construct a hypothesis as to the grammar internally represented. We could try to do the same at intermediate stages, thus gaining further insight into the growth of language.

In principle, it is possible to obtain as complete a record as we like of the experience available to the person who has achieved this steady state. We make no such attempt in practice, of course, but we can nevertheless focus on particular aspects of this experience relevant to specific hypotheses as to the nature of S_s and S_0. Assuming a sufficient record E of relevant experience, we can then proceed to construct a second-order hypothesis as to the character of S_0. This hypothesis must meet certain empirical conditions: It cannot be so specific as to rule out attested steady states, across languages; it must suffice to account for the transition from S_0 to S_s, given E, for any (normal) person. We may think of this hypothesis as a hypothesis with regard to a function mapping E into S_s. For any choice of E sufficient to give rise to knowledge of some human language L, this function must assign an appropriate S_s in which the grammar of L is represented. We might refer to this function as "the learning theory for humans in the domain language"—call it LT(H,L). Abstracting away from individual differences, we may take S_0— which specifies LT(H,L)—to be a genetically determined species character. Refinements are possible, as we consider stages of development more carefully.

More generally, for any species O and cognitive domain D that have been tentatively identified and delimited, we may, correspondingly, investigate LT(O,D), the "learning theory" for the organism O in the domain D, a property of the genetically determined initial state. Suppose, for example, that we are investigating the ability of humans to recognize and identify human faces. Assuming "face-recognition" to constitute a legitimate cognitive domain F, we may try to specify LT(H,F), the genetically determined principles that give rise to a steady state (apparently some time after language is neurally fixed, and perhaps represented in homologous regions of the right hemisphere, as some recent work suggests). Similarly, other cognitive domains can be studied in humans and other organisms. We would hardly expect to find interesting properties common to LT(O,D) for arbitrary O,D; that is, we would hardly expect to discover that there exists something that might be called "general learning theory." As far as I know, the prospects for such a theory are no brighter than for a "growth theory," intermediate in level between cellular biology and the study of particular organs, and concerned with the principles that govern the growth of arbitrary organs for arbitrary organisms.

Again, we may refine the investigation, considering intermediate states as well.

Returning to the case of language, to discover the properties of S_0 we will naturally focus attention on properties of later states (in particular, S_s) that are not determined by E, that is, elements of language that are known but for which there appears to be no relevant evidence. Consider a few examples.

THE STRUCTURE-DEPENDENT PROPERTY OF LINGUISTIC RULES

Consider the process of formation of simple yes-or-no questions in English. We have such declarative-question pairs as (1):

(1) The man is here—Is the man here?
   The man will leave.—Will the man leave?

Consider the following two hypotheses put forth to account for this infinite class of pairs:

H_1: process the declarative from beginning to end (left to right), word by word, until reaching the first occurrence of the words *is, will,* etc.; transpose this occurrence to the beginning (left), forming the associated interrogative.

H_2: same as H_1, but select the first occurrence of *is, will,* etc., following the first noun phrase of the declarative.

Let us refer to H_1 as a "structure-independent rule" and H_2 as a "structure-dependent rule." Thus, H_1 requires analysis of the declarative into just a sequence of words, whereas H_2 requires an analysis into successive words and also abstract phrases such as "noun phrase." The phrases are "abstract" in that their boundaries and labeling are not in general physically marked in any way; rather, they are mental constructions.

A scientist observing English speakers, given such data as (1), would naturally select hypothesis H_1 over the far more complex hypothesis H_2, which postulates abstract mental processing of a nontrivial sort beyond H_1. Similarly, given such data as (1) it is reasonable to assume that an "unstructured" child would assume that H_1 is valid. In fact, as we know, it is not, and H_2 is (more nearly) correct. Thus consider the data of (2):

(2) The man who is here is tall.—Is the man who is here tall?
   The man who is tall will leave.—Will the man who is tall leave?

These data are predicted by H_2 and refute H_1, which would predict rather the interrogatives (3):

(3) Is the man who here is tall?
   Is the man who tall will leave?

Now the question that arises is this: how does a child know that H_2 is correct (nearly), while H_1 is false? It is surely not the case that he first hits on H_1 (as a neutral scientist would) and then is forced to reject it on the basis of data such as (2). No child is taught the relevant facts. Children make many errors in language learning, but none such as (3), prior to appropriate training or evidence. A person might go through much or all of his life without ever having been exposed to relevant evidence, but he will nevertheless unerringly employ H_2, never H_1, on the first relevant occasion (assuming that he can handle the structures at all). We cannot, it seems, explain the preference for H_2 on grounds of communicative efficiency or the like. Nor do there appear to be relevant analogies of other than the most superficial and uninformative sort in other cognitive domains. If humans were differently designed, they would acquire a grammar that incorporates H_1, and would be none the worse for that. In fact, it would be difficult to know, by mere passive observation of a person's total linguistic performance, whether he was using H_1 or H_2.

Such observations suggest that it is a property of S_0—that is, of LT(H,L)—that rules (or rules of some specific category, identifiable on quite general grounds by some genetically determined mechanism) are structure-dependent. The child need not consider H_1; it is ruled out by properties of his initial mental state, S_0. Although this example is very simple, almost trivial, it illustrates the general problem that arises when we attend to the specific properties of attained cognitive states.

THE SPECIFIED SUBJECT CONDITION

Let us consider a slightly more complex example. The sentences (4) and (5) are near synonyms:

(4) Each of the men likes the others.
(5) The men like each other.

More generally, the pairs *each of the men . . . the others* and *the men . . . each other* are interchangeable without change of meaning (to a good approximation). In some contexts, however, this is not true at all. Consider, for example, the sentences of (6):

(6) (a) Each of the men expects [John to like the others].
    (b) Each of the men was surprised at [John's hatred of the others].
    (c) Each of the men liked [John's stories about the others].

Replacing *each of the men . . . the others* by *the men . . . each other* in (6), we derive, respectively, the sentences of (7) (with the automatic change of verbal inflection, which we may ignore):

(7) (a) The men expect [John to like each other].
   (b) The men were surprised at [John's hatred of each other].
   (c) The men liked [John's stories about each other].

But the examples of (7) are not near synonyms of the corresponding examples of (6). In fact, they are not well-formed English sentences at all, though if forced to assign an interpretation, we might do so—presumably, the interpretations of the corresponding examples of (6). The grounds for this judgment cannot be "semantic incoherence" or the like; look again at sentences (6a–c), which are perfectly coherent but do not, for some reason, express the meaning of (7a–c). How does the speaker of English know this to be true? Why does his grammar, in state S_s, determine these facts?

The answer, I believe, lies in a general principle of language structure that I will call the "specified subject condition" (SSC). This condition concerns rules that relate X and Y in a structure such as (8), where the bracketed embedded structure is a sentence or a noun phrase:

(8) $\ldots X \ldots [\ldots Y \ldots] \ldots$

SSC asserts roughly that no rule can apply to X and Y if the embedded phrase contains a subject distinct from Y.

Consider now sentence (7a). The brackets enclose an embedded sentence; hence (7a) is of the form (8). Take the reciprocal phrase *each other* to be Y and its proposed antecedent, *the men*, to be X. But the embedded sentence contains a subject *John* distinct from *each other*, so that the relation between X and Y is blocked by SSC. The same is true of other cases of so-called "bound anaphora." Note that the sentence (9) is quite all right, because the reciprocal phrase *each other* is itself the subject:

(9) The candidates expect [each other to win].

What of (7b)? Exactly the same condition will block (7b) if we take *John* to be the "subject" of the noun *hatred* (as it would be in a corresponding sentence *John hates . . .*) in the noun phrase contained within brackets. Similarly, (7c) is accounted for if we take *John* to be the "subject" of *stories* in the bracketed noun phrase. Observe that sentence (10) is well formed, because the embedded noun phrase contains no subject at all, and thus no subject distinct from *each other* (Y of (8)):

(10) The men heard [stories about each other].

Notice that the notion "subject" involved in SSC is rather abstract, a generalization of the corresponding notion of traditional grammar. There are good reasons, quite independent of these considerations, for generalizing the traditional notion in this way.

SSC applies not only to bound anaphora, but also to rules of quite different sorts. Consider, for example, the *wh*-questions of (11):

(11) (a) Who did the men hear [stories about]?
     (b) Who did the men hear [John's stories about]?

(11a) is a grammatical sentence of English, but (11b) is not, because the rule of interrogative-formation is blocked by SSC ((11b) might also be blocked in a style that imposes more stringent conditions on stranding of prepositions).

This explanation is controversial, and I am now avoiding many further questions and a few problems. But I believe that it is essentially correct.

We may now ask exactly the same questions raised with respect to the structure-dependent property of rules. How does the language learner know that SSC applies to the bound anaphor *each other* but not to *the others* in (6)? Again, it cannot be imagined that the language learner is taught these facts or the relevant principles. No one ever makes mistakes to be corrected. As in the case of the structure-dependent principle, passive observation of a person's total performance might not enable us to determine whether the principles are in fact being observed (just as experience would not suffice, normally, to provide this information to the language learner), though "experiment" will quickly reveal that this is so. The only rational conclusion is that the SSC and the relevant abstract notion of "subject" and "bound anaphor" are properties of S_0, that is, part of LT(H,L).

It remains to determine the difference between the bound anaphor *each other* and the free anaphor *the others*, the difference that is revealed in a comparison of (6) and (7). This is straightforward. Notice that the antecedent of *each other* is strictly determined by a property of the grammar of sentences, whereas the antecedent of *the others* may, in general, be determined outside of the sentence in which it appears, by some feature of situational context or background knowledge. Thus the sentence (12) is quite possible, but (13) is not:

(12) The others left.
(13) Each other left.

The sentence (12) may appear in a discourse, if the participants know somehow what set is being referred to; for example, in the discourse (14):

(14) Some of the men stayed. The others left.

In contrast, there is no discourse in which (13) may appear. Correspondingly, in sentences such as (4) and (6), the phrase *the others* might be unrelated to the phrase *each of the men*. Consider the discourse (15):

(15) Each of the women likes some of the books. Each of the men likes the others.

We may understand *the others* to refer to the other books. There is no such possibility if (4) is replaced by (5) in (15). Thus it was not quite correct to say, as I did before, that (4) and (5) are near synonyms. They do not have the same range of meaning, as these examples demonstrate.

These are among the basic properties that distinguish free from bound anaphora. A person must have knowledge of this distinction to know the range of application of SSC. Again, it seems that such knowledge must be a property of S_0, though as in the case of many other genetically determined properties (for example, the onset of puberty, the termination of growth) the appearance of this mental characteristic may be delayed many years after birth, and may be conditional on the triggering effect of relevant experience (again, as in the case of other innate processes and structures).

"Mentally Present" Subjects

Let us consider next the following slightly more complex examples. Consider the sentences (16) and (17):

(16) John seems to each of the men [to like the others].
(17) John seems to the men [to like each other].

Sentence (16) is well formed, but (17) is not. What is the explanation for this fact?

Again, the answer is provided by SSC. The bracketed expressions in (16) and (17) do not have the full form of sentences, since they lack a subject. But they are understood as sentences with subjects, or, to use the traditional term, they each have an "understood subject," namely, *John*. The understood subject *John* of the embedded sentence fragment of (17) suffices to block the rule of reciprocal interpretation, by SSC, just as the subject *John* of the embedded sentence blocked the same rule in (7a).

The only difference between (7a) and (17) is that the subject is physically present in the former case, but only "mentally present" in the second. As the example shows, mentally present subjects behave just like physically present ones with respect to SSC.

As in the earlier cases discussed, it is unimaginable that every speaker of English who can distinguish between (16) and (17) has been taught that mentally present subjects suffice to put the principle SSC into operation, or has been exposed to relevant experience. Once again, we could not know, from passive observation, that a person is aware of the relevant principle (unconsciously, to be sure). Furthermore, if English did not abide by this particular principle, it would be no "worse" a language; rather, in this pseudo-English, (17) would mean (16). Every speaker who has reached his steady state does know the principle that mentally present subjects suffice to put SSC into operation. We apparently must assume, again, that the principle is a property of S_0, coming into operation at some point in mental development.

ON THE NOTION "SPECIFIED SUBJECT"

In the preceding examples, SSC served to block the application of rules to an embedded sentence or noun phrase with a subject distinct from the phrase (Y of (8)) to which the rule applied within this embedded structure. Other examples show that the "specified subject" must also be distinct from X of (8). Consider, for example, the following sentences:

(18) (a) John seems to the men [to like each other].
       [same as (17)]
     (b) The men seem to John [to like each other].
     (c) John ordered the men [to kill each other].
     (d) John promised the men [to kill each other].

Sentences (18b) and (18c) are well formed, and have about the same meaning as the corresponding sentences with *each of the men . . . the others* in place of *the men . . . each other*. But (18a) and (18d) are not well formed. The explanation is transparent. In (18b) and (18c) the understood, mentally present subject of the embedded sentence fragments is identical to the antecedent *the men*, and therefore SSC does not apply, as it does in (18a) and (18d), where the mentally present subject is distinct from the antecedent. We see, then, that a "specified subject" in the embedded phrase of the sentences in (18) is one that is distinct from

X of (8). Just what "distinct" means here must be made more precise; I omit this refinement here.[1]

Again there is no *a priori* reason why any of this should be so, nor is it imaginable that the principle has been learned or derived from some sensorimotor construction or the like.

In all of these cases we are, it seems, dealing with knowledge that derives "from the original hand of nature," in Hume's phrase—that is, "innate knowledge." In order to avoid a pointless terminological dispute, I will avoid the term, simply noting that an inquiry into language leads us to attribute to the invariant state S_0 certain properties such as structure-dependence of rules, SSC, the notions of "bound anaphor" and "abstract subject," the condition that mentally present subjects behave like physically present ones with respect to SSC, the conditions on the specified subject, and so forth. More generally, we have tacitly presupposed throughout this discussion a certain framework of rules and principles, all of which must be attributed to S_0 as part of the schematism that determines the form of the resulting knowledge of language. Specific details result, of course, from experience.

As humans functioning in a social environment, we are naturally concerned with differences among individuals and cultures, and tend to ignore or be unaware of uniformities. The latter are regarded as "natural" or "necessary" or are just taken for granted, just as we take for granted "obvious" properties of the natural environment. But a scientist who is trying to understand the nature and origin of human cognitive capacities must, in contrast, be concerned with just those invariant properties that he may safely and properly ignore in his interaction with other people. His task is to determine LT(H,D), for each D; in particular, to determine LT(H,L), the "learning theory" for humans in the domain of language, a property of the initial state S_0. I have suggested some of the characteristics that it seems appropriate to attribute to S_0. These characteristics are rather abstract; they are what I have called elsewhere "formal universals," conditions on the form and function of the system of rules and principles that constitutes our theory of the structure of some cognitive domain. In comparison, there is, to my knowledge, much less to say about "substantive universals," fixed elements that enter into particular grammars.

These examples have been drawn from the domain of syntax and semantic interpretation of syntactic structures. One may find similar examples in phonology and phonetics, or in semantics proper. For example, consider the intricate properties of rule ordering and application in phonology that have been investigated in recent years. As in the cases just discussed, it seems that these are unlearned, hence properties of S_0. Or consider some of the usages that are permissable in cases of "systematic ambiguity" as compared with "accidental" or "syntactically determined" ambiguity. Compare examples (19) and (20):

(19) (a) John wrote a book.
    (b) This book weighs five pounds.
(20) (a) Flying planes are a nuisance (are dangerous).
    (b) Flying planes is a nuisance (is dangerous).

In (19a), the word *book* has an abstract reference. In saying sentence (19a), we may have no concrete object in mind (in fact, John may have just written the book in his head, committing nothing to paper). If there are two copies of the book before us, I can point to either one and say, "John wrote this book," but I cannot conclude that John wrote two books. In (19b), in contrast, the reference of *book* is concrete, or at least it would normally be. Thus there is a certain ambiguity in the usage of *book;* it can be used with either abstract or concrete reference. Though in the current state of descriptive semantics, caution is necessary, it still seems a fair guess that this ambiguity is quite systematic, not an idiosyncratic property of the word *book,* as it is an idiosyncratic property of the word *trunk* that it may refer to an oversize suitcase or an appendage of an elephant.

In the sentences of (20), the phrase *flying planes* is used in two ways, to refer to certain objects that fly in (a) and to the act of piloting in (b). But this ambiguity is syntactically determined, not a general property of phrases with these semantic functions.

The two sentences of (19) can be "combined" in a relative clause construction on *book,* despite its ambiguity, as in (21):

(21) (a) John wrote a book that weighs five pounds.
    (b) The book that John wrote weighs five pounds.
    (c) This book, which John wrote, weighs five pounds.

In (a), for example, the reference of *book* is abstract in the main clause and concrete in the embedded relative clause, but the sentence is well formed. In contrast, there can be no such relative clause construction as (22), based on (20):

(22) (a) Flying planes, which is a nuisance, are dangerous.
    (b) Flying planes, which is dangerous, are a nuisance.

The property of systematic ambiguity just noted, while rather

curious, seems quite general. Consider the following sentences
(23):

(23) (a) John's intelligence, which is his most remarkable quality, exceeds his foresight.
   (b) The temperature, which was 70 degrees this morning,
will rise rapidly.
   (c) The price of bread, which was fixed at $1.00 a loaf by
the monopoly, will rise rapidly.

In (23a), *intelligence* refers to a quality in the embedded clause
and to a degree of intelligence in the main clause. Examples
(23b) and (23c) illustrate a different sort of systematic ambiguity.
Terms such as *temperature* or *price of bread* designate functions, which may rise or fall, and so on. But terms designating
functions can be used ambiguously to designate their values as
well. Thus in (23b) and (23c) the terms in question designate a
function in the main clause and its value at a certain point of
time in the relative clause, but the process of relativization
nevertheless is not blocked.

Presumably, what I have called "systematic ambiguity" is
determined within the lexical component of the grammar, by
general and perhaps universal principles. Syntactically determined ambiguity (or idiosyncratic lexical ambiguity, as in
the case of *trunk*) is not established by general lexical principles.
Thus in the case of *book, intelligence, temperature,* or *the price
of bread,* there is a single formal element with a fixed (range of)
meaning, so that relativization is permitted. But in the case of
flying planes or *trunk* we really have two formal elements with
the same phonetic form; thus relativization is impermissible.

It seems reasonable to surmise that general principles of semantic representation, elements of the initial state S_0, are involved in these judgments. As is generally the case in dealing
with examples drawn from the domain of meaning and reference, these cases are less striking than the syntactic or phonological cases, perhaps because the domain of semantics is simply
less rich in deeper principles or perhaps because these principles,
whatever they may be, have so far eluded us. If there are semantic principles of the depth and generality of those that are
now partially understood in the domains of syntax, phonology,
and semantic interpretation of syntactic structures, then these
principles too will be natural candidates for the learning
theories for humans in particular cognitive domains, hence
properties of the general initial cognitive state.

The pattern of inference in the preceding examples is, I believe, entirely legitimate, though of course nondemonstrative. In each case, we begin by determining certain properties of the attained linguistic competence, the attained steady state S_s. We ask how these properties develop on the basis of an interplay of experience and genetic endowment. The properties were sought and selected in such a way as to minimize the likely role of experience, and thus to reflect genetic endowment as closely as a property of an attained steady state can do so. Thus, in the cases in question, it seems most unlikely that relevant experience is directly available, in all (or perhaps any) instances in which the steady state is attained by a language learner. It might, of course, be argued that relevant evidence is *indirectly* available, in the sense that experience has led to the development of certain generalized capacities of which the linguistic property in question is a special case; I presume that something of the sort is proposed in the "constructivist" theory. But no specific proposals exist, to my knowledge, concerning such "generalized capacities," and it does not seem very likely, to me at least, that the linguistic properties in question reflect constructions of sensorimotor intelligence or the like.

In the examples just reviewed, I have not hesitated to propose a general principle of linguistic structure on the basis of observation of a single language. The inference is legitimate, on the assumption that humans are not specifically adapted to learn one rather than another human language, say English rather than Japanese. Assuming that the genetically determined language faculty is a common human possession, we may conclude that a principle of language is universal if we are led to postulate it as a "precondition" for the acquisition of a single language. Thus, SSC may be proposed as a universal principle on the grounds that investigation of English, along the lines just reviewed, leads us to postulate this principle as an element of the initial state S_0, a precondition for language learning, a property of the general language faculty, one faculty of the mind.

To test such a conclusion, we will naturally want to investigate other languages in comparable detail. We may find that our inference is refuted by such investigation. Consider, for example, the following argument, patterned on those presented above. We may have sentences such as (24) and (25), but not (26):

(24) (a) John, who likes math, goes to MIT.
    (b) People who like math are likely to get jobs.
    (c) John, who goes to MIT, likes math.
    (d) People who go to MIT are likely to get jobs.

(25) People who like math who go to MIT are likely to get jobs.
(26) John, who likes math, who goes to MIT, is likely to get a job.

In short, restrictive relative clauses can "stack" (as in (25)), whereas nonrestrictive relative clauses cannot (compare (26)). We may, as before, inquire into the origin of this principle. A reasonable proposal is that it is a general principle of language, determined by the language faculty. Thus, as before, it is difficult to believe that relevant information is invariably presented to individuals capable of making these distinctions in English. But in this case, the conclusion is too strong, it appears. It seems that in Japanese and Korean, for example, nonrestrictive relative clauses *can* stack, giving an analogue to (26) (furthermore, the two types of relatives do not seem to be distinguished in these languages). Therefore, we must search for some modified form of the original proposal to explain the property of English just noted, perhaps in terms of some other feature of the languages in question that determines whether relatives may or may not stack.

Our earlier inferences, being nondemonstrative, are subject to the same kind of check. The structure that we attribute to the genetically determined language faculty must meet two empirical conditions: it must be sufficiently rich and specific to account for the attainment of linguistic competence in particular languages, but it must not be so rich and specific that it excludes attested cases. The theory of "universal grammar" must fall between these empirical bounds.

When a particular proposal concerning universal grammar is advanced, we must subject it to empirical confirmation in this dual manner. In principle, straightforward tests are possible; namely, we might raise a person in a controlled environment in which information concerning the proposal in question is lacking and then determine whether behavior conforms to the proposal or not. Of course, such experiments are excluded. Part of the intellectual fascination of the study of language is that it is necessary to devise complex arguments to overcome the fact that direct experimentation is rarely possible. This unavoidable contingency in no way threatens the empirical status of the questions raised, though it does affect the credibility and force of particular theories.

Perhaps a comment might be in order on the matter of empirical confirmation of grammars. In the preceding discussion, I have based my argument on data from English; for example, the fact that the well-formed interrogatives are those of (2) and not (3), the fact that (7a) is not a paraphrase of (6a) (and, in fact, is not well formed), and so on. These factual observations are not the result of careful experimentation, though there would be no problem of principle in devising experiments to provide such observations over quite an interesting range. Of course, any proposed experiment would have to meet certain conditions of adequacy. Suppose that someone devised an experimental procedure, offering an operational criterion of "well-formedness," that assigned this property to the forms of (3) rather than (2). We would know that he had simply devised a bad experiment; his "operational criterion" was not a criterion for well-formedness, whatever else it might have been. It is very easy to design bad experiments, which provide meaningless results; to design experiments that provide useful data is much more difficult.

A related problem is that experimental data necessarily relate to behavior (performance) and thus bear only indirectly on the nature of the linguistic competence—the knowledge of language—that is only one factor in performance. The problem, of course, is not unique to the study of language. In physics, and indeed throughout the natural sciences, the problem always exists of determining how given experimental evidence bears on theories that involve crucial idealizations. From these inescapable contingencies of rational inquiry one cannot, of course, conclude that experimental data—in this case, studies of performance—are irrelevant to the postulated theories, nor has this absurd proposal ever been advanced, to my knowledge. Rather, we always face the problem of determining the import of observations on theoretical constructions, whether these observations derive from experiment or simply introspection.

Ultimately, we hope to construct a comprehensive integrated theory of performance that will spell out in precise detail the interaction of various systems, with knowledge of language (linguistic competence, grammar) among them. Observations of performance bear directly on this comprehensive system, hence indirectly on its postulated components. At the moment, we have only the glimmerings of such a comprehensive integrated theory, and therefore must always view observations of performance with care, naturally. Again, I note that this is true whether these observations derive from introspection, psycholinguistic experiment, neurophysiology, or whatever. All such observations are in principle of great importance and interest. Their bearing on theories of cognitive structure and function is rarely crystal clear and is often quite obscure.

These general observations, which should be fairly obvious, have often been made in the past. Still, there persists much misunderstanding about what has been proposed. As a case in point, consider the paper "Logic and the Theory of Mind"* by Carol Fleisher Feldman and Stephen Toulmin, which appeared in the *Proceedings of the Nebraska Symposium on Motivation* (1974–75). Feldman and Toulmin assert that I have dealt with the "evidential problem in a dismissive manner," taking the "extreme position" that the "language behavior of laboratory subjects . . . can neither verify nor falsify the 'psychological reality' of structures in Chomskian grammar," thus regarding "observable data about behavior" as "unsuitable evidence" in contrast to " 'intuitions' of a native speaker" which are the "only appropriate substitute." This step, they conclude, "revolutionize[s] the ground rules of scientific inquiry."[2] But in fact this point of view is one that I have always explicitly rejected, for just the reasons outlined here.

It is quite true that no observations, whether of introspection or experiment, can conclusively verify or falsify the hypotheses of linguistic theory. It is also true that experimental results must meet certain conditions of intuitive adequacy to determine their import; consider, again, a hypothetical experiment that would class (3) rather than (2) as well formed. Furthermore, as I have repeatedly stressed, all observations must be judged with care for their relevance concerning theoretical hypotheses, for the reasons just outlined. Far from "revolutioniz[ing] the grounds of scientific inquiry," these comments simply indicate that inquiry into language is quite comparable to all nontrivial research in the natural sciences, in that it is always necessary to evaluate the import of experimental data on theoretical constructions, and in particular, to determine how such data bear on hypotheses that in nontrivial cases involve various idealizations and abstractions. But that experiment and observation of behavior can provide "suitable evidence" is a truism that I (and others) have never questioned and have repeatedly stressed.

I have touched on only a few examples. In each case, when we investigate the particular properties of human cognition, we find principles that are highly specific and narrowly articulated, structures of a marvelous intricacy and delicacy. As in the case of physical organs, there seems to be no possibility of accounting for the character and origin of basic mental structures

* Editor's note: This article, which was then in the course of publication, was made available to the participants of the colloquim by Stephen Toulmin.

in terms of organism-environment interaction. Mental and physical organs alike are determined, it seems, by species-specific, genetically determined properties, though in both cases interaction with the environment is required to trigger growth and will influence and shape the structures that develop. Our ignorance—temporary, let us hope—of the physical basis for mental structures compels us to keep to abstract characterization, in this case, but there is no reason to suppose that the physical structures involved are fundamentally different in character and development from other physical organs that are better understood, though a long tradition has tacitly assumed otherwise.

What of other cognitive abilities and achievements—say, the growth of our system of "common-sense" beliefs about physical space and the objects in it, about human action and the structure of personality, the nature and function of artifacts, and the like? Or what of the principles, now unknown, that underlie what Peirce called "abduction," that is, the principles by which humans construct scientific theories to explain phenomena that intrigue them? I see no reason to doubt that here too there are highly specific innate capacities that determine the growth of cognitive structures, some of which remain unconscious and beyond the bounds of introspection, while others, probably quite different in kind, are explicitly articulated and put to test. Our ignorance of these matters is profound, but it may be that the results of investigation of such relatively well defined cognitive domains as human language will suggest a useful model for further inquiry.

In these two papers most of the essential points of each position are already brought into focus. In order to provide the reader with a guideline for the ensuing discussions, some key points deserve to be singled out and briefly analyzed in the light of further developments. It appears from the start that a major controversial issue between Piaget and Chomsky stems from their divergent assessment of the roots of necessity (logical or factual) and of the nature of that fixed nucleus about whose existence they both agree. For Piaget, constructive consistency and an evolving combination of substructures, constrained by their interlocking (fermeture) within cognitive domain, are much firmer grounds on which to base arguments about necessity than the random mutations of a neo-Darwinian process. Innateness is to him a weaker argument and also, apparently, one that is bound to lead to an endless regression back to bacteria or viruses. For Chomsky, species-specific innate structures, expressible through formal (rather than substantial) language universals, are the obvious way of accounting for the spontaneous, uniform, and complex character of the rules of sentence production and comprehension. Innateness is not problematic as a principle; the difficulty arises when one tries to translate this principle into observational criteria that can fit into the framework of the natural sciences. Anatomical structures are, however, in no better position with respect to a detailed, predictive account of their origins and their evolution through phylogenesis.

The next chapter deals with these issues, and the biologists will have their say. It can be anticipated that Piaget's interpretation of basic evolutionary mechanisms and his emphasis on "phenocopy" will be difficult to accommodate within the firm strictures of contemporary biology, as is emphasized by Jacob in his remarks and by Danchin in his discourse on the notion of phenocopy (see Appendix A). The compromise proposed by Changeux, which is so warmly welcomed by Piaget (see his "Afterthoughts" in Chapter 13), concerns a quite different matter, and this is perhaps worth pointing out. Changeux's concept of "genetic envelope" matches well in fact with Piaget's concept of epigenesis as presented in this chapter and evoked in the following, but the envelope itself is framed by heredity, having evolved in the most respectful obedience to neo-Darwinian rules of mutation and selection. The compromise is between developmental plasticity of neuronal networks (this plasticity being delimited, however, by a species-specific genetic envelope) and specificity of the final steady state. This is, in fact, nothing but an extension of selective theories into the once sacred domain of cognitive development and its neuronal hardware. Now, no compromise is possible if the interpretation of the concept of phenocopy implies, as Piaget suggests, a "feedback" mechanism, subtle and mediated though it may be, acting between expression and genes, between phenotype and genotype. Different, external, stands are taken about this controversy by Bateson, Toulmin, and Wilden. Their concern is the inadequacy of neo-Darwinian approaches to account for the evolution of complex structures—both biological and behavioral-cognitive structures. However, as stated above, this is an "external" critique and touches the Chomsky-Piaget confrontation only marginally.

Another key point, concerning not the necessity issue, but the patterns of explanation of any constructivist theory, will assume a decisive importance in what follows. It is raised in Chapter 2 by Fodor and then fully stated in his paper "Fixation of Belief and Concept Acquisition" in Chapter 6. Fodor and Chomsky claim to demonstrate the logical impossibility and the experimental inconclusiveness of all learning theories that imply "acquisition" in the strict sense of genuinely new structures and new operations being appropriated by the subject through his interactions with the environment. In contrast, Piaget, Papert, and Cellérier, each from a specific point of view, maintain that learning theories implying acquisition of true novelty are not only logically defensible, but empirically demonstrable. The deepening of this debate will lead to a thorough analysis of the acquisition concept and to a reexamination of the entire problem of induction (see Chapter 12). The Chomsky-Putnam-Fodor debate in Part II, which took place subsequent to the meeting, has considerably sharpened the philosophical edges of this first panel discussion.

The points of convergence should also be stressed, since they are much less frequently evoked but form the implicit background against which the entire debate takes shape, as well as the sharing of values that makes the flow of communication possible. As Piaget says, the rejection of empiricist theories of cognition and of behaviorism is the most important single point of convergence between himself and Chomsky and, I can add, between them and all the other participants. Representatives of animal psychology, such as Premack; of ethology, such as Bischof; of artificial intelligence, such as Papert; of biology, such as Monod, Jacob, Changeux, Danchin, and Dütting; and of the philosophy of science, such as Fodor, Putnam, and Toulmin, will expound a variety of attitudes, methodological stands, and intelligibility criteria, but at least two common implicit assumptions are retained: (1) nothing is knowable unless cognitive organization of some kind is there from the start; and (2) nothing is knowable unless the subject acts, in one way or another, on the surrounding world. As to the modes, origins, degrees of universality, constitutive traits, and describable properties of these cognitive structures, varying opinions will be expressed; this is precisely the core of the debate.

CHAPTER TWO

About the Fixed Nucleus and Its Innateness

Piaget's acknowledgment of his admiration for Chomsky and the emphasis he puts on "the essential points on which I think I am in agreement with him" are the opening sentences of the meeting. The debate proper starts right here, since the papers we have read in Chapter 1 were written before the meeting and were circulated in advance. The present chapter includes the first panel discussion, which is basically focused on the nature of the fixed nucleus, its variability and its origins. Granted that "something" is innate, the controversial point is the specificity of this core arising "out of the hands of Nature" (in Hume's words, quoted here by Chomsky). Being an anti-empiricist and an antibehaviorist, Piaget has always rejected all models based on associationism. His notion of pattern, or scheme, as a basis of assimilation and then, on top of it, of accommodation places the endogenous activity of the subject in open, constructive exchange with the environment. According to Piaget, the hallmark of cognitive development is a "construction of the new," where novelty is conceived both as unprecedented for each subject and "open to further constructions." Through assimilation, some structure without is turned into some corresponding structure within. Once assimilated, the new construction belongs to the subject and can enter, as a component, into more complex constructions, and can then possibly pile up onto the next level according to a combinatorial algebra of constructions of constructions. The subject's global self-organization is the variable product of integrated local patterns of self-equilibration. For Piaget—as I have em-

55

phasized in the Introduction—this process is, at its core, a biological model. *Cognition is a subdomain of the class of biologically adaptive interadjustments between an organism and its environment.* This is where Piaget's reliance on the concept of phenocopy or, as he surmises, on the less committal concept of "genetic assimilation" (coined by C. H. Waddington) become so crucial.

Part of this chapter is devoted to the argument on phenocopy, where Piaget's biology is shown to be somewhat at odds with the biologists' biology (see the interventions of Jacob and Changeux).

Chomsky relies on less controversial biological metaphors, describing language acquisition in terms of "maturation" or "growth." Language is not, properly speaking, an "organ," Chomsky specifies in answering Bateson's blunt question; nonetheless, he feels that the growth of linguistic competence and performance should be approached in much the same way as the anatomist-physiologist studies the growth and functioning of the liver or the heart. Between these two "extreme" positions, that is, cognition as "order from noise" (according to Piaget) and language as an "organ" (according to Chomsky), Cellérier attempts to establish a more acceptable middle point.

The search for a compromise between constructivism and innatism takes its beginning from Cellérier's "hill-climbing" strategies in this chapter, proceeds in the next with Papert's perceptron, and oscillates up and down all through Chapters 4 and 5. Fodor's arguments against such a compromise, reported in Chapter 6, will baffle such hopes for quite a while. Eventually, from different standpoints, Putnam and Petitot will each persuasively argue against Fodor's demonstrations that, on purely logical grounds, a "richer" conceptual system can never grow out of a "poorer" one. The fortunes and misfortunes of the compromise reflect faithfully the swinging balance of consensus to one or the other scientific research program.

Introductory Remarks

Jean Piaget

I should like to begin by expressing to Noam Chomsky the admiration that I have for his works and listing the essential points on which I think I am in agreement with him. These points are so essential and so fundamental that the question of the heredity or innateness of language appears very minor to me. First of all, I agree with him on what I see as Chomsky's main contribution to psychology, which is that language is the product of intelligence or reason and not the product of learning in the behaviorist sense of the term. I also agree with him on the fact that this rational origin of language presupposes the existence of a fixed nucleus necessary to the elaboration of all languages, and presupposing, for example, the subject-to-predicate relation or the ability to construct relations. Finally, I naturally agree with him regarding the partial constructivism of his works, that is, the transformational grammars. I think, therefore, that we agree on the basic points, and I do not see any major conflict between Chomsky's linguistics and my own psychology. I can go so far as to say that on the issue relating to the relationships between language and thought, I consider myself to be in symmetry with Chomsky.

Why, then, is there a disagreement on the question of the innateness of the fixed nucleus? First, I would like to say that I believe I understand why Chomsky proposed this hypothesis: simply because it is a very common opinion to presuppose that a behavior is more stable if it is firmly rooted, that is, if it is hereditary and not simply a product of autoregulation. In other words, Chomsky's fixed nucleus would appear more stable, more important, and thus of higher value, if it were hereditarily fixed. If that opinion were true, I myself would adhere to the innateness of rational and linguistic structures. However, we know today that the problem of the innateness of behavior is a much more complex problem than that of any morphological character of the organism, and that it is very difficult to agree on innateness when one is dealing with the development of behaviors. It was a long time ago in psychology that McGraw wrote in *Carmichael's Manual*[1] that the alternative between maturation and experience was a false alternative that complicated discussions instead of enlightening them. In ethology as well, we have become very careful today for the same reasons; in this domain, we no longer speak of instinct in the same sense as that of Konrad Lorenz, because we have not found any stable limits between what is innate and what is acquired. Wickler, one of Lorenz's successors from Seewiesen, recently wrote an article[2] in which one passage really struck me: he said that the development of specific behaviors (for the term *instinct* is now replaced by the term *species-specific behavior*) is not only a product of selection, but in many cases, a product of phenocopy, a problem with which I will deal later on.

In regard to the innate fixed nucleus of language, I have been impressed with the recent works of Roger Brown,[3] Lenneberg,[4] and McNeill,[5] who became converted to explaining it by sensorimotor intelligence; McNeill in particular had been initially a very strong defender of innateness, and subsequently changed his opinion. Furthermore, I should like to recall the very profound remark made by James M. Baldwin[6] (obviously not a very recent remark), who said that the child is older than all the adults and that he is anterior to prehistoric man himself, which is perfectly obvious. Consequently, what is general in the child is not necessarily inherited from the adult. For instance, while studying in Geneva notions of physics held by young children, I discovered numerous examples of explanations of movement by Aristotle's *antiperistasis,* a hypothesis according to which the air that flows back behind a body whose own motion creates that airflow, pushes the body forward; this *antiperistasis* is a common notion in a 7- to 9-year-old child. I have also discovered in detail the notion of *impetus* as conceived by Buridan, hence of "impulse" as a necessary intermediary between force and movement. Now, it is perfectly clear that there is no hereditary link between Aristotle and Buridan, or between the little Genevans on whom I conducted my research in Geneva and the little Poles studied by Szeminska[7] in Poland.

In the case of Chomsky's innate fixed nucleus, it seems to me that a major objection is added to the difficulty: this innateness is not needed to ensure the formation and the stability of this nucleus; sensorimotor intelligence is sufficient for that. Sensorimotor intelligence, which can be studied between birth and the age of 1½ to 2 years (that is, the beginnings of language), is distributed according to six successive stages which are characterized by schemes of action interrelated by virtue of a process of extremely regular autoregulation, with corrections, reinforcements, and so on. It is only at the sixth of these stages—that is, when the assimilation of objects to the schemes of action is able to be completed by an assimilation of objects themselves, in other words, by means of representation—that language begins; and at this sixth stage, these beginnings of language profit from a whole construction achieved previously and to which I shall refer later.

But what especially bothers me about the innateness hypothesis is that the current explanations of the neo-Darwinians concerning the formation of any new character trait in the organism are based solely on notions of mutation and selection. Now, a mutation necessarily occurs at random; therefore, if there were innateness, reason and language would be the result of selected accidents, but selected subsequently, after the fact, whereas the formation itself would be the result of mutations and would therefore occur at random. I claim that in that case, it would be tantamount to shaking the solidity of the fixed nucleus, and generally speaking the solidity of knowledge, instead of consolidating it, as one might wish to do by invoking the innateness hypothesis. Konrad Lorenz, who was both a Kantian and a biologist, understood this very well when he said that Kant's a priori notions are the equivalent of what is innate from the biological point of view, adding nevertheless: this is true, but heredity is specific, therefore it can vary from one species to another and thus has nothing necessary. He eventually translated Kant's a priori categories into simple "innate working hypotheses." I absolutely refuse, for my part, to think that logico-mathematical structures would owe their origin to chance; there is nothing fortuitous about them. These structures could not be formed by survival selection but by an exact and detailed adaptation to reality.

But let us suppose now that this innateness is demonstrated. The following could happen: genes or loci could be discovered that would allow the reality of such innateness to be demonstrated. In that case, I would answer that this is not a random mutation, but that the only possible explanation would have to be sought in the direction of phenocopies, that is, in the phenomenon that I have endeavored to explain as follows: The notion of phenocopy is a biological process in which certain behaviors—for it is mostly valid in the area of behaviors—or else a certain form or a morphological structure is first acquired by the phenotype, but without being genetically determined. The phenotype, by contrast, modifies the internal environment and the upper levels of the epigenetic environment, and in this way, the variations or the mutations which can occur in the genome will be selected, not by the external environment, but by that internal or epigenetic environment which will then channel it in the same direction as the trend already acquired by the phenotype; in other words, there would be a genetic or gene-linked reconstruction of an acquisition made by the phenotype. Therefore, demonstrating innateness would still not be proof of a random mutation. You will answer me, of course, that I have no competence in biology; I am only a novice in that field, a novice, however, who has recently received two or three encouragements: the main one is to be found in the book written by the late Waddington, which was, regrettably, his last one, *The Evolution of an Evolutionist.*[8] He devotes the entire ninth chapter to the example of my Limnea living in ponds or in the large lakes of Sweden or Switzerland;[9] he sees there the best example of what he calls "genetic assimilation," which is an equivalent of phenocopy. Waddington calls the Limnea the best case of genetic assimilation because it was observed in nature and not produced in a laboratory, as for example in the case of drosophila. Likewise, in a recent ethology symposium in Parma,[10] the Italian geneticist, Francesco Scudo, referred to these same studies on Limnea and to other similar works in order to explain their possible meaning in the case of the formation of an innate behavior. In other words—and I am approaching my conclusion—there are two things to consider: (1) there is no clear and total opposition, with well-defined boundaries, between what is innate and what is acquired: all cognitive behavior includes a portion of innateness, in its functioning at least, whereas the structure appears to me to be constructed bit by bit by autoregulation; (2) the real problem is not to decide whether such a fixed nucleus or other cognitive structures are innate or not; the real question is: what has been their formation process? And, in the case of innateness, what is the biological mode of formation of that innateness? Are we dealing with random mutations, or with more complex processes like that of phenocopy to which I just alluded?

If it were a question of phenocopy, it goes without saying that the initial construction would be the result of behaviors, and, consequently, innateness becomes useless again because, among the kinds of acquisition of behavior assured by the phenotype of any species, some give rise later on to a phenocopy, but a very large number of others do not give rise to any such gene-linked reconstructions—the phenotypic action and behavior are simply formed anew at each generation without necessitating a hereditary fixation.

I will conclude my discussion by saying that innateness appears useless to me as far as our present goal is concerned, which is to emphasize the stability and the importance of cognitive structures and, in particular, of the fixed nucleus in the field of linguistics. I believe that the processes of autoregulation are as stable and as capable of providing the same importance in any formation as heredity itself. The following remark must be made, however, as a final note: as a rule, autoregulation in the organism limits itself to preserving a certain state of equilibrium and, in the case of deviation or of a new formation, to bringing it back to its initial state; whereas, on the contrary, autoregulation in the realm of behaviors constantly pushes the organism—or the subject, if a cognitive behavior is involved—toward new extensions. The physiological organism has no reason at all to change; and as Monod very aptly wrote, there is no "necessity" in evolutionary changes. Conservation is the supreme rule for physiological equilibrium. Whereas, on the contrary, as soon as we approach the field of behavior, we find that two goals are being pursued: the first one is the extension of the environment, that is, the surpassing of that environment which now encompasses the organism, through explorations and research in new environments; the second goal is the reinforcement of the organism's power over that environment. An autoregulation that is capable of preserving the past as well as constantly surpassing itself through the double end of extending the environment and reinforcing the organism's power, appears to me, when we are dealing with behaviors and cognitive processes, a much more fundamental mechanism than heredity itself.

Discussion

Jacob   I would like to make two quick biological remarks. The first one concerns phenocopies. Phenocopies in biology are modifications due to the environment that imitate genetic effects. For example, it is taking a specimen that should become a female and drowning it with testosterone, which makes it phenotypically male. But this represents only a slight variation within the realm of what the genotype allows. In the case of the small animals from the bottom of Lake

Geneva, the observed variations are always those allowed by their genotype. One always remains within the working margin authorized by the genes, and one simply has a slight variation due to temperature, osmotic pressure, and so forth.

The second biological remark I would like to make concerns the mechanism of autoregulation: *there is regulation only on structures and with structures that exist and that are there to regulate,* structures which, in biology, are themselves constrained by genes. They adjust, of course, the allowed working margin, but it is, once more, the genotype that prescribes the limits. In other words, in all cases, including those that were given by Piaget, the problem is only pushed back one notch; we haven't gotten rid of it. When you say phenocopy, it is within a genotype; you allow a small working margin for regulation and adaptation, but you certainly need, at least for all biological mechanisms, a genetically determined structure.

Piaget I would like to make three remarks. The first one is that I am surprised at the very limited instance of phenocopy that Jacob gives us, and in any case, it does not apply to the abyssal Limnea, since, particularly in that case, there was no fixation; it was only a phenotypic variation that returned to the original type as soon as the environment was changed. On the other hand, in the case of the littoral Limnea, the environment agitated by the wind and the waves of the large lakes causes the appearance and the formation of new genotypes which did not belong to the norm of reaction of the genotype of the species, a new genotype . . .

Jacob A phenotype . . .

Piaget No, a genotype. In regard to those contracted Limnea found in agitated sites, there are sites where the change remains at the phenotypic stage, but in the most agitated parts of the lake, and only there, these variations became hereditary; and when the same specimens are raised in an aquarium or in stagnant ponds, they completely retain their contracted form. I say "became" to simplify, but there is, of course, in this case a replacement of the phenotype by a genotype of the same form, and that is what I call "phenocopy."

Jacob Then it is not a phenocopy. The definition of a phenocopy is the phenotypic imitation of another genotype.

Piaget I would like to question this point . . . When Lorenz gives an example, he calls it "genocopy" to indicate the difference; he gives the example of birds whose crests have a

specific function in certain behaviors and become a hereditary organ in other situations . . . Anyway, this is a mere detail. If the term *phenocopy* gives rise to alternative definitions,
then let us simply speak of genetic assimilation in the sense
used by Waddington, who also admits that there can be replacement of a phenotype of the same form. Jacob's main objection, on the contrary, is that naturally the self-regulatory
mechanism presupposes genetic structures, *in the case of
morphogenesis;* but the essential characteristic of behavior is
precisely *to transcend itself constantly and to change autoregulation into auto-organization leading to new structures.*
My hope is that this will be found in biology as well as in
psychology. In psychology, autoregulation is not a return to
a previous state determined by any genetic structure but is
always a "passing beyond."

Now, as for the relation between phenocopy and genome,
I would like to remind you of Paul Weiss's profound remark:[1]
that when we say "related to the genome," this may have two
completely different meanings: the first one being "determined by the genes" and the second one "compatible with
the genes," which is not the same thing. It is precisely in the
case of phenocopies that *there are new hereditary formations
compatible with, but not determined by, previous genes.*

I have taken my definition of phenocopy from three
sources: Lorenz, who has not inconsiderable knowledge of
genetics; Hovasse, from his chapter on evolution in the
Encyclopédie de la Pléiade; and especially Mayr, who, in the
large work, *Animal Species and Evolution,*[2] defines phenocopy as the replacement of a phenotype by a genotype of
the same form, and states that it is a common process, but
genetically obscure. In another passage of the same chapter,
he gives the same definition when speaking of such processes,
whose mechanism remains unknown.

Changeux I think there is controversy here because it looks
as if you are dealing with two species of Limnea with different
phenotypic variability. What is genetically determined is the
potentiality of a given Limnea to have different shapes, and
this potentiality is more limited in one species than in the
other one: that defines the *genetic envelope* of this character
you are looking at. But, as Jacob said, this phenotypic variability *takes place within the given genotype and is limited by the
genotype.* Now, the word *phenocopy,* "copy," exists for me
only in the mind of the observer: the word *copy* means that
as observers we compare the two objects.

Piaget All this exists only in the mind of the observer, but I would say the same about the notion of potentiality, which is the most dangerous of notions. This is an Aristotelian notion which is of the "dormant property" type and which acquires significance only when one has measurement (potential energy, for example).

Toulmin I do think that at this point, in talking about evolutionary questions, we might set Piaget's anxieties about the "randomness" of mutation at rest. This does seem to me a red herring, which we ought to clear out of the way as soon as we can. It is a red herring that Chomsky is also drawn to in his paper, so it is worth being careful about. Consider the process by which a certain feature that appeared originally in noninheritable forms as a result of muscular effort or extension in a phenotype appears in some later generation for quite different reasons, in consequence of a genetic change. Anything of intellectual significance about this latter change must then be understood as having occurred for reasons of an ecological kind, having to do with *adaptation*—reasons that have to do (in Piaget's own phrase) with "adaptation to reality at the biological level." All the same, this transition from the phenotype to the genotype could never take place unless there were a pool of mutations from which an ecological selection could determine the form of a new genome. Where these mutants ultimately come from—whether they are random, or whether they are (for example) the effects of x-ray irradiation—is of no significance to the question that Piaget is concerned with. And he is worrying needlessly by placing so much stress on the supposed "random origin," which he regards as a serious objection to all sorts of genetic explanations of the basis of different cognitive structures.

Chomsky First, on what Toulmin very correctly left aside for the moment as a side issue, let me just say that there are plenty of real issues, and just to avoid non-issues let me simply say that the remarks that I made in my opening paper about evolution have no relation whatsoever with the red herring at issue.

Let me just say what I see as the question. First, is there a fixed cognitive structure, a fixed nucleus (*noyau fixe*)? The answer is yes—we all seem to agree on that. Second, on the question we are discussing, does this fixed nucleus—which I guess is what I have been calling universal grammar in this specific case—does it arise as a result of structural properties of the organism that are genetically determined, or does it arise in each particular case through self-regulating mechanisms? We ought to know how to pursue the answer to that question, not by philosophical discussion, but by looking at specific properties of the fixed nucleus and asking how they might arise from self-regulating mechanisms, from sensorimotor constructions, and so forth. Now, just to state my own view, it seems to me inconceivable that there is any significant relationship between these specific structures and any structures of sensorimotor intelligence or general properties of self-regulatory mechanisms. However, I am entirely open-minded on this issue: if somebody could show that some of the elementary properties of language that I discussed in my paper do result from self-regulatory mechanisms I would be delighted, but I don't anticipate it.

Another point that I think ought to be stated a little more sharply is this: the issue is not to account for the stability of the fixed nucleus; rather it is to account for its specific character. Piaget is quite right to say that there are many possible explanations for stability, but that is not even in question; the question is how do we account for the specific structures that we are led to attribute to the mature organism (and indirectly to the neonate) through the study of what it does, the way it acts, and so on. I think we ought to be able to try to find the answer to that problem by looking at the specific cases and looking at all the possible explanations, exactly as we would deal with the quite comparable question of the structure of the liver or the heart or the complex mechanisms of the visual cortex. We wouldn't have philosophical debates about them; we would simply ask whether the specific structures which we are led to believe exist and function in such and such a way with particular properties in organisms are genetically determined or result from the activity of individual self-regulatory mechanisms.

Piaget   I will attempt to respond to Chomsky later by trying to show how sensorimotor intelligence prepares the semiotic function in general (see Chapter 7).

Wilden   I would like to ask three "metaquestions," if the term is permitted—questions about the kind of questions we are discussing.

In discussing genetics, development, and the organism, what relationship are we actually talking about? What epistemological assumptions are we working with? What I am hearing, whether it be from Jacob, from Piaget, or from Chomsky, is a discussion that implicitly assumes a primacy of the organism over its environment. This is an epistemological position that is at least 100 years old, and we seem to have forgotten that it was *invented*, not discovered. I don't think there are any evolutionary or ecological grounds for continuing to assume that this position is valid, and I note that a number of biologists, ecologists, and others—on both sides of the Atlantic—have been moving away from it in recent years, partly because of the influence of nonmechanistic approaches related to cybernetics and systems theory. So, taking the relational position of *both* organism *and* environment, my first question is: How much of the "fixed nucleus" or the "genetic structure" is "in the organism" and how much of it is "in the environment"? The only way that I can see us dealing adequately with this question is from a system-environment position in which the "prototypical structure"—to use an expression of Piaget's—is that relationship itself, and not *either* the "organism" *or* the "environment."

The second question is related to the first. What, at the epistemological level, does the use of the metaphor "genetic determination" actually imply? It seems to me to be a residue of mechanistic determinism, implying a one-way relationship between the genetic program and both the environment it is in and the environment (within the developing organism) it is in the process of creating. We ought surely to be talking about the *constraints* on the relative *semiotic freedom* of the expression of the genetic program. Some of those constraints develop as a result of the expression of the program, which seems to be hierarchically arranged; some are properties of the environment or milieu in the ordinary sense.

The third question concerns another metaphor that I have heard repeatedly: the metaphor of "self-regulation." This is in reality a transitive expression, an expression requiring some completion. But it is being used here, as elsewhere, as if it were *intransitive,* that is, complete in and of itself. In this sense, the term "self-regulation" betrays an ideological and epistemological association with the dialect of atomism or individualism in academic discourse.[3] It betrays the fundamental epistemological misconstruction characteristic of both "mechanism" and "organicism" as we know them: the misconstruction (*méconnaissance*) of the system-environment relation to which I have already referred. The third question, then, is "self-regulating *in relation* to what?" By itself, the expression is a logical and ecological absurdity. Nevertheless, it seems that this question about relation is never answered. In fact, I have some doubt that the question is even *perceived* as one, much less *recognized*.

Chomsky All this still doesn't deal with the question that I am raising, namely, what is the origin of the various specific structures that are complex in detail and extensively articulated?

Cognitive Strategies in Problem Solving

Guy Cellérier

According to Toulmin, because the theoretical differences between innatism and constructivism are "so extreme," we may be "tempted simply to choose up sides," which, he says, would result in "a barren confrontation" (see Chapter 13). Of course I agree with Toulmin: if we are going to argue in the abstract, whenever we "observe" two consecutive states of knowledge in some cognitive domain and agree that the second state has in some sense more *structural* content than the first, the innatist can argue that the new rules are only the actualization of preexisting rules that were already present in a virtual form, whereas the constructivist will argue that they have actually been generated here and now. The constructivist will try to make this idea plausible by showing that the new rule could have been composed by some simple evolutionary transformation or combination of the rules that were present in the preceding state. If the innatist is kindly disposed, he will imitate the turtle in Lewis Carroll's dialogue between the turtle and Achilles and say "I grant this," but then he will add: "but the transformation rule itself was already there." The constructivist will do the same: he will grant this, and add: "but it has been generated by some higher level constructive transformation on preceding transformation rules," and so on—and the discussion can regress in a rather barren way.

If this type of argument had been going on between two Scholasticists, there would have been no logical or empirical grounds for the regression to stop. I believe we are slightly better off nowadays because both participants in this kind of dialogue, whatever their views may be on the neo-Darwinian theory of evolution, would agree that cognition is mechanistically related to the functioning of the brain and that the brain itself is a *construct* of biological evolution. This means that even a radical constructivist will allow for some *initial innate structure* in the central nervous system, and this would transfer the problem of how the structure was generated to the biologists and stop the logical regression. The constructivist will try to do this as late as possible in the discussion, whereas the innatist will try to do it as soon as possible. I will now try to show that in this context "soon" is "late," just as "half empty" means "half full." This looks *a priori* quite easy to do, because who knows what the middle of a theory can look like? It is, of course, anywhere between its endpoints, and since I have the floor now, I get first choice of where it is. But first I am going to compare the theories more or less point by point, in a discussion on the comparative anatomy of the theories.

To start with, both Chomsky and Piaget agree on the existence of a *non-empty* "genetically determined initial state S_0," followed by a sequence of intermediate states and a final relatively stable state S_s, stable at least for the observable development of language (perhaps less so for mathematics). Also both agree that part of the content of these states is not innate but *acquired, that is, "learned" in an external environment characterized by "problems."* The classic question is how much of this content is innate and how much is acquired. I believe it is more pertinent to ask what *kind* of content rather than how much. The minimal content we can give S_0 is just enough to make the central nervous system a functioning organ. The modern equivalents of the empiricists' *tabula rasa* are entities like universal machines or universal postcanonical systems or—perhaps closer to the letter of the theory—perceptrons. But even these very general systems must have some initial internal structure wired into their (possibly biological) implementation, to allow them to function as *interpreters* or to "learn" by adjusting thresholds under reinforcement. Since neither Piaget nor Chomsky is an empiricist, both of them agree that S_0 must contain not only a structure independent of the environment (that is, in the sense that a universal machine is not adjusted to a specific problem-environment) but a more specific structure that must allow the central nervous system to work adaptively in a given problem-environment or cognitive domain. This problem-bound knowledge can in principle be of two kinds: it may describe either the content or the form of the problem-environment. This distinction is, I believe, quite clear in both Piaget's and Chomsky's views, and the relative importance of form versus content is also the same in both views.

In Chomsky's viewpoint, S_0 contains mainly abstract characteristics: ". . . 'formal universals,' conditions on the form and function of the system of rules and principles that constitutes our theory of the structure of some cognitive domain"; S_0 may also contain " 'substantive universals,' fixed elements that enter into particular grammars." However, there is much less—according to Chomsky—to say about these universals (if I understand him well) in regard to their number and functional importance.

In Piaget's view, the initial form of intelligence, sensorimotor or practical intelligence, is developed from a nucleus of innate, preadapted sensorimotor action programs. These programs, says Piaget, organize and coordinate particular actions and perceptions that are adapted to the specific content of the environment in which they function. These particular elements contain the knowledge of this specific content. But Piaget adds that in order to assemble these particular elements into working programs, a more formal knowledge of the structure of the problem-space is required. This formal knowledge is contained in what Piaget calls general coordinations of action, which are general coordination processes that characterize all motor or mental composition. These general coordinations are basic to all the ensuing constructions of intellectual structures, and they are independent of whatever particular actions or primitives are being combined.

Thus, I think that here again the two views are highly congruent: Chomsky's distinction between formal and substantive parallels that of Piaget between general and particular. I will try to show that their function in the "theory of development" is the same in both cases. In their chapter in the *Handbook of Mathematical Psychology*, Chomsky and Miller describe a part of the child's learning mechanism for language and say, "It would have to include a device that accepted a sample of grammatical utterances as its input (with some restrictions, perhaps, on their order of presentation) and that would produce a grammar of the language (including the lexicon) as its output."[1] This mechanism should be guided by "heuristic principles that would enable it, given its input data and a range of possible grammars, to make a rapid selection of a few promising alternatives, which could then be submitted to a process of evaluation."[2]

This is of course a sketchy description of the mechanism, but I think it can be characterized in a perhaps more baroque but more general formulation as a variety of "hill-climbing" problem-solving system, using a width-first, generate-and-test method, in the search space of grammars. I am using the term "hill climbing" in the usual sense in artificial intelligence as an "adaptive" or "self-optimizing" servomechanism. Minsky defines it very neatly in "Steps towards Artificial Intelligence." The hypothesis is that we want to get to the top of a hill in a dense fog, and he then says, ". . . the obvious approach is to explore locally about a point, finding the direction of steepest ascent. One moves a certain distance in that direction and repeats the process until improvement ceases."[3]

In a similar manner, Piaget's central constructive mechanism, which he calls the "equilibration" process, may be recast in the same mold. Its main function is to move the learner from states of lesser cognitive equilibrium to states of greater equilibrium in the search space of logico-mathematical structures. The self-optimizing character is quite explicit in his formulation.

Thus the learning theory part of both views consists of a "hill climber." Again, a hill climber needs some internal structure, independent of the environment, to make it a functioning system. It also needs some specific knowledge of its problem-environment to make it work adaptively. More precisely, it has to be placed in some *initial position* on the adaptive surface and not out of the problem-space, and its generator must be constrained to make only legal moves, that is, it can only step *on* this adaptive surface. However, to make it an efficient problem solver, the generator must be further constrained to produce not all legal moves around each point but *only a subset* of "promising" or "plausible" moves around a given position. This heuristic orientation of the generator is the most delicate part of the learning theory. Now, this "constriction," if I may use this term, is performed in very much the same way in both views: an initial position is defined by the *particular* actions or *substantive* universals, and the generator is constrained to perform legal moves by the *general coordinations* or by the *formal* universals (in both cases, it is assumed implicitly that the hill climber possesses a minimal structure independent of the environment).

However, it is in the heuristic part that the first really important divergence appears. Piaget uses a heuristic that he calls "reflective abstraction," which is in part very similar to a major heuristic that appeared in the evolution of genetic systems: sexual reproduction that entails the Mendelian combination of whole chromosomes, and the recombination of parts of chromosomes by crossing-over. This constrains the generator to produce the next state by using the successful parts of the present state and its *vicinity*. This means that the next step will not be taken before some neighboring states have been explored to some extent; we get functional plateaus where exploration occurs and is followed or paralleled by reorganizations and recombinations, and the choice of a next adaptive step is accomplished among the reorganizations.

As far as I can see, there is nothing similar in the grammar generator of Chomsky; we may perhaps imagine that its set of legal moves to guide its explorations is much smaller and generates only highly pertinent states, which of course makes the problem much more trivial, or that in certain classes of states a pertinent innate rule that defines what to do next is triggered, and so on (whatever we imagine is not that important).

But in the case we are discussing now, we are left with the problem of explaining how this innate heuristic was acquired during biological evolution. At this level we cannot resort to scholastic regression, in the sense that we can no longer resort to an innatist solution. As far as I can see, there is nothing in the contemporary theory of evolution that allows us to assert plausibly that the evolution of species is the result of the execution of a preexisting master plan. The genetic system of a species is described as a self-optimizing device that must construct its own heuristics as it goes along. In this sense any innatist view is ultimately constructivist, and it must face exactly the same problems as Piaget's constructivism when it is asked where its constructive mechanisms and their heuristics come from in the first place. I also believe it will have to speculate along very much the same lines. In fact, it already does so. I know Piaget is not going to like what I am saying, because he has what I will call a "private gentleman's disagreement" with Darwin on the specific mechanisms that implement the hill climber in the Darwinian model. However, the kinds of questions a biologist will have to ask (questions like what is the adaptive value, what is the origin in a previous structure of a specific component) about the phylogeny of cognition and about the view of both the evolutionary mechanism and the developmental sequence that the Darwinian theory will support—this type of question, I think, is very close to Piaget's constructivism, at least in spirit if not in the letter.

From the evolutionary point of view, I see no incompatibility between innatism and constructivism, but rather a relation of division of labor, not only in regard to the construction itself but in regard to the explanations we have to give: we must consider the cognitive part of the central nervous system as a fast problem solver whose hardware is the output of a much slower one, the genetic system. The Darwinian argument will be that anything that facilitates the functioning of cognition will result in a selective advantage. For instance, the development of complex cognitive systems can be both oriented and subdivided into subsystems by "innate advice" appearing at strategic points in development. If we consider psychogenetic states from this point of view, they seem to be characterized by the successive appearance of qualitatively different modes of functioning that might well be based in part on something like *successive maturation of specialized hardware.* As an example of this I will give a semi-hypothetical maturation sequence that goes like this: you have in the infant gross movements of the arm, followed by fine movements of the fingers, followed by locomotion. This sequence would both direct what problems should be solved here and now, and also reduce the total problem of movement in space, to an ordered learning sequence of smaller and more manageable problems.* I have the impression that the developmental sequence that we see from the innate nucleus of sensorimotor programs to sensorimotor intelligence (structured by something like conditioning or, in a more general sense, learning) and then to the appearance of representation, followed by the appearance of capacities like reversibility or hypothetico-deductive reasoning, will have the same kind of function. The semiotic function, for instance, is certainly species-specific, and to make it available at the right moment in time, that is after some sensorimotor experience has been acquired, would be a good heuristic because it would constrain all the limited computing power of the infant's brain to the exploration of one limited problem-space first; then when this has been properly explored and when a set of smoothly working routines has been established, we can start executing them "mentally" on symbols and anticipating their probable results.

To sum up my main point, I believe that the problem of the evolution of cognition is of such difficulty that we will need simultaneously the full power of Darwinian and constructivist theories to account for it.

* Editor's note: See in this regard the exchange between Piaget and Thom in Appendix B.

Discussion

Chomsky Let me mention again, without pursuing the issues that will come later, the points in which I consider that Cellérier went further than I would at least.

First, in regard to the matter of choosing sides: I don't feel inclined to choose sides in this at all. I think that the two strategies suggested by Cellérier pose the issue in a way which it would be well to get away from. He proposes two strategies: attributing a maximal amount of initial structure to S_0 versus attributing a minimal amount of initial structure to it. I think that the right strategy would be to try to attribute the true structure to the initial state. Here I think one ought to treat the question of, say, the nature of language without prejudice and exactly as one would treat the question of some physical organ of the body. If we looked at the heart or at the visual cortex, it wouldn't make sense to propose these two strategies: clearly any such system results from genetically determined and environmental factors. It wouldn't make sense to oppose two strategies, one maximizing and the other minimizing the genetic contribution; rather, a physiologist would say, "Let's find what this contribution is."

In regard to the analogy Cellérier draws between a grammar-generating device and the hill-climbing system, I would like to step back from that analogy too: I think that hill climbing is one technique that is very special and possibly correct (though I am rather skeptical) for gaining cognitive structures sometimes; but whether it is *the* method here, I'm rather skeptical. In fact it seems to me possibly more likely in this case to be a *matter of successive maturation of specialized hardware* (to use one of Cellérier's expressions). It seems to me highly plausible that what we call (probably using a bad metaphor) language learning (my feeling is that we should call it language growth or something like that) does involve development of specialized hardware or of a specialized system that comes into operation, perhaps in the way in which sexual maturation takes place at a certain age for reasons that are probably deeply rooted in genetics, though naturally external conditions have to be appropriate. So I'm very skeptical that hill climbing is the right model or even that learning is the right metaphor. It is perfectly true that we talk about this as learning, but that is because there is a tradition in assuming that what goes on in the mind involves an organism-environment interaction whereas what goes on in the body is somehow determined physically. For all I know, that methodological assumption could turn out to be true, but I have never heard any argument for it and I don't believe it is true.

Now, suppose we are led tentatively to attribute such and such innate structures to the organism. I agree that there is a question of explaining how they evolved. But I don't see how that question is fundamentally any different or more complex (it is certainly less complex) than the comparable problems that you can raise about the physical characteristics of the body. If someone argues, as I assume any physiologist would, that the specific structures of the visual cortex are genetically determined, or that the fact that we have a heart, or the fact that we have arms rather than wings, is genetically determined, no one goes on to argue that this cannot be so because explaining the evolution is too hard a problem. Nobody has the slightest idea of how to explain it; we can say, "This happened and it was adaptive," and so on, but there are no general principles from which one can, at the moment, carry out a deduction which says that from some earlier stage we will get this particular phenomenon, given that physical fact. That is not to say that it is inexplicable, but just unexplained, and as far as I can see, no more unexplained in the particular case of language than in the case of the physical organs of the body. It is often argued that somehow those principles that are proposed for mental organization are of such order of complexity that it is incomprehensible that they could be determined by evolution. Implicitly there is some metric of complexity which I don't perceive or share, along which these proposals involve complexity that goes far beyond the physical properties of the body. As far as I can see that is not true: the most complicated ideas that have ever been proposed regarding mental organization seem to be extremely trivial as compared to the complexities involved in the physical structures of the body which remain unexplained, though they are not inexplicable in the same sense.

A final remark: implicit in the whole discussion there was a sort of parallel which Cellérier presented and then withdrew between learning and evolution. I would like to question again whether that is productive; it seems to me that what happens in what we call learning is a very complex process which probably does involve what we can call "successive maturation of specialized hardware" (and it probably involves that crucially), and there is nothing comparable to that in evolution. So, it seems to me that these processes are so different on all grounds that there is no point in drawing some kind of connection between them.

Atran   I also think that the analogy between a child learning language and Minsky's hill climber moving toward the summit in a haze is of little value. If, as Cellérier argues, the exploration is only local, then how could the hill climber ever know his path was the best? He could only know that it was apparently a good path relative to the others that he had *actually* considered. It might be, however, that his path was a poor one with respect to others he might not have considered. Moreover, there may be any number of summits, also surrounded by dense fog, which he is not aware of. It seems clear, then, that the climber cannot be sure that he has actually advanced unless he has some reasonably coherent picture of the shape of the hill, or the range of hills, beforehand. The local exploration, that is, experience, would simply help him to discover whether or not he has deviated too far from the course already mapped out.

Piattelli-Palmarini   I think there is little doubt here among the majority of us that some kind of isomorphism can be found between the explanation of why the heart is there, how it works, and so on, and why certain specific linguistic properties are present; but I wonder if Chomsky thinks that the same categories of explanation are there at work; I don't say higher or lower, I just wonder whether or not one can apply the same explanatory categories to explain some physiological mechanism or to explain the sort of structures Chomsky is after.

Chomsky   I would like to go back to that phrase which I like, "successive maturation of specialized hardware." I think that this is a good metaphor which holds rather well for the embryological development of organs or for later development and also for the growth of mental structures—what we call learning. There is a very traditional assumption, which can be traced all the way back to the scholastic dogma, attributing to Aristotle certain doctrines about the emptiness of the mind; this assumption says that learning involves continual repetition of a very simple set of operations. I think it was a big step forward when psychology discarded that concept, which for centuries stopped progress in the study of the nature of the mind.

We should next explore the question of what the special mechanisms are that come into operation at various stages of growth. There are various ways of looking at this: through experimental investigations of children solving problems, which is a fine way to look at it; you can also look at it by the study of the characteristics of the achieved final state. Each of these methods provides some information, but there are other ways, no doubt. In principle, if we could carry out experiments with humans as we do with lower organisms we could study the question very directly: we would know exactly how to proceed; we would construct controlled environments and we would see what happens to an organism growing in these controlled environments, or we would carry out experimentation directly into the brain, for example. All of these methods of course have to be excluded for obvious reasons, and therefore we will have to work with indirect approaches; but I don't think that changes anything in principle. It makes our work more interesting and exciting. It seems to me that the very same categories of explanation apply at this level, at least as far as we know, for the investigation of the growth of both physical and mental organs like language.

Bateson   You think that language is an organ?

Chomsky   I think that as long as we are speaking with metaphors, it is better than the ones that have been used (of course it is not an organ in the sense that we can delimit it physically). But I think that the growth of this capacity has the general characteristics of the growth of organs. It may very well be that the growth of language essentially terminates around puberty. There seems to be some evidence concerning the possible existence of specialized face-recognition devices that evolve in parts of the brain that may in fact be homologous to the language areas, and these facial recognition capacities appear to grow during the later prepubertal period, supposedly after the language capacities are fixed in the left hemisphere. It is not at all beyond our understanding of the growth of physical structures to interpret the growth of language very much along the same lines and to try to isolate those successive stages and successive structures which develop in an appropriate environment but whose character develops in a manner essentially independent of that environment. In other words, their character is determined even though an appropriate environment is required for the character to be realized, just as is true for embryological development.

Danchin   I agree that one should study the heart and the brain with the same methods, but nevertheless I think that the heart and the brain are quite different because one inherits the same heart as one's father, but one doesn't inherit the memory of one's father.

Chomsky There is a large amount of the structure of the brain that is quite independent of the particular memories stored in the brain. And of course the heart also depends, for example, on the particular nutritional environment in which the embryo develops. We, as human beings, naturally pay tremendous attention to the variations in the way the cognitive structures represented in the brain develop in different individuals. We don't happen to pay much attention to the differences in size and function of the heart because it doesn't interest us so much. But as scientists there is no reason for us to take that point of view: if, say, a Martian superorganism were looking at us, it might determine that from its point of view the variations of brains, of memories and languages, are rather trivial, just like the variations in the size of hearts, in the way they function, and so on; and it might be amused to discover that the intellectual tradition of its subjects assumes otherwise. But then we can easily explain that, because we are quite naturally concerned with what from another point of view would be considered slight differences between individuals, differences that are enormously important for our daily lives. We shouldn't as scientists look at humans with that natural prejudice of daily life.

Bateson I think we should consider these metaphors very carefully; that's why I am interested in the distinction of levels, and Cellérier seemed to agree with one based on phylogeny, learning and morphogenesis, and perhaps environment. Now, what we are being told, as I understand it, is to think of learning, and specifically the learning related to language, as being more like morphogenesis than it is like an evolutionary phylogenetic process. That is really the issue (after all, morphogenesis is determined by genes; phylogeny is not). So let's now look at that metaphor and consider what the difference might be between the two sources of metaphor. In morphogenesis, the characteristic of the whole process is the buildup of interactive stresses of relationships between parts, where there is a building up of quantitative tension which, if it breaks, breaks always to a prepared understructure.

Chomsky I think that's too simple. Isn't it true, for example, that there are very specific genes that will trigger very special developments at a late stage of morphogenesis if that stage is reached, and then lead to very complex structures?

Bateson   Certainly, but you are moving along a homeorhetic* track where compensations are already intervening, so that within certain limits a normal pathway will be followed. Even if the growth goes over an edge and brings in a new element, it is still going on along a predictable track (internally predictable).

Chomsky   Even though there will be considerable variation depending on the environment, I agree with what you are saying, but if one were arguing that the growth of arms rather than wings is to be studied on a traditional model of learning which really is like the model of evolution, what you would say is that the embryo is endowed with appendages which it tries out, and if they go up in the air they become wings, and if not, they become arms. Of course, nothing like that really happens.

Fodor   We know that the child has certain data about the body of utterances produced by its language community, and about the situation in which these utterances are produced; nobody denies that, nobody doubts it. The child ends up with a body of information, which allows him to speak the language. To look at it from the point of view of a problem-solving system is plausible (and in fact exactly accurate, I would say) in order to characterize the intervening processes as inferences from those data to that body of beliefs. Now, the question is whether or not the inferential mechanisms are specialized and innately determined. That seems to me to be exactly the question, and I don't see why we are talking about how children don't learn to develop wings.

Sperber   In many respects, we are listening to a pseudo-debate. At first glance, it seems that we are dealing with two symmetrical and opposing positions, basically that of Piaget and that of Chomsky, between which one would have to make a choice; but a closer look shows that this symmetry does not exist. The case is not that there are, on the one hand, constructivist hypotheses, and on the other hand, innatist hypotheses on language learning, but rather that there is a constructivist *a priori* that rejects all innatist hypotheses, and

---

* Editor's note: Bateson introduces here a term originally coined by the British embryologist Conrad H. Waddington, meaning "compensated change." It mimics and generalizes the notion of homeostasis (coined by Walter Cannon in the late 1920s), making it more dynamic.

an open attitude that accepts innatist hypotheses as well as constructivist hypotheses provided they explain something and are not immediately invalidated. Chomsky's discussion offers some examples of well-argued innatist hypotheses, and in general, there is no reason to reject *a priori* this type of hypothesis, that is, to exclude that the mental equipment utilized by the child to learn a language possesses a certain number of genetically determined properties. The so-called innatist position is simply, in this respect, an open attitude, and as with all open attitudes, it does not need any particular justification. Once again, this attitude does not consist of granting a preference to innatist hypotheses, but simply considering them as admissible.

The constructivist position, on the contrary, consists of immediately rejecting all innatist hypotheses, or at least, in giving a marked preference to all noninnatist hypotheses. This prejudice goes so far as to prefer the consideration of a still unformed constructivist hypothesis to an already formed and explanatory hypothesis that has innatist implications. To be sure, it often happens that a scientist is led to prefer the consideration of a hypothesis to be constructed to an existing hypothesis; if this did not occur, science would scarcely progress. But as long as the scientist remains at this stage and has not constructed his new hypothesis, he hardly has good reason for having his project preferred over the existing hypothesis; he is still at the laboratory stage and not at the public debate stage. Such is precisely the situation of constructivists in regard to language learning, except for the minor distinction that they do not set a new project against old hypotheses but, on the contrary, an old project (which has remained in the form of a project) against new and viable hypotheses.

Moreover, even if constructivism had a better developed description of language learning, it would not follow for all that that innatist hypotheses are to be excluded in principle. One would only have in this case two sets of hypotheses to confront, and a real debate would be possible whose outcome would not depend on any *a priori* arguments.

But this is not where we stand. Chomsky has offered data that each learning theory must account for as well as innatist hypotheses that account for these data. If the constructivists have neither supplementary data that invalidate these hypotheses, nor alternate hypotheses, all we can do then is to take note of their reticence and their hope to find something better someday; but to pursue the debate as if we were faced with two symmetrical positions would be a waste of time.

Cellérier   My immediate reply is that a bad explanation is more satisfying than none at all: the innatist position is no explanation at all.

Sperber   In what way is it no explanation at all? You do accept the existence of a cardiovascular system explained by an innatist hypothesis, don't you?

Chomsky   An innatist hypothesis is a refutable hypothesis. Any hypothesis which says that such and such a property of language is genetically determined is subject to the most immediate refutation of the strongest kind. Such hypotheses have been refuted over and over again in the past by just looking at the next phenomenon in the same language or the next language. That is why it has been so hard to formulate specific hypotheses about genetically determined structures.

Cellérier   But you are really showing that the hypothesis is not general...

Chomsky   If the hypothesis is refuted for the next language then it is wrong. Assuming, of course, the uniformity of species (I am just taking that for granted, that there aren't subspecies of humans), then if somebody proposes the property P and says that all he can suggest is that that property P is genetically determined, then he will be subject to the most immediate refutation by looking at the next language where somebody may show that it doesn't conform to the property P. I gave examples in my paper of a very reasonable inference to a universal property of language (the stacking of subordinate clauses; see Chapter 1) which is known to be false and which requires that we set up some other property.

Cellérier   But if you find a universal property you still can't show it is innate.

Chomsky   You can't demonstratively prove it is innate—that is because we are dealing with science and not mathematics; even if you looked at genes you couldn't prove that. In science you don't have demonstrative inferences; in science you can accumulate evidence that makes certain hypotheses seem reasonable, and that is all you can do—otherwise you are doing mathematics. But I think we can find a lot of evidence that is convincing, although it is certainly much less convincing than it would be if we could deal with humans the way we deal with fruit flies. We can't do that, so therefore we are forced to have arguments that are much more indirect and complex, inferences that are only partially supported, open questions that we know how to investigate in principle but are barred from investigating; these are the contingencies of research on humans, but there is no point of principle raised by that, there is no philosophical or epistemological issue—it is just a question raised by the ethics of experimentation on humans. I think that every characteristic of explanatory hypotheses that I know of is met by specific proposals about innate structure, except that the requirements are met less well than they would be if we could experiment with humans.

Piaget I would like to make a brief remark concerning what has just been said: "general" and "innate" should not be confused; the whole weakness of the works of Jung lies in the fact that he believed that because a myth is general it corresponds to an innate archetype. Now, first of all, generality alone is no proof of innateness; and second, the question is to know whether generality is common to all levels of development or whether it becomes so. In many cases structures become general, but they do not appear as general before the proper level comes under consideration, before we hit upon a level that can be studied very easily through experimentation.

Chomsky I agree with both of these points: the fact that a thing is general is only evidence that it is innate, but it doesn't demonstrate that it is innate. If something is not general then it is certainly not innate. But what we are interested in discovering here is properties that are biologically necessary, and generality is a necessary but not a sufficient property. Again, we run into the difficulty that we can't do experimental control; to distinguish between something that is just general and something that is biologically necessary, the obvious experiment is to construct a perfectly controlled environment; since that is ruled out we have to find out indirect ways of overcoming this nondemonstrative inference. The second point that I think is valid is a point I would like to emphasize, namely, that there are certain properties that are general and, I assume, biologically determined, but only at specific levels of development. For example, at a particular advanced level of development of some organ, some complicated thing will happen necessarily at that level, and correspondingly I would assume that specific properties of language structure, for instance, simply won't come into operation at all unless a certain level of complexity has been reached. I think that all the things we are talking about will ultimately be explained in terms of properties of the brain; however, we cannot speak of the physical structure of the brain because of our ignorance, and therefore we can only speak of some of the conditions that the physical structures must meet, however they meet them. We simply don't have the kind of evidence to tell us how the abstract structures might be represented in the concrete physical system. However, that doesn't mean we should stop working on the problem. I think we can go rather far in terms of the limited sorts of evidence available to impose some fairly narrow and specific conditions on what this physical system must be doing. But there are a lot of questions that we will never be able to answer.

Jacob   I would simply like to reemphasize the fact, since we have been concerned with development here, that we do not know much about the development of physical structures. One can describe, as Chomsky does for linguistics, a state S_0 which passes to a state S_x. S_0 is a single cell, the fertilized ovum. S_x is, in the case of man, something on the order of 10^{13} cells. This means that there is not enough genetic information in the genome to describe in detail the totality of the individual, to describe each cell and to specify, for example, that the 2,327th cell will be in contact with the 242,000th cell, and so forth. What we do know is that among the 10^{13} cells, there is a repertoire of approximately 200 cellular types. It is the number and the distribution of these 200 types that determine the differences of form from one mammal to another or from one vertebrate to another. Genes do not contain the detailed description of the individual; they contain a program that specifies cellular structures and the number and position of the cells. But at this time no one knows the internal logic of this program. One can attempt to assimilate a cell to an automaton, to say that a cell has a constant and a variable part, the constant part being the genotype and the variable part, the macromolecular types contained in it. This amounts to saying that all the cells of an individual have the same genes. But from one cellular type to another, it is not the same genes that are in the "on" or the "off" position. One can also say that in all likelihood cells have a certain number of successive binary choices during their life span, during ontogenesis. After each choice, a new choice must be made, so that cells pass through a series of successive states. In this way, the same signals can be utilized several times, since they have different meanings according to the state of the cells; hence the possibility of having a very complex system of differentiation by means of a combinatorial system of signals in a limited number. It seems, therefore, that genes contain a certain number of specifications for successive choices, and that is about all we can say at the present time.

Some Clarifications on Innatism and Constructivism

Guy Cellérier

I will endeavor here to clarify some superficial misunderstandings in order to concentrate on some points of the argument for innatism that leave me somewhat unconvinced.

STRATEGIES

In characterizing the innatist and constructivist strategies, I was not suggesting a choice between them, but merely describing positions in fact already chosen by Piaget and Chomsky themselves. When Chomsky then asserts that "the two strategies . . . pose the issue in a way which it would be well to get away from," I am in complete agreement with him, as I believe that *the full power of both evolutionary theory and genetic psychology will be necessary to account for the interactive development of the innate and acquired features of language.* However, when Chomsky goes on to say that the right strategy is to "treat the question of . . . the nature of language without prejudice and exactly as one would treat the question of some physical organ of the body," such as the heart, I can only conclude either that he does not believe the development of the heart to be innately determined, or that he does, and is thereby reverting to one of the two strategies he has just declared "it would be well to get away from," which is a contradiction. Both terms of the alternative introduce an inconsistency in Chomsky's defense of innatism.

HILL CLIMBING

My point in regard to hill climbing is the following: all goal-oriented or adaptive processes (problem solving, inference making, equilibration, or the working of the genetic system of a population) may be described, at some level of abstraction, as hill climbing in some symbolic problem-space. No analogy between language acquisition and hill climbing is intended; my concern is with generalizing the definition of hill climbing and using it as a schema for a general adaptive cycle which, by proper adjustment of its generating and testing procedures, may be made to range over the whole set of problem-solving methods, from random trial and error to completely preprogrammed behavior leading to the goal with no search. This provides a convenient common framework in which to express and compare the structures of innatism and constructivism. Thus I agree with Chomsky when he steps away from the unintended analogy, though I remain convinced that his and Miller's characterization of language acquisition was very much closer to constructivism than the purely innatist position he defends today.

Morphogenesis versus Phylogenesis of Language

Although Bateson and Fodor use different words, I believe they are in fact saying the same thing. To say that language acquisition is "more like morphogenesis" (Bateson) is equivalent to invoking, as Fodor does, a problem-solving or specialized inferential mechanism that is innately determined and that gives rise subsequently to a mental organ (a "body of beliefs") that is innately determined. To say that it is "more like phylogenesis" is to affirm that the mechanism is multipurpose and innately determined. However, its output is not innately determined, since a new factor (random variation, in the case of Darwinian evolution) intervenes in its generation. It follows that the alternative is not between specialized and innate, and its converse. Whatever the mechanism is, whether it is specialized or not, it is genetically determined: no neural circuits will grow without genes to specify their anatomy, interconnection, and physiology. The alternative thus becomes: is the mechanism a composer of programs or merely an executor? In the latter case, it is like morphogenesis, during which no new genetic programs are created and only preexisting ones are executed; in the former case, it is like phylogenesis, where the genetic system has the function of a genetically determined, general purpose, self-programming system of problem solving, whose output is new genetic programs. If we adopt Chomsky's morphogenetic view, man becomes the passive plaything of genetic predestination and environmental determinism, whereas in Piaget's view a strong measure of free will and creative autonomy is maintained; in his words, "No child is born either good or bad, whether from the intellectual or the moral point of view; he is the master of his destiny." This I believe is the main underlying issue. Since the nature of the genetically determined initial state S_0 of the human brain is unknown at this date, both views may still legitimately be entertained. The second view, in fact, constitutes the basic assumption of psychology, namely, that a cognitive structure is acquired through the individual's psychogenetic experience. This assumption is epistemologically fundamental, since if it is replaced by its Chomskian converse, "All cognitive structure is acquired through phylogenetic experience during the evolution of the species," the object of psychology vanishes and psychology is reduced to biology.

SPERBER'S ACCUSATIONS: A PLEA OF NOT GUILTY

The preceding remarks may shed some light on Sperber's contribution to the debate.* I fear that he may have confused the issues, or their proponents, or both. The notion that "the mental equipment utilized by the child to learn a language possesses a certain number of genetically determined properties" which he ascribes to Chomsky, is in fact Piaget's, whereas in Chomsky's version "a certain number" is replaced by "all," since the environment provides no equipment, but only content for it to process. This basic misconception clearly weakens his indictment of ideological prejudice against constructivism, and that of preferring "the consideration of a still unformed constructivist hypothesis to an already formed and explanatory hypothesis that has innatist implications." Since S_0 is unknown, the same may be said of innatism, hence *in pari turpitudine* the case should be dismissed. However, since it will serve to introduce my next point, I will briefly discuss it now.

Our ignorance of the nature of S_0 being profound, a psychologist working on the basic assumption that some of the elements of the mental equipment of the child may be acquired (in the sense of being a construct of the individual and not of the species) does not know beforehand if a given element is innate or acquired. He will therefore first endeavor to find a constructivist explanation for it; this is not a matter of ideological prejudice or preference, but of consistency with his hypothesis. If and when he ascribes to this element an innate origin, it is both an acknowledgment that it has no constructive explanation in the domain of psychology, and an assertion that a biological explanation is necessary. However, merely asserting that an

* Editor's note: See also Sperber's paper in Chapter 11.

element is innate, without producing the results of a genetic study or at least a plausible phylogenetic derivation, is simply giving it no explanation at all, neither a psychological nor a biological one. It is taking as given what is to be explained, a *petitio principii*. This is the exact position occupied by Chomsky and his followers, as I shall now argue.

PROOFS OF INNATENESS

When a biologist decides that an anatomo-physiological trait is innate, he does so on the basis of a body of theory and experiment which is singularly lacking in Chomsky's presentations. Moreover, I suspect that the methods he advocates, and even proposes to generalize to the study of other cognitive domains, are incapable in principle of producing such a body of evidence. The choice of universality as a criterion for innateness does not seem sufficient by contemporary biological standards. All organisms follow the laws of gravitation, but still we do not conclude that these laws are innate. Sickle cell anemia is not universal, yet we conclude that it is innate. In short, universality is not even a necessary condition, and its pursuit, even if we grant the uniformity of the human species, will lead on the contrary to ignoring traits that are in fact innate, but are produced by the alleles of a given gene. Finally, "the contingencies of research on humans," though they do not allow breeding experiments and "perfectly controlled environments," have not forced biologists to use "much more indirect and complex arguments" in their study of, say, the heredity of human blood groups, where this type of argument and experiment have not proved necessary to date. If one wishes to "treat the question of . . . the nature of language . . . exactly as one would treat the question of some physical organ of the body," resorting to standard biological practice would seem entirely sufficient to the task of proving the eventual innateness of certain linguistic traits: they should, after all, follow Mendelian laws of transmission, be subject to recessiveness and dominance, mutation and recombination, and so forth; and if they do, empirical evidence will show it conclusively.

FODOR'S ANTI-DESCARTES POSITION

Fodor's position that we can only learn or conceive of what we already know,* since any concept that we form must be as-

* Editor's note: Cellérier is also referring here to Fodor's presentation to be found in Chapter 6.

sembled from concepts and relations we already possess, has the flavor of the well-known proposition that "all books are already contained in the alphabet." As the reciprocal of this proposition is equally true, we may deduce that "the set of all books is equal to the alphabet," namely, "there exist 26 books" and "the alphabet is an infinite set." Applied to biology, Fodor's theorem leads to even more startling conclusions, one of which peremptorily dispels all further reflection on this subject. The first is that Darwinian mechanisms are incapable of producing the sequence of forms leading to species like *Homo sapiens;* from this follows the proposition that "all species and their subsequent forms are contained in the primitive protogenetic alphabet," with conclusions analogous to those of the preceding example. The second conclusion is that species like *Homo sapiens* do not in fact exist; I will call it Fodor's *cogito ergo non sum.*

Reading these first two chapters makes it clear that basic research strategies differ and shows how each different approach, founded on characteristic presuppositions, results in a different delimitation of relevant fields of inquiry and brings with itself idiosyncratic criteria of relevance and intelligibility standards. The following chapters will further clarify the diversity of options and will spell out the specificity of each approach. Chomsky's plea for moving away from statements on general strategies and centering the discussion on what is "the true nature of the initial state" will meet many sympathetic ears. The main axes of development will now concern developmental mechanisms, the foundations of learning theories, and the interactions between cognitive invariants and cultural variables. Bärbel Inhelder and Piaget will delve into the contents and style of their long experimentation with children; Seymour Papert will bring into the picture the principles of artificial intelligence and will open a very exhaustive, sometimes highly polemical discussion with Chomsky and Fodor on what a learning theory should look like; Jean-Pierre Changeux will then explain in detail how contemporary neurobiology can contribute to the clarification of underlying mechanisms in terms of neuronal network growth. The debate on language and cognition, whose explicit or understood subject is man, will be enriched by Papert's discussion of complex machines (in Chapter 3 and in subsequent chapters) and in Chapter 9 by the astonishing description of cognitive competence in a nonhuman primate (the chimpanzee) given by Premack. These analytical developments are bound to raise more complex and more fundamental problems, which will lead to a recurrence of methodological confrontations, especially in Chapters 6 and 12 of Part I, and their prolongation in Part II. The critique of both constructivist and generative approaches as being too "individualistic" is voiced by Toulmin, Godelier, and Wilden, from different points of view, and the role of cultural and social interactions in the development of language, cognition, and symbolism is discussed in Chapter 11.

CHAPTER THREE

Artificial Intelligence and General Developmental Mechanisms

Chomsky has repeatedly stated (see Chapters 1 and 2) that he does not expect to see a "general learning theory" being produced and proving both informationally rich and refutable or confirmable by experiment. Cellérier has argued against Chomsky's negative heuristic, contending not only that a general learning theory can indeed exist, but that it is already available, at least as a first good approximation. Marvin Minsky and Seymour Papert of the Laboratory of Artificial Intelligence at MIT are credited with this accomplishment.

In this chapter, Papert draws a clear sketch of the principles that have guided his and Minsky's experiments on computer simulations of higher cognitive functions. The visible result of their work is a device known (after Rosenblatt) as a perceptron, which is capable of formulating simple hypotheses from regular exposure to raw data and then testing these tentative hypotheses against further relevant data under a suitable reinforcement schedule fed back into the machine by the experimenter. The advantage of an artificial rudimentary "learning subject" like a perceptron is free access to all its constitutive parts and to all its constitutive relations, that is, the complete description of its initial state (S_0).

Papert challenges the innatist hypothesis put forward by Chomsky and, in the course of the ensuing discussion, by Fodor, presenting the perceptron's "discovery" of Euler's theorem. When asked to analyze irregular patterns and to assign numerosity or to evaluate the overall degree of connectivity of such patterns, the machine performs perfectly well by "learning" a rule (Euler's theorem of the total curvature of simply connected figures). Now this rule was not a built-in property of the perceptron, Papert affirms, and therefore not part of its initial state (S_0). What is innate (that is, what is part of the wiring diagram of the machine) is only a general, nonspecific ability to calculate local primitives (for example, square versus non-square, round versus elongated, and so forth), not Euler's theorem, nor connectivity or numerosity as predicates ascribable to the whole pattern.

Chomsky and Fodor are charged with committing a fallacy, the "innatist fallacy." Of such a crime they will plead innocent again and again, in spite of its being charged by Cellérier, Papert, Toulmin, and Putnam. The fallacy, to put it in simplified terms, is to ascribe to the brain what is only an abstract property of its operations. As Putnam says (see Chapter 17), if the geography of the White Mountains can be said to be in my mind, and therefore somehow represented in my brain, that does not imply that the geography of the White Mountains is itself a description of my brain. And in Mehler's terms, if eye color is innate, that does not imply that the genes are themselves colored. In the following chapters, less provocative and more subtle formulations of the alleged innatist fallacy will be presented and discussed. The contours of agreements and disagreements on general learning theory and innate cognitive structures will become clearer and increasingly more sophisticated.

The Role of Artificial Intelligence in Psychology

Seymour Papert

I will now try to show some ways in which artificial intelligence (AI) is able to elucidate a debate in theoretical psychology such as the present one between Chomsky and Piaget. As a first step I want to guard against common misunderstandings of the role of AI in relation to traditional psychology.

The most important of these misunderstandings sees AI as methodologically similar to behaviorism, in that both are sometimes presented as seeking greater rigor by limiting the domain of psychological investigation: behaviorism by excluding reference to mentalism, AI by refusing theoretical models that cannot be simulated on a computer. This view of AI as a limitative theory is completely false, as is the associated belief that AI imposes "simple" models on complex phenomena. Quite on the contrary, AI seeks to be expansive by adding new and powerful kinds of mechanisms to the theoretical repertory of the psychologist, and the models it constructs are very much more complex than those of traditional psychologies. The perception of the models as "simple" can often be traced back to ignorance of computer languages, which leads people to confuse English-language descriptions of AI theories with the theories themselves.

AI has thrusts in three directions which relate to controversies in psychology and linguistics about the property of innateness. Two of these are easy to state: The first tends to reduce the set of structures considered to be innate by showing how they could be acquired through the operation of more powerful developmental mechanisms. The second thrust goes in the opposite direction; paradoxically, by understanding very powerful developmental mechanisms one is able to see how certain structures totally unsuspected by traditional psychology could, if they were innately present, play the role of seeds for the growth of mental functioning.

These two thrusts find a direct translation in terms of the present debate. I believe that Chomsky is biased toward perceiving certain syntactic structures as "unlearnable" because his underlying paradigm of the process of learning is too simple, too restricted. If the only learning processes were those he seems to recognize, these syntactic structures might indeed have to be innate! Allowing a richer set of learning methods certainly does not in itself prove that the principles in question are, in fact, "learned"; proving the existence of such learning would at the very least require a rather complex empirical investigation. But I will argue that a stronger learning theory shifts the balance of plausibility toward conjecturing that syntactic structures are "learned," and so toward adopting a research strategy that looks for how this could happen rather than following a strategy of assuming "innateness."

As an integral part of my argument, I will give some hints (the most I can do in a short exposition) of kinds of structures that computational thinking leads us to recognize as being almost certainly necessary to the operation of so complex a computer as a brain. These structures are not specifically linguistic and so bring us in contact with another, perhaps more fundamental aspect of the Chomsky-Piaget debate: the extent to which the operation of language shares common structures with the rest of the intellectual system. Piaget finds this sharing to be extensive, in contrast to Chomsky's "organicist" tendency to see mental functions as more sharply distinct, organized into organs of the mind (to use his analogy) much as the heart, the liver, and so on are distinct organs of the body. The contribution of AI to this area is to show how computational primitives are fundamentally important to all the mental functions: by seeing all the "mental organs" as computational processes, we are inclined to see them as less fundamentally different from one another than are hearts and livers.

The highly metaphorical flavor of these last remarks leads to the third, and more subtle, thrust of AI: to prune psychological language of prescientific metaphors by developing a more precise terminology, conceptual framework, and, indeed, a new set of "metaphors" in the form of well-understood situations against which general ideas can be tested for intellectual coherence. To understand this, consider the reactions one might have to Chomsky's assertion that such things as the "SSC" (specified subject condition), the "abstract notion of 'subset,' " or "bound anaphor" are properties of the genetically determined initial state of the newborn. One could argue about the assertion's truth or plausibility; but it might be more fruitful to ask how metaphorical these assertions really are: what does it mean to say that the notion of "subject" or "anaphor" is part of the infant's initial state?

Easy answers lead to conceptual difficulties. Is it being said, quite literally, that these notions in the form we know them in adults are in some sense (what sense?) present in the newborn? Or is it being said that some precursor of the notion is present in the newborn—something of an unspecified kind that will grow as a seed into, for example, the notion of "bound anaphor"? The literal choice is certainly hard to swallow without a theoretical framework to explicate (among other puzzles) what could be meant by grammar in a prelinguistic subject. On the other hand, the "seed" version is in itself a very weak, almost trivial, statement with which no one would quarrel and which certainly does not justify Chomsky's strident criticisms of Piaget, AI, and the like.

The same dilemma appears in more sophisticated informational reformulations of the question as a kind of determinism:

can one deduce from the initial state of the baby the fact that his adult language will exhibit the SSC? If one means this in the strict sense that allows us to deduce the property "blue eyes" from the presence of certain genes, it become very hard to believe. If, on the other hand, we weaken it to make it credible, it becomes difficult to know exactly what is being asserted. (This line of argument is certainly not alien to Chomsky's way of thinking; he used it most persuasively in his critique of Skinner on language.)[1]

The first of some more technical comments, to which I now turn, is intended mainly to illustrate more sharply the need for greater clarity about what it means to be innate. I will do this by describing an automaton, a machine that we understand quite thoroughly, and asking questions about what is and what is not innate in the machine. If the question is unclear even in this "toy" situation, how much more clarification does it need in the complex situation of human development?

The machine in question is called a perceptron. Its structure is quite simple: It has a retina on which pictures can be projected, and the purpose of the machine is to recognize whether or not this image has a certain property called "the predicate" (for example, *is a square*). It has a large number of submechanisms, each of which can compute the answer, to be expressed as "yes" or "no," to any well-defined question about a tiny region of the retina. Collectively these submechanisms (called the "local function") cover the whole retina, but none of them has any global knowledge. In particular, none of them can see the whole figure.

There is also a central organ, which has access to the answers given by the local mechanisms; but this organ is constrained to a particular simple algorithm to generate the global decision (for example, *is it a square?*) from the local functions, namely, the "linear threshold decision function": the binary yes/no outputs of the local functions are represented as 1 and 0, respectively; the machine forms a weighted sum of these numbers using weighting coefficients characteristic of the particular perceptron; it then makes its decision according to whether the sum comes out to be more than or less than a certain quantity called the "threshold."

Finally, the perceptron is equipped with a "learning mechanism," which works like this: when the machine says "that's a square" it will be told whether it is right or wrong, and if wrong, will use this feedback to alter its weighting coefficients (in a manner whose details are not relevant here).

What can a perceptron learn? The answer is not always immediately obvious, either from an examination of its "innate structure" or from simple experiments. It is easy enough to see that a perceptron can learn to distinguish between dichotomies such as a *square* versus *triangular;* in this case the local functions recognize the presence or absence of at least one angle that is not a right angle, and so the hypothesis *square* can be eliminated on local grounds. But there are cases in which it is much harder to see whether the global decision is reducible to such local ones. The classic example is the predicate *is connected.* The picture on the retina is assumed to be a black figure on a white ground, and the question for the perceptron is whether the black figure is made of one or several pieces. Is such a decision reducible to local observations? Intuition still says that a perceptron should not be able to tell whether there is only one blob or several. But a deep mathematical theorem by Euler can be adapted to show that the perceptron can learn any predicate like *the number of blobs is less than K.*

Let us now imagine an investigator who does not know the Euler theorem and happens to be concerned with whether blob-numerosity (in the sense of the predicate just mentioned) is innate in the perceptron. One can easily imagine such a person being very puzzled when shown the wiring diagram of the perceptron. He would see nothing there which (to his mind) even remotely resembles numerosity. He might conclude that something must be missing from our wiring diagram (so one of the cautioning morals of the story is that one has to be very careful about conclusions like this). But the more important, if more subtle, conclusion is that even with *full knowledge* (of the wiring diagram and of the mathematics), it is not at all clear whether one ought to say that numerosity is innate. In some senses of "innate" it is, and in other senses it is not. The conclusion for me is that we need a much more carefully elaborated theoretical framework within which to formulate the real questions that lie behind formulations such as, "Does the subject X have the notion Y?" or "Is Y a property of the initial state of this subject?" or "Is Y innate?"

One of the purposes of such a theoretical framework would be to replace notions such as "notion" by something more technical. It is quite sobering to take stock of how much of the language used today in serious discussions of the mind is not very different from that of Aristotle. Of course, Chomsky himself has contributed enormously to changing this state of affairs *within linguistics;* but this makes it all the more paradoxical that his *psychological metalanguage* is so pretechnical. Let me develop the point by contrasting the way Chomsky and Piaget formulate a question about the development of what is popularly called a "notion."

A naive perception of Piaget sees him as saying: nothing is innate, everything emerges from development. Of course, this is absurd if pushed undialectically to the limit; but what he does teach us is this: if you make a list of structures and notions and rules (or whatever you call them) found in adult intelligence, and if you ask which of them is innate, the answer will be *none*. The point behind the apparent contradiction is simple enough: everything has a developmental history through which it emerges from other, very different things. Whatever it is that is innate, we can at least be sure that it is *not* (and probably does not even resemble) any discrete part of the adult mind. The principle might seem quite obvious; but whereas it is exemplified in a deep and subtle way in Piaget's total work, it is violated by the very form of Chomsky's suggestion that developed entities such as "the specified subject condition (SSC)" or "the notion of bound anaphor" (these are his actual words) might be "properties" of the initial state. In fact one can see a large part of Piaget's work as the search for *intermediate entities,* which can play the role of precursors of the structures we find in the adult, or even the child of any particular age. Thus the question "Is the notion of 'number' innate?" is displaced by seeing how it grows out of various precursors whose existence was not recognized by Aristotle or any other pre-Piagetian psychologists. The technical spirit of Piaget's work is reflected in the fact that the abstract noun *number* occurs much more prominently in the title of his book about it[2] than in the text: the pretechnical concept "number" now serves only as an indicator of a direction for research whose actual dimension cannot be specified by the pretechnical intuition of "number." I argue (and this has some irony in the context of the present discussion) that the power of Piaget's contribution would scarcely be altered if the intermediate objects he has discovered are proved to be "innate"; the hard and deep work was discovering the precursors. When we transpose the observation to the problems raised by Chomsky, the observation turns into the suggestion that the hard work here will be discovering the precursors out of which the SSC and similar structures emerge. And then we will have to understand the precursors of those precursors and, by a longer or shorter chain of genesis, eventually arrive at the properties of the initial state. This is what developmental studies are about;

it is a long, arduous, and technical path. It seems to me very remarkable that Chomsky should, by contrast, take a position that essentially declares: I, Chomsky, cannot see how the SSC can be learned, so all reasonable men should conclude that it is innate.

But what leads Chomsky to this position? If I claim that he is in an absurd position, the onus is clearly on me to explain this mystery. So I turn next to sketch my theory of Chomsky. The theory pivots around a claim that Chomsky, despite his well-known criticism of Skinner and of behaviorism in general, has remained wedded to a behavioristic position in one crucial area, namely in his model of learning. I will develop this point by sketching a taxonomy of developmental theories in which Skinner, Chomsky, Piaget, and Simon will be explicitly located. As a first step I recall, with slight modification, Chomsky's notation. The baby is born in state S_0 and eventually comes to state S_f. S_0 and S_f are deep structures and thus not directly visible. It is consequently possible, in principle, for different observers to argue that behaviorists typically underestimate the complexity of S_f. One can classify developmental theories according to how much of the complexity of the human mind they attribute to S_0 and to S_f and to the component of mental function responsible for development. For example, Skinner believes that it is possible to explain the passage from S_0 to S_f by a very simple general developmental mechanism (GDM). Both Chomsky and Piaget have used forceful arguments to persuade us that S_f is certainly more complex than Skinner believes, and probably too complex for a simple GDM to guide its growth from the kind of S_0 Skinner would admit. The difficulty facing Skinner is a mismatch between his simple S_0 and the putatively complex S_f. There are in principle three (nonexclusive) reactions to this apparent mismatch: One can postulate that S_0 is more complex than Skinner thought, which is the route taken by Chomsky; one can postulate, as Piaget does, that the GDM must be more powerful than Skinner believed; finally, one could deny the mismatch, for example by arguing as Herbert Simon does that S_f really is structurally simple after all and thus that S_0 and the GDM can both be simple as well[3] (although, of course, Simon's GDM and S_0 are radically different from Skinner's).

I will devote the rest of my discussion to developing the idea that Chomsky seems to be tacitly committed to a very Skinnerian kind of GDM and illustrating some ways in which Piaget's developmental mechanisms and also the emerging viewpoint of AI can be understood as more powerful mathematical and epistemological principles rather than more powerful biological mechanisms. In this regard, it is appropriate to look at Chomsky's exact words (see Chapter 1):

> Again, it cannot be imagined that the language learner is taught these facts or the relevant principles. No one ever makes mistakes to be corrected. As in the case of the structure-dependent principle, passive observation of a person's total performance might not enable us to determine whether the principles are in fact being observed (just as experience would not suffice, normally, to provide this information to the language learner), though "experiment" will quickly reveal that this is so. The only rational conclusion is that the SSC and the relevant abstract notion of "subject" and "bound anaphor" are properties of S_0, that is, part of LT(H,L).

The point of the quotation is to draw attention to the underlying model of the learning process, which has the following characteristics of typically behaviorist models: the emphasis on teaching, either explicitly or by correction of mistakes; the apparent rejection of "experiment" as applicable to the child's learning of language; and the assumption that what is being learned is the thing itself (the adult structure) rather than some developmentally deep structural precursor. Since the point is central, let me put it differently. Of course the child does not learn the SSC by being taught in any direct sense; this is not the way any fundamental structures or skills are ever acquired. And of course the child does not learn the SSC by passive observation. Piaget has removed any lingering tendencies people might have had to see the child as *ever* engaging in "passive observation." So I would have thought that the "only rational conclusion" from Chomsky's set of statements is that the child discovered the SSC through "experiments." If asked where the ability to do experiments came from, I would be a little more inclined to grant that *this* is a property of S_0. We certainly know that recognizable precursors of components of the complex activities involved in experimenting are visible in very young babies.

But of course, it is not sufficient to say that the child learns by doing experiments. We need to understand the conceptual framework within which such experiments can be conceived and interpreted. So again and again, we come back to the central problem of discovering the intermediate intellectual structures.

Piaget's contribution to this problem is much deeper than any particular structural analysis he makes of any particular aspect or stage of intellectual ability. One can disagree with his specific analyses of stages or aspects (indeed, he himself often does) but still appreciate the very original paradigm he has given to developmental psychology. To emphasize an analogy with Chomsky, we can describe this as the concept of deep structure in the developmental domain. I myself like Piaget's phrase: "There is no genesis without structures; there are no structures without genesis" *(pas de genèse sans structures, pas de structures sans genèse)*. You cannot understand the genesis of number by trying to trace surface forms such as actual uses of numbers themselves. One has to look for a system of deeper structures, of which Piaget's "grouping" *(groupement)* should be seen for purposes of the present discussion as an example to illustrate in a very general way what kind of entity such a structure might be. But one will not find intelligible structures without focusing from the outset on the problem of genesis.

I will make this idea more concrete by stepping back and looking at a formulation of what I think should be the key problem of learning theory: to reduce the sense of miracle induced by the power of the mind both to think and to grow. Euler's theorem did this for the hypothetical student of perceptrons in my little computational parable. I would like now to sketch a real example, for which credit goes to Piaget and to Bourbaki. We will see at the same time how epistemological and mathematical insights meld with psychological/developmental thinking.

I am sure that the Bourbaki group did not think of their theory of structures as a contribution to the theory of learning, nor do textbooks of psychology include Bourbaki in their list of learning theorists. Yet if the task of the theory of learning is to reduce the apparent mystery of the acts of learning, Bourbaki made a significant contribution by developing a perception of mathematics which happens to make it appear much more learnable than it did before. This is not mere appearance: certain insights into the nature of number reveal aspects of its structure that play a significant role in all processes of learning. One (out of many) of these could be called the principle of *factoring*: structures that can be seen as being composed of simpler but still significant parts (substructures) tend to be more learnable. One could order foundational theories of arithmetic along a learnability dimension: number "à la Peano" or recursive function theory stands at the unlearnable end; number "à la Russell/Whitehead" is more learnable; number "à la Bourbaki/Piaget" is very much more learnable; and AI extensions of this last perception go still further.

One can argue about whether Piaget's theory of the antecedent structures of informal mathematical thinking is exactly the same as Bourbaki's theory of formal mathematics; but the significant circumstance is already there in the fact that they are close enough for such questions to be asked. And for our present purpose, the point of all this discussion is to illustrate a kind of explication of learning that falls outside the behaviorist GDM and seems not to be considered by Chomsky. Of course the example is from mathematics rather than linguistics, but the question is whether similar structural analyses will reduce the apparent degree of unlearnability of properties of language.

Grounds for optimism are to be found in the recent tendency to intermarriage between AI and styles of linguistic theory related to systemic and case grammars, and to a much tighter interconnection between syntactic structures and cognitive (some would say "semantic") structures. Since I can discuss only one example, I choose in the interests of simplicity the very general one that Chomsky calls "the structure-dependent property of linguistic rules." One possible answer to the question of how the child learns so easily to develop structure-dependent rules of language is that he has already come to do this outside of language; another possible answer is that the nature of computational processes dictates that rules will be structure-dependent. Now I grant that either of these conjectures is compatible with some sense of innateness of structure dependence. But it would not be a *linguistic* rule that is innate but some more general precursor, and this in itself is a significant shift away from Chomsky's position toward a more Piagetian one.

At last we come to the final link in my chain: the emergence within AI of a structure dependence general enough to induce language, visual perception, common sense reasoning, and, indeed, all information processing in men and in machines. A technical account of such a theory is impossible to give here and, indeed, has not been described in detail as a topic in itself. But it is a pervasive theme of research in AI and readers can find more detail in other sources.[4]

Discussion

Chomsky Papert claims that I don't see any way of explaining the final state in terms of a behaviorist type of general developmental mechanism, and therefore I conclude it is innate. What I actually say is that I don't see any way of explaining the resulting final state in terms of any proposed general developmental mechanism that has been suggested by artificial intelligence, sensorimotor mechanisms, or anything else; and that remains precisely true. At that point Papert objects, quite incorrectly, that somehow the burden of proof is on me to go beyond saying that I see no way of doing something. Of course, that's not the case: if someone wants to show that some general developmental mechanisms exist (I don't know of any), then he has to do exactly what Rosenblatt (who invented the perceptron) did, namely, he has to propose the mechanism; if you think that sensorimotor mechanisms are going to play a role, if you can give a precise characterization of them, I will be delighted to study their mathematical properties and see whether the scope of those mechanisms includes the case in question. Similarly, you are mistaken if you think that the mechanisms here relate in some way to the acquisition of structure-dependent rules—they don't at all. The fact that you can describe or even discover hierarchical organization tells you nothing about whether the rule in question should observe a hierarchical structure in this case or should observe the property *leftmost* in this case. If anyone thinks there is such a general developmental mechanism, fine, propose it, make it explicit, then I and others will investigate it to see whether there is any relation whatsoever, be it direct or metaphorical, to the concrete problem of attaining the final state. Since that has not been done in artificial intelligence or in studies of sensorimotor intelligence anywhere to my knowledge, I can't do what I did, for example, twenty years ago when the theory of finite-state Markov sources was proposed. This is an example similar to that of the perceptron: a specific theory was proposed about the nature of grammatical structures,[1] and it was then possible to investigate its mathematical properties and to demonstrate that no conceivable realization of that structure, no matter how much time you allowed, could in fact have certain properties that languages have.[2] So once somebody had proposed the theory of finite-state Markov sources as a generalized superdevelopment of the most complicated behaviorist theory of chaining that had ever been invented—in fact a theory even including Lashley-style rhythmic properties—then it was possible to study that theory and in this case to demonstrate that the theory, and correspondingly any of its subtheories, were demonstrably false. Now, when theories are not proposed, of course all you can say is: "I don't see any conceivable way in which these ideas relate to a given consequence"; but I don't accept that the burden goes beyond that—the burden there has to fall on the person who believes that the principles really exist, and if somebody can present, for example, a theory of sensorimotor constructions in a form explicit enough to investigate the possibility of obtaining the "specified subject condition" in those terms, I would be delighted to investigate it similarly in this case. As for the general theory of structure, that is exactly what generative grammar has been concerned with for twenty-five years: the whole complicated array of structures beginning, let's say, with finite-state automata, various types of context-free or context-sensitive grammars, and various subdivisions of these theories of transformational grammar—these are all theories of proliferating systems of structures devised for the problem of trying to locate this particular structure, language, in that system. So there can't be any controversy about the legitimacy of that attempt; in fact, that is what all the work in formal linguistics has been about for a certain number of years.

Papert   What I am trying to do is to situate Chomsky and Piaget in terms of a wider context. It could be put in this way: although it is true that transformational grammar looks for a certain kind of structure, it looks toward linguistic examples as its main source for formulating the kinds of structures that it wants. As opposed to this there are others, including specialists in artificial intelligence and Piaget, who look at the structure of mathematics itself for examples from which you might draw a general theory of structures. This is a trend that is going on now, and if one wants to make sense of these debates and different points of view, one has to have a wider perception of the goal that all these researchers are pursuing.

Chomsky   The theory of structures developed in generative grammar was within a particular mathematical theory, namely, recursive function theory; that is, the theory of subrecursive hierarchies is precisely what offered the framework for investigating the different types of linguistic structures. Now, maybe we shouldn't have looked at the theory of subrecursive hierarchies but at some other mathematical theory; but the idea of looking at mathematical theories for ideas about the class of structures, *that* is relevant . . .

Papert   No, that is not the point: the idea is not to look to mathematics for mathematical theories of structure, it is to look at the structure of mathematics in the same way that you look at the structure of language, as the object of the theory of structures. For example, it is very important in Piaget's way of thinking, and for the plausibility of Piaget's explanation of the development of mathematical thinking in children, that something like the deep discoveries made by the Bourbaki group be true. Bourbaki, by revealing certain things about the structure of mathematics that were not quite clear before, altered the apparent degree of complexity involved in learning mathematics. Since then we have had a quite different perception of the evolution of mathematics, either historically or in the individual.

Chomsky   I think all this is really, as Toulmin said previously, a red herring. There is no such thing as *the* structure of mathematics: you can find within mathematics all sorts of different types of structures which you can study historically, non-historically, or whatever. But the theory of subrecursive hierarchies barely existed as a structure of mathematics twenty-five years ago, and therefore you couldn't look for detailed suggestions there as to the relevant types of structures; it provided at most a general framework. As for what Bourbaki investigated, algebraic structures or topological structures, fine, if those are relevant to this issue, let's see how; let's see how the investigation of topological structures, for example, relates to the problem of the existence of structure-dependent rules. But I will repeat the statement that Papert does not like: that I don't see any possible conceivable connection between them; if you think that that statement is wrong, then show me even the most remote connection between them.

Papert   The connection between Bourbaki and structure-dependent rules in language cannot be immediate. But since you deny any conceivable, even remote, connection between them, let me repeat one of the connections I have stressed. Arithmetic as axiomatized by Peano would seem quite as unlearnable as any rule of language as axiomatized by Chomsky. Along comes Bourbaki/Piaget, and the situation changes in arithmetic. Peano was not wrong as a formal mathematician; he was wrong as a developmentalist. Perhaps the linguistic correctness of your theories of language does not alter the possibility that you are wrong as a developmentalist.

Chomsky That was not my question. My question has to do with the point that you originally raised, namely, that somehow the kind of investigation conducted by Bourbaki leads to a theory of structures that relates to the question of why there are structure-dependent rules in grammar; and I say there is no conceivable connection there, although I think there is some connection with another part of mathematics, for example, the theory of subrecursive hierarchies. Now, I'm not wedded to that theory: if you find some connection of the theory of topological spaces, for instance, to the problem of structure-dependent rules, fine, but it's pointless just to say that there might be such a connection.

Atran It seems to me that this interest in the Bourbakian structures follows from some very peculiar assumptions and leads to some rather dubious conclusions. According to Piaget's doctrine that he calls "genetic epistemology," and I assume this is what Papert is really referring to, each advance made toward a foundation theory in mathematics is, by that very fact, a more comprehensive theory of cognition. Moreover, if a mathematical model is developed which is not meant to be a foundation theory it is still, by definition, part of the structural movement. This must be the case if, as Piaget claims, "logico-mathematical knowledge does not succeed in detaching us from reality or the world of objects," and if every logico-mathematical deduction represents a "theory of the physical phenomena after the event."

Now it is quite possible that the Bourbaki effort to analyze mathematically significant notions in terms of certain historical precedents or of structures that are basically heuristic provides some account of the thinking involved in the construction of certain mathematical systems. If so, this represents a contribution to that part of the mind concerned with the construction and interpretation of mathematical systems. Biologists would then be justified in beginning a search for the neurophysiological bases of these systems in a region of the brain specified by the complex genetic program of human beings.

For Piaget, however, a Bourbakian structure like the group is today the foundation of algebra; it is, according to Piaget, already being used in an important way in physics, and very likely the day will come when it acquires a central role in biology as well. Such "facts" as these thus seem to suggest to Piaget that the mother structures of the Bourbaki group correspond to coordinations that are necessary to all intellectual activity. But even though groups were the first general algebraic structures to be investigated, they are no more basic or essential to algebra than other general structures. Each kind of algebraic structure captures some interesting set of uniformities characteristic of a related collection of mathematical systems; however, there may be as many "basic" or general structures as there are interesting uniformities among any of the various systems that already exist or that may be created in the future.

Perhaps certain groups, with specific properties, will be useful in describing certain areas of physics, biology, or cognition. Most of the significant theories of science, however, do not depend in any nontrivial way on groups or on any of the other Bourbakian structures. Consequently, Piaget attempts to increase the importance of the group by providing it with a significance that lies outside the concerns of algebra. Using metaphors drawn from the equilibrium theory of gases and the regulatory and structural function of genes, he proposes that the structural coherence of the group is maintained by autoregulation; mathematical notions of closure, identity, and transformation are equated with self-maintenance, reversibility of processes, and formation. For the working mathematician, this definition of the group would appear quite arbitrary and can be completely ignored. Such ad hoc efforts to generalize precise notions by analogy can only lead to trivialities.

It must be admitted, nevertheless, that the general ad hoc approach characteristic of genetic epistemology may occasionally lead to interesting results. Because structuralism sets itself the task of constructing formal languages as an empirical program, there is a constant effort to try out the whole range of mathematical structures on various domains of cognition. This process could conceivably lead to an interesting explanation of phenomena; this may be the case, for instance, in the apparent success of a grouplike structure, called "grouping" (*groupement*), in accounting for displacements in a perceptual centration. Usually the attempt to extend important results to other domains, such as language or mathematics itself, only serves to obscure the significance of the original findings. The fact that some success is possible with such an approach, however, means that a refutation of the premises of structuralism does not necessarily hold for particular consequences. But the reasoning that those premises entail often makes it difficult to separate the significant from the trivial.

In Seymour Papert's presentation we have read some state-ments that deserve to be singled out, because much of the fol-lowing discussion will revolve around them: "If you make a list of structures and notions and rules (or whatever you call them) found in adult intelligence, and if you ask which of them is innate, the answer will be none . . . *The hard and deep work was discovering the precursors. When we transpose the observation to the problems raised by Chomsky, the observa-tion turns into the suggestion that the hard work here will be discovering the precursors out of which [linguistic] structures emerge. And then we will have to understand the precursors of those precursors and, by a longer or shorter chain of genesis, eventually arrive at the properties of the initial state. This is what developmental studies are about."*

This is the core of the compromise between Chomsky's in-natism and Piaget's constructivism as forwarded by its propo-nents. Let's first adopt an innatist view with regard to nonspe-cific, undifferentiated, multipurpose primitives *or* precursors; *then let's embrace a strictly constructivist view to account for the more complex cognitive or linguistic structures arising out of these precursors in the course of development. We will see that such a "division of labor," as Cellérier has called it, be-tween innatism and constructivism has appealed to many, in-cluding Monod (as witnessed by his reply to Fodor in Chapter 6). Now, granted* this, *options can further diverge as to the in-nateness of the developmental pathways themselves. Piaget re-jects the hypothesis that the sequence of stages representing successive integration-plus-differentiation of primitives is itself the product of some genetically determined program, whereas Monod explicitly endorses such a view.*

Chomsky and Fodor are more trenchant, however, and their disagreement blocks the argument at a much earlier state; they maintain that cognitive development is not an "enriching" process at all, but rather consists of a progressive specialization, channeled by the environment. In other words, the task of any developmental theory in the field of cognition and language, as seen by Chomsky and Fodor, is not to account for a step-wise construction of more powerful and specific structures out of raw primitives (be it through trial and error or hill climbing) but rather to account for the organism's inborn predisposition to select quickly and without mistake a specific working hy-

pothesis (structure dependence, SSC, understood subject equivalence, systematic ambiguity, and so forth). Learning is, to them, plugging in the right device at the right time, using the structure of the incoming information only as a test for highly specific filters that are already built in.

Chomsky explains in the next chapter why such an "extreme" innatism appears to him plausible—indeed, the most plausible hypothesis that is compatible with a wealth of linguistic, psychological and neurophysiological data. Fodor will present his own analogous point of view in Chapter 6.

CHAPTER FOUR

Initial States and Steady States

The present chapter consists basically of Chomsky's plea for "the Cartesian mind." His presupposition is that cognitive and linguistic structures are in principle "explicable," though as yet "unexplained," in terms of the expression of a genetic program universal to the human species. His discussion in this chapter is so clear and exhaustive that any external comment would be, at best, redundant. However, Chomsky does mention a most revealing experiment in neurophysiology that is pivotal to his arguments and that may be unknown to the general reader. I assume that a brief account of Hubel's and Wiesel's findings may be welcome to those who, unlike most participants in the meeting, are not familiar with it. The reasons why these findings are apt to support Chomsky's model of the mind and why they reinforce the notion of learning as "selective stabilization of functioning synapses" (adopting the felicitous expression of Changeux and Danchin)* also need to be made explicit.

Towards the middle of the sixties, neurophysiologists such as Jerry Lettvin, Humberto Maturana, David Hubel, and Thorstein Wiesel developed an ingenious technique for determining how single nerve cells in an animal's visual system respond to specific patterns (horizontal lines, vertical lines,

---

* See J. -P. Changeux, P. Courrège, and A. Danchin, in *Proceedings of the National Academy of Science U.S.A.* 70:2974–2978, 1973; and J.-P. Changeux and A. Danchin, "Apprendre par stabilisation sélective de synapses en cours de développement," in *L'Unité de l'homme*, ed. E. Morin and M. Piattelli-Palmarini (Paris: Editions de Seuil, 1974).

sharp angles, moving spots) in the visual field. The interesting result was that even within a few hours after birth, particular neurons were specifically preset to react (that is, to send a train of electrical impulses) only to a well-specified class of visual stimuli. For example, neurons that are innately preset to react when a horizontal stripe is presented before a newborn kitten will remain silent when the same animal is exposed to vertical lines, and vice versa. Even more interestingly, Hubel and Wiesel were the first to demonstrate that a given class of specialized neurons can become totally inert if the kitten is brought up, from birth onward, in a "deprived" optical environment (for example, a tall cylinder painted with only vertical or only horizontal stripes and nothing else). Only the class of neurons corresponding to the pattern effectively shown by that environment will remain active, whereas all other optical neurons will become inactive because the corresponding synapses will degenerate. Such loss of visual competence can be irreversible. These and numerous other experiments of the same kind are directly relevant to the central topic of this debate because they have demonstrated, or at least made plausible, the following inferences: (1) highly specific perceptual filters are already present at birth (evidence for innatism); (2) these filters shape the visual world into orderly geometrical figures (the Cartesian mind); (3) the geometrical figures without (structures of the external world) elicit specific responses within (orderly patterns of neuronal activity) but do not determine the form of the response (evidence against "assimilation" and in favor of a simple triggering of preset mechanisms).

Therefore: (1) experience of the surrounding environment results in a selection of "relevant" stimuli according to discriminative criteria which "are there" beforehand, that is, which are innate (learning as a selective process); (2) the actualization of a given cognitive structure is made at the expense of other competing possible structures which become irretrievably lost in the course of development (fixation of synapses by actual functioning and degeneration of the inactive ones).

This last point has been widely developed by Changeux and Danchin in their theory of selective stabilization of functioning synapses and by Jacques Mehler in his theory of "knowing by unlearning."* On the basis of these premises, however

---

* J. Mehler, "Connaître par désapprentissage," in *L'Unité de l'homme.*

sketchy and imprecise, the reader may now be in a better posi-
tion to grasp Chomsky's arguments and their far-reaching
consequences.

The Linguistic Approach

Noam Chomsky

I will just refer to my paper (see Chapter 1) and bring out some
of the general points I was trying to make, leaving the details
to the paper. The general approach I'm taking seems to me
straightforward and unsophisticated, but nevertheless correct.

Let's start by noting that we belong to a certain species, and
we can assume uniformity, idealizing away from variation. This
species has what we can call an initial state, that is, a state
prior to experience, fixed for the species and called S_0. We discover through investigation that in particular cognitive domains, for example in the domain of language but not only
there, the individual goes through a series of states and reaches
what is in effect a steady state, which is a state that doesn't
change very much except in marginal respects. In the case of
language, it seems that the steady state is invariably attained
about the time of puberty. We can then ask ourselves what is
the nature of the steady state attained and what must have been
the character of the initial state for that steady state to be attained, given the nature of the existing experience. One needn't
be interested in this question, but I am interested in it. The
most interesting question from this point of view is what is the
nature of the initial state, that is, what does human nature consist of in this respect? Evidently experience is required to attain the steady state, so we can think then of the initial state
as being in effect *a function that maps experience onto the*
steady state. We can express the idea in this way without losing
any generality, and this formulation permits any degree of interaction as well as complexity, new devices at later stages, and so
forth.

This function, which maps experience onto the steady state,
the function that in effect characterizes the initial state, can be
quite properly thought of as a learning theory, that is, this func-

tion is simply *the* learning theory for human language. As I mentioned in my paper, I don't see any particular reason to believe that there exists such a thing as a learning theory; it seems to me a very odd idea that such a thing should exist, rather as if there existed something like a growth theory for organs. Of course there is a level at which a growth theory does exist, namely, cellular biology, but I don't see why there should be one above that level.

Similarly, if we study the development of cognitive structures I think that we will discover separate learning theories; no doubt they will have some properties in common, but I assume that they will be quite specific to particular cognitive domains and particular species, or at least if this is not the case it will be surprising and it will be necessary to demonstrate it. The common assumption to the contrary, that is, that a general learning theory does exist, seems to me dubious, unargued, and without any empirical support or plausibility at the moment.

Let's look at this particular question and ask what is the nature of the learning theory for human language, that is, what is the acquisition function that maps experience onto the final state, or to put it differently, what is the nature of the initial state S_0 (these are all different ways of formulating the same question).

One can make a variety of different proposals on this point, and through the history of the last several hundred years one can find a number of general attempts to approach the question I put in these terms. For example, one might argue that there are general developmental mechanisms (GDMs) which constitute in effect the initial state and which therefore constitute the function that maps experience onto the state attained. If I understand the ideas put forth about constructions of sensorimotor intelligence, they essentially fall into this category; similarly, Papert's remarks about GDMs fall into this category as well (see Chapter 3). These I take to be proposals about the properties of the initial state, namely, that the initial state is characterized by a system of GDMs which will give rise to the final state, given experience. Now, if someone presents such a system it can be investigated; if someone proposes a GDM in a specific enough form so that it is possible to draw out consequences from the proposal, then we can investigate the adequacy of such a system. Prior to the presentation of any such GDM, I am afraid I have to resort to the comment that Papert dislikes so much, namely, that in the absence of any concrete proposals that can be investigated, I see no plausibility to the suggestion.

There are people who have actually made such proposals. For example, Patrick Suppes at Stanford has presented a very explicit and interesting proposal based on the Suppes-Estes statistical sampling theory, which gives a general developmental model for attaining a final state on the basis of experience.[1] This is a proposal that one can investigate, and that is precisely what Suppes did: it was clear and explicit enough to investigate, and he showed that this system could attain in the limit a finite-state Markovian system which produces symbols from left to right. That is interesting because we know that such a system is inadequate for language, that is, we know that the systems that can in principle be attained within this model are not the systems that are attained *in fact* by humans; therefore we have an explicit refutation of this theory of developmental mechanisms. To say that we refute the theory is to make a positive comment about it, that is, this theory was presented in a clear enough way so that it was possible to determine whether or not it is correct, or at least on the verge of being correct. It is a merit of a theory to be proved false. Proposals that do not allow such a determination, or the determination of whether or not evidence bears on them, do not have that merit. The proposal that I just mentioned is the most sophisticated suggestion that I know of regarding general developmental mechanisms.

If you go back in history there are other proposals. For example, Hume had some specific proposals which are much denigrated these days, although I don't know why—I think they are good because they are concrete. He listed the mechanisms that he felt belonged to what I am calling the initial state: contiguity, resemblance, perceived cause and effect, and he made an explicit claim that the systems of knowledge that we have can be attained on the basis of these general developmental mechanisms. This is a moderately explicit theory; it was developed further in subsequent associationist theories, and it can be submitted to investigation, but it is so evidently false that there is no point in pursuing it. But at least it was concrete enough to investigate.

Descriptive linguists of the 1940s made very explicit proposals about what one could think of as developmental mechanisms (which they didn't regard as such), namely, the so-called discovery procedures for grammars, which became rather sophisticated. One could investigate these proposals, and one could prove again that they could not in principle lead to the steady state attained—and that is interesting.

If you want my judgment about this whole issue, of course you cannot demonstrate that general developmental mechanisms do not exist—that's impossible—but I think that the efforts that have been undertaken have in fact proved abortive, and I don't think there is a particular reason to believe that this is a plausible way to proceed.

There is historically another general approach to this whole question, which in the modern period is traceable back to Descartes. He makes the following kind of observation: Suppose I draw a triangle on the blackboard; Descartes says that anybody looking at that figure will see it as a distorted triangle. The question is, according to Descartes, why is that true—why do we regard that figure as a distorted triangle and not as a precise example of what it is? That sounds like a somewhat silly question, but as with a lot of silly questions, it is in a way rather deep. Why do we see this thing as a distorted triangle? Descartes' answer is that the nature of the mind is such that regular geometrical figures are simply produced as models for the interpretation of experience; the mind just has that character, and if you were to develop a science of the mind, you would develop it in terms of such a geometry. Hence we are compelled to regard any figure that we see as a distorted regular geometrical figure because that is simply the way that the mind functions. We have here another kind of approach to S_0; what it says is that S_0 has certain specific structural conditions that are imposed on any system that is acquired. Of course in this case S_0 and the steady state S_s are presumably identical for Descartes, but that doesn't matter; one can also talk about systems in which, perhaps, the initial conditions simply involve regular geometrical figures, and some pattern of experience leads to the attainment of a more specific state (I don't know if that is true in this case). As far as the Cartesian type of approach is concerned, I think that is the right one. One can then go ahead and investigate it in various ways; one can investigate it through psychological means, and one can look for neurological mechanisms. In this particular case, it seems rather plausible to me to interpret the very exciting work of the last ten or fifteen years on the visual cortex as presenting a neurological basis for a kind of Cartesian theory of mind. Thus the experiments of Hubel and Wiesel,[2] experiments which lead to a picture of the visual cortex as carrying out primitive analyses in terms of line, angle, motion, and so on, produce a concrete physical system which has many of the properties of the postulated Cartesian mind and offers perhaps the beginning of an explanation as to why we see that object as a distorted triangle. This approach seems quite reasonable to me.

Coming back to language, if human beings were mice we would know exactly how to proceed to investigate any particular hypothesis at this point; however, since direct and intrusive methods are obviously excluded for humans, we have to use another type of approach. The natural way to proceed, if we are trying to determine the nature of S_0, is to try to find some property of the steady state that is minimally affected by experience, a property for which E (experience) is reduced as close to zero as possible. Of course, in order to demonstrate that there is no relevant experience with respect to some property of language, we really would have to have a complete record of a person's experience—a job that would be totally boring; there is no empirical problem in getting this information, but nobody in his right mind would try to do it. So what we can try to do is to find properties for which it is very implausible to assume that everyone has had relevant experience. In my paper (see Chapter 1), I gave a number of examples of these, and I had thought that I might be able to talk now about some of the more complicated ones, but after the previous discussion I thought that it might be a good idea just to talk about the simplest example and to try to bring out the logic of that.

The most simple example that I can conceive, an almost trivial one, is the following: Consider sentences like "The man is tall," for which we form corresponding questions: "Is the man tall?" by moving the word "is." From examples of this kind we can make certain inductive inferences, which enable us to ask questions of a more complicated kind. Consider, for example, cases like "The man who is tall is sad." From simple examples of this kind, we might make two different types of induction: we might assume that what is going on here is that the leftmost occurrence of the word "is" is moved to the front, and pursuing that hypothesis we would get "Is the man who tall is sad?"; or we might construct the hypothesis that the first occurrence of "is" that follows the subject of the sentence is moved to the left, in which case we would get "Is the man who is tall sad?". Clearly, we make the second inference (there are, of course, other possibilities, but let's limit ourselves to these two). One is an induction over the property *leftmost*, the other an induction over the property *follows the first noun-phrase*. What we see is that people make the second type of induction. Why? This is not a trivial question. I am very dubious about notions of absolute simplicity or the general theory of simplicity, and so on, but if somone wanted to propose such notions (which I do not), he would certainly say that *leftmost* is a simpler property than *follows the first noun-phrase,* for a very obvious reason, namely, that the property *leftmost* is completely definable in terms of the physical symbols themselves. To understand the property *leftmost,* all you have to know is the physical symbols and their order, whereas to know the property *follows the first noun-phrase,* a certain abstract mental processing has to intervene which tells you that this thing (the man who is tall) is a unit of a particular type. Of course, there need be no physical demarcation; this unit doesn't have a space after it or anything like that—there is a continuum of sound. "Follows" is a concrete physical notion, but the concept of "first noun-phrase" or "subject" is a highly abstract notion, so complex that in fact nobody knows how to describe it properly. Thus, supposing that there is a hierarchy of inductive processes, if a scientist from Mars were to look at examples like these and were to ask the question that any scientist would raise, namely, how to go on to the next case, he would of course first take the property *leftmost,* not the property *follows the subject.* Indeed, in any kind of hierarchy of inductive processes, the former is the obvious property to examine first, because it is a concrete physical property that doesn't involve subtle, complex, unknown kinds of abstract mental processing.* It is certainly true that children never make mistakes about this kind of thing: no child ever tries the Martian hypothesis first, then is told that is not the way it works and subsequently goes to the other hypothesis. The process of language learning does not resemble the way in which a scientist would study the question, by trying the elementary inductive processes first and then going on if this fails to more complex assumptions. This raises the question of why induction makes use of this very complex property and not the very simple one.

I said in my paper that from passive observation of what people are doing we could hardly know whether they are using this hypothesis or that one, because in fact the more complex cases that distinguish the hypotheses rarely arise; you can easily live your whole life without ever producing a relevant example to show that you are using one hypothesis rather than the other

* Editor's note: For a detailed counterargument see Putnam's paper in Chapter 14 of the present volume. Chomsky's rejoinder to the critique expressed by Putnam is to be found in his "Discussion of Putnam's Comments" in Chapter 15.

one. The examples cited are the only kind for which the hypotheses differ, and you can go over a vast amount of data of experience without ever finding such a case. Thus in many cases, the Martian scientist could not know by passive observation whether the subject is using the first hypothesis or the second one. The proposals that were previously attributed to me were described in the wrong terms: I did not say only that the child could not generally determine by passive observation whether one or the other hypothesis is true; what I said is that *we could not know by passive observation whether in fact a person is using one hypothesis or the other because the evidence is essentially not available,* just as for the most part it is not available to the child in terms of direct linguistic experience. Nevertheless, the fact is that the inductive operation does proceed without error, and even without trial, to the second hypothesis. How can this be explained?

First of all, I will mention some approaches that don't offer a valid explanation. Compare Papert's work on the recognition of the "arch" pattern. We can construct a program that will deal with this structure in terms of groups of elements in a hierarchical structure; we can also construct a program that deals with this as a linear array in sequence. Since we can do it either way, we can in principle carry out the induction either way. We can describe the linguistic structure in either way: We can describe it as a linear array of words, and in this case we use the property *leftmost* as the basis for induction, or we can describe it as a hierarchical structure, in which case we use the property *follows the subject* if that is the way the hierarchical system works. We learn nothing from the fact that it is possible to construct programs to look at things hierarchically, because it is also possible to construct programs to look at things linearly. The issue is, in this case, do we look at the sentences in a linear or a hierarchical manner in order to carry out the induction? The existence of a program that will do one or the other is irrelevant to the question of explaining how the inductive step is taken.

A more relevant question would be this: in other cases do people in their inductive behavior regard systems as hierarchically or linearly structured? Unfortunately, this question doesn't get us anywhere because they do both. There are cases in which people deal with properties like *leftmost* (they may regard an array of elements as linear and consider the physical arrangement of the elements), whereas there are other cases where people take into account all kinds of hierarchical structures in visual space or whatever. What we have to ask is what is the property in the initial state S_0 that forces us, in this specific linguistic case, always to go to the hierarchical abstract rule and always to neglect the more elementary linear physical rule? Several answers have been proposed to this question: the right one, I think, is the one which is implicit in the theory of transformational grammar, which in effect asserts that there is a notation available for describing linguistic rules that does not permit the formulation of the property *leftmost*. In fact, to formulate the property *leftmost* within the framework of that notation, you would have to use quantifiers in structural descriptions of rules, and that is not permitted. Alternatively, in terms of that notation, to describe the property *leftmost* would be extremely complex (involving quantifiers), whereas to describe the property *follows the first noun-phrase* would be very trivial.* Of course these are properties of the specific theory and the notation it provides, not general properties of systems of representation. It is a property of one very concrete specific theory that within it, to formulate the property *leftmost* requires the use of quantifiers, whereas the property *follows the first noun-phrase* can be formulated without the use of quantifiers. So there is a very specific theory of representations in terms of which *follows the first noun-phrase* is a more elementary property than *leftmost;* but that happens to be a property of *this* specific concrete theory and not a consequence of any general theory of representations and structures. Of course this property has many consequences elsewhere; it has vast consequences for grammar, where, applied to other linguistic structures, the use of the category *leftmost* (that is, rules involving the use of quantifiers) should always be less accessible than properties like *follows the first noun-phrase.* This hypothesis is one that is rich in empirical consequences and to my knowledge true.

Just as Descartes is saying that we perceive figures in two-dimensional visual space in terms of regular geometrical figures and distortions of them because that is in the nature of the mind, what I am suggesting here is that the very explicit and specific theory that makes the formulation of one property far more complex than the formulation of another is a characteristic of the mind. Perhaps somebody will find the physical basis for it someday. I would assume that we can regard ourselves as talking about the brain, in the same sense that we regard Descartes'

---

* Editor's note: This assumption is challenged by Putnam in his paper (Chapter 14) and developed further by Chomsky in his reply to Putnam.

theory of perception as talking about the brain, but now we do it at an abstract level because we have no analogue to the Hubel-Wiesel mechanisms.*

Discussion

Wilden A point of information, in order to understand a further dimension of the example you are using: What happens to the meaning of the sentence if you add a "not" after the second "is" and then make the same transformation as before? You will see then that the transformation no longer produces the same kind of result. The reason for this difference appears to stem from hierarchical functions in the sentence, and specifically from the hierarchical situation of syntactic negation (that is, "not" as distinct from "no") in linguistic utterances.

Chomsky What you get is "Isn't the man tall?"

Wilden That is not the point of my question. Let me rephrase it. You have set up a transformation based on moving the expression "is" so as to produce a question. In your example, "The man who is tall is sad" is transformed into: "Is the man who is tall sad?" What I am suggesting is that if you insert "not" into the example and then make what appears on the surface to be the very same transformation, you do not obtain the same results. Let the original sentence be: "The man who is tall *is not* sad." Move the "is not" to create a question, and the result is: "*Isn't* the man who is tall sad?" By means of what appears to be a simple syntactic reordering, the semantic structure of the sentence has changed. The question is why? Why has the semantic level changed?

Chomsky That is true, but the semantics has nothing to do with it!

Wilden The semantics has everything to do with it! The object of my question was precisely to bring out this point: Just what is the relationship between syntactic structure and semantic structure? And why do we find these apparent interferences of one with the other?

* Editor's note: See the editorial comments at the beginning of this chapter.

Chomsky   Semantic considerations arise in a different connection. We are talking here about a system of rules that gives us the surface forms of sentences, and the theory in question says that the surface forms of sentences are given by, let's say, derivations, each derivation being a sequence of abstract representations of phrase structure; let's call them K_1 to K_n, each of these being a representation of the phrase structure of the sentence, and the move from K_i to $K_i + 1$ taking place by means of one of the transformations that is expressible in our notation. The last of these phrase structure representations is what is sometimes called the surface structure, while the first one is sometimes called the deep structure. Now, the particular rule that I was talking about is one that gives you the surface structure from a slightly more abstract representation of what I present here as a sentence. The question you are asking is what is the meaning of this whole thing.

Wilden   No, I am not concerned with "the meaning of the whole thing." The actual meaning of this sentence is of no concern to me at all. I am not asking questions about the meaning of this or of any other particular sentence. I am asking a question about *relationships*. In this example, my question is concerned with what happens to your theoretical explanation of transformations when one begins with an example which includes an expression—in this case "not"—which is clearly of a different level of logical types (to quote Russell) from that of all of the other expressions in the sentence. That is what I meant by my earlier reference to hierarchies.

Chomsky   The answer to that question is that if you introduce the word "not," then the whole unit, for reasons that I won't bother explaining here, goes to the front.

Wilden   And the sentence changes its meaning.

Chomsky   Yes, but that has no relevance at all until we turn to the next question that one can ask, namely, how are derivations associated with meanings?

Wilden   If I may be permitted to insert a clarification at this point, it seems to me that our obvious inability to agree on what this question is actually about is the result of our speaking different dialects in the discourse of science. You are speaking in linguistic terms; my question was posed in the metalinguistic terms of semiotic communication. I leave the matter there and let Chomsky continue.

Chomsky The next question one can ask is how derivations are related to meanings through the surface structure. There is one type of semantic relations, sometimes called case relations or thematic relations (things like agent, instrument, and so on), which seems to have to do with the initial (deep) structure; but in every other respect, and certainly with respect to notions like negation and, in fact, all logical structure, meaning is directly determined by the surface structure. Correspondingly, we would expect the meaning of those sentences to differ under this theory, because the meaning would depend on the configuration of the surface structure, which happens to have "not" in different places. You can find very striking cases where the meaning changes, depending on the application of transformations. Take the sentence "Many arrows didn't hit the target" and compare it with its passive: "The target wasn't hit by many arrows"; these sentences have totally different meanings, totally different truth conditions, and so forth. This follows from a very reasonable theory of surface structure interpretation of logical particles. So the question is a perfectly legitimate one, but it has no bearing on the issue.

Wilden It does have some bearing. Unfortunately, your example about the arrows, although perfectly legitimate in itself, is not of the same type as the example produced by my insertion of "not" into the sentence you began with. In other words, in your example of negation in the active and passive forms of the sentence about the arrows and the target, the expression "not" does not undergo any change in function after the transformation, whereas in my example "not" does change function, and the sentence changes its meaning because of it. To put the issue as simply as possible: When "The man who is tall is not sad" becomes, by the simple process of positional change, "Isn't the man who is tall sad?" then the negative declaration in the original—which in Jakobson's terms refers only to the level of the code, and not to the communicational circuit between senders and receivers—not only becomes a question, but also introduces a *shifter*. The shifter indicates the relationship of the sender to the message and thence to the receiver, as well as to the code. And the shifter in the question is the word "not." How is it that what appears to be a simple *syntactic* shift can result in the introduction of not just a different meaning, but what is in effect a new *semantic dimension* into the sentence? The "not" has changed its characteristics and its function. What I am now wondering is whether, in such examples, we are not in fact faced with a hierarchy of logical determination in communication (and not only in language), a relationship between levels of communication and a relationship between the message and its environment—in other words, a relationship or relationships which are not taken into account by the way in which you are explaining these forms of transformation. That is not an easy question, and I know that we won't find a simple answer to it.

Chomsky It's a good question; I think the answer is no, for the reason I have just described, namely, that *insofar as logical particles are concerned (like negation, quantifiers, anaphora, scope and so on), the meaning is a function of the surface structure, including the form of the sentence and its actual bracketing into phrases.* The two sentences "Isn't the man who is tall sad?" and "The man who is tall isn't sad" have a different physical shape, and different physical arrangements, and from these physical shapes and arrangements we can infer the meanings, getting the differentiated meanings that you talked about. The point is that there are interactions among order, logical particles, and quantifiers, all of which have to do with surface structure, and the more elements of this type that you introduce into a sentence, the more the meaning is likely to change, depending on the transformations that take place, as a result of the simple fact that the meaning is directly determined from the surface structure.

Returning to my paper, at this point I went on and gave more complex examples; I will mention one and will give an analogue in French. One of the examples had to do with what I call the *specified subject condition;* briefly, that has to do with the following kind of configuration. Suppose we consider something like: "We expect John to like each other"; why can't we say sentences like that? We can, however, say "We expect each other to win." Why doesn't the first sentence mean "Each of us expects John to like the others"? It could mean that—the meaning is perfectly sensible—so why doesn't the sentence have this meaning? There is nothing semantically incorrect about it. Let's take another sentence: "We like each other"; this sentence means "Each of us likes the others." Correspondingly, why doesn't the sentence "We expect John to like each other," by induction, mean "Each of us expects John to like the others"? This sentence is fine, but "We expect John to like each other" doesn't mean that; somehow, the induction, the generalization is blocked. The generalization that says "replace *we . . . each other* by *each of us . . . the others*" is blocked in this case. Again, this is the kind of thing that nobody is taught, so once more the question arises, why don't we make the natural generalization? I think that the answer lies in a very general condition of rules which says roughly that if an embedded sentence has a subject, only the subject is accessible to the rule. This sentence has a subject, *John*; therefore only that subject is accessible to any rule, and particularly the rule of reciprocal interpretation.

Therefore, I think that just as it is reasonable to assume that the specific notation which gave the appropriate hierarchy to the inductive possibilities is simply part of S_0, correspondingly it is perfectly reasonable to assume that the specified subject condition is part of S_0. If somebody believes that this condition or anything remotely like it arises from general developmental mechanisms, all he has to do is present the mechanism that leads to the condition that if that embedded sentence has a subject, then only the subject is accessible to the rule.

Papert   What do you mean exactly by "accessible to the rule"?

Chomsky   Consider a rule that relates two phrases—for example, the rule for reciprocal interpretation takes a plural noun-phrase and it takes the phrase *each other*, which can be anywhere in the sentence—and it says that these two elements are related by the principle of reciprocal interpretation, which essentially gives the meaning *each of these . . . the others*. Now, here the rule cannot apply to the noun-phrases *we* and *each other* in "We expect John to like each other"; that is, *each other* is not accessible to the reciprocal rule. Why? Because the embedded clause "John to like each other" has a subject, *John*, and the principle says that if the sentence has a subject, only the subject is accessible to the rule.

Papert   I think Piaget has often proposed such principles.

Chomsky   I will simply assert that there is no proposal in the literature from which one can deductively conclude that the specified subject condition operates in English. If you have an example to the contrary I'd like to study the deduction; but frankly, I don't expect to see one.

Returning to my paper, what I then went on to point out is that really the issue is far more complex than this, and I gave the following example: take the sentence "John seems to the men to like Bill." Now let's try "John seems to the men to like each other." The first one is correct; the second is not. Why doesn't the second sentence mean "John seems to each of the men to like the others"? Now the sentence "John seems to each of the men to like the others" is a perfectly fine sentence in English; so why don't we carry out the induction from "We like each other" to "John seems to the men to like each other" to give the meaning "John seems to each of the men to like the others"? What blocks that induction? Notice that the specified subject condition (SSC) as so far formulated doesn't block it because there is no subject in this case, and therefore the SSC does not block the induction, at least so it appears. Nevertheless, this example looks very much like the other, so we may argue that if the SSC was correctly formulated it ought to cover this case.

A natural way to give a correct formulation is to use a concept of traditional grammar, namely, the concept of *understood subject*. If you think about the following sentence: "John seems to the men to like Bill," traditional grammar would say that the word *like* does have a subject, that is, an understood subject, namely *John*, since it is John who is doing the liking. This concept of understood subject is very complex and very intricate and depends on all sorts of complex semantic properties of words, but it is a very important concept. What apparently is the case is that the SSC does not care whether the subject is physically present or whether it is only mentally present. Let us say rather that at one of the levels of this abstract system of representations it is physically present, in the computational systems which, according to our theoretical hypothesis, the mind is employing. Thus at a certain level the subject is really there, and this fact turns out to be crucial.

What apparently is the case, judging from examples like this (and there are many others), is that the rule is not permitted to apply to an element if there is a subject either physically or mentally present in the sentence in which that element appears; that is the real principle. Notice that there is nothing logically necessary about that principle; English would be a perfectly fine language if it didn't have that principle, only in English you would then say "John seems to the men to like each other." There would be no problems about communication; all the properties would be acceptable. *It just wouldn't be a human language;* it could be the language of another organism, namely, an organism whose initial state would not include this principle. One could conceive of an organism exactly like humans, but minus the specified subject condition, and it would talk with a fine language which it could use for all possible purposes. In fact, we could observe that organism for a very long time and not even know that it is not using the SSC, because these questions generally don't even arise. Similarly, physicists could observe the natural world for a long time and not know that certain physically interesting properties have ever been realized—that is why people do experiments. Likewise, if you were simply to observe the flow of experience, to make a movie of people talking for instance, you might not know whether they are using the SSC at all, and certainly not if they are using it in the special sense where mentally present subjects act like physically present subjects. Yet the fact is that everyone, without ever committing an error, uses that condition even if they have had no relevant experience whatsoever. We could prove this by taking a total record of a person's experience and showing that he never produced any such examples or had any specific training concerning them, but I don't think that is a worthwhile experiment because it is obvious what the result would be; however, it is an experiment that someone could carry out if he doesn't believe what I am saying. What is obvious, I mean, is that there would never be any relevant experience. Someone who thinks the contrary is true should study children and discover the moment when they are presented with experience that tells them that mentally present subjects act like physically present subjects. This is an answerable question. It could be that children do try to say things like "John seems to the men to like each other," but they are told they can't do that and then they conclude in some way that mentally present subjects are not like physically present subjects; but surely that doesn't happen.

Let's turn to something that illustrates the operation of this principle in a totally different domain, in a different language —French in this case—in which apparently you can say things like "J'ai laissé Jean manger X" or "J'ai laissé manger X à Jean." If you have a quantifier, for example "tout" instead of X, then there is a rule that says that "tout" can be moved, which ought to give these two sentences: "J'ai tout laissé Jean manger" or "J'ai tout laissé manger à Jean." According to my sources, the second sentence is correct and the first one isn't; why is there that distinction? In the first case there is a subject in the embedded sentence; therefore, by the SSC, only the subject is accessible to a rule that moves an element, and thus you can't move the word "tout" just as you couldn't interpret the reciprocal phrase "each other," when there was a subject. In the second case there is no subject, but rather something that functions as a subject in a prepositional phrase ("à Jean"); since there is no subject, the SSC doesn't apply, therefore "tout" is accessible to the rule, and therefore it moves. So it is perhaps the same condition, but operating in a totally different domain where its effects are quite different from the earlier case I discussed.

There are a lot of cases in which that same, quite abstract condition has empirical consequences as to what is possible or is not in language. To the extent that that condition leads to empirical consequences, it is very easy to prove that it is false, if that is the case; but my point about that condition is that it is a highly specific one which, as far as I know, has no analogue in any other cognitive domain. There is no general principle of cognitive structure from which one can *deduce* that this principle holds for language. For this reason, I think it extremely reasonable to postulate that we have here a highly specific linguistic mechanism specific to this cognitive domain, which is part of S_0.

One can go on with many other examples of this kind, but all these examples are misleading in one important respect (and in rereading my paper I noticed that it is misleading in that respect), namely, what I gave there looks like a list of properties that belong to S_0. What I failed to say, and should have said, is that this list of properties forms a highly integrated theory. It may not seem so when they are just listed as examples, but in fact they all fall together in a very natural way; they don't logically follow from one another, but they are so close in form when you actually formulate them correctly that they really flow from a kind of common concept, an integrated theory of what the system is like. This seems to me exactly what we should hope to discover: that there is in the general initial cognitive state a subsystem (that we are calling S_0 for language) which has a specific integrated character and which in effect is the genetic program for a specific organ (here it is the program for the specific organ which is human language). It is evidently not possible now to spell it out in terms of nucleotides, although I don't see why someone couldn't do it, in principle. Likewise, it seems to me that someone who did not know the laws of physics *could have* hoped in the seventeenth century that the theory of perception could be spelled out in terms of properties of the brain. Similarly, we are in a position like that of Descartes with respect to visual perception. We can say what the genetic program must look like (of course this a scientific and not a mathematical "must"—we are dealing with a hypothesis about reality) but we cannot yet say what the genetic program is—which does not mean that we *could not* in principle say what it is. One has to make a sharp distinction between notions like "inexplicable" and notions like "unexplained." At the moment there is no explanation, in terms of the biological structure of the organism, for the genetic program for this particular human language, and of course that is true of any other organ as well. To say that there is no explanation at the moment means, to me, that there is no set of principles by which we can deductively conclude this or that. There is no explanation at the moment for the fact that the heart is what it is, or the liver. That is not to say that it is inexplicable. It is possible that the principles are actually known but we don't know how to draw the conclusions because it is too complicated.

Now, if that is true for the liver, why shouldn't it be true for the brain? The liver, I am told by neuroanatomists, has about the same number of cells as the brain, but the brain is far more complex as an organ. So why should we expect that the genetic components of the brain should be easier to account for or to deal with than the genetic components of the liver, which are also unexplained but not inexplicable? The answer is that there is no reason at all to believe that. When people say, as I think Toulmin is saying (see Chapter 13) if I read him correctly, that to assume these properties in S_0 is to attribute to it a structure so specific that the burden on evolutionary theory is too heavy—if that is asserted, I simply deny it. First of all, I don't think that the structure assumed here, that is, the SSC, is more complex than the structure we presume to be true of the liver; in fact, if we were really to explain in detail the functioning of the liver, I'm sure that we would have properties at least as complex as the SSC—even far more complex—yet nobody is troubled by the fact that we leave it to the theory of evolution to explain why the liver is what it is. We don't assume that the child learns to have a liver, and similarly, I don't see the reason why much simpler properties should impose an unsupportable burden on the theory of evolution; quite the contrary, even if we could advance this study to the point where we really had a much more complex theory, and I think we are ultimately going to discover a far more complex theory of what the initial state must be. A theory of the brain should surpass in complexity a theory of the liver. We assume that the liver is a much less complex organ than the brain, despite the fact that it has approximately the same number of cells.

As a final remark, it seems to me that no burden of an unacceptable nature is imposed on the theory of evolution in this case—quite the contrary. It is possible, of course, that my argument may be wrong, since it is not a demonstrative argument, but I think there is plenty of evidence for it. Furthermore, I think it's the kind of thing we ought to expect to find. We ought to expect to find that highly specialized structures, like the general mammalian structure for the visual cortex which leads to "Cartesian" properties, or the very specific structures of particular cognitive organs like the brain, are just the reflection of a genetic program. This explains why we have these highly complex and remarkable systems that develop in a curious fashion along patterns of inductive inference which seem very strange from the point of view of scientific induction but which nevertheless are uniform, very specific, and highly complex in the results to which they lead.

Dütting   I have difficulty in accepting your explanation of the SSC. It seems that in the two sentences, "Each of the men likes the others" and "The men like each other," the meaning is different. Why do you need the SSC condition, if it is a semantic problem?

Chomsky   What I said was that the two sentences are synonymous. That's a good first approximation, but still somewhat inexact. What I should have said is that the two sentences have a fixed relationship in meaning which comes very close to synonymy. Let's call the relationship in meaning between the two "R." The relation R holds between the two sentences, which is to say that the pair of phrases "The men . . . each other" can be interchanged with the pair "Each of the men . . . the other(s)," preserving the relation R over a very large domain. However, there are cases where this is not true, in certain contexts. Now, why is this so? That is the problem that has to be explained, namely, why does the pattern of generalization break down in this case? The answer that I suggested to this problem is the SSC. There is also a difference between "the other" and "the others." So let's say "the other" is related by R to "each other" and "the others" by R' to "each other." We can then ask the same question at a slightly more complex level: Why is neither the relation R nor the relation R′ preserved?

Suppose we agree that the SSC is the reason why the generalization breaks down. Then a paradox presents itself: namely, the sentence "Each of the men expected John to like the other(s)" is perfectly correct, but the sentence "The men expected John to like each other" is not. The reason is the SSC. However, assuming that the rule relating "the men" to "each other" is blocked in this case, how do you explain why the rule relating "each of the men" and "the others" is not blocked in the other case? Why are the two cases different? Why isn't the SSC refuted by the perfectly good sentence "Each of the men expected John to like the others"? The reason is that another reciprocal rule applies in this case which says that "the others" is not the same as "the rest of the men." Some rule is applying; why isn't it blocked?

This is an important question; its answer hinges on the very great difference between "each other" and "the others." "The others" is not related by bound anaphora, a rule of sentence grammar, to "the men." (This becomes clear if you notice that "the others" can begin a sentence, whereas "each other" cannot; for example, I can say, "Some of the men are happy. The others are sad," but I can't say "Some of the men are happy. Each other are sad.")

Premack Chomsky's first example, "The man who is tall," reminds me of a logically parallel case from a simpler system concerning a chimpanzee and the rule for pluralization that she apparently learned. In Sarah's language the plural is formed by adding a piece of plastic which we call the plural particle or "pl." In training her, we contrasted singular forms such as "apple is red" with plural forms such as "apple banana is pl red," where "is + pl" = "are." Although Sarah learned the training sentences and went on to pass the usual transfer tests involving new sentences, it dawned on us that there might be other tests she could not pass. For from the training we had given her, she could have learned either of two rules, only one of which was correct. She could have learned to use a physical feature comparable to the physical feature in Chomsky's example, namely, applying a plural particle whenever there are two words to the left of "is." Or she could have induced a rule based not on a physical feature but on a grammatical one, namely, applying a plural particle when the subject is plural. When we tested her with sentences of the kind, "red apple? fruit" versus "orange grape? fruit," we found that she answered correctly, replacing "?" with "is" in the first case, and with "is pl" in the second. Thus the chimpanzee induced a rule based on a grammatical feature, not a physical one, despite the fact that the physical feature might be considered simpler than the grammatical one, and the training given the animal was equally compatible with both alternatives.

Sperber   I would like to make two remarks that refer directly to Chomsky's discussion. First, there is no final state for all the domains of knowledge. For example, encyclopedic knowledge accrues throughout life. Second, Chomsky suggests that he can construct a special theory of learning for each domain of knowledge. I do not disagree with this point, but I would like to know how Chomsky would determine what constitutes a truly autonomous domain under the jurisdiction of a proper theory of learning.

Chomsky   As far as the first question is concerned, of course that is true: encyclopedic knowledge does not stop growing. Of course, that is true for language as well; for example, you keep learning more and more words, but the system doesn't fundamentally change. We simply don't know whether that is true for what you call encyclopedic knowledge. It might very well be that up to a certain point, whatever that may be, people are developing systems for organizing information, and that after that point they are just adding information to the systems. (I don't know if that's true, but I wouldn't be surprised if that were the case.)

About the second point: how do we decide when we have identified an autonomous domain? Well, we can't decide a priori; we can only decide when we have an organized system. When we come across an integrated system with special properties and internal interconnections, and so forth, *then we can reasonably postulate that is a system.* Of course that is an idealization, just as to talk about the heart is an idealization. Why do we say that the heart is an organ? In principle, we can put it in an entirely different way; and in fact, that idealization is misleading at a certain stage of investigation, where we want to talk about the integration of this system into other richer systems, some mental, some physical, and so on. So it is a legitimate but at some point misleading idealization, like other idealizations that demarcate subsystems for investigation. As for other cognitive domains, I think there are other areas where one can make a guess at least. Let's take music, for example, which to all appearances constitutes a system; or mathematics. I don't have enough information in these areas, but my feeling is that if one looks at the history of mathematics, what one sees is that for very obscure reasons, as a byproduct of something else, there developed in the course of human evolution this truly weird capacity to deal with abstract properties of the number system. Now, this is a capacity that has no selective advantages in itself; it may be a byproduct of something that does. But in any event, at some stage in human evolution a kind of dual capacity emerged to deal abstractly with problems of three-dimensional space and properties of the number system, and out of that amazing capacity developed 2,000 or 2,500 years of mathematics which, in a certain sense, finally led to a kind of consummation at the beginning of the twentieth century. At that point, roughly speaking, I think it would be fair to say that classical mathematics came close to being exhausted in the sense that the problems of number theory and of classical analysis were just too difficult for any mere human being; if they hadn't been, Gauss would have solved them. What happened at that point is that classical analysis and number theory became in a way the special province of an exotic group of people who, from an evolutionary point of view, were freaks, special geniuses who emerged. This domain was just too difficult for the working mathematician to work on. The result was that a number of other branches of mathematics developed, perhaps because classical mathematics became too difficult. This is, of course, a vast oversimplification, but I think it is a rough account of what happened, and what it seems to me to suggest is that a specific human cognitive capacity, which one could investigate, was pursued nearly to its limits in the development of classical mathematics and was then more or less exhausted.

Like all theoretical models, the "Cartesian mind" postulated by Chomsky is supported by some constitutive metaphors whose analysis can be quite illuminating. Chomsky describes the process that is responsible for the attainment of the final steady state S_s starting from the initial state S_0 as a "mapping function." S_0 is in effect "a function which maps experience onto the steady state." If one keeps in mind the perceptual mechanisms "à la Hubel-Wiesel" (also summarized in my comments *at the beginning of this chapter), it is clear why the notion of mapping is so important for Chomsky. Mapping means imposing a lawful point-to-point correspondence between patterns belonging to two different spaces (the "real" space and the "image" space or map). Experience is said to be "mapped" onto the steady state, therefore to be actively processed by the subject according to rules which are imposed by the subject, are universal, and are susceptible to be made explicit. In contrast to the constitutive metaphors of the Piagetian system, the Chomskian notion of mapping is projective and not introjective; it is conceived as a complete system of rules available to the newborn baby, and not as a stepwise construction through trial and error.*

In accordance with the neurophysiological discovery of preset filters, the environment is given a structure, not explored to derive structures from it. The environment channels the mapping from S_0 toward S_s; it does not instruct the subject on how to do it. According to Chomsky, the subject is "exposed" to relevant information and the underlying structures are then "revealed" by the action of the environment. The predominance of optical metaphors (projective and photographic) is in perfect harmony with the rationalistic character of his basic conceptions. As we have seen in the Introduction, the rationalistic outlook of Chomsky differs from the "vitalistic" outlook of Piaget. Nowhere else in the book is Chomsky's basic attitude so completely and analytically expounded as in this chapter. The full significance of the following discussions, including the one with Putnam in Part II, will not be appreciated if Chomsky's positions, as expressed here, are not kept constantly in mind.

CHAPTER FIVE

Cognitive Schemes and Their Possible Relations to Language Acquisition

The differences in presuppositions, aims, and styles of explanation between constructivism and innatism have already been highlighted in the preceding chapters. In the present chapter the discussion moves somewhat deeper into the rationale of the disagreement between Chomsky and Fodor on one side and the Geneva school on the other. Bärbel Inhelder offers a further, most persuasive argument in favor of a reconciliation between her approach to language learning and that of Chomsky. The examples she quotes are drawn from semantics, that is, from linguistics proper. This time the argument for a compromise is based on the pertinent field of sentence production and on the understanding of the meaning of sentences. Inhelder sees a direct relation—even a substantial identity—between specific linguistic structures and other nonlinguistic cognitive operations. The semantic operations she describes appear to be based directly on the child's appraisal of the external structure of the world. Such a provocative and definitely pertinent move elicits a significative reply from Chomsky: "One cannot deny that there are some properties of what people do in regard to language that relate to other aspects of their cognitive development . . . [but] I want to find those properties that cannot be plausibly related to other aspects of cognitive development . . . because I am interested in human nature."

The difference in basic strategies of research is seen clearly here, as well as the choice of what is the proper object of Chomsky's inquiry. Could there be, after all, that "division of labor" propounded earlier by Cellérier—the constructivists choosing to explore those linguistic properties that are also common to other cognitive domains, the innatist focusing instead on those linguistic structures, specific to the human species (hence Chomsky's reference to human nature), that have no conceivable counterpart elsewhere in the subject's cognitive repertoire? This distinction, which seemed to allow a peaceful split of two overlapping domains, is nonetheless challenged by Chomsky, who attributes to Piaget the position, irreconcilable with his own, that "all of the properties of language use and structure derive from sensorimotor construction." The controversy is now at a turning point.

Language and Knowledge in a Constructivist Framework

Bärbel Inhelder

In their respective papers, Piaget and Chomsky, one defending constructivism, the other adopting an innatist position, presented very different points of view, which could hide the fact that in reality they were attacking the same adversary: empiricism in all its forms and nuances. Did not Chomsky in one fell swoop do away with the behaviorist approach of *Verbal Behavior*,[1] and did not Piaget dedicate decades of epistemological argumentation to giving the coup de grace to logical empiricism?

All the resources of the child's environment cannot of themselves explain the spontaneous creativity inherent in the formation of his language and thought during the first years of his life. In their study of sensorimotor programming, of linguistic structures, and of the reasoning process, Piaget and Chomsky did not limit themselves to a simple recording of the obvious forms of thought and language; they both attempted to analyze their underlying structures, but by different means.

Whereas Piaget endeavored to bring out the most general structures that account for the categories of knowledge, such as permanent object, space, time, causality, and so on, Chomsky grappled with the problem of universal forms that are language-specific. Indeed, did he not say that, although it was pure speculation, in his opinion "there exists an autonomous system of formal grammar which is in principle determined by the faculty of language and its universal components"?[2] For Piaget, language is part of a more general cognitive organization that has its roots "in action and in sensorimotor mechanisms that reach deeper than the linguistic reality";[3] more specifically, language is one of the elements of a cluster of signs resting on the semiotic function and in which symbolic play, deferred imitation, and mental imagery participate.

The fundamental difference between Chomsky and Piaget lies in the fact that the latter considers all cognitive acquisition, language included, as the product of a progressive construction, beginning with the evolutionary forms of biological embryogenesis and culminating in contemporary scientific thought; and Piaget also rejects the hypothesis of preprogramming in the strict sense of the term. But let me immediately make clear that what is innate for Piaget is a general ability to recombine the successive levels of a more and more intensive cognitive organization. For this reason, among others, he considers representation beyond the here and now as the culmination of sensorimotor intelligence. This does not at all mean that Piaget sees in the latter a sufficient preparation for all future linguistic achievements and abilities—as Chomsky seems to imply when he states: "Nor is it imaginable that the principle has been learned or derived from some sensorimotor construction or the like" (see Chapter 1).

When developmental psychology demonstrates the chronological unfolding and the filiations of behaviors, one does not presuppose that a previous behavior is in itself capable of producing subsequent behaviors. Each sensorimotor and semiotic level seems to be ruled by evolutionary principles, but the analogy is not necessarily one of identity, and the reconstruction at a higher level is not tantamount to a pure repetition of what has been accomplished at a lower level. Did not Brown write: "In sum, I think that the first sentences express the construction of reality which is the terminal achievement of sensorimotor intelligence . . . Representation starts with just those meanings that are most available to it, propositions about action schemas involving agents and objects, assertions of nonexistence, recurrence, location, and so on"?[4]

Whereas Brown and others emphasize the relationships that exist between sensorimotor development and the *semantic content* of utterances, others search for structural[5] or dialogical[6] relationships. According to Sinclair, "At the sensorimotor level, the child can establish connections of order, time, and space; he can classify objects—in other words, he can use a class of objects for the same actions or apply sets of programmed actions to a single object. He is able to connect objects with actions, as well as to interconnect actions among themselves. The linguistic equivalent of such structures would be concatenation and categorization, especially the essential categories of P, SN, and SV as well as functional grammatical relationships: subject of, object of, etc."[7] Sensorimotor schematizations would thus provide the child with heuristic procedures allowing him to approach the syntactic and dialogical structures of his language.

Neither Piaget nor Chomsky has taken as his main line of study the relationships between language and thought. For Piaget, language is a necessary but not sufficient condition for the construction of logical operations. It is necessary, he says, "because without the system of symbolic expression which constitutes language, the operations would remain at the stage of successive actions without ever being integrated into simultaneous systems or simultaneously encompassing a set of interdependent transformations. Without language, the operations would remain personal and would consequently not be regulated by interpersonal exchange and cooperation. It is in this dual sense of symbolic condensation and social regulation that language is indispensable to the elaboration of thought. Thus language and thought are linked in a genetic circle* where each necessarily leans on the other in interdependent formation and continuous reciprocal action. In the last analysis, both depend on intelligence itself, which antedates language and is independent of it."[8] Chomsky, on the other hand, feels that drawing a clear distinction between the linguistic and nonlinguistic components of knowledge can prove to be impossible. An effective language could only be the result of the interaction of several mental faculties, one of them being the faculty of language itself. No concrete cases could be described as being simply the product of the faculty of language; nor could specific actions result uniquely from the exercise of linguistic functions. Questions of this nature emerge, according to Chomsky, no matter what aspect of language one tries to elucidate.

The more we progress in our knowledge of the language development of the child, the more we become aware of the in-

* Translator's note: Piaget uses the term "genetic" in the sense of "developmental" and not in the sense that biologists use the term. See Piaget's article "Language and Thought from the Genetic Viewpoint," in *Six Psychological Studies*, for a clear definition of the "genetic viewpoint."

tense activity he puts forth to discover the rules and functions of his own linguistic capacity. It is legitimate to think that this activity of linguistic discovery, in its turn, has a repercussion on the development of his knowledge in other domains.[9]

Contrary to Chomsky's assertion that there is no general theory of cognitive learning, I am convinced for my part that the learning experience corresponds to a very broad process, whether it is a question of logico-mathematical knowledge, physical knowledge, or knowledge whose object is one's mother tongue.

Piaget himself has never dedicated to language acquisition research the amount of study he has given to other fields of human knowledge. However, a whole team of researchers in Geneva has devoted itself to that task. I will briefly discuss a few results of these psycholinguistic studies which, when compared to our recent research on the processes of discovery in the child, illustrate our point of view according to which very profound analogies between the genesis of language and that of thought would exist.

One of the first questions that arises concerns the attempt to know which cognitive structures would explain the difficulties encountered by the child and how these are overcome in the acquisition of certain of the semantic and syntactic aspects of language.

Let us begin with an example of a syntactic nature. Many researchers have demonstrated that the structure of the passive voice is understood relatively late by the child. Whereas some attribute this late acquisition solely to the underlying linguistic complexity, the Genevan psycholinguists tend to find the reason for it in difficulties of a cognitive nature:[10] that is, difficulties in preserving the meaning in the face of word-order operations, in making inversions, and so on. Such problems go far beyond the specific case of the passive voice and involve any change in normative order (see, for example, Ferreiro[11] on the inversions of temporal relationships). It is certainly not by chance that these difficulties are all overcome around the age of seven, which is the period of the onset of concrete operations.

The relationships between language and knowledge are still more striking in the area of semantics. It has been amply demonstrated that, in spite of early utilization of some "linguistic markers," the function of these markers changes considerably during the child's development. In a study on the evolution of verbal markers in the child, Bronckart was able to show that the first temporal inflexions have an aspectual meaning.[12] It is only around the age of eight that the temporal utilization of uniform markers is stabilized. The whole question is to know why the child first chooses aspectual meaning. In general, during the period of cognitive development he centers his initial attention, as we know, on the conditions and the results of actions before he can account for their transformations. Many researchers concur in leading us to believe that the laws of reason would tend to explain in part the evolution of the markers of a semantic nature.

The attempt to establish the relationship existing between the syntactico-semantic structures of language and those of thought in formation is one of the ways to consider the problem. A complementary approach consists of attempting to bring to light the networks of cognitive processes that the child brings into play both to learn his language and to understand his immediate universe.

The progress made by the child in the discovery of his universe results from the overcoming of the conflict created by the confrontation of different procedures destined to resolve problems of a physical or linguistic nature. We assume that the overcoming of conflicts takes place in a similar manner in both areas. In a study on the process of learning the notion of length from discrete quantities, Bovet constructed situations that provoked conflicts between ordinal and numerical sets.[13] Now, the youngest children were content with a simple juxtaposition of the two systems of sets, but later on they became aware of their contradiction and discovered compromise solutions. (For example, in order to make two paths of the same length, they simultaneously observed the ordinal boundaries between a straight and a zigzag line, and the number of segments by breaking some of the elements in two.) It is only during the learning process that they succeed in discovering the conditions necessary for the equality of lengths.

A study on the acquisition of gender markers in French has cast light on a similar phenomenon.[14] When confronted with situations of discordance between grammatical and natural gender, or between grammatical gender and phonological ending, little children do not experience any conflict. For example, they use the masculine gender to refer to a female person while continuing their discourse with feminine pronouns. As in the preceding example, they juxtapose different procedures. When a conflict is felt, they again adopt compromise solutions: they change the gender of the article so that it agrees with the phonological ending of the suffix, or vice versa. Thus *"une bicron"* be-

comes either "*le* bicron" or "*la* bicron*ne*." (In order to emphasize the function of the procedure selected, nonsense words are
used.) Although phonological procedures remain dominant,
nonetheless when the child goes beyond his compromise solutions he becomes capable of coordinating the various procedures
with one another.

I have cited only a few examples of ongoing research. The
entire body of results, of which these constitute only a small
example, urges us to question Chomsky's claim that innate capacities of a high degree of specificity exist in order to account
for the principles through which men construct scientific
theories to explain phenomena that intrigue them (see Chapter
1). The evolution of the construction of knowledge and mental
procedures, whether one means those that explain the physical
universe or those that the child creates for himself in order to
grapple with his language, has, on the contrary, a high degree
of generality. Although it is true that the Genevan research has
mostly centered on the general aspects of behavior, in no way
do we consider that language is only one of the manifestations
of thought or that its specific aspects are reducible to the laws
of reason.

In the context of the ongoing debate, is it not surprising to be
able to recall the words of a Genevan psycholinguist, words that
tend to suggest, as I believe, that the perspectives of Chomsky
and of Piaget are not as contradictory as they are trying to make
us believe: "It is Chomsky's work that is making possible the
study of language acquisition within a Piagetian framework"?[15]
And it is not only in Geneva that these points of similarity have
been considered. Did not Cromer conclude his discussion by
asserting that "perhaps Chomsky and Piaget are both right"?[16]

Discussion

Chomsky Let me first try to make a simple logical point, without trying to resolve the issues. Suppose I were to say that
something in the room is green, and suppose somebody were
to respond, "Well, that is not so because there is something
that is white"—that wouldn't convince me that I was wrong
in saying that something in the room was green. Correspondingly, if I say that some properties of language use and struc-

ture are determined in the initial state by language-specific principles, it does not convince me that I am wrong if I am told that some aspects of language use and structure are related to other aspects of cognitive development—that is a simple point of logic.

There are two proposals that have been made from the Geneva group presentations: one is Inhelder's statement that *some,* but not all, of the properties of language use and structure derive from sensorimotor construction; I don't dispute this statement in any way. The other proposal is that of Piaget, in which *all* of the properties of language use and structure derive from sensorimotor construction, or to put it in Piaget's logically equivalent terms, "This innateness is not needed to ensure the formation and the stability of [the fixed] nucleus; sensorimotor intelligence is sufficient for that." This second assertion seems false to me: I know of no reason to believe that the principles of sensorimotor construction or any other general developmental methods will suffice to account for all properties of the fixed nucleus. But one cannot deny that there are some properties of what people do in regard to language that relate to other aspects of their cognitive development. That is specifically why I have been interested in trying to find the properties of language structures and their use in the area of semantics (where there are a number) and in the area of syntax and phonology; precisely, I want to find those properties that cannot be plausibly related to other aspects of cognitive development, and I want to do this because I am interested in human nature.

Papert I suppose that most of the examples that Inhelder gave could be evaded by the issues that were debated because of the green and white principle. But she did touch on some issues that overlap closely with the actual examples given by Chomsky in his paper. One of these is the importance in the sensorimotor area of schematization in terms of subject-action. Such schematization makes Chomsky's second type of rule (the structure-dependent one) *logically simpler* than the first type. The general process of assimilation of something into an existing scheme implies that a hypothesis formulated in terms of that scheme would be the simpler hypothesis. Similarly, even for the specified subject condition, if the rule is formulated in terms of an element of the schematization, for example the subject, that would be a more natural form of rule. One last very common example, which

Inhelder did not mention directly: she showed once again how the subject, through schematization, is always dealing with a mentally present rather than physically present object, or dealing with the mentally present object as if it were physically present. This is a major theme of the development of sensorimotor intelligence, which directly elucidates some of the aspects of language that Chomsky finds so mysterious.

Fodor Before this discussion goes off in too many different directions, one ought to distinguish *the subject of a sentence* from *the person who utters it*. If I say "Give the apple to me," the implicit subject of the sentence is *you*, the direct object is *apple*, and I only come in as an indirect object. We must not get confused about the difference between "subject" in the sense of egocentrism and "subject" in a sense of subject of the sentence. Once we have made that distinction, there is simply no relation between a constraint definable over the subject of the sentence and an obsession of the child with himself.

Piattelli-Palmarini It seems to me that the examples of language abilities connected with cognitive abilities reported by Inhelder have mainly to do with semantics—is there any evidence of other cognitive abilities linked with those formal universals of which Chomsky is speaking?

Inhelder There are some rules of transformation which are also fundamental and which, from the viewpoint of the construction of the subject's logic, can find their equivalent as rules; but on the other hand, there are, of course, the semantic aspects, and in this respect, I think what is important is that the child discovers also the whole interplay of meanings, as early as the sensorimotor level.

Piattelli-Palmarini But Chomsky's rules are of another kind.

Chomsky This topic interests me very much, and I have the feeling that if one were to look at those things one would also find aspects of semantic structure which cannot be accounted for in terms of sensorimotor intelligence, but which involve very specific modes of cognitive organization. I think there are such examples as soon as we begin to look, although I don't think they are as striking as the syntactic examples (I have one in my paper, in fact, that has to do with semantic ambiguity). But even if we take something as "simple" as the notion of the integrity of an object (and that is a very complex notion), it was said in the past, for example by Russell, that a nameable object can be anything that meets the condition of spatiotemporal contiguity. This is plainly false: if you begin to look at it more carefully you find that you can have noncontiguous things which are objects; for example, a Calder mobile can be a nameable object. On the other hand, the collection of leaves on a tree is not an object—why? As far as I can tell, it is because when we look at such cases, as adults at least, the notion of human will and creation plays an essential role in determining what is recognized as an object. If it is true that part of the definition of an object involves the notion "created by an act of human will," and if one wants to account for that alleged fact on the basis of constructions of sensorimotor intelligence, one will have to go beyond the stage of approximative analogies and give a deductive explanation—and I insist on that—a demonstration that from some property of sensorimotor interaction, one can deduce that part of the definition of an object must be "created by an act of human will." In other words, one must progress from demonstrable properties of sensorimotor construction to the conclusion that part of what characterizes the integrity of a physical object is, as I have described, an act of human creation. That would explain this purported fact from the theory of sensorimotor constructions; anything short of that would not count as an explanation. What won't count as an explanation is the observation that elsewhere in human behavior the notion of human will plays a great role.

Monod   I am thinking of an experiment that is theoretically very simple: if the development of language in the child is closely related to sensorimotor experience, one can suppose that a child born paraplegic, for example, would have very great difficulties in developing his language. Did the Geneva school develop an interest in such cases? I think that the Geneva school has always worked with normal children, and it seems to me that there would be a great deal to be learned from children having impairments as serious as paraplegia.

Inhelder   Until now nothing has been done with cases as serious as these; much has been done with older people who have lost some of their functions, which is something completely different. As a rule, one must have a minimum of movement; obviously one must be able to bring objects close to one another . . .

Monod   If I understand the Piagetian theory correctly, one must be able to exert an action on external reality for this to develop.

Inhelder Yes, but it can be acoustical, visual—or it can be multiple.

Fodor In the extreme case, if all that is required to engage sensorimotor intelligence is one instance of moving something (for example, moving a glass from one place to another), how do you distinguish between *learning* and what the ethologists call a *triggering function*? If anything would do it, if for instance moving your eyes once would do it, then what is the distinction between *construction* due to sensorimotor intelligence and simply *releasing* by a motor gesture?

Inhelder In the whole field of newborn perception, you have all kinds of strategies developed very early that one can follow; it is more than just a triggering function.

Fodor That doesn't answer the question, which is: what would you do in the case of extremely reduced capacity? I thought the answer was that you need do very little, just move the eyes. But then, why not say that any case of ethological triggering, any case where an arbitrary action is innately connected with a highly developed scheme of intelligence would count as learning? But that merely trivializes the doctrine that intelligence arises out of sensorimotor activity, and there is really hardly anything left.

A crucial point has been raised by Monod through his Gedankenexperiment: *if it is true that language development in the child is strictly associated with sensorimotor activities, then children suffering from extreme motor disabilities should not be able to talk, or at most, should develop very poor language. Inhelder replies that such experiments have not yet been carried out by the Geneva group, but that she expects, even in those extreme cases, that language would be fairly complete. A variety of "actions" can serve the purpose, be they acoustical, visual, or tactile. Here the innatists, such as Jerry Fodor, drive their wedge: if the "precursor" is almost anything, then this "anything" is rather a* triggering action *in the ethological sense than a primitive or precursor in the constructivist sense. Inhelder replies that the sensorimotor precursor schemes are somewhere in the middle, more complex and specific than a simple triggering action, but not so specific as to be reduced to a purely muscular action or to require perfect easiness in limb movements. The relationship between schemes, triggering actions, and precursors will be discussed by Premack in Chapter 9, and by Piaget and Bischof in Chapters 7 and 10.*

CHAPTER SIX

On the Impossibility of Acquiring "More Powerful" Structures

The extreme but very consequential stand which is outlined here by Jerry Fodor and which is expounded in due detail in his essay, **The Language of Thought,** *is a stumbling block to all those who, like Papert, Inhelder, Cellérier, and Piaget himself, are in favor of a "compromise" between innatism and constructivism. The grounds for such a compromise have been tentatively, though recurrently, identified in the domain of cognitive "primitives," that is, those early and still poorly differentiated processes out of which specific language structures and specific cognitive strategies might develop. Granted that* some *structures are innate, it is not on the side of complex, highly specific linguistic rules such as the specified subject condition (SSC) or bound anaphora that one has to look. These rules may be the terminal, sophisticated outcome of a vast class of interactions among simpler primitives, that is, a repertoire of general-purpose computational abilities to be found at the common root of a variety of linguistic and extralinguistic competences. Such a conclusion, which has been offered repeatedly by the Geneva group and by Seymour Papert, forms in addition the building block of Putnam's contribution to this debate. When Piaget insists on the demarcation between properties of the cognitive system which are "compatible with the genes, but not determined by them," when Cellérier confines the genetic component to a "general-purpose self-programming problem solver" capable of creating genuine novelty (see Chapter 2), when Papert claims that all that the genetic specification can allow for is computational*

142

"primitives," the core issue is again and again one of conciliating specificity (of invariant structures) with flexibility (of the overall performance range).

Admitting that a finite set of multipurpose precursor operations (and nothing else) is innate, the stepwise differentiation and integration of such basic structures by the action of the external environment can account for the variety of cognitive and linguistic abilities, making of innatism and constructivism two faces of the same coin. This, in its simplest terms, is the "compromise" between Chomsky and Piaget propounded by many authors. Fodor's argument frustrates these conciliatory hopes at a very fundamental level, pushing the innatist approach into an almost paradoxical position. Nothing new, he contends, can be "acquired" during cognitive development, and this for purely logical reasons. The growth of language, apart from obvious accretion of vocabulary, and the growth of knowledge, apart from obvious accretion of information, are to be seen as the unfolding of predetermined developmental stages involving specialization and restriction of competence. The compromise already rejected by Chomsky on grounds of weakness of the proposed constructivist hypotheses (see Chapter 6) is rejected here by Fodor on more general grounds, because of the inherent fallacy of the concept of "acquiring a more powerful structure." The implications of Fodor's argument concerning the philosophy of mind will appear in sharper focus in his "Reply to Putnam" in Part II.

Fixation of Belief and Concept Acquisition

Jerry Fodor

It seems to me that there is a sense in which there *isn't* any theory of learning, and this is quite compatible with Chomsky's point that maybe there is no general learning mechanism that applies equally to perception, language, and so on. I'll argue not only that there is no learning theory but that in certain senses there certainly *couldn't* be; the very *idea* of concept learning is, I think, confused.[1]

That is a contention that goes against the dominant thought of the last 300 years or so, in both psychology and philosophy. The sort of picture that one is invited to have in philosophy and psychology is that there exist two rough alternatives: there is the nativist alternative, which is methodologically very obscure and maybe unscientific and unintelligible, but in any case, very low down on the hierarchy of possible theories; then there is the learning alternative. The latter is at least supposed to be clear— that is, we know what it would be *like* to have a theory of learning; we know what it would be like to explain something in terms of learning. The only question is, with what generality can we do so?

Yet it seems to me that nobody has ever presented anything that would have even the basic characteristics of a theory of learning in the sense of a theory of concept acquisition. The reason people *think* that there is such a theory is that they confuse a theory of *concept acquisition* with a theory that has a quite different kind of logical structure, what I will call a theory of "fixation of belief." Although there are no theories of concept learning, there *are* theories of fixation of belief, and I think they are very deep and very important. The trouble is that to get any of them to work you have to be radically innatist about the origin of concepts. In short, no theory of learning that anybody has ever developed is, as far as I can see, a theory that tells you how concepts are acquired; rather, such theories tell you how beliefs are fixed by experiences—they are essentially inductive logics. That kind of mechanism, which shows you how beliefs are fixed by experiences, makes sense only against the background of radical nativism. That is the position that I am going to try to argue for.

For reasons of space I can't set out my point of view in great detail, and I certainly can't make a general case; what I will do is give a sketch of the kind of argument that I have in mind and then give two applications: one to what is known as *concept learning experiments* in psychology (I have in mind the kind of things that Vygotsky, Bruner, and others have done), and the other to what I consider to be a way of reading the Piagetian system.

Let me say, in the first place, something that I think everybody has always assumed is true in one form or another about theories of learning: I take it that anybody who has ever given a theory of learning in terms of mental processes (anybody who has ever said anything about what the information flow in learning is like) has said, in effect, that learning is a matter of inductive extrapolation, that is, of some form of nondemonstrative inference: It follows that a learning theory is some function that takes you 'from some sets of beliefs about your experiences into some sort of general beliefs; and secondly, that any such theory must acknowledge, among the processes involved in learning, hypothesis formation and confirmation.

Let's see how this works. Consider the so-called concept learning experiment. The subject enters an experimental situation and the experimenter puts a stack of cards in front of him: there are, let's say, red circles, green triangles, blue tetrahedrons, and so on. The colors and shapes of the objects on the cards are allowed to vary freely. What the subject has to do is to sort the cards into piles which are called "plus" and "minus" (which might also be called "satisfy the experimenter" and "don't satisfy the experimenter," or "reinforced" and "unreinforced," and so forth). Every time the subject (S) sorts the cards, the experimenter (E) tells him whether he is right (for example, he says "You're right," or he nods his head, or he gives the subject an M&M). Eventually, S comes to sort "correctly," that is, to place in a given pile all the cards that E wanted there, and only those cards.

This kind of experiment is sometimes thought of as involving *language* learning as well as *concept* learning. You can turn it into a language learning experiment in the following way: instead of being asked to put the card into one or the other pile, the subject is told to say a nonsense word like *miv* if he thinks the card is of one kind and to say *non-miv* if he thinks it is of the other kind. You can then think of this either as an experiment in which you learn the word *miv,* or as an experiment in which you learn the criterial attributes that define the concept *miv.*

Now, let's consider the theories of what happens in the experiment. There is only one theory that I know of, and it goes like this: the organism (child, adult, rat, or whatever) comes to develop some such hypothesis as "X is *miv,* if and only if X is . . . ," and then he fills in the blank on the right-hand side with a specification of the attributes that are criterial for being *miv,* say, red and square. All the experiment tells us is how (for example) various choices of the attributes, or various choices of the reward, or various relations between the two, affect the subject's convergence on accepting the right hypothesis. What it *doesn't* tell you is where the hypotheses (and the concepts that they deploy) come from! If you think about the classic concept learning experiments, I think you will see that that is true of every one of them.

To summarize, everybody agrees that S eventually ends up sorting into *mivs* and *non-mivs* correctly, and that he does so as a consequence of his history of being told which particular cards are *miv* and which aren't. There exist, moreover, prototheories of this process; theories that tell us, in effect, with what probability a given body of experience with the cards will lead to the fixation of one or another belief about the extension of *miv*. Such theories have, as I remarked previously, the general character of inductive logics: that is, they map pairs consisting of hypotheses ("X is *miv* if X is . . .") and sets of data-statements ("Card number 17, which I was reinforced for calling *miv*, had a red square on it") onto a number which can be interpreted as the degree to which that body of experiences tends to fix a belief in the truth of that hypothesis. Our psychology of learning details this mapping: it tells how the degree of fixation of belief varies with variations of experimental parameters. I claim that all theories of learning do this, and that none do anything else (that is, anything else revelant to the present discussion).

The difficulty with such a theory is, however, that it says nothing about the origin of concepts. In particular, it assumes as "given" the "criterial attributes" which form the hypotheses that are "fixed" in the experimental situation. In consequence, a theory of how our beliefs are determined by our experiences is not a theory of the source of our inductive hypotheses. On the contrary, it presupposes the availability of such hypotheses (and, of course, of the experiential data) and tells us only how the likelihood that one or another hypothesis will be accepted by an organism varies with one or another aspect of the organism's experience of its environment. I am saying that an inductive logic (that is, a theory of the fixation of beliefs; that is, a theory of learning in the only sense in which there *are* theories of learning) can't tell you how the concept *miv* is acquired because it presupposes the availability of that concept when it assumes that *miv* occurs in the confirmed inductive hypothesis. As far as I know, nobody except the nativists has addressed the question of how the concept *miv* (that is, *red and square*) is acquired, and what they have said is that it *isn't* acquired.

I am not, of course, arguing that we should abandon the notion that a learning device is, in essence, an instantiated inductive logic. Rather, the point is that to let such a device do what it is supposed to do, you have to presuppose the field of hypothesis, the field of concepts on which the inductive logic operates. In other words, to let this theory do what it is supposed to do you have to be in effect a nativist. You have to be nativistic about the conceptual resources of the organism because the inductive theory of learning simply doesn't tell you anything about that—it presupposes it—and the inductive theory of learning is the only one we've got.

Now I want to say something about how this whole way of looking at things applies to the Piagetian theory, at least as it is interpreted in certain places in the States; say, in my office. It seems to me that the following is at least one way of formulating the Piagetian view: Suppose you are Kant and are interested in writing the "First Critique," that is, you are interested in characterizing the computational capacities of the organism in terms of some very general constraints on the character of the concepts available to it. One way of reading the Piagetian position is to say that if you did that for several different time slices of the organism (instead of just considering the adult), what you would get is a fundamentally different galaxy of constraints on the organism's concepts. Moreover, this difference would have the following important characteristic: the logic instantiated by the system of concepts at any i^{th} stage is *weaker than* the logic instantiated by the $i - 1^{th}$ stage (I take this to be implied by such remarks as children at certain stages "don't have" transitive concepts, or "don't have" reversibility, and so on). In short, if you look at the organism as a succession of logics, then it is a succession of increasingly powerful logics, and powerful in some fairly rigorous sense: as for example that the set of truths that could be expressed by using the concepts available at i is a subset of the set of truths that could be expressed by using the concepts available at i + 1.

Let's suppose for the moment that in fact the organism does decompose in exactly that way; that a developing child is a series of logics such that each logic literally contains the preceding one, and "contains" is an asymmetrical relation. The logics, then, get stronger; that is, each successive one has the former one as a proper part. Let's suppose that is true. Now, what I want to argue is that if it is true, then Piaget must not, in point of logical necessity (not empirical necessity) be a *non-nativist* about changes of stage, that is, about the mechanisms that take you from one stage to the other. In particular, I want to argue that according to this viewpoint, the change of stage *cannot* be a learning process. It is an argument fundamentally analogous to the one I made when I discussed concept learning.

Why can't it be a learning process? Well, let's assume, once again, that learning is a matter of inductive inference, that is, a process of hypothesis formation and confirmation. Then the least you would have to be able to do at stage 1 is to characterize truth conditions on formulas containing the concepts in stage 2. You have to be able to do that because in stage 1 you have to have hypotheses about when these concepts are instantiated; as I said, hypothesis formation and confirmation is the only model of learning we've got.

The point is that we have a succession of stages of increasing power and we are going to have learning, that is, hypothesis formation and confirmation, mediating the relation between the stages. Now, how is that going to work? It is immediately obvious, from the following example, that it *can't* work.

Suppose we have a hypothetical organism for which, at the first stage, the form of logic instantiated is propositional logic. Suppose that at stage 2 the form of logic instantiated is first-order quantificational logic. The particular example does not matter in any respect, except that I want it to be clearly a case of a weaker system at stage 1 followed by a stronger system at stage 2. And, of course, every theorem of a propositional logic is a theorem of first-order quantificational logic, but not vice versa.

Now we are going to try to get from stage 1 to stage 2 by a process of learning, that is, by a process of hypothesis formation and confirmation. Patently, it can't be done. Why? Because to learn quantificational logic we are going to have to learn the truth conditions on such expressions as "(X) F_x." And, to learn those truth conditions, we are going to have to formulate, *with the conceptual apparatus available at stage 1,* some such hypotheses as *"(X) F_x" is true if and only if* . . . But of course, such a hypothesis can't be formulated with the conceptual apparatus available at stage 1; that is precisely the respect in which propositional logic is weaker than quantificational logic. Since there isn't any way of giving truth conditions on formulas such as all "(X) F_x" in propositional logic, all you can do is say: they include F_a and F_b and F_c, and so on.

If you think about this, you will see that this is an entirely general form of argument, one that shows that it is *never* possible to learn a richer logic on the basis of a weaker logic, if what you mean by learning is hypothesis formation and confirmation. Yet I say again that learning must be nondemonstrative inference; there is nothing else for it to be. And the only model of a nondemonstrative inference that has ever been proposed anywhere by anyone is hypothesis formation and confirmation.

I take it from this that there literally isn't such a thing as the notion of learning a conceptual system richer than the one that one already has; we simply have no idea of what it would be like to get from a conceptually impoverished to a conceptually richer system by anything like a process of learning. Thus there is an important sense in which the nativist hypothesis is the only one in the field, and the situation has been put exactly backwards over the last 300 years. The only intelligible theory of enrichment of conceptual resources is that it is a function of maturation, and there simply isn't any theory of how *learning can affect concepts.*

Discussion

Papert   Winston's model of learning[1] has the following form: make a hypothesis and from that compute a modification of the hypothesis. So it is not a matter of selection or confirmation; it is a process of successively modifying it. I don't know if I believe Winston's theory of learning, but it certainly doesn't fit your categorization of what a theory of learning has to be.

Fodor   It doesn't make any difference that I can see. You say that in the process of going from here to there, you can have feedback loops, but that doesn't change the logical situation. The feedback, after all, must be directed toward rejecting the hypothesis if it is false or accepting it if it is true; in both cases the hypothesis has to be available to the learning system until it is modified in terms of a better hypothesis, and then *that* hypothesis has to be available. It just confuses the issue to ask whether or not there are feedback mechanisms involved. Assuming that the mechanisms are a kind of inductive logic, any kind of inductive logic is going to have this problem.

Piaget   I was very much interested by Fodor's presentation, and I fully agree with Fodor on the first part, that is, on the impossibility of explaining language development by means of a theory of learning in the usual sense of the term; but the way he reduces my ideas to a theory of learning appears to me quite exaggerated, and I do not recognize myself in this interpretation. What is very correct is the idea that each structure becomes a subset of a richer structure. What I have endeavored to do (which is an idea in the back of my mind that I have not, I think, explicitly formulated) is to show that cognitive development in the child—that is to say, the construction of successive structures—is analogous to what is found in history with the formation of mathematics, which is always a generalization of a weaker structure leading to a stronger structure, of which the first one becomes a substructure, a subset. Then, applying Fodor's theory to the history of mathematics would be tantamount to saying that nothing has ever been invented, that everything is always contained in the previous state, and that, consequently, mathematics in its totality is predetermined and innate. Now, this innateness of mathematics is for me a real problem: at what age are we going to discover the appearance of innateness of negative numbers, of complex numbers, and so forth—at age 2, 7, 20? And, most of all, why on earth would this be special to the human species if we have here necessary innate structures? For my part, I have a difficult time believing that Cantor's theories or today's theories of categories are already preformed in bacteria or viruses; something must have developed . . . Now, Fodor, if I understood correctly, spoke of Kant. For my part, I consider myself to be profoundly Kantian, but of a Kantianism that is not static, that is, the categories are not there at the outset; it is rather a Kantianism that is dynamic, that is, with each category raising new possibilities, which is something completely different. I agree that the previous structure by its very existence opens up possibilities, and what development and construction do in the history of mathematics is to make the most of these possibilities, to convert them into realities, to actualize them. Then, what was given—and I agree with Fodor on this point—is that *the previous structure already contained something of the subsequent one, containing it not as a structure, but as a possibility.* What is this possibility; what is the set of all possibilities? I believe that the set of all possibilities is as antinomic a notion as the set of all sets. I believe that the "possible" is a process that progressively enriches itself: a weak structure opens up only few possibilities; a stronger structure opens up a large number of possibilities. There is an adjunction, a creation of new possibilities, and it is in this sense that I find innatism difficult to accept and constructivism much closer to what we see both in the development of the child and in the history of mathematics. The two points of view appear absolutely parallel and convergent to me. When I reason in terms of genetic psychology, I always keep in the back of my mind something based on the history of sciences or the history of mathematics, because it is the same process.

Fodor   One thing I will not do is argue with Piaget about the exegesis of his books. But let me make a couple of points about individual arguments. First, the nativist isn't committed to saying that viruses know about set theory any more than he is committed to saying that viruses have legs; it hardly follows from the fact that viruses don't have legs that legs aren't innately specified. It is true, and I think this is profoundly paradoxical but I think probably right, that in any theory of the modification of concepts available to us, there is no such thing as a concept being invented. It is obviously also true that there must be *some* sense in which our conceptual repertoire is responsive to our experiences, including the experiences of the species in doing things like inventing mathematics. What that implies, it seems to me, is that a theory of the conceptual plasticity of organisms must be a theory of how the environment selects among the innately specified concepts. *It is not a theory of how you acquire concepts, but a theory of how the environment determines which parts of the conceptual mechanism in principle available to you are in fact exploited.* I don't know whether or not such a theory can be made to stick, but I simply don't see that it is an incoherent notion in principle, and whether it can be made to stick is something that we can find out by trying (as we tried to do for several hundred years with the alternative theory, and to utterly bankrupt consequences, it seems to me).

I wanted to say something about the notion of potentiality, because what I have been saying could be confused with a banal thesis that's not worth discussing. The banal thesis is just that you have the innate potential of learning any concept you can in fact learn; which reduces, in turn, to the non-insight that whatever is learnable is learnable. I hope that is not what I have been arguing (it is surely not what I intended to argue). What I intend to argue is something very much stronger; the intended argument depends on a certain view on what learning is like, that is, the view that everybody has always accepted, that it is based on hypothesis formation and confirmation. According to that view, it must be the case that the concepts that figure in the hypotheses that you come to accept are not only *potentially* accessible to you, but are *actually exploited to mediate the learning* (that is, in the confirmation of the hypothesis). The point about confirming a hypothesis like "X is *miv* if and only if it is red and square" is that it is required not only that *red and square* be *potentially* available to the organism, but that these notions be effectively used to mediate between the organism's experiences and its consequent beliefs about the extension of *miv*. That's a much much stronger claim about the accessibility of concepts prior to experience, a much stronger claim than the mere tautology that you can potentially acquire any concept that you can potentially acquire.

If anything like this is true, then one has to alter the way we look at the phenomenon of plasticity, as Chomsky did (I think very properly and profoundly) in the case of language. Prior to Chomsky's works, the puzzle was taken to be: How is it that there are *any* relationships between languages at all? Because after all, the organism is flexible in an arbitrary way, environments can presumably differ in an arbitrary way, and thus the existence of any universals of language is a puzzle that will have to be explained. Once a sort of nativist theory of language is accepted, the puzzle is the reverse; it is then a matter of making enough room in the innate structure of the organisms to account for the fact that their behavior differs, that it is susceptible to the effects of the environment. I think that is the way we will have to look at learning in general: The problem is to account for plasticity, not for generality; that is to say, the problem is to find enough looseness in the innately available conceptual mechanisms of the organism to be reflected in congruences between particular facts about the environment and particular facts about the beliefs of the organism. I think, as far as I can see, that some model of fixation of belief along the lines of inductive logic has got to be right, if only for lack of alternatives. But that model, as I said, is one that assumes the most radical possible nativism: namely, that any engagement of the organism with its environment has to be mediated by the availability of any concept that can eventually turn up in the organism's beliefs. The organism is a closed system proposing hypotheses to the world, and the world then chooses among them in terms explicated by some system of inductive logic.

Wilden I am surprised that anyone should consider an organism a closed system. Thermodynamically speaking, it is a system open to the input and output of both materials and energy. But these inputs, as patterns of variety, also carry with them the information without which the organism could not continue to survive for one minute in its environment. Without going into details, one has only to consider what Herbert Simon,[2] among others, has termed the "alphabetic currency" of interchange between organism and environment expressed by means of the amino acids. Bateson[3] and others, including myself, have tried to deal in other ways with the numerous different levels of this and other kinds of information exchange. Thus the organism is open in three senses: open to material forms of order, open to energetic forms of order, and open to informational forms of order. I suspect that to a very significant degree, and without singling out any particular statement by any particular participant here, this question of the "organism-environment" (or "system-environment") relation is symptomatic of deeply rooted epistemological differences between a number of us, differences that would require discussion at a level which, in relation to our general level of discussion, we would have to call "metatheoretical."

I am specifically concerned at the moment with Fodor's "succession" of logics and with his use of the terms "weaker" and "more powerful," in a genetic or developmental sense, to describe them. Possibly this implicitly "evolutionist" usage is connected epistemologically with the similar usage of such terms by Piaget, which I have attempted to analyze and criticize elsewhere.[4] I think that Fodor has his succession of logics in development inside out or upside down, and that this is the result of the exclusionary and highly restricted conception of logic that has been dominant in our culture for several centuries. Fodor is talking about a whole subsystem in its multidimensional communicational relationships with its various environments, not only local, but also past, present, and future. In contrast, his *analysis* speaks only of a highly limited aspect of all those ecological relations. Fodor has said that as one moves through this developmental (or constructed) succession of logics, the later stages appear "logically richer" and "more powerful" than the earlier ones. Such a statement is valid and is no source of difficulty if we substitute for both of the expressions Fodor uses a single one: "syntactically more powerful." The reason for this substitution is that at all the other levels of relation, that is, those which for one reason or another have been excluded from his analysis, an inverse sequence is taking place. As the syntax of the particular logic he describes becomes more powerful because of the positional manipulability it provides, it grows at the same time *semantically* and *pragmatically* weaker. (I use these expressions in a semiotic rather than a linguistic sense, since what I understand Fodor to mean by "semantics" is that limited domain of digital *signification* usually called "meaning" in English, whereas from the semiotic perspective "semantics" considers meaning as the ground of signification, to be characteristic of analogical communication—or in another terminology, of the domain of the so-called "paralinguistic.") Fodor is in effect talking about the relationship between analogical logic and digital logic, but without taking the former adequately into account. In other words, I am suggesting that it is illegitimate to impose the restrictions on logic and communication that Fodor's analysis and schema do indeed impose. I also have the impression that Fodor is compounding the original error by implicitly sanctifying the semantic and pragmatic impoverishment of the digital domain by an all-encompassing use of the term "more powerful." What I am saying, then, is that since logic, communication, and language are *not* purely digital, Fodor's succession of logics is invalid.

Fodor   I think that there clearly are cases in which one system is more powerful than another in the sense that the more powerful system can represent continuous function and the other one can't. But it is equally clear that not *all* the cases are of this sort.

Wilden   Are we talking about syntax—ordering—or semantics and pragmatics—the exchange value and the use value of signs and signifiers? In what sense do you mean "more powerful"?

Fodor   We are talking about semantics. In one sort of system, the variables can range over continuous domains, whereas in the weaker system they do not. That is *one* kind of case, but certainly not the general case. The fact that quantificational logic, for example, is semantically richer than propositional logic has absolutely nothing to do with the continuity or discreteness of the state of affairs it represents.

Dütting   It is my feeling that concepts are growing in the sense that raw semantic features are added at each developmental stage, acquired by interaction with the world which then allows generalizations. In this sense, I agree with Wilden. Why shouldn't you call this a type of learning since it is not, strictly speaking, simple logic?

Fodor Semantic features, at least in any sense I know of, are just predicates. If that is correct, then the previous argument applies exactly, because precisely what you can't do is to introduce a predicate that is not definable in terms of the predicate previously available; that is the problem. That is why anybody who has ever talked about semantic features, including, by the way, people like Locke, has always assumed that the set of defining features is available to the organism from the beginning. The only disagreement is that Locke thinks that the set of primitive features is exhausted by the sensory features; but Locke has no theory about where these semantic features come from, other than that the sensorium of the organism is innately given. No one, to my knowledge, has ever proposed a non-nativist theory of where primitive features come from, and that strikes me as suggesting that there couldn't be such a theory.

Monod I would like first to find out if I understood what Fodor said, and also to ask some naive questions. I'm not sure whether or not I understood Fodor's point. If we take two systems, S_1 and S_2, one of which is more powerful than the other, then S_2 is able to express all the relationships in S_1, but S_1 cannot possibly do that for S_2, by definition. Therefore— and it is here that I am not quite clear about what Fodor meant—since S_2 cannot possibly have ever derived from S_1 and is not contained in S_1, then S_2 has to have stemmed from some sort of innate evidence. Actually Fodor didn't say this, but I think he did imply it. The point, it seems to me, is how can you generate S_2 since you cannot possibly derive it from S_1?

Fodor If you grant that then you have no need of my arguments. What I was arguing against was the position according to which you start at S_1 and by some computational procedure you get to S_2. If you grant that you can't do it, then there are various possibilities: God does it for you on Tuesdays, or you do it by falling on your head, or it is innate.

Monod This is where my rather naive proposal comes in. Of course one can show that one gets to a complete paradox because we can imagine that there may exist a system S_3 which may not have been invented yet, which would contain S_2

and S_1, and so on, indefinitely. As far as we know, there may be logicians a hundred years from now, and we can conclude that it is very probable that they will derive systems like that ad infinitum.

Fodor   There is a total misunderstanding between us, and it is undoubtedly my fault. I am not talking about the evolution of the discipline of logic; in other words, I am not talking about the situation in which a logician given only a logic of one formal character thinks about it for ten years and envisages a more powerful formalism. I am talking about the following problem in psychology: imagine that the conceptual system of an organism at a certain time, a certain stage of its development, is formalized as a logic. In other words, imagine that we know what its conceptual system looks like: we know what the elements are, we know about its semantics, and we know what combinatorial mechanisms are available. So that is what the organism looks like if it is represented as an algebra at the stage S_1; and then we find as an empirical fact that it gets to S_2. Now the question is: how did the organism get to S_2? Various things might have happened: maturational events might have occurred which have nothing to do with any learning process or any computational procedure. It is simply that its brain rewires itself, as I said, "on Tuesdays"; this is perfectly possible. Indeed, I think that this must be what happens in some cases of "cognitive development." But another possibility is this: some learning process takes place—this is the classic story—and this learning process essentially involves hypothesis formation and confirmation.

Monod   I think I agree with you there, and I don't want to distort what you said—on the contrary. You call S_1, S_2, S_3 "logics." Why don't you consider the possibility that in fact the word is not well applied? There is a substructure to all of this, which I would call elementary universal innate logic, and it is from this very simple elementary universal innate logic that you construct different combinatorial logics by using more and more sophisticated methods of derivation. In other words, the word "logic" does not really apply to these combinations.

Fodor   "Conceptual system" would do, or "the program of the organism at time T," but they are equally bad metaphors.

Monod   What I am in fact asking is whether you would agree that we use the word *logic* in two rather different meanings.

One of them serves to define those different mathematical or logical systems which can actually be constructed in more or less arbitrary ways, but which one cannot construct without always using the same innate elementary steps, which I would agree are innate. And these are the steps or the elements of logic that are postulated as innate by Descartes himself.

Chomsky I think that's what Fodor is saying: that the resources of all of the innumerable systems that ever may be invented by this genotype, those resources are already fixed.

Monod I will go even further by trying to begin to give an answer to the question that Piaget presented earlier: must we say that the whole of modern mathematics and classical mathematics and Euclidean mathematics is in fact innate? Of course not. But the logical elementary procedures that allow us to construct these mathematics, I would say, must be innate.

Piaget I think the question raised by Monod is very important; it essentially touches on the big difference between what I call structure, on the one hand—that is, what the subject is able to do and construct—and the thematization of this structure and its formalization, on the other. Then, even if one does not know logic and does not formalize the structures that one utilizes, these structures bring about constructions, each one raising new possibilities that lead you to the next step, where you use the new structures. The fact that you do not know how to formalize these structures if you are not a logician does not have the least importance when they are applied to experience or to the problem we are discussing here. Thus to say that the point of departure is innate (I have my doubts about that, because I am satisfied with just a functioning that is innate) does not have the least importance. The question is to know how a structure originates from another one, and in this case, observation shows at all levels, in the scientist as in the child, that any structure at all is going to create others by the possibilities it raises.

An example taken from the current history of mathematics is the manner in which the Bourbaki group have constructed their formalized, thematized structure, using instruments that were actually, without their being aware of it, correspondences of both morphisms and categories. The next step was to find out how they had constructed their structure and the instruments they had used as means of action, but not yet as formalization and thematization. From the discovery of their means of action, one passed to the next step, that is, the discovery of the theory of categories and morphisms.

Atran It must be admitted as historical fact that the theory of generative grammar owes its existence in part to investigations into the foundations of mathematics. Ever since Descartes, it has been realized by some that language possesses a truly "creative" aspect which allows infinite use of finite means. It is only in recent years, however, that the new understanding of recursive mechanisms and the nature of algorithms has made it possible to focus on this aspect and to attempt to formulate, in a precise way, the mechanisms that each language makes available for the free and unbounded use of language. In the early days of transformational syntax, the kernel structure, which formed part of the algebraic models of such mechanisms, was the subject of some speculation. The kernel comprised only one part of the model and had no priority over other syntactic, semantic, or phonological mechanisms in the actual production of sentences. More recently, speculation about the empirical nature of the kernel has been largely abandoned; it seems to have been more an interesting part of the particular model used than of the phenomena which that model attempted to describe.

Although algebraic linguistics has its origins in the work on mathematical foundation theory, their respective interests have markedly diverged. Most of the models available to linguistics are too powerful, in that they allow innumerable "imaginable" languages that are not human languages in a psychologically important sense. Consequently, the central task facing algebraic linguistics is to introduce formal constraints that would preclude the formulation of all but human languages. There is no reason to believe, however, that knowledge of the mechanisms of sensorimotor coordination or of any other cognitive domain could guide the linguist to a discovery of the appropriate restrictions.

Fodor's critique of current theories of learning, which admittedly "goes against the dominant thought of the last 300 years or so, in both psychology and philosophy," is a major challenge not only to the "compromise" between Chomsky and Piaget, but to the Piagetian system as a whole. This challenge will be taken up again in the course of the debate. Even though some of the implications of Fodor's radical innatism have been overlooked and some of his implicit assumptions have undergone undue distortion, the relevance of his argu-

ment is so compelling for anyone interested in the theories of language and learning that it is worthwhile to draw a better chart of the dividing lines between the main schools of thought represented here. Given the sharp demarcation that is now emerging between constructivism and innatism, it is legitimate to assimilate Fodor's and Chomsky's basic stands in order to see how they both contend with the line of reasoning shared by the Geneva school and Papert.

Piaget appropriately states that it is undeniable that new concepts and more powerful cognitive schemes are acquired *de facto* in the course of time both by individuals and by the scientific community at large. The history of mathematics (in Piaget's eyes, a privileged domain in the totality of human achievements) ostensibly consists of a progression of more and more powerful generalizations embedding previous conceptual frameworks as subdomains. Piaget purports to demonstrate that the historical development of mathematics and the ontogenesis of cognition are closely related, that they are isomorphic rather than simply analogous. If the acquisition of new concepts and of more powerful systems of logic cannot be accounted for in one domain, it has to be, on equal grounds, inexplicable or even impossible in the other: hence Piaget's *reductio ad absurdum* of Fodor's thesis. Monod sees a way out of this apparent paradox and argues for a theory of environmental enactment of innate combinatorial dispositions. New logics, he suggests, could be produced via new assemblies of innate building blocks of computational operations. However, Monod's position differs from Piaget's constructivism in one crucial respect (approaching therefore Fodor's innatism), namely: the rules of assembly can themselves be innate and selected by the environment. Granting this, the constructivist theory and Monod's proposition are indistinguishable from one another. However, Piaget flatly denies the innateness of the developmental cognitive pathways, leading to "more and more sophisticated methods of derivation," as Monod puts it. For Piaget, necessity and universality stem from constructive constraints, not out of the genetic endowment; they belong to the "structure of the environment" as much as they belong to the blueprint of the organism. At this precise point is the main, irreconcilable split between innatism and constructivism. Does it make any sense to attribute a certain structure to the environment? If the answer is yes, what is the meaning of the "assimilation" of such a structure by the organism? The nativist option is radical: the environment has its own structure,

*but all of the organism's structure comes from "within," from
the cognitive subject, and it grows according to the species-
specific, predetermined schedule, with the outer structures im-
pinging only after having been decoded by the organism's
selective filters. The environment (that is, observations, communicative exchanges, and information flows) can trigger or
delay, catalyze or suppress cognitive achievements, but it can
never mold them by transferring onto the organism some inherent structure of its own. Fodor goes so far as to suggest to
Piaget a pattern of explanation that is a sort of inverted image
of the one heretofore propounded by genetic epistemologists:
if the child indeed acquires more powerful cognitive structures,
then "Piaget must not, in point of logical necessity (not empirical necessity), be a non-nativist about changes of stage . . .
the change of stage cannot be a learning process." Piaget's rebuttal that his own theory cannot be "reduced" to a mere
theory of learning in its strict sense is legitimate, but it does
not answer the question.*

*The following chapters will bring further clarifications to
this controversy, although often obliquely. Before we join the
discussants again and give the floor to Piaget for a more detailed statement of how he sees the interrelations between
cognitive operations and linguistic structures, let us stop a
moment to briefly summarize Fodor's and Piaget's stands concerning the history of science and see where and why they
diverge. The Geneva school seems to be in a position to refute
Fodor's innatism only if the following arguments are simultaneously proved right, on logical (and not empirical) grounds:
(1) the growth of knowledge, as rationally reconstructed through
the history of science, and the ontogenesis of cognitive structures, as rationally reconstructed through experiments in child
psychology, are deeply analogous or even rigorously isomorphic; (2) the innatist approach is in principle (and not only
provisionally) incapable of accounting for the growth of scientific knowledge, and in particular for the development of
mathematical thought; (3) therefore, the innatist approach is
in principle inadequate to account for cognitive development.
This is the argumentation developed by Piaget in the present
chapter. There are a few points that should be briefly analyzed.
First of all, modern epistemology, through the work of Popper,
Kuhn, Lakatos, Elkana, Putnam, and many others, in spite of
internal differences and local disagreements, supports Fodor's
view of conceptual development as essentially based on "fixa-*

tion of beliefs," "nondemonstrative inference," and "hypothesis formation and confirmation."* *Scientific progress is far from being always a step-by-step improvement of conceptual power, whereby each new phase includes the previous ones as subdomains. Moreover, innatist stands are explicit in much of Popper's later writings, and the neo-Darwinian account of how hypotheses are tested and rejected through mutation-selection (the "amoeba to Einstein" argument) is recurrent in all his work. Beliefs and expectations, expressed in terms of hypotheses, are prior to observation; and as Fodor points out in his reply to Papert in this chapter, the fact that empirical evidence feeds back into the conceptual stock in terms of reassessing beliefs or selecting hypotheses leaves the problem of their origins unanswered. To consider that the stock of concepts, beliefs, and expectations is there from the start (that is, genetically fixed), is a strategy of inquiry that many modern epistemologists, and not only Fodor, support. The assumption expressed by proposition (2) is untenable. There seems to be no reason in principle to bar the way to a satisfactory innatist explanation of the growth of scientific knowledge, including mathematics.† Point (1) summarizes one of the most cherished lines of inquiry of the Geneva school and constitutes a sophisticated reedition of the belief that ontogenesis (individual cognitive development from birth to adulthood) parallels phylogenesis (historical development of scientific knowledge).‡ The backbone of Piaget's theory of cognitive epigenesis is made up of explanatory categories such as "equilibration," "self-organization," and "self-adjustment," concepts that betray the fundamental heuristic role played by evolutionary models. But such models are at root anti-Darwinian. The principle of selection, implying the sorting out under environmental constraints of particular processes already present from the start, cannot be accommodated into the Piagetian scheme. The parallel between ontogenesis and phylogenesis is highly questionable, but even granting that cognitive development and the historical progress of scientific domains can be matched to each other*

---

* The most representative work on this subject is the collective volume *Criticism and the Growth of Knowledge*, ed. I. Lakatos and A. Musgrave (Cambridge: Cambridge University Press, 1970).

† For a history of mathematics as seen in a non-Bourbakian and non-Piagetian framework, see I. Lakatos, *Proofs and Refutations: The Logic of Mathematical Discovery* (Cambridge: Cambridge University Press, 1976).

‡ See the remarks made by Mehler in his conclusion to this volume.

almost point to point, it still needs to be proved that a radical innatism and a mutation-selection hypothesis cannot in prin-ciple provide a joint pattern of explanation for both. There is no reason to exclude such possibilities on logical grounds. Thus, inference (3) eventually collapses even if (1) is held true.

Finally, Fod̥ ̃ in no way excludes on logical grounds that more powerf̥ ̃ ̃lisms or genuine novelty can be achieved by professio̥ ̃ ̃ ̃or by the child at certain stages). He only demo̥ ̃ ̃ ̃ical grounds, that this cannot be the ou̥ ̃ ̃ ̃cess whatsoever. If, for instance ̥ ̃ ̃ ̃main of the theory of sets, ̥ ̃ ̃in of the theor̥ ̃ ̃here has beer ̃ ̃im- pli̥ ̃ ̃cepts ir̥ ̃ ̃l than the ̥ ̃nate. This ̥ ̃tentially ate that con- before the . These prob- ̥d in Part II.

CHAPTER SEVEN

Language within Cognition

In addition to further clarifications on why Piaget thinks that language is "all of a piece with acquisitions made at the level of sensorimotor intelligence" and on why Chomsky persists in denying it, the present chapter introduces another relevant hypothesis. The new important piece of the Piagetian puzzle is what he calls the "semiotic function." The distinctive traits that Piaget attributes to the symbolic or semiotic function are as follows: its possibility of being integrated with schemes of assimilation pertaining to the sensorimotor level (the symbolic schemes can merge with a purely "active" logic); imitation (conceived as an intentional and adequate replay of the behavior of objects through bodily movements); interiorized imitation (engendering internal images and mental representations); evocative play; and delayed imitation (reenactment of schemes in the absence of the corresponding object). Piaget considers language to be a particular case of the semiotic function. At any rate, he stresses, the appearance of the semiotic function at about age 2 is the "context in which language begins." The synchronism between these two abilities, Piaget contends, "cannot just be the outcome of a random process."

Chomsky replies that although it is evident that the child is doing all sorts of other things and developing all sorts of other abilities that are synchronous with or immediately preceding the appearance of language, this does not prove that language in any way depends on them. Even the weaker hypothesis, that somehow (that is, by indirect connections) the appearance of sensorimotor or general cognitive abilities is a precondition for

163

language, is refuted by Chomsky in terms of Monod's criteria
(see Chapter 5). Indeed, blind children or even paraplegics show
no significant impairment in their linguistic performance.

Dan Sperber, a cognitive anthropologist, then goes as far as
denying the meaningfulness of the notion of a "semiotic function." Subsuming both language and, say, imitative play under
the heading of a semiotic function appears to Sperber no less
arbitrary than subsuming "all the protuberant parts of the body
. . . [under] a special branch of biology" (his argument is fully
developed in Chapter 11). A preliminary exchange between
David Premack and Chomsky in this chapter anticipates the
problems posed by experimental interspecies comparisons in
the domain of cognitive competence; such topics will be fully
discussed in Chapter 9.

Schemes of Action and Language Learning

Jean Piaget

I would like to explain in a few words why I believe language to
be all of a piece with acquisitions made at the level of sensorimotor intelligence. In fact, sensorimotor intelligence already
possesses a logic, but a logic in action, since there is not yet
either thought, representation, or language. But these actions
are coordinated according to a logic that already contains multiple structures, which will develop later in a spectacular manner. First there is, of course, a generalization of actions. For example, take a child in front of a hanging object: he tries to grasp
it and fails, but this makes the object swing; then he becomes
very interested, he continues to hit it to make it swing, and after
that, every time he sees a hanging object he pushes it and makes
it swing. Here is an act of generalization that obviously shows a
beginning of logical generalization or intelligence. The fundamental phenomenon at the level of this logic of actions is the
phenomenon of assimilation, and I will define assimilation as
*the integration of new objects or new situations and events into
previous schemes;* I define "scheme" as the result of those generalizations of which I just gave an example when talking about

the hanging object. These schemes of assimilation are somewhat like concepts, but of a practical kind. They are concepts in the sense that they imply comprehension (comprehension as opposed to extension, to use the French vocabulary of logic);* they are concepts of comprehension, that is, they bear on qualities and predicates, but there is no extension yet. In other words, the child recognizes a hanging object, this is comprehension, but he does not have the means of representing to himself the totality of hanging objects. And if there is no extension, it is for lack of evocation, for in order to be able to represent to oneself the totality of objects with the same quality, one must naturally have a capacity of evocation, in other words, representation. This will be the role of the symbolic or semiotic function, which will come into existence much later on, but which is not present at the beginning, hence the limitations of these practical concepts which I call schemes of assimilation.

In contrast, if there is not yet any extension, there are coordinations of schemes, and it is these coordinations that are going to constitute all of sensorimotor logic. Here is an example of coordination: let us imagine an object placed on another one; the relation "placed on" can be coordinated with the action of "pull," and the child will pull toward himself an object placed on the blanket in order to be able to reach it. As for the way to verify if there is indeed coordination, one needs only to place the object a bit farther than its base; if the child continues to pull, this means he did not understand at all and there is no coordination, whereas if he waits for the object to be on top and then pulls, there is indeed coordination. In addition, one finds in this sensorimotor logic all sorts of correspondences or practical morphisms, morphisms in the mathematical sense; one finds relationships of order, of course: the means precede the arrival at the goal, and they have to be ordered in a certain sequence; one finds interdependencies, which means that a scheme can be interlocked with another as a particular scheme or a subscheme. In short, one finds a structure that announces the structure of logic.

Let us return to my first problem: how will the subject pass from this logic of action to a conceptual logic? Conceptual logic is, for me, the logic that comprises representation and thought, thus concepts defined in extension and not only in comprehension. This passage to conceptual logic is essentially a trans-

* Translator's note: In French logico-mathematical terminology, the word "comprehension" is frequently used to convey the notion of "intension" as opposed to extension.

formation of assimilation. Up to now, assimilation was the integration of an object to a scheme of action; for example, this object can be grasped, that other object can be grasped, and so on —all the objects to be grasped are assimilated, incorporated into a scheme of action which is the action of grasping. Whereas the new form of assimilation that is going to develop and allow conceptual logic is an assimilation between objects, and no longer only between objects and a scheme of action; in other words, the objects will be directly assimilated to each other, which will permit extension. But this presupposes evocation, of course; for this, there must be a necessity to evoke, that is, to think of something that is not actually and perceptibly present. Now, where does this evocation come from? It is here that we see the formation of the symbolic or semiotic function I just mentioned.

The symbolic or semiotic function is formed during the second year and appears to me to be of great importance for our problem. Naturally, language is a particular case of this function, but it is *only* a particular case—particularly important, I do not deny—but a limited case within the totality of manifestations of the symbolic function.[1]

Chomsky perhaps will object that this is semantics, and that semantics is less interesting than syntax as far as our problem is concerned, but I claim that there is a syntax here, a logical syntax of course, since we are dealing with coordinations of schemes, coordinations playing a basic role in the logic to come. Imitation appears to me to play a very large role in the formation of the semiotic function. I mean by imitation not the imitation of a person—the child may not imitate someone's gesture— but the imitation of an object, that is, the copying by gestures of the characteristics of that object (for example, the object has a hole that must be enlarged, and this enlargement is imitated by the motion of opening and closing the mouth). This imitation plays a very large role because it can be motive at the outset, as in the case I have just mentioned, but it continues later on as an interiorized imitation. I claim that the mental image is nothing more, at the beginning, than an interiorized imitation that creates the ensuing representations.

Another form of symbolic function is symbolic play. There is, of course, some playing before the age we are concerned with; a baby plays very early, but his initial games are games involving the repetition of an action that is serious elsewhere. The child can exercise his ability, for example, by swinging a hanging object; then he simply plays with it for the pleasure of exercising his ability. This kind of play is a game of simple exercise or repetition in which there is as yet no symbolism, whereas at the level we are now examining, symbolic play begins, that is to say, play that evokes by means of gestures a situation that is not current, not perceptible.[2]

A third example that I would like to cite is deferred imitation; we call in psychology deferred imitation that which begins in the absence of the model.

Here is the context in which language begins. You can see my hypothesis: that the conditions of language are part of a vaster context, a context prepared by the various stages of sensorimotor intelligence. Six of these stages can be distinguished, which are notably different in terms of their successive acquisitions, but I found it sufficient to characterize sensorimotor logic in a rough way and then the appearance of this symbolic function. It is at this moment that language appears, and it can profit from all that was acquired by sensorimotor logic and by the symbolic function in the broad sense that I give to this term, of which language is only a particular case. I think, therefore, that there is a reason for this synchrony, and that there is a link between sensorimotor intelligence and language formation. I further believe that the formation of the symbolic function, which is a necessary derivative of sensorimotor intelligence, allows the acquisition of language, and this is the reason why, for my part, I do not see the necessity of attributing innateness to those structures (subject, predicate, relationships, and so on) which Chomsky calls the "fixed nucleus." I agree with Chomsky as to its necessity, but I do not believe in innateness given the fact that there is everything that is needed, it seems to me, in what I just said to explain its formation. In other words, and here I totally agree with Chomsky, language is a product of intelligence rather than intelligence being a product of language. These are the few facts I wanted to present to you for the discussion on the relationships between language and intelligence or thought.

One more point: this synchrony is meaningful as a synchronization because in the hypothesis of innateness, one does not see why language would not appear six months earlier or a year earlier or later. Why this synchronization? It does not appear to me to be the result of chance. Furthermore, if one wants to introduce innateness into language, why not introduce it into the symbolic function in its totality, and finally into anything that is general?

Discussion

Chomsky There is no question at all that the child is doing many things before he learns language. The question that has to be raised is what is the relationship between the things the child is doing prior to the development of language and the particular aspects of the structure of the system that develops. Now, Piaget's position is radically different from Inhelder's position, and I think that is an important point to keep in mind because a lot hinges on it. Inhelder's position is that certain aspects of the nature of language relate to constructions of sensorimotor intelligence or other elements of intellectual development. I have no argument with that position. But Piaget's position is much stronger: he feels that it is unnecessary to postulate an innate structure to account for the particular aspects of the semantic structure of language or, he would doubtless say, of its syntactic or its phonological structure (I'm just projecting from what he said).

Piaget I have already said that all behaviors contain something innate and something acquired, but that we do not know where the separation should be placed. I have never denied that there was something innate as far as functioning (but not structure) is concerned; no one has ever been able to make an intelligent man out of an idiot.

Chomsky I agree, but that is inconsistent with your other point of view, because if there are elements of innateness involved in the structure of language, then it is false that it is unnecessary to postulate innate structures. We can't have it both ways—it is one or the other. At any rate, let's put aside the issue of logic and turn to the concrete question at hand.

We agreed that a certain number of things happen prior to the development of language; we want to know what is the relationship, if any, between these things that happen prior to the development of language and the system that emerges. And just to correct something that I think has been a persistent misunderstanding throughout much of this discussion, it is not true that I (or linguists in general) have special reasons for wanting to exclude semantics or pragmatics or whatever from the discussion. In fact, the examples in my paper all have to do with semantics in some manner (see Chapter 1). So I wouldn't agree with Piaget's remark or other remarks made earlier that to me syntax is intrinsically more interesting than semantics. Nevertheless, there is one respect in which this is true, and it is an important point that has a bearing on this discussion: Why is syntax, or the areas of interaction between syntax and semantics, more interesting? The reason is that in these areas there are results, there are principles that have been proposed, and naturally the field becomes intellectually more interesting to the extent that one obtains results. There are other areas of semantics in which we would like to have results—we would like to have principles about the nature of the concepts of language— but unfortunately such results are lacking beyond the most superficial level. *It is for this reason, and this reason alone, that many areas of semantics are not of much interest to me in relation to this discussion.* Now, we might ask why we don't have results in these other areas. It is possible that there are no results to be had, that is, it may be that semantics, over much of its range, is just an uninteresting subject, that there is nothing deep to discover in it. Or it is possible that there is something deep to discover in it and we haven't yet found it. But whatever the answer might be, I think that for the purpose of this discussion we should be concerned with those aspects of language for which we possess significant results, that is, some nontrivial general principles of considerable empirical import and explanatory power that are not superficially obvious (I have mentioned a few principles that I think are of this sort and that involve syntax and semantics).

If we focus on the areas in which there are a certain number of results (and as I suggested earlier, what we have is a picture of an integrated system with some moderately complex principles that lead to rather surprising phenomena and offer an explanation of an interesting range of facts), the question we have to ask is as follows: how is the specific structure of this particular mental organ related to the things that the child is doing before the system emerges? There are a number of possible answers to this question: one answer might be that there is no relation; the fact that there is a temporal succession, a regular progression, is not very impressive. Sexual maturation follows the acquisition of language, but we would not conclude from that that the acquisition of language determines the form of sexual maturation, for instance. There are a number of reasons why things happen in a regular order, which may have to do with the development of dendrites, for example. Lots of strange things are happening in the brain between the ages of 2 and 4; there is a very rich growth of dendritic structures, and this may have something to do with the fact that language is developing. Lots of other things are happening about which very little is known, but certainly it would not be at all surprising if the regular progression that we observe relates to biological phenomena having to do with this extraordinarily complex physical organ about which remarkably little is known, perhaps because of its complexity. So the order of progression seems to me to show very little.

Let's return to our question: what is the relationship between these early achievements of the child and the specific structure of the system that emerges? One could, perhaps, eventually adopt, at least sometimes, Piaget's stronger position, namely, that all aspects of this mental organ are determined by the constructions of sensorimotor intelligence (this is what I take to be the meaning of the statement that it is unnecessary to postulate any specific forms of innateness). From my point of view, the arguments against that position are, for the moment, overwhelming; it seems to me that in all the cases in which there is a principle that seems plausible with regard to the nature of this system, that principle has no demonstrable (or even suggestive) relationship to the constructions of sensorimotor intelligence. Therefore, the strong form of the thesis seems to me unacceptable. I have no objection if someone proposes it as a hypothesis with regard to something that may be discovered in the future, but I see no force whatsoever to that hypothesis today. What about a weaker concept? Could it be, for example, that the constructions of sensorimotor intelligence are a necessary condition for the emergence of language? There are different ways for investigating that, for example the way Jacques Monod suggested earlier (see Chapter 5). If in fact the constructions of sensorimotor intelligence are a necessary condition for the development of language, then it should turn out that insofar as those sensorimotor constructions are impeded, the intelligence that leads to the acquisition of language should also be impeded; and if they are drastically reduced, language ought to be virtually eliminated. So if one adopts this weaker position (one that may be true, but I have no doctrine on the matter), which claims that the constructions of sensorimotor intelligence are a necessary condition for the acquisition of language, then one must make a certain number of conjectures and go on to investigate them, for example the case of paraplegics.

I don't know if anyone has investigated this, but my own prediction is that it would turn out that there is no relation whatsoever, or at best the most marginal relation, between even extreme defects that would make it virtually impossible for a child to develop and do all the various things that Piaget was discussing, and his acquisition of language. Again, I don't know if this has been studied systematically, but there are at least some suggestive results. For example, there have been numerous studies on the rate of acquisition of language in blind children, who have, if not one hundred percent reduction, at least a significant reduction in their capacity to develop constructions of sensorimotor intelligence, especially those constructions that involve the visual world. Yet in this case it appears that blind children acquire language more rapidly than sighted children, which isn't so surprising in certain respects because they are more dependent on it. In any event, there is no linguistic impairment in such cases, and if a child were paralyzed, for example, my prediction would be that it would have no noticeable effect on his language development. If this is true, it is hard to see in what sense one might maintain the weaker thesis, namely, that the constructions of sensorimotor intelligence are a necessary condition for the acquisition of language. However, this thesis might be true in a still weaker sense, as Fodor suggested earlier: it could turn out that the development of schemes of action has a *triggering function*. This is something that is understood in biology—for example, let's take something that is analogous in some way to the problem of acquisition of language: the Hubel-Wiesel structures, the structures that underlie visual space.* Since the studies begun ten or fifteen years ago on determining the reactions of single cells with microelectrodes, a vast amount of information has been accumulated about the highly specific structure of the most superficial processing in the visual cortex. One of the by-products of this work has been the theory that these structures degenerate; they simply don't function unless there is a certain triggering experience. In other words, unless the kitten has patterned stimulation presented to it at the appropriate age, these systems will simply degenerate—a neuronal degeneration takes place. Diffuse light will not suffice to keep the systems functioning, and naturally blindness will

---

* Editor's note: These experiments are summarized in the editorial comments at the beginning of Chapter 4.

destroy them very significantly. Of course, the pattern of stimulation does not determine what the system does; the latter is just going to do essentially what it is designed to do. Experience won't turn a kitten into an octopus. But the pattern of stimulation will determine the activation of the system. It's a little bit like turning on the ignition in an automobile: it's necessary that you turn the key for the car to run, but the structure of the internal combustion engine is not determined by this act. This structure will do what it has to do when you start it with the key. It is perfectly possible and conceivable that certain kinds of interaction with the external world serve a triggering function for the acquisition of language; this is a still weaker theory, in terms of what one might propose, and I have no idea whether it is true or false. There is no reason to believe it at the moment, to my knowledge. The only reason that has been proposed, as far as I can see, is the matter of orderly progression, which as I have said is not very important evidence in my view, and also the fact that there are some not very general similarities between some of the things that happen in language and some of the things that happen elsewhere: representation, schemata, embedding, temporal order, and so on. However, as soon as we look at any of the particular aspects of language, whether semantic or syntactic, about which there are any nontrivial results (again, by that I mean principles of some generality that have an explanatory power), it appears that there is no resemblance, no similarity, no relationship between these principles and any known constructions of sensorimotor intelligence. That is not to say that somebody may not discover such relationships someday; I just don't *see* any relationship, and to my knowledge, no one has offered a plausible case that there is such a relationship. I would say, then, that a rational approach would be to assume that in the domain where we have some nontrivial results concerning the structure of language, the principles of organization that determine the specific structures of language are simply part of the initial state of the organism. As far as we know these principles don't generalize, that is, there are no known analogues in other domains of intelligence (it is possible that such analogues are partially there, but this remains to be seen). I think that it is rational to draw this conclusion on the basis of what little we know. And furthermore, to pick up a remark of Fodor's, this is in a way the null hypothesis. Even if there were no evidence at all, I would say that it is a reasonable conjecture because it is very hard to imagine anything else. For example, if there are constructions of sensorimotor intelligence or particular concepts that develop in particular ways, then I would think, as Fodor argued, that *in those cases too we will just have to assume that the concepts themselves are essentially innately determined, since we know of no other way of accounting for their acquisition.* Thus the discovery (if it is a discovery; to me it seems to be) of what I regard as strong evidence that particular aspects of language are innately determined simply seems to me to be a confirmation of the null hypothesis, interesting but not surprising.

Inhelder   I would like to ask a somewhat more general question: do you think that severely handicapped people can develop an articulated language irrespective of any possible deficit of thought?

Chomsky   I think that can hardly be true because language is so deeply involved in many aspects of thinking. I don't think that thought is just a silent speech, but nevertheless, a substantial part of what we call thinking is simply linguistic manipulation, so if there is a severe deficit of language there will be a severe deficit of thought. I don't know what more can be said than that.

Fodor   I think there is a silly mistake that one keeps finding oneself making, that is, to cite the banality that language rests on conceptual development: nobody would learn the word "cat" unless he knows what a cat is. Clearly, you can't learn a word that expresses a concept that you don't have. The question is whether or not anything *deeper* than that is being asserted.

Even when Piaget says that he agrees with an interpretation like Chomsky's and mine—that language rests on intelligence rather than the other way around—I sense a pair of options *neither* of which I would like to take: it seems to me quite unlikely that there is any interesting sense in which language is a construction of our general principles of intelligence, and that is almost as unlikely as the theory that intelligence is a construction out of the general principles of language.

Chomsky   Such a view could only be held by a real Watsonian, somebody who believes that language is silent speech.

Papert   There are deaf children who don't speak, but who think pretty well.

Chomsky   I take it for granted that thinking is a domain that is quite different from language, even though language is used for the expression of thought, and for a good deal of thinking we really need the mediation of language.

Sperber There is one of Piaget's arguments which, it seems to me, Chomsky has not completely answered. If I understand Piaget correctly, he is not satisfied with noting the simultaneity of the appearance of language and that of symbolic activity. In his view, this simultaneity takes all its importance from the fact that *he sees in these two phenomena two aspects of the same semiotic function.* A correspondence *both* in time and in function has a stronger argumentative value than a single correspondence in time, which is the only one considered by Chomsky in his answer.

Having said that, even if Piaget's argument were thus given all its strength, it would still be too weak to be convincing. Both imitative activity and language activity have in common the fact of being expressive behaviors. But does this common point suffice to postulate a *common function,* the semiotic function? I think it is extremely doubtful. For example, no one is going to think that all the protuberant parts of the body—nose, ears, fingers, or whatever—have a common function and ought to constitute a special branch of biology. In the same way, the existence of an expressive characteristic common to both imitative behavior and language is not sufficient to justify the hypothesis of a semiotic function per se. It is, moreover, a hypothesis that I have attempted to refute more fully and directly in my book, *Rethinking Symbolism.*[1] Even if we were to give back to Piaget's argument all its initial strength, it would still not be strong enough.

Chomsky I agree with that, and I would go on to say that perhaps another way of putting it is that the semiotic function is something that I would have excluded from the discussion, in order to follow the ground rules that we should keep to areas where some nontrivial principles have been discovered. I don't think that this is the case for the semiotic function.

Papert I'd like to ask a simple question: weren't you taking rather lightly the coincidence referred to by Piaget when you said that it is not important that sexual function occurs later than language development? It comes not only at the same time but in rather close coordination.

Chomsky That's true of language too. According to what the experts tell me, it is apparently true that the onset of puberty marks the period at which the right hemisphere can really no longer take over the language functions in cases of severe aphasia. In other words, severe aphasia that destroys the language areas of the brain can be compensated for by the right hemisphere in a child, and when there is a serious lesion, complete destruction, or surgical elimination of the left hemisphere, the right hemisphere will take over up to a certain point, but not after puberty. So one might argue that there is really a deep connection.

Papert But what do you think of Hermine Sinclair's claim that there is really a very close parallelism between the development of syntactic complexity and that of intelligence?[2] For example, the severely mentally defective children she studied, who were many years late in developing the concept of conservation (and some of them never developed it), never used the passive construction either. Of course, you could say that they never had any reasons to use passive constructions because their very limited kind of mental capacity didn't require it. Nevertheless, this particular construction, which I suppose you would call a very central rule of transformation, seems to be delayed in precisely those cases in which the development not of sensorimotor intelligence perhaps, but of typical Piagetian operations, is also delayed.

Chomsky I haven't heard about that result, but it does surprise me a little because it has been claimed in the literature that even subjects affected by Down's syndrome use rules like passive transformation. What has been found over and over is that there seems to be a remarkable lack of correlation between the development of basic structural features of language and even very severe impairments of other kinds of intellectual ability. But quite apart from that, I would be inclined to think, even without any investigation, that there would be a correlation between linguistic performance and intelligence; people who are intelligent use language much better than other people most of the time. They even may know more about language; thus when we talk about a fixed steady state, which is of course idealized, it may very well be (and in fact there is some evidence) that the steady state attained is rather different among people of different educational level, even if there is no reason to believe that there is a difference in intelligence. I will give you an example: Carol Chomsky did some work on the acquisition of moderately complex linguistic structures,[3] as in sentences like "I asked him what to read" and "I told him what to read." If I say "I asked him what to read" then *I* am doing the reading; if I say "I told him what to read" then *he* is doing the reading. This is a case where there are some lower-order general principles that account for differences in interpretation. She discovered that principles of this kind apparently develop in a more or less regular order, approximately between ages 5 and 10. That was an interesting discovery. Zella Luria had some of her students replicate this work, and one of them discovered that the students in the class where the material was being presented were all nodding their heads at the right point when the examples were discussed, but then when she talked to them later, a number of them didn't understand what was being discussed; they were just nodding their heads because they didn't want to appear stupid. It turned out that many of them didn't understand the examples. She then did a study on adults to find out whether they were in fact making these distinctions, and it turned out that there were a remarkable number of adults, at least on the basis of the most sophisticated tests they could devise, who were not making these distinctions.[4] This is very hard for me to believe, and I must say that there may even be some data that are inconsistent with it. For example, I've been told that someone did an experiment with college students of two different ages, and it turned out that there was a considerable increase in the performance level when these distinctions were used, which is hard to reconcile with the belief that a fixed percentage of subjects don't understand the distinction at all. All of this is extremely contradictory, and one could even conclude that people just have a hard time passing such tests.

In any event, it is entirely conceivable that some complex structures just aren't developed by a large number of people, perhaps because the degree of stimulation in their external environment isn't sufficient for them to develop. That wouldn't be too surprising. If we really look into the details of the development of this particular system we might find successive thresholds of this kind, but I would expect to find exactly the same thing in the study of any physical organ. The way in which an organ develops is going to depend on all sorts of factors in the environment, but I think what we would expect to find, and do find over and over again, is that the fundamental organizing properties, the general features, simply are not up for grabs but rather are fixed; and I think I would want to go along with Fodor in saying that the specific properties are also fixed.

Premack On the basis of Chomsky's remarks there seem to be at least two varieties of innatism, one in which the factors that participate in language owe a great deal to genes but are nonetheless general—a part of intelligence at large—and a second in which the debt to the genes is equally large, but the factor is special to language. My impression is that Chomsky dismisses the first alternative too quickly. He talks of the language organ and rules out certain results that could support the first position on the grounds that they are trivial. I am not sure what Chomsky means by "nontrivial results," but I think that, for example, the relation that Piaget was talking about between representational competence and language can be said to support the first position. Thus, for example, one can show by very direct procedure whether or not such competence is present, whether or not the memory system possesses a certain quality, whether or not the internal representation of which the memory system is capable has such and such a quality; one can then show that unless these conditions are met in a given species, it is not possible to inculcate a lexicon. This does not tell us what we would like to know, namely how the memory system is organized, but it is a first step and, I think, a nontrivial one; it is a relation between a kind of competence that is very basic to language, involving the whole task of representation and the various forms it takes, and the fact that there can or cannot be a lexical function in the series.

One can pursue this issue further by a slightly more complicated demonstration. If you can find evidence for causal analysis in a species, then you can find types of sentences that use causal notions. But if you cannot find evidence for causal analysis in the species, then it does not seem possible to find ways of instilling this in the expressive behavior of the species.

Chomsky This is a little bit like Fodor's point that if you don't know what a cat is, you don't know the meaning of the word "cat."

Premack I think that is banal, and that this is perhaps less so. You can use entirely nonverbal evidence to raise the question: is this a species that engages in causal inference?

Chomsky And if it is not, you certainly won't have the concept of cause in the language, but that is like saying that if a person is color-blind, he is not going to use color terms properly.

Premack Fine, but if the semantic concepts are not present, then we won't find them in the language—that's part of the argument.

Chomsky   Yes, but it isn't really interesting. It is certainly true that if a subspecies of humans develops in a remote place, let's say in New Guinea, and they are color-blind, we wouldn't be surprised to discover that they don't have color words in their language. Similarly, if through some mutation another subspecies of humans developed who were causality-blind— who couldn't perceive causality—then (assuming they could survive somehow) we would know that they would not have causal notions in their language. But I think that the first part of Premack's remark is very much to the point, and I don't disagree with it. Let's put aside the word "trivial"; I know that it may sound contentious (I meant it in a technical sense and nothing else). What I mean by a nontrivial result is one that has some explanatory force over a range of empirical facts and that can be refuted. Now, I see nothing of that nature when we talk about matters like the representing function; I don't know how to refute it, or how to say what it is, although I agree that something like that must exist. But don't forget that I do not contend that every aspect of what we call language has, so to speak, a specific box in the brain, which is used just for that aspect; on the contrary, I have argued just the opposite for years and years. George Miller and I did some work years ago in which we tried to explain acceptability judgments in terms of properties of the memory system;[5] that study may be right or wrong, but its purpose was to try to show how a whole variety of linguistic judgments can be explained in terms of independent properties of memory. We even tried to argue that the reason we have a transformational grammar is related to the fact that the system of memory includes long-term memory and short-term memory, and that this system is far from unreasonable. Whatever one may think of that argument, it still proves that I am ready to admit that some aspects of language are related to some aspect or other of the rest of intelligence. That will certainly prove to be true.

But I will return to what I said before: that in the area of trivial or nontrivial results—in the technical sense—I know of no serious analogues concerning language, and furthermore, I don't expect to find them. My only doctrine on this subject is that we must study language with the same approach that we take toward the problems of natural science, and nothing more. It seems to me that if we study language in this manner, without dogmatism, then we will see that at this stage of investigation *there exist, at least, nontrivial results concerning the nature of language and that they have no analogue elsewhere,* which, in fact, is not at all surprising.

Premack Assume for the moment you were shown by non-verbal research procedures the richness of internal representation, the extent of power or weakness of the representations that the species has stored, and that you were then fairly well able to predict the power of the word, that is, the extent to which the word can serve as an information retrieval device. If there isn't good storage in the first place, it would be unreasonable to anticipate that the word can retrieve very much information.

Chomsky I agree with that, but it seems to me like the color-blindness argument.

Premack This seems to me to go beyond the problem of knowing whether the concept is there as a precondition for acquiring a label for the concept. It goes without saying that this is so. Nevertheless, it seems to me that the whole matter of conceptual structure is more important to the argument for general factors than you are willing to admit.

Another point: you said that there is no hope for the possibility that one will find in nonlinguistic domains the kind of formal properties one finds in language . . .

Chomsky I didn't say that; I said that I didn't *see* any hope for that.

Premack That seems to me a very premature judgment. I agree with you when you say that there is no nontrivial evidence from nonlinguistic domains in regard to formal structures, but precisely because there isn't any, because the kind of investigation that one needs in order to make the decision is not at hand, I think it is premature to conclude that the formal structures one knows to exist in language will not be found elsewhere, in another species or perhaps even in other human domains. Let's wait and see.

Chomsky On this point I agree with Premack. I think he is right in talking about two different problems that enter into this whole innateness controversy. The first is the question of the genetic determination of structures (for me, at least, this point is established beyond any reasonable question, although of course it is an empirical issue). The second problem concerns specificity. This is an interesting question, and the right way to investigate it is exactly the way Premack describes. If someone thinks that there are general mechanisms of that sort, then the thing to do (and I really urge this) is to take some other cognitive domain, delimit it in any way you like, and try to study its structure in the same way you study language, in the sort of naive way which to me is simply normal scientific procedure, and which should not be glorified with fancy terms. In other words, one should *try to characterize the final state attained, particularly if it is a steady state and therefore likely to show something interesting about the species, and then try to formulate hypotheses from the steady state attained about the properties that must have been necessary to account for its attainment on the basis of experience.* Trying out that kind of inquiry, we would then have other information about a new S_0 and would compare that with the S_0 that we have for language. I don't see any particular reason to expect the same result, but if that happens, I would be very pleased.

Premack   That is one way to proceed; the other way is to do a cross-species study.

Monod   I would like to ask a question relating to cross-species investigation; it relates to what Piaget said earlier. I suspect that in listening to Piaget, Premack with his experience with young chimpanzees must have recognized many phenomena that he has seen developing in the young chimpanzee. Now, if I understood him correctly, Piaget almost equated the development in the child of these analogous computational capacities with the child's capacity to express some of the results of this computation in the form of language. The point is that in Premack's experience, from what I know of his work, there are many of these types of analogous computational capacities that his little ape Sarah does, yet she doesn't speak. Premack has succeeded in making her do something that is like speech, but it is certain that she doesn't do anything like that spontaneously. She got there thanks to Premack, but there is no kind of spontaneity in the development of this capacity in the chimpanzee.

Toulmin   What counts as spontaneity? If you look at the Gardners' work,[6] you find a great deal of spontaneity.

Monod   Let's put it like this: does Premack recognize traits of Sarah in Piaget's children? I, for one, certainly do.

Premack   Monod's point is very well taken, and the mystery that it raises might be put this way: what language-like competence does the ape have before man has intervened? We find considerable evidence for representational capacity, for the ape's ability to use one thing to stand for another, and even some evidence for spontaneous symbolization. But we find very little of the latter, and it is troublesome for me to find the evidence for the existence of a capacity along with so little evidence for the use of the capacity. I have always assumed that an integral part of a capacity is a disposition to use the capacity.

Monod   A man named Descartes said that.

Premack   It is not impossible that apes possess a level of symbolization the extent of which remains to be discovered. So whether there is a real mystery remains to be found out, and we are looking at that now. The ape has very well developed computational capacities that appear to make little connection with its communicative capacities—at least this is so if one believes that its natural communication is limited to affective states. We are now doing experiments which fortunately do not require us to be able to say how they communicate with one another in order to specify what kind and complexity of information they may be able to communicate. There may turn out to be a more important linkage between computational and communicative capacities than we thought.

Chomsky   I find this kind of work fascinating, and I think that what they are going to discover (and have already discovered in part) is a high order of intelligent behavior on the part of apes involving social communication, sensorimotor constructions, notions of causality, and so on. But what they are not going to discover is the possibility of imposing on that species, however hard they try, a system that has *any* of the properties of language in the domain that I'm talking about, that is, in the domain where there are nontrivial results. I don't expect that they are going to be able to impose on that species a system that has, for example, recursive rules meeting the condition of structure dependence (to take the most simple property of human language).*

Let me just mention another of Premack's findings that I find very fascinating. Glass, Premack, and Gazzaniga have found something that I would have certainly predicted or would have liked to find true: they have discovered that in

* Editor's note: The capacity of apes to handle structure-dependent transformations is again brought into focus by Putnam in Chapter 14 and discussed further by Chomsky in his reply to Putnam (Chapter 15).

the case of severe global aphasics (people who apparently have almost total destruction of the physical basis for language capacity) they were able by using Premack's techniques to induce a system very much like the one that the chimpanzee acquired.[7] Some other studies that I know of have suggested the same thing.[8] I think that is the kind of result one would expect, because what it means is that a chimpanzee is very smart and has all kinds of sensorimotor constructions (causality, representational functions, semiotic functions, and so forth), but one thing is missing: that little part of the left hemisphere that is responsible for the very specific structures of human language. That is exactly what ought to come out if the specific structures of human language are genetically determined, and therefore I would take it to be further evidence that this is the case. This additional evidence also refutes the belief that the emergence of these specific structures is in any way connected with—and certainly not a product of—sensorimotor intelligence.

An interesting remark was made in the preceding discussion, first expressed rather bluntly by Fodor, then taken up by Chomsky. When asserting that language depends on other cognitive or sensorimotor abilities, one should be careful to avoid a truism: as Fodor says straightforwardly, "Nobody would learn the word 'cat' unless he knows what a cat is." In Chomsky's terms, if a species (or an idealized human tribe) is colorblind, we will certainly not find the notion of certain colors in its expressive repertoire. This is surely true, but trivial. Premack, who demonstrates that chimpanzees are able to make causal inferences (see his presentation in Chapter 9) and that they are able to manipulate successfully an abstract causal connective, tends to see the truism as not so trivial, after all. What puzzles Premack is the relationship, if any, between a capacity and the propensity to use that capacity; this is what Monod calls the dilemma of Descartes. Reformulated in this way (in what way the actual use of a concept depends on the "possession" of it), the truism becomes much more problematic. Subtler versions of this "truism" will be presented and discussed in Chapter 9 and in Part II.

Finally, it should be stressed that Monod asks a question that has puzzled many of us for some time: does the astounding competence shown by chimpanzees in the domain of symbolic languages (sign language in the case of the Gardners, the use of abstract token symbols in the case of Premack) corre-

spond to human linguistic competence? Chomsky answers flatly: no. The evidence he produces derives from Premack's own studies on human subjects affected by global aphasia. Given that (1) these subjects have suffered vast brain damage extending over practically the entire speech area, and (2) they are nonetheless capable of learning to use efficiently a symbolic language analogous to the one Premack has taught to his chimpanzees, Chomsky therefore concludes that "real" human language and these other abilities are distinct and independent. The absence of "that little piece of the left hemisphere" renders a subject incapable of producing a language resembling human language. A chimpanzee and a global aphasic can do marvelous things—they can have representational abilities, handle complex strings of symbols, engage in causality judgments—but they just cannot speak.

The cogency of Chomsky's argument is indeed impressive. In the course of the debate this style of explanation will, however, be challenged again and again.

The next chapter deals precisely with the structure of the brain and the logic of its developmental mechanisms.

CHAPTER EIGHT

Properties of the Neuronal Network

That the linguistic structures underlying "all humanly accessible grammars" are in the ultimate analysis grounded upon specialized brain structures is something that Chomsky considers as a "refutable, empirical hypothesis" (see Chapter 2). He also contends that language should be studied with the same "unprejudiced" methods that biologists adopt in studying the liver or the heart. Therefore, it is of special relevance to the present debate that a molecular neurobiologist such as Jean-Pierre Changeux be given the floor and asked to consider in some detail the perspectives of innatism and constructivism as seen from his point of view. Changeux, Danchin, and Courrège have developed one of the most complete and original theories now in existence on the growth and development of neuronal networks. As I have already emphasized (see my editorial comments in Chapter 4), the pivotal concept of their theory is that of "selective stabilization of the developing synapses by functioning." Closely dependent on the concept of a "genetic envelope," the notion of selective stabilization leaves ample room for neuronal plasticity, thereby conciliating genetic determinism and individual variability.

Changeux starts by presenting a simple "fact": the specificity of all neuronal contacts cannot possibly be dictated by the genes. A simple calculation of the amount of information theoretically required to spell out each of the 10^{14} synapses shows that the genome of a mammalian species, let alone man, can contain only a fraction of this information. What is dictated by the genes is the "genetic envelope," that is, a range of

184

possibilities, a class of "potentially accessible structures" plus a detailed schedule concerning the successive degrees of connectivity of the system as a whole. This is a strategy of minimization, allowing for a maximum of useful information with a minimum of genes. Changeux's model, allowing for both determinism and plasticity, is put forward as a "compromise" between innatism and constructivism.

Piaget, as we will see in his "Afterthoughts" (Chapter 13), is wholeheartedly in favor of Changeux's model. In the course of the following chapters, we will see that there are, nonetheless, many controversial points clustered around this compromise.

Genetic Determinism and Epigenesis of the Neuronal Network: Is There a Biological Compromise between Chomsky and Piaget?

Jean-Pierre Changeux

It is a difficult position for a neurobiologist to present facts or interpretations from his own field of research in the exceptional context of an encounter between Chomsky and Piaget. These two eminent scholars have devoted years to the two most complex and elaborate behavioral abilities of humans: cognition and language. Since my own experience in this domain is negligible, I will limit my presentation to a few examples concerning the biology of the brain and of the peripheral nervous system in vertebrates.

It is hoped that despite their simplicity, these examples might be of some help in the understanding of sophisticated behavioral processes. First of all, they might constitute elements of more complex systems that govern these processes. It is well accepted that the chemical nature of the genes and their expression in man is the same as that in colibacillus; likewise, one cannot escape the fact that human brain is made up of neurons as in the nervous system of other organisms, and that the properties of these neurons exert rigid constraints on all its performances. Another often mentioned reason to turn to simple systems is that they can lead to "structural analogies" with more complex systems. To look for a "structural convergence," however, may easily lead to a blind alley. To cite one example among many: nothing came out of the attempts to find fundamental relationships between gene coding and information storage in the brain.

In this respect, one should be aware of the danger, emphasized by Louis Althusser, of establishing a relationship of "exploitation" of one discipline by another. In both Piaget's and Chomsky's introductory papers (Chapter 1), a tendency exists to exploit biology in favor of psychology and linguistics. It is easy to say that human language is a genetically determined faculty; it is certainly much less easy for the biologist to demonstrate the genetic determinism of the simplest behaviorial ability. The difficulty becomes even greater when one has to offer explanations for the genetic determinism of brain connectivity even in a small mammal like a mouse or a cat. As a neurobiologist, I agree entirely with Chomsky when he says that the development of language acquisition should be studied like the development of any other physical organ. But it is going too far to say, as he does in the discussion (see Chapter 2), that the environment does not introduce any more complexity into the brain than into any other physical organs. The metaphor brain-liver may be useful for an audience of linguists, but it is misleading for psychologists or biologists. Indeed, the neuron as a cell is far more complex than a hepatocyte. A neuron can often communicate with several thousand other cells, which obviously a hepatocyte cannot do. The essential functions of the nervous system, and in particular those relevant to learning, are determined by these intercellular relationships.

This tendency to exploit biology is also found in Piaget's paper. The distinction between "general heredity" and "specific heredity" or the mutations "particular to the human species" are concepts that have no evident biological signification, despite the fact that "mutation" and "heredity" are well-defined biological concepts. In a more general manner, even though biological metaphors are sometimes useful, they rapidly become dangerous. One should avoid falling into what I would call "biologism"; rather, one should deal first with the complexity of the nervous system and look for authentic biological explanations (instead of abusing the currently available ones).

Complexity of the Functional Organization of the Central Nervous System in Vertebrates

When one reads in Piaget's paper that "the functioning of intelligence alone is hereditary and creates structures only through an organization of successive actions performed on objects," one realizes that the distinction is not made explicit between three evident but fundamental levels: (1) *anatomy*, the neuronal network; (2) *activity*, the train of impulses that travel in some particular circuits of the neuronal network either spontaneously or as a consequence of an interaction with the environment; and (3) *behavior*, the operations performed by the organism on the environment consecutive to a particular activity.

Language and cognition are mostly described and studied, as operations of behavior, in terms of a set of "visible relations," as Maurice Godelier would say, between organism and environment. Despite its splendid organization, the human nervous system is rarely regarded by the linguist or the psychologist with any more curiosity than he would give to a *black box*, and only the rules of input-output relationships are described in the normal adult or in the course of development. In fact, there exists an underlying organization on the basis of which this apparent organization has to be explained, and this organization lies in (1) the anatomy of the relevant neuronal circuits, (2) the activity of these circuits, and (3) the signals that the organism receives by its sense organs. A satisfactory description, and therefore an explanation, of any behavioral act should by obligation include these three underlying levels of organization, and in particular the first two. In principle, one should be able to compute any behavioral act from the knowledge of the anatomy, the activity, and the signals that trigger it. This is indeed a formidable task in practice, but *a priori* possible in theory, and it is actually becoming successful with some simple (or simplified) systems.

The powerful and inescapable constraints imposed by anatomy and activity on behavior make hazardous any movement in the opposite direction that would aim to infer the underlying organization—anatomy, activity, and genetic determinism—of behavior. As pointed out by Chomsky, "Part of the intellectual fascination of the study of language is that it is necessary to devise complex arguments to overcome the fact that direct experimentation is rarely possible"; fascination for some, deception for others. Is this why the words "infer" and "inference" occur frequently in Chomsky's paper? In the past decades, this inductive method has appeared to be rather unsuccessful in the neurosciences.

The reasons for the limited success of such inferences lie basically in the anatomical organization of the nervous system. Apparently simple operations of behavior, such as the movements of the eye or the killing of a mouse by a cat, in fact involve the recruitment of a large number of neurons (thousands, even millions) from many different areas of the brain. In addition, no simple rule appears to exist in the macroscopic and histological organization of such centers in the brain. Why should there be any logic, for instance, in the presence and the role of subcortical structures in highly "corticalized" mammals, except for the very fact that these structures existed in the brain of more primitive animals from which they evolved? A given behavioral act may indeed engage, *simultaneously* and *necessarily*, groups of neurons which appeared at different periods in the evolution of vertebrates. The stabilization or selection of these centers had its own logic at the time they were formed. But this logic becomes masked by millions of years of history that followed under the influence of eminently variable ecological conditions. To some extent, the "arbitrary nature" of the anatomy reflects the historical variability of the environment. Anatomy cannot be inferred from anything other than its direct investigation.

At the level of the cell, simple and general rules of architecture appear, however: for example, the subdivision of the neuron into soma, axonic and dendritic prolongations; the manner in which it interacts with other cell bodies through synaptic contacts; the convergence or divergence of nerve terminals on or from a given cell body; and the establishment of loops making possible the Piagetian reflectings *(refléchissements)* and the setting of correspondence between levels *(mise en correspondance de niveaux)*. This is why, in our experimental and theoretical work, we have selected the cell as the basic level for the study of the nervous system. The cell is, in fact, located at the point of convergence of two lines of research: that of the molecular biologist, who considers it as a system of macromolecules in interaction, and that of the neurobiologist and the embryologist who, on the contrary, see it as the basic unit from which the organ or the organism is constructed.

In any case, at the starting point of any experimental approach to a biological phenomenon, a critical choice exists: It is that of the *level of organization* which will serve as a reference in a qualitative "cleavage" of the biological object. Such cleavage should lead to the delimitation of its constitutive elements, to the definition of rules of organization and rules of interaction in a form that is simplified but sufficient to explain the global functioning.

GENETIC DETERMINISM OF THE FUNCTIONAL ORGANIZATION OF THE CENTRAL NERVOUS SYSTEM

Piaget, criticizing the preformationist attitude, writes about the cognitive functioning of the child: "If mathematics were preformed, this would mean that a baby at birth would already possess virtually everything that Galois, Cantor, Hilbert, Bourbaki, or MacLane have since been able to realize. And since the child is himself a consequence, one would have to go back as far as protozoa and viruses to locate the seat of 'the set of all possibilities' " (see Chapter 1). Indeed, it is the task of the biologist who accepts that the major patterns of functional organization of the brain are genetically determined to find an explanation, or at least plausible models, for this determinism.

Darwin writes that "heredity is the law." The development of the nervous system is subject to it, as is the development of the whole organism, and it is the task of anatomists and of ethologists to look for its invariance through generations, whatever the environment.

The only exceptions to this stability are variations of the genome, which are spontaneous and rare—mutations whose evolution can be followed in the course of experiments on hybridization. It is striking that one of the first demonstrations of Mendelian laws in mice was established by Yerkes at the beginning of the century with a behavioral mutant: the "dancing mouse," which appeared in the Middle Ages due to Chinese breeders.[1] In man, to quote a well-documented example, the family heredity of a manic-depressive psychosis follows that of a dominant gene linked to the X chromosome.

Anatomical or functional alterations, sometimes very discrete, underly the hereditary variations of behavior. Thus, Sidman has recognized that the motor incoordination that accompanies the "staggerer" mutation in the mouse corresponds to the loss of a main category of synapses in the cerebellum.[2] The connectional organization of the nervous system down to the synaptic level is thus subjected to the omnipotence of the genes.

If one accepts this point of view, a new difficulty arises. If the functional organization of the nervous system, down to its slightest details, is subject to such a strict genetic determinism, is there a sufficient number of genes in the chromosomal apparatus to account for it?

The human body has about 200 different cell types: neurons, muscle cells, gland cells, and so on. In the human brain there are more than 10^{10} neurons, and about 10^{14} or more synapses. Each one of these neurons or synapses is engaged in a characteristic function. A high degree of cross-linking exists between cell bodies organized in well-defined patterns. To this extreme complexity and to these large numbers one classically opposes the small amount of genetic information available in the nucleus of the egg: 3.0×10^{-6} µg of DNA in the nucleus of the human spermatozoon; 6.0 µg in the nucleus of a somatic cell like a liver cell or a fertilized egg; approximately the same quantity, in the same cells, in the cow, the mouse, or the chimpanzee. If one takes for the definition of a gene the amount of DNA necessary to code for a protein of molecular weight 100,000, that makes about one million genes. In fact, a large fraction of chromosomal DNA, about 40 percent, exhibits repeated sequences (that is, seems to be redundant), and the number of "true" structural genes coding for proteins is estimated to be in the range of 10,000 to 30,000. The function of the rest of the DNA, redundant or not, is not known but is thought to consist of regulatory genes.

In any event, the formidable structural complexity of the central nervous system stands in contrast with a very small amount of coding information. How, from such a limited number of genes, can one generate the complexity of the brain?

Setting Up Neuronal Somas The setting up of neuronal somas is a process of embryonic development. Following Morgan, Jacob, and Monod, and others, the differentiation of the diverse classes of cells from the egg can be viewed as a selective regulation of gene activity. For instance, Kaufman[3] and Wolpert[4] have built models of gene regulation that show how one can create significant diversity from a limited number of genes and with a limited number of signals. The principle is that at any stage of its development each embryonic cell has very few alternative courses open to it. The choice between these alternatives can be guided by simple yes/no signals which might vary, for instance, with the *position* of the cell in the embryo, its past history, and so on. The essential point is that the choice, once made, will control what option becomes available for the next decision. Single genes might therefore determine a decision as important as an imaginal disk of drosophila becoming an antenna or a leg (the mutation *Aristopedia* causes a fruit fly to grow a leg where there should have been an antenna). Starting from a sequential expression of genes and from simple combinations one can generate an enormous complexity. One can observe here a formal analogy with linguistics, which has often been pointed out by molecular biologists. The rules might be very simple: for instance, twenty yes/no signals can generate in such a way 2^{20} (that is, one million) different messages, hence one million ways to assign the final state to be reached. This is just a very theoretical example and still a model; at present, the signals involved in embryonic cell-to-cell communication are not known. Nevertheless, this schema is plausible and could account for the positioning of the main categories of neuronal somas, the various areas and centers of the brain.

Development of Nerve Connections   There is every reason to think that the differentiation and the positioning of the principal categories of neurons do not differ significantly from those of the 200 other cell types of the organism. However, the final network, as mentioned previously, is particular to the nervous system and is of a higher order of complexity. How do the 60,000 fibers of the optic nerve of the frog reach their respective targets in the optic tectum? More than ever, the scarcity of genes makes itself cruelly felt; it singularly limits the number of models that come to mind to explain a process which, we must admit, escapes us for the time being.

Several hypotheses have nevertheless been proposed: according to Sperry,[5] nerve fibers in the process of growth bear chemical marks that are complementary to those of their neuronal targets. The two partners recognize each other and assemble themselves with a selectivity that depends strictly on the capacity for adhesiveness existing between cell surfaces.

According to Jacobson[6] and Gaze,[7] it is the differential growth of nerve fibers that brings about the appearance of an order. Reaching the target neurons at different moments, they "number" them in sequential order.

The little that we know about synaptic development indicates that each of these hypotheses is partly true. There is no doubt that nerve endings in the process of growth must recognize their targets according to their cell surfaces, but probably not with the degree of selectivity that Sperry's hypothesis implies.

A third mechanism has, since Ramon y Cajal and Marinesco,[8] retained the attention of generations of neurobiologists. In one way or another, the state of activity of the developing nervous system participates in the setting up of the final connectivity. This last hypothesis led to some research that I performed in close collaboration with Philippe Courrège and Antoine Danchin.[9] I will give only a very brief summary of this work here.

The first series of facts which must be taken into account, and which has already been mentioned, concerns the genetic determinism of the nervous system. This determinism is almost absolute in a small invertebrate, a nematode or a crustacean; it is less strict in the brain of a vertebrate. Let us examine in detail the arborization of a given neuron from the adult brain of genetically identical individuals, for example, from a parthenogenetic fish. One will find that these cells are "almost" superimposable, but not "exactly" so. As Cyrus Levinthal pointed out,[10] a minor but significant fluctuation manifests itself at the level of the precise number of synaptic contacts, the level of the orientation of axons or of dendrites. However, this fluctuation manifests itself only in a very narrow area; it is limited by a "genetic envelope."

In the second place, the first synaptic contacts are not stable in the course of their formation. A *labile* state precedes the rigid state of the adult.

In the third place, spontaneous regressive phenomena are often observed in the course of development. Ramon y Cajal[11] noted that in Purkinje cells of the cerebellum of the newborn infant, the axon presents twenty to twenty-four collateral branches; at the age of 2 months, only four or five of them remain. Similarly, in the first stages of innervation of striated muscle, each muscle fiber receives several functional and redundant nerve endings; only one of them persists in the adult. In a different field, Jacques Mehler emphasized the fact that the development of certain perceptive and cognitive processes in man is accompanied by a spontaneous loss of competence.[12]

The fourth and last point of these biological premises, and the most important one, concerns the effect of the environment on certain sensory areas of the cerebral cortex. As shown by Hubel and Wiesel,[13] Barlow,[14] or Michel Imbert,[15] the neurons of the visual cortex area of the cat have a functional specificity. For instance, they respond to signals coming from one or both eyes, or to shining points moving about the visual field, with a privileged orientation. It is now well established that an incomplete visual experience interferes with the development of this specificity.

"Selective Stabilization" of Synapses as a "Gene-saving"

Mechanism Considering these biological premises, several general attitudes are possible. According to one interpretation, interaction with the external world does not enrich the system in any significant way; its action would be limited to triggering preestablished programs. It would stabilize a synaptic organization that had already been genetically specified. This is the attitude adopted by Hubel and Wiesel, Chomsky, and Fodor.

On the other hand, the "empiricists" postulate that to a large extent, the activity of the system specifies the connectivity, for example by orienting the growth of the nerve terminals or by tracing pathways in more or less random networks.

As a compromise between these two attitudes, we have postulated ("selective stabilization hypothesis") that the genetic program directs the proper interaction between main categories of neurons, for example via the mechanisms discussed above. However, during development within a given category, several contacts with the same specificity may form; in other words, a significant but limited "redundancy" of the connectivity exists. The early activity of the circuits, spontaneous (in the embryo) or evoked (after birth), would increase the specificity or the organization of the system by reducing this transient redundancy.

This selective stabilization hypothesis has been formalized and applied to several systems. One of its advantages is that it may permit a significant economy of genes. Indeed, it is not impossible that some of the genes that dictate, for example, the general rules of growth, the stability properties of the immature synapses, the regulation of their stability by the activity of the immature synapse, or the integrative properties of the post-synaptic neuron may be shared by different categories of neurons or even be common to all neurons. The set of genes involved (the genetic envelope) should therefore be smaller than if each synapse were determined individually. The genetic envelope offers a hazily outlined network; the activity defines its angles.

The selective stabilization of developing synapses by activity would become a critical step in synaptic development, ensuring the coupling between activity and connectivity. The biochemical model that can be proposed for it draws its inspiration both from the chemical cybernetics of the bacterial cell and from that of the synapse. The receptor protein of the neurotransmitter plays the principal role in this model.

In the immature cell, the molecule of the receptor exists in a labile and mobile form. Its life span is only a few hours, and it diffuses by translation on the surface of the neuron. As soon as the cell becomes active, the synthesis of the molecule stops. From then on, two categories of signals govern its evolution toward a form that is at the same time stable and localized in precise points of the cell surface. To begin with, the transmitter becomes liberated by labile nerve endings; later on, one or more intracellular signals are sent toward the interior of the cell by the receptor protein once it is activated. This last type of signal ensures a functional coupling between the first synaptic contacts. The combined arrival of these two types of signals on the same molecule of the receptor freezes it into a state which, if not "eternal," is at least much more resistant to degradation. If one of these two signals is lacking, an area of the stable receptor either is not formed or regresses.

Nervous activity is expressed by different concentrations, by various rhythms of production of the transmitter and of the internal signal. It is clear that under these conditions, the receptor will accumulate under certain synapses and not under others. The nerve endings located above surfaces rich in receptors would, in turn, be subject to a stabilization received from the receptor.

Whether it is true or false, this schema has, at least, the merit of suggesting experiments. It allows us to envisage seriously the possibility of understanding a property that is particular to the cerebral computer, and of modifying, within very narrow limits, its own wiring, as a consequence of the circulation of signals.

This theory of learning is a "selective" theory. It is radically opposed to "instructive" theories, which postulate, for example, that nervous activity directs the growth of nerve endings toward the appropriate targets. It does not require the appearance of new molecular species, as postulated by Hyden,[16] Ungar,[17] and even Szilard.[18] On the contrary, according to this theory, "to learn is to eliminate."

REMARKS ON EVOLUTION

In organisms simpler than man, such as many invertebrates or primitive vertebrates, the genetic determinism of the functional organization of the nervous system is almost absolute.

In the high vertebrates and in some invertebrates (like the cephalopods), learning represents a minor but significant failure in this determinism. Learning allows a broadening of the ecological niches that the organism can explore. Through learning, the organism adapts itself and renews at a faster rate the communications it exchanges with its environment. The establishment of the nervous system in a primitive organism takes place almost exclusively through an *internal* and autonomous combination of genes and intercellular signals. In the higher vertebrates, the organism becomes receptive to *external* and mobile combinations of signs that it can also produce. Circumscribed by the limits of the transient redundancy of the developing synapses, these external combinations may henceforth evolve on their own; a culture becomes implanted.

The acquisition of new performances through learning is accomplished in extremely brief intervals. A much longer time would be required for the same performances to develop by means of the evolution of the genome. One understands why, once it appeared, the faculty of learning became stabilized. According to the theory developed here, the cost in genes for the acquisition of this "cellular" capacity must not have been very high. For reasons that are as yet not clear, the total stock of genes remained at a constant and relatively low value in the course of the evolution of mammals. In spite of that, the complexity of the nervous system continued to increase. With the internal programming of the system becoming more and more difficult, the genetic determinism broke down and the redundancy of the connectivity became amplified. Learning may be viewed as the result of an increasing complexity of the system with a constant number of genes.

There is no necessary reason to postulate that the genetic mechanisms that governed the evolution of the genetic envelope of the central nervous system in mammals are of a different nature than those brought into play for the rest of the organism, despite the fact that the signals that regulate their phenotypic expression may have peculiarities of their own. The genes that code for the nervous system are made up of DNA just like those coding for the liver cell.

Modern theories of evolution are based on the spontaneous and random mutations of the DNA molecule and on the recombination of its segments; obviously, these views are valid in the case of the higher vertebrates, and it seems difficult to imagine, at present, a molecular mechanism for Piaget's mutations "particular to the human species."

On the other hand, the factors that determine the stabilization of a gene fluctuation in a natural population remain quite obscure. Is natural selection of any necessity? If one sides with the modern theorists of evolution such as Kimura,[19] the random distribution of genes within a heterogeneous population, following, for example, geographical isolation, would be sufficient to explain the diversification of species without the intervention of selection. The "behavior" of the organism may, however, exert significant though indirect effects on the evolution of the gene pool of the population through, for example, sexual behavior or social rules. "Artificial" selections may even take place and can lead, for instance, to domestication. To the extent that a wolf can be trained to live with man, the domestic dog becomes a "phenocopy" of the trained wolf. In this respect, *the so-called phenocopy corresponds to a decrease in the genetic potentialities of the organism.* This is also the case with Piaget's Limnea (see Chapter 2). The form that "adapts" to different environments by a change of shape may exhibit several different phenotypes, while the so-called "phenocopy" stabilized by heredity expresses only one of them in different environments. It is easy to conceive of the phenocopy as deriving from a polymorphic type as a result of a loss (or an inactivation) of the genes that determine the other phenotypes and as a result of the "constitutive" (unregulated by the environment) expressions of the remaining genes. The phenocopy *would not correspond to the acquisition of a new competence, but to a loss of genetic potentialities.*[*]

The theory of the selective stabilization of synapses has an interesting consequence regarding the variability of the central nervous system phenotype, that is, the topology of nerve connections in the adult. A limited redundancy in the developing synapses exists at critical stages of growth, but all individuals may not experience *exactly* the same interaction with the environment nor *exactly* at the same time. The theory predicts that the acquisition of a given input-output relationship may take place in different individuals along different neuronal pathways and may be printed as a different pattern of connections. In a genetically homogeneous population, the type of connectivity in adults is expected to vary from one individual to another, due to a limited but significant "fluctuation" of the connectivity. In natural populations, the fluctuations of the connectivity become superimposed on the fluctuation of the genetic material. Several generations are required to stabilize the hereditary variations of the genome. In contrast, the trace of the environment is imprinted in the nervous system in a much shorter time span. In the course of the life of the individual, the fluctuation of the connectivity prolongs and subsumes the genetic fluctuation of its ancestry.

Finally, I would like to say that these views represent a kind

---

[*] Editor's note: See also Danchin's comments in Appendix A.

of compromise between the views of Piaget and those of Chomsky. The existence of a transient redundancy in the development of neuronal networks is now well documented. The problem still remains of determining to what extent the activity of the developing network contributes to the observed decrease of redundancy. Does this epigenetic step correspond only to a triggering of already programmed functions? Or is there an increase of specificity, and therefore of order, consecutive to the interaction with the environment which is significantly more important in the brain than in any other physical organ? These are questions that should receive a definitive answer in the years to come.

Discussion

Piaget I warmly thank Changeux for having analyzed in such detail the possible compromises between Chomsky and myself. For my part, I have attempted in this colloquium to find such a compromise by admitting the heredity of functioning in the constructions themselves. I don't know anything about neurology, but while reading a work by Paul Weiss on the development of the nervous system, I was greatly impressed by his refusal to admit a fixed programming and by his insistence on demonstrating possible individual variations along the way.[1] In regard to the search for a compromise such as Changeux wishes, I would like to make one remark. It was said previously that mathematics is innate. Now, what is innate in mathematics? The simplest thing would be natural numbers, but as you well know, natural numbers lead to the notion of infinity, which is not concrete. It is not a real number that can be determined, like the number 14; the infinite is a continual construction. Thus, when we say that natural numbers are innate, what is innate is not the numbers as such but the process that constructs the number.

Dütting I have two questions: (1) Does neuronal plasticity increase in the evolution of higher organisms? (2) Is a functional verification necessary for the stability of the final networks? If the connections between the visual centers and the brain are established and then the vision is suppressed during the critical period, do these connections degenerate seriously?

Changeux   In regard to the first question, I would like to make a final remark concerning phylogenesis. As stated previously, the genetic stock doesn't seem to change very much during the course of the evolution of vertebrates, even though the complexity of the nervous system seems to change quite markedly. The increase in complexity gives to the organism the possibility of exploring the environment and has been, as a consequence of that fact, selected. The complexity of the central nervous system increases without a relative increase in the genetic information; the capacity to learn becomes a by-product of the complexification, with a constant number of genes. It is possible that the capacity to learn has not been selected as such but has simply resulted from the fluctuation introduced into the system, since it is not possible to program everything in a punctual way. Then, if you combine a little bit of instability of the synapse with a few biochemical rules, you can explain how you can order the system.

This leads to the second question, which has to do with the Hubel and Wiesel interpretation.* I think that here the question is not yet settled; after the pioneering work of Hubel and Wiesel there is still a discussion about how specific the connections are from the beginning. The work that Michel Imbert has been doing clearly indicates that a fraction of the neurons is entirely specified.[2] In fact, the question of whether or not there is also another fraction that is not specified interests us very much because the nonspecific cell reacts in all directions, and in addition, the receptor field of these cells is larger than it is in the specific cells. You can really imagine that you have a reduction of the number of synapses, but this is not the point of view of Hubel and Wiesel: what they say is that there is a functional verification that is wired in the system for specificity, that the system has to be stabilized by a functioning that conforms to its construction; if it is not, then it degenerates. I think that the other point of view (order from fluctuations) is different, because it suggests that if you have a multi-innervation of the system, you have more possibilities but less order in it; thus it represents another hypothesis to ask whether it is indeed the actual kind of signal that you introduce into the system which creates the specificity.

Monod   We know there are approximately 10^6 genes that one could theoretically use, given the amount of DNA in the cells. In fact, we know that only a fraction of the DNA is

---

* Editor's note: See the editorial comment at the beginning of Chapter 4

functional for structural purposes, so there are probably only 10^4 structural genes available. In any cell you will need to recruit a certain fraction of these genes to assume the normal functions that any cell has to assume. 10^3 genes is about enough to account for the biochemical functioning of elementary cells such as bacteria. Now, you need ten structural proteins to give its label to that particular cell. These ten structural proteins can be chosen from the 10^4 that are not used. Therefore, you have a choice of something like 10^{40} different labels, which is indeed quite a bit more than is necessary to build the central nervous system. How, then, do you make the choices? 10^{40} is not much different from 2^{130}, so you need 130 bits, or binary choices, to arrive at a label, using only a small fraction of the information of the genome to make the right choices, even for the specification of an extremely complex organ.

Chomsky I have one comment and one question. The comment has to do with complexity. I think it is worth stressing that in this discussion concerning the innate capacities of the central nervous system, one needs to add very little to the assumed complexity of the organism in order to account for language-specific structures. What one needs to add is a *minute element, so minute that it is undistinguishable at the level of our discussion;* so whatever complexity is determined for the organism, that complexity plus the infinitesimal epsilon we are talking about doesn't change the issue. So far, at least, the whole quantity of speculations that anyone has engaged in are minute as compared to what we have to assume just to account for the simple facts of physical organization.

As for the question I wanted to ask, isn't it true that there is experimental work coming, I think, from the Hubel and Wiesel laboratory, showing that if a kitten is exposed to horizontal stripes there will be a radical increase in the number of horizontal receptors?

Changeux This falls within the range of controversial questions. To specify the orientation of a neuron and to add an epsilon is something that you might consider trivial, but in fact, you might need to introduce only a very small, admittedly, but highly specific amount of information, that is, a precise sequence of impulses, which could be a very delicate thing to determine. The question that was discussed previously is precisely this: how can one estimate quantitatively the degree of organization between S_0 and S_f, and the degree of organization of the signal that one introduces, and is it really possible to explain S_f from S_0, starting from the organization of S_0 plus something?

Chomsky   I don't think that is the right question. What we have to ask is this: how much extra complexity is added by consideration of this specific transition from S_0 to S_f, over what we have to assume anyway just to account for the fact that we are human beings with a particular physical structure? If we were to try to describe the physical structure of the organism in the way in which we try to describe language, we would have such a huge mass of specifications that the extra amount that we were just discussing would not even be noticeable. So, whatever the answer might be to the problem of how specificity is determined, it will not answer the question that we are discussing now.

Changeux   I agree with Chomsky up to a certain point: when you look at the development of a network, if new waves of synapses or neurons are added one on top of the other in proceeding from S_0 to S_f, it is clear that you cannot explain this as simple addition of information from the outside in terms of activity. The question is really, for highly integrated operations of the central nervous system, to determine whether you actually have qualitative changes in the category of synapses you are making, and I still think that this is an open question.

Changeux emphasizes that "according to this theory, 'to learn is to eliminate.' " The selective theory of cognitive development presented by Changeux matches beautifully with the theory in psychology, independently formulated by Jacques Mehler, of "knowing by unlearning." Seen in evolutionary terms, as Changeux invites us to do, the selective mechanisms arise out of the logic of a thrifty genome: ". . . the total stock of genes remained at a constant and relatively low value in the course of the evolution of mammals. In spite of that, the complexity of the nervous system continued to increase . . . Learning may be viewed as the result of an increasing complexity of the system with a constant number of genes." The theory of selective stabilization of synapses seems to offer an admirable complement to Chomsky's innatism and Fodor's concept of "belief fixation." On what, then, does the compromise with Piaget rest? Changeux specifies that his selective theory must necessarily accommodate for a "transient redundancy in the development of neuronal networks." Whether the decrease in

redundancy corresponds to "*a triggering of already programmed functions . . . [or to] an increase of specificity, and
therefore of order, consecutive to the interaction with the environment*" is left an open question. With almost Newtonian
scruples, Changeux does not venture into the area of hypotheses concerning the a priori plausibility of an innatist explanation (in terms of order from fluctuations). His "suspension of
judgment," however, concerns the detailed mechanisms of an
epigenetic step at a very precise transitory phase of neuronal
development. Changeux's approach to the process of learning
as a whole is a selective one. In response to a question,
Changeux again takes up the argument that "*the capacity to
learn has not been selected as such but has simply resulted
from the fluctuation introduced into the system.*" Is this what
Piaget, after von Foerster, calls "order from noise"? Is such an
order anything but unpredictable selection at the microscopic
level?

In addition, Changeux offers a second type of explanation:
"*. . . thus it represents another hypothesis to ask whether it is
indeed the actual kind of signal that you introduce into the
system which creates the specificity.*" In the whole of the debate, the two "programs" have never come so close. What I
have called in the Introduction the "crystal program" and the
"order-from-noise program" are put side by side, translated
precisely by Changeux into hypotheses on synaptic mechanisms, and then left undecided. The two options materialize
in the form of alternative explanations of what happens, during certain stages of neuronal development, to the interacting
neurons. On the one hand, we have the hypothesis of a "triggering" of predetermined (that is, genetically specified) functions; on the other hand, we have the distinct hypothesis of a
specificity somehow injected into the system from the outside,
via particular classes of stimuli. These two options, as
Changeux suggests, may turn out not to be mutually incompatible, but rather complementary (whence a "compromise"
between innatism and constructivism). The final decision
must, however, be made on the basis of experimental data.

One last point needs to be stressed. Chomsky assumes that
the specificity and the innateness of linguistic structures such
as the specified subject condition, understood subject equivalence, and others are perfectly compatible with the "thrifty
strategy" of genes as described by Changeux. What you need is
an extra epsilon of information, says Chomsky, an infinitesimal addition to the "mass of specifications" already needed by

the overall structure of the organism. In other words, the burden imposed on the genetic stock by the addition of specifically human linguistic structures to the mass of "current" specifications is seen by Chomsky as negligible. Prudent once again, Changeux prefers not to pass judgment on these hypotheses and leaves the question open. To give a definitive answer to two or three such questions would be the equivalent of settling a dispute that is at least two hundred years old.

CHAPTER NINE

Interspecies Comparisons of Cognitive Abilities

In his book Intelligence in Ape and Man,* *published after this symposium, David Premack explains that his motivation in studying the cognitive capacity of chimpanzees was to obtain a description of our own capacities as seen by another species. To some extent Premack is starting a Copernican revolution in psychology: it is no longer a human investigator describing the cognitive structure of another organism, but the reverse. Self-knowledge as imposed by the Socratic motto is pursued through an indirect, painstaking, and unprecedented strategy.*

An intense flow of communication is first established between the experimenter and the ape, whereby problems are posed, questions asked, and capacities measured and refined. The dominant mode of interaction is clearly the cognitive one. In contrast to more "playful" and "spontaneous" styles of dialogue established with chimpanzees by other animal psychologists such as Allen and Beatrice Gardner, Premack admits here that "my chimpanzees, poor things, are the victims of a very scholastically inclined experimenter." This pedagogical bent is congruent with Premack's interesting assumption that "it is replay, and, of course, problem solving, that language serves uniquely well, and these functions are no less basic than social communication." Indeed, the latter, Premack specifies, "can get on nicely without language."

Once the regular "classroom" interaction is established between the experimenter and the chimpanzee, a lot of interesting things happen. Premack describes his methodology

* D. Premack, Intelligence in Ape and Man (New York: Halsted, 1977).

203

*in detail in his book. In this chapter he describes some aston-
ishing results (perception of causal links, symbolic replay, hints
of structure-dependent transformations, and so on) obtained by
careful "interrogation" of his chimpanzees. The conclusions
that he draws concerning the cognitive structures available to
the chimpanzee and the epistemological presuppositions that
have oriented his research deserve a brief commentary here.*

*In the first place, Premack rejects, on the basis of solid
experimental evidence, three hypotheses: (1) that cross-modal
associations (visual-auditory, visual-tactile, olfactory-visual,
and so on) are unique to man; (2) that categorial perception is
unique to man; and (3) that brain lateralization is unique to
man. As he says, "All three are rather good examples of what
one means by innate factors, but they do not appear to be
language-specific factors, or in any case factors unique to man."
Second, instead of pursuing a search for a general developmental mechanism or a general learning theory, Premack takes the
more cautious path of attempting to identify "factors that both
participate in human intelligence and play a role in language"
—factors such as representational capacity, accessibility of
knowledge, causality, and synonymy. It turns out that all these
factors are present, in an unsuspected degree, in the chimpanzee. This finding appears to Premack to be, at least potentially,
very important and relevant to the problems raised in this
debate between Chomsky and Piaget. For instance, representational capacity appears to Premack to be "a more pivotal capacity than either syntax or intentionality." Echoing a previous
remark made by Piaget, when referring to the all-important
"semiotic function" of which Piaget considers human language
to be a subdomain, Premack states: "If we view language as a
family of representational systems of which human language is
one variant, we can retrieve the study of language from its
ethnocentric limitations." To which he adds a methodological
stand, a sophisticated one at that: "It is profitable to take this
view even though, on this planet, such a family may have only
one natural member, that is, speech." The careful interspecies
comparison of cognitive abilities can, therefore, lead to the
perception of human language, unique as it is, as a member of
a potentially vast class, even if this class, for contingent reasons
(ascribable to the vagaries of phylogenesis), contains only that
member. Such a methodological stand is rich in consequences,
suggesting further experiments and criteria of interpretation of
available data. The second part of Premack's paper and the
ensuing discussion spell out these consequences in detail.*

Finally, I would like to attract the reader's attention to the antibehaviorist argument that Premack develops in the last section of his paper. Originally formulated by Premack's "old teacher" Herbert Feigl (one of the most authoritative epistemologists and philosophers of science of our time), the argument attempts to revalue "weaker tests" as a sufficiently reliable basis to infer the existence of a given capacity. The behaviorists' obsession to obtain only irrefutable evidence by strong negative tests (to prove that such and such an experiment is totally compatible with the absence of a given capacity) has paralyzed animal psychologists for a long time. It is indeed possible, according to Feigl and Premack, to "get at what's what" by avoiding the limitative criteria of "nothing but" and "something more" (that is, behaviorist sterility and pure armchair speculation). What is at stake here, as is well known to philosophers of science, is a demarcation criterion between the best available evidence and the best conceivable evidence. Experimental scientists, unlike pure mathematicians, have to be content with the former and avoid being paralyzed by the utopia of the latter. This chapter, like the rest of Premack's work, shows us where intelligent, rigorous, and creative use of available evidence can lead.

Representational Capacity and Accessibility of Knowledge: The Case of Chimpanzees

David Premack

Unfortunately, I will have little to say about the question that is of uppermost interest to many of us, namely, does human syntax arise from genetically unique linguistic factors or from general cognitive factors? Ten years ago the former view would have been strongly supported; today it is in decline. The change in view has led to new research; it is now possible to give a richly detailed account of the development of mother-infant preverbal communication. But there is no demonstration that the preverbal communication is a necessary condition for adult syntax.

Moreover, for ethical reasons we cannot find out in a simple, direct way (we cannot withhold preverbal communication from human infants) and thus an answer will depend on finding indirect test models. In the meantime, it is already clear that preverbal communication is not a sufficient condition for adult syntax. Preverbal communication has been shown in the mother-infant dyad in monkeys,[1] let alone apes; and indeed, as regards early social communication, it may be difficult to tell one primate from another. Yet only one primate develops natural language. It seems to me questionable whether the social communication view of language now replacing the unique factor view is any better founded than its predecessor. There is a sense in which the transition we are now witnessing is the replacement of one vogue by another.

Another quite different approach to resolving the issue would be to obtain grammars for any nonlinguistic domain—play, tool making, art—that is sufficiently well formed so that units could be identified and the sequences of units thus determined. A comparison of the formal properties of the grammars for the nonlanguage cases with those of the grammars for language should help to decide how much the behaviors of language and various kinds of nonlanguage may have in common. Although the proposal to do this has come from several quarters,[2] to my knowledge it remains to be done. Recently Kim Dolgin, Dan Osherson, and I have taken the first steps toward doing this specifically for play, in both chimpanzees and children. There are at least two possible outcomes that would be of interest. If we were to succeed in actually writing a grammar for play, then the desired comparisons with language could be made. Alternatively, it may not be possible to write a grammar for play; the problem of units may be insuperable, or there may be other difficulties. If so, and if we could show that the difficulty was not trivial but arose from deep factors, there would be a suggestion that play and language are not comparable systems, and thus are not likely to influence one another. This, of course, is only a possibility—a remote one, perhaps—but I mention it to flesh out the possibilities that accompany this comparison, for the range seems to be greater than has been considered.

There are a few pieces of evidence of a circumstantial nature that I think bear on the question, not of innate factors but of innate factors that are linguistically unique: I will mention three. First, it has been claimed that cross-modal associations are difficult, if not impossible, in nonhuman species.[3] This claim has been falsified not only in apes[4] but more recently even in monkeys (which, it is my intuitive impression, are farther from the ape than the ape is from man). Cowey and Weiskrantz recently reported a nice experiment in which they showed visual-tactile associations in monkeys.[5] In the ape, not only visual-tactile associations but the most interesting case, visual-auditory, can be demonstrated. We recently found that apes with whom speech had been used informally in the course of their formal training on plastic words could subsequently comprehend speech alone. The comprehension was very limited, was largely confined to words, and was far less accurate than for the plastic words, but then their "training" on speech was also limited and entirely incidental. In any case, the claim restricting cross-modal association to man can be retired.

A second claim that may also be heading for retirement is that categorical perception is unique to speech sounds, on the one hand, and to man, on the other. This two-headed claim is the basis of the view that man is uniquely equipped with speech detectors. It appeared that this claim was corroborated when Eimas and others found categorical discrimination of speech sounds in human neonates.[6] But the relevance of the infant data for the assumption of species-specific speech detectors has been called into question by additional data of two kinds. First, nonhuman species have been found to discriminate certain speech sounds in a categorical manner. Rhesus monkeys[7] and chinchillas,[8] whose inner ear structure resembles man's, discriminate the voice-voiceless distinction in the contrast between /t/ and /d/ in essentially the same categorical manner as the adult human speaker. Second, categorical discrimination is not only not unique to man, but also not unique to speech sounds. Human adults discriminate between a bowed and a plucked instrument in a categorical manner.[9] We await additional tests to see if the claim for speech detectors being unique to man can be reconstituted on a more subtle basis. But in the meantime, there is the suggestion that we should think not in terms of speech detectors but of auditory hardware that was on the evolutionary shelf for some time before it was picked up by man and incorporated into language. Thus there exists an innate factor, but not a language-specific innate factor.

Third, quite recently, there have been at least two reports of anatomical lateralization in apes. Lemay and others have reported hemispherical differences in the ape's brain similar to those in man, though far less marked; they also reported the absence of such differences in the monkey.[10] Now of course, we do not know whether or not the anatomical difference in the ape is associated with a functional difference, or if it is, whether the difference is comparable to the one in man. From time to time, Gazzaniga and (more recently) Levy have threatened to hunt for functional lateralization in chimpanzees, and on the condition that they leave their drills and knives home, they have been welcomed. Incidently, early studies did not show handedness in the chimp; that is, individual chimps are handed but the distribution of handedness in the population was random. It could do no harm to look again, however, since this is the result of an early study.

In summary, three factors—intermodal association, speech detectors, and anatomical brain lateralization—can no longer be unequivocally assigned uniquely to man. Two of the three factors clearly participate in language; the third may not. All three are rather good examples of what one means by innate factors, but they do not appear to be language-specific factors, or in any case factors unique to man.

I will try to talk (very programmatically, I'm afraid) about factors that seem to characterize human intelligence and see whether we can find these factors elsewhere. I think that there are two ways one can make the argument about innate factors and the necessity for them. One is the argument that Chomsky has made in a very elegant presentation: there are some formal properties of language, but there doesn't appear to be any general developmental mechanism (GDM) that could generate these factors. This is a legitimate form of argument, but a bit at the mercy of what the next bright fellow might do. Even now, a clever young man, let's call him Goldschmidt, may be sitting in his attic, figuring out how to build GDMs that will realize Chomsky's formal properties. I prefer an approach that is less dependent on what Goldschmidt may or may not do—an approach that says: here are the elements that participate in human intelligence; this is the time at which we find them in the infant; it is too close to zero for experience to play a profound or exclusive role; and moreover, this is the distribution of these elements over the species. So, Goldschmidt, you have a delightful hypothetical GDM, but it is irrelevant to this particular argument.

Let's look at three or four factors that both participate in human intelligence and play a role in language. Consider representational capacity, accessibility of knowledge, causality, and (time permitting) synonymy. Memory is obviously critical for both language and representational capacity. So the first question we might ask is, what is the quality of information a species can store? If a species cannot store a powerful representation of the world, then even though we might, in some sense, teach it words, the words would be ineffective; they could not be used to retrieve much, since there would not be much information stored in the first place. The power of the word is limited by how much information the species can store.

POWER OF THE WORD

To assess the chimpanzee's ability to remember the attributes of objects, on the one hand, and the amount of information it could associate with their names, on the other, we used fruits and plastic objects as "names" for the fruits. We divided the fruit into a number of pieces; we gave the chimpanzees one piece and then asked them to identify other pieces that belonged to the same fruit. We assumed that if one knew a great deal about an object, one should need only a small sample to identify it. If given only a stem or a seed or even a taste, an informed animal should be able to identify the fruit from which the sample was taken.

What is the difference between what an animal can perceive about an object and what it can reconstruct from memory? When an animal is required to match apple and redness, the object and the color sample match, giving a measure of perception. If, however, the sample remains red but the apple is now painted white, the object and the color sample will no longer match. Instead, they only match on the basis of information reconstructed from memory. Tests that require reconstructing information from memory do not specifically depend on distorted alternatives, however. The relation between stem and peel, stem and seed, seed and peel; color and shape, shape and size; and color and stem, shape and seed, and so on, are all undistorted cases of this kind. Items in these pairs do not share common features but are related simply through being attributes of the same object.

In the present tests, fruits were divided into four canonical components and two features: wedge, stem, peel, and seed; color and shape. Taste was added as the one nonvisual attribute. Eight fruits were divided in this manner: banana, orange, apple, lemon, peach, pear, grape, and cherry. The chimpanzee was given one or another of the features as a sample, along with two other features as alternatives, and was required to select the correct alternative. For instance, the animal was given an apple seed as the sample, along with an apple stem or a pear stem, and was to select the apple stem.

After completing the series of approximately twenty-four individual tests with each of the four subjects, we were able to rank-order the components and features according to their informativeness. Not surprisingly, the whole fruit was the most informative cue. Color and peel were next, followed closely by taste, after which there was essentially a tie between shape, wedge, and stem, and last came seed, the least informative cue of all. Sarah, impressively, was able to use all the cues correctly, but the other three chimpanzees were best able to identify the source of the attribute of a fruit from its color or peel, and least able from its seed.

In the next test series, actual parts of the fruit were given as samples, and the alternatives were plastic words that named the fruits. The results of these tests were unusually clear-cut. Words provided as much information to the animal as did the presence of a whole fruit; furthermore, words were more informative than actual parts of the fruit. In another test series, we used names of colors rather than of objects and obtained identical results. For instance, we could substitute the word *red* for an actual instance of red in the matching test without loss of accuracy. Since in the ape, the word substitutes vigorously for its referent, it seems proper to speak of the "power of the word" for the chimpanzee and not only for man.

The fact that fruit and color names could serve as substitutes for their referents, without any loss of accuracy, shows that a major consequence of giving arbitrary items (such as pieces of plastic) linguistic prerogatives is the transfer to the arbitrary item of some or all of the information that an animal has concerning the associated object. Under what circumstances does this transfer of information take place? Perhaps it occurs only after the piece of plastic has been used in a wordlike way, to request or describe the object a certain number of times. That would be the only tenable hypothesis if the only way to produce names was by associating them with their referents in one linguistic context or another. However, we already know that this procedure can be short-circuited. Names can be generated more directly by instructions of the form "X is the name of Y," where X is a previously unused piece of plastic and Y an unnamed object. Following an instruction of this kind, Sarah used X in all the ways she used names introduced in the more standard fashion. Thus the effect of instructions such as "X is the name of Y" must be to transfer to X some or all of the information the chimpanzee has stored in his memory about Y. This fact clarifies some of the power of language and at the same time suggests the kind of intelligence a species must have in order to acquire it.

To qualify for language, a species must be capable of storing a rich representation of Y; if not, the information transferred to X would be weak, and the name would be a poor substitute for the referent. In addition, instructions of the form "X is the name of Y" must have the force of transferring to X some—ideally all—of the information that the subject has stored about Y. These are not the only capacities a species must have to qualify for language, but they are two that seem to be basic.

Sarah was capable of displacement, of comprehending statements about "things that are not there." When given the instruction "brown color of chocolate" as a means of introducing "brown" and subsequently told "take brown," she performed correctly, choosing the brown disk from the four offered. The chimpanzee's ability to comprehend statements about "things that are not there" derives from its demonstrated ability to store adequate representations of items and to use words to retrieve the stored information. In substituting, say, the word *apple* for an actual apple without loss of accuracy in all the matching tests, it gave direct proof of this ability. Displacement is not a uniquely linguistic phenomenon but the consequence of a certain quality of memory.

REPRESENTATIONAL CAPACITY

Let us turn now more directly to representational capacity. Although the language-trained ape has so far shown painfully little syntactic competence, it has shown a remarkable representational capacity. Beguiled by the linguist on the one hand and the semiotician on the other, we have tended to overlook representational capacity, which in my view is a more pivotal capacity than either syntax or intentionality.

Representational capacity is the ability to judge the relationship between actual events and representations of them. For instance, one can place a red card on a green one and ask the chimpanzee "Is red on green?" or "What is on green?" ("? red on green" or "? on green"). In answering these two question forms correctly, the chimpanzee demonstrates that it recognizes the relation between them, a red-card-on-a-green-card, and the representation of the item, "red on green." The chimpanzee can even answer questions in the absence of the colored cards, demonstrating that it can remember visual situations and recognize representations of the absent situations.

If we view language as a family of representational systems

of which human language is one variant, we can retrieve the study of language from its ethnocentric limitations. It is profitable to take this view even though, on this planet, such a family may have only one natural member, that is, speech. Nevertheless, we can imagine other variants; we can find suggestions of other variants (in the developmental stages of the acquisition of speech by children and in pathological human populations); and we can train or synthesize other variants in nonhuman species as we are now doing with apes. While holding this relaxed view of language, however, it is still questionable to consider bee communication as language. Ordinarily, the contrast between bee and human language is made on the grounds that only one of the two systems is learned, but this is a dubious contrast, since critical aspects of human language, including parts of both syntax and phonology, are probably not learned. More important, even if the bee's unique system *were* learned it probably would not qualify as language. The two systems can be better contrasted by asking if the bee shows any suggestion of representational capacity.

Suppose a scout bee were to gather information about the direction and distance of a food source from its hive. The bee encodes this information in its dance, and a second bee decodes the dance; but could the bee, when shown its own dance, judge whether or not this dance accurately represented the direction and distance of the source of food? Could the bee recognize that dance as a representation of its own knowledge? If a bee could judge between the real situation and a representation of that situation, it would be possible to interrogate the bee, just as we can interrogate the ape. A species that can be interrogated, such as the chimpanzee, is well on its way toward being able to make true-false judgments. But I know of no data that even faintly suggest that the bee can recognize the dance as a representation of its knowledge. While we wait for the critical experiments to demonstrate such an ability in the bee, we must adopt an agnostic position with regard to the language ability of bees; we must take the position that the bee has a code, a correlation between items inside and outside its body—not necessarily a language, since language depends on representational capacity.

A problem also arises from the tendency to call the elements of the bee's dance *symbols*. With the chimpanzee, it is possible to decide in a straightforward manner whether or not a language element operates as a symbol. If a small blue piece of triangular plastic is consistently associated with an apple in the chimpanzee's daily experience, whenever the chimpanzee later wants some apple, he will put the blue piece of plastic on his writing board and be given an apple. If an apple is present and the trainer asks the chimpanzee "What is this?" (in effect), the chimpanzee will answer by placing the blue plastic on the board. How do we decide if the chimpanzee is using the plastic shape as a symbol? We can perform two tests on the chimpanzee, obtaining what amounts to a features analysis of apple. Like us, the ape sees the apple as red (rather than green), as round (not square), as having a stem (rather than not), and so forth. When we replace the apple with the triangular piece of blue plastic, once more offering the same alternatives and now obtaining a features analysis of the would-be word, we get the same answers as before. The ape tells us that the blue plastic triangle is red, round, and has a stem, and so on. The chimpanzee's analysis is compatible with the view that the ape is judging not the plastic triangle itself, but what the blue triangle stands for.

If the ape could provide no further evidence of linguistic function, we would have to scale down our interpretation of these results; but we accept the interpretation (though only tentatively at first) because the linguistic performance of the ape does not end here but goes on to approximate ever more complex human performances. For example, just as at one stage the ape is able to make judgments about the agreement between an item and a representation of that item, so at a later stage the ape (Sarah) can make judgments about the agreement between two representations. She subsequently made judgments about the relation between sentences such as "apple is red" and "red color of apple." Thus a capacity for judging between two nonlinguistic items (as in the causality tests; see the section on causal inference) advanced to making judgments between one linguistic and one nonlinguistic item, and culminated finally in synonymy, where the chimpanzee compared two linguistic representations for similarity.

These are only some of the several tests that show the ape to have an impressive representational competence. Now, if you believe as I do that competence means in part an indigenous disposition to exercise the competence, then it is embarrassing to find so little evidence for spontaneous symbolization in the ape. Thankfully, there is a little evidence of this kind from Sarah, not enough to conceal the embarrassment but enough to suggest where we might look to find more. Sarah was offered a photograph of a chimpanzee face that was cut up into eyes, nose, and mouth, to see if she could reassemble it, which she proved able to do and which is interesting in its own right.

While being given these tests she was also given an opportunity to wear hats and to view herself in a mirror, which she very much enjoys. Incidentally, the ape, unlike the monkey, can recognize the image in the mirror as itself; the monkey stares at the mirror while continuing to handle the mirror, but after about ten hours the chimpanzee ceases to handle the mirror and begins to handle itself while looking in the mirror.[11] Now, at a time when Sarah was looking in the mirror while wearing hats, and having a lot of fun, she was subsequently given a disassembled face of a chimpanzee. She put in the eyes, the nose, and the mouth, making her usual veridical reconstruction; then she paused, picked up the mouth, turned it over, and put it on top of the head like a hat. When we repeated the procedure in an experimental way, we found that we could evoke the symbolic play reliably, provided only that we preceded her puzzle experience with an opportunity for her to view herself wearing hats.

In producing a visual form comparable to the one she had seen earlier in the mirror, Sarah would seem to have been engaging in a complex version of a form of behavior in which she had engaged since infancy. For example, when Sarah was about 18 months old, a woman entered the nursery wearing a distinctive wool skirt. Sarah palpated the skirt for a moment and then rushed over to her bed and stroked her blanket, which was also wool. Having no language at the time, Sarah had no other way in which to announce or celebrate the discovery of an equivalence. Sarah went even further with the chimpanzee face, for there she did not merely detect an equivalence—she produced one, or at least helped it along. The face in the mirror and in the picture were only partly comparable; she changed the one, making it more like the other.

All of this behavior would seem to be an example of a basic disposition that takes many forms, and that can be described in several ways. One can speak of a disposition to discover (or produce) equivalences; to imitate oneself; to reproduce previous experience, sometimes with a change in mode. Thus, we see children play and at the same time speak, describing their play, and we see the same thing in the chimpanzees; they too play and then describe their play with the plastic words. Indeed, of all the devices that might be used to reproduce previous experience, none could be more efficient than language. Language is the ideal replay device. People emphasize social communication in discussing language, yet social communication can get on nicely without language. It is replay, and, of course, problem solving, that language serves uniquely well, and these functions are no less basic than social communication.

Let us turn now to one of the most critical and least understood aspects of intelligence, the accessibility of knowledge. Piaget has, of course, dealt with this problem as he has dealt with most problems of intelligence, so I shall do no more than sketch the problem in order to show its relevance to the animal case.

THE ACCESSIBILITY OF KNOWLEDGE

Is access to a cognitive map a sufficient condition for the use of an actual map? Since we have good reason to suspect that it is not, we must explain why a species could have a maplike representation of its home terrain in its head and yet not recognize the relation between its cognitive map and an actual map. The question need not be restricted to maps, of course. Why is it that some species can recognize representations, including representations of their own knowledge, and others, apparently, cannot?

From the ape's success in remembering the location of hidden objects, we infer that it has a cognitive map.[12] Yet we can make the same inference for other species as well, since spatial relations is one of the most widely demonstrable forms of knowledge. Rats[13] and even insects[14] have been shown to have information of this kind.

The differences in the ability of various species to use external representations may be due to three factors. The first factor is the form of the information and the level at which it is stored. If the bee's dance, for instance, did not code for direction specifically but rather coded the distance, the quality, and/or the quantity of the food source, these factors could be attributed to motivational systems, controlled by the gut, taste receptors, or other visceral sites, with little, if any, neural representation. Second, regardless of how information is stored, species may differ in the extent to which they have access to it. This factor could not only influence the ability of the species to use maps or language, but also affect the degree of self-reflective behavior in which it could engage. Third, even if information were stored in a favorable form and a species had good access to it, we, an alien species, might be unable to design an appropriate map, one that would resemble the form of information stored by the species. At present, we are far from being able to decide which, if any, of these factors—form, access, or appropriateness—may account for the limitations of various species. Perhaps the ability of a species to use either maps or language depends primarily on the presence of at least two different forms of representation or information storage. This attractive suggestion was offered by my colleague Dr. Randy Gallistel during a conversation over lunch. If a species can store information not only in pictorial form (to which insects may conceivably be restricted) but also in propositional form (demonstrably the case for man and chimpanzee), then the same information could be stored in both forms. Cases of this kind could provide the opportunity for a species to translate one form of internal representation into another.

Experience and instruction may help an animal to recognize the relation between an item and a representation of that item, since, in principle, this is similar to the ability to recognize the relation between two equivalent internal representations. Certain kinds of information may naturally lend themselves to an image of maplike form, other kinds to a propositional form (these extremes may never be represented in both ways). Still others may be intermediate with respect to form, and may be represented both as image and as proposition more or less automatically, depending on the occasion.

In 1932, Tinklepaugh conducted a series of memory tests with apes and monkeys using a kind of information that could be easily modulated so as to potentiate an image-form of storage on one occasion, a propositional-form on another, and possibly both forms on further occasions.[15] Tinklepaugh tested the apes by arranging sixteen pairs of containers in a circle (with a diameter of 7 meters), baiting one container of each pair while the ape observed from the center of the circle, and then, after varying delays, releasing the ape to find the baited containers. The sixteen containers, consisting of a variety of painted and unpainted wooden boxes, tin cans, and cups, were not confined to a special order from trial to trial, and baiting of the containers was essentially random. For an animal to succeed in this experiment, it seems that an image-form would be the most practical form of storage. The circular arrangement of the containers would make the coordinate system on which maps are based less suitable, since half the pairs of containers would have the same value on the abscissa and the other half the same value on the ordinate, a factor that would reduce their identifiability.

A propositional form of storage also seems unsuited for the Tinklepaugh experiments. It could be used, in theory, but the lack of systematic relations between the type of container and the baiting system greatly reduces the advantages of a propositional format, which works most efficiently if information is patterned or systematic. For example, if for all the tin containers, the left member of each pair were baited, and for all the wooden containers, the right member of each pair were baited, then the information could be stored economically in a propositional format. Moreover, this propositional format does not seem to involve any predicates foreign to the conceptual nature of the chimpanzee. In fact, Sarah was successfully taught quantifiers—the use of various modifiers comparable to "wooden containers" and "tin containers"—and although she was not taught "right-left," she learned to label distinctions such as "top-bottom," thus storing information of a kind not unlike that required for the Tinklepaugh studies.

In principle, it would seem possible to change the animal's form of storage—image, map, propositional—by modulating several parameters: the degree of pattern in the information, the shape of the geometrical arrangement, the reliability of the position of the containers after baiting is complete. At intermediate values of these parameters, animals capable of more than one form of storage may be inclined to use both forms, setting up an equivalence between two different internal representations. This strategy may help the animal to recognize the relation between a situation and the external representation of the situation. Although this hypothesis seems to elude a direct test at the moment, indirect tests are possible and may lead to more satisfying demonstrations later.

CAUSAL INFERENCE

In acquiring language, one acquires labels for existing concepts; this proposal can be tested with admirable directness in many cases. Can the animal discriminate between conditions that exemplify "same" and "different"? "all" and "none"? "red" and "black"? If so, according to the proposal, it should be possible to teach the animal names for "same-different," the quantifiers, and the like. Not all concepts are as simple as these, however, and some of them must be approached differently. For instance, we approach the "if-then" or conditional relation by observing that the conditional sentence is a way of expressing a causal relation: "If you drop that, it will break." "If you smile at Mary, she will smile back." "If you touch that, you'll get burned." These sentences and the infinitely many possible others like them express a causal relation between the antecedent and the consequent. Only a species that made a causal analysis of its experience would use sentences of this form productively.

Hence, we designed a simple visual test to answer the question: does the subject make a causal analysis of its experience?

The subject was given an intact object, a blank space, and the same object in a changed or terminal state, along with various alternatives, and was encouraged to complete the sequence by placing one of the alternatives in the blank space. For example, the subject was given items such as an intact apple and a cut apple, a dry sponge and a wet one, and a clear piece of paper and one with writing on it. The three alternatives given the subject consisted of a knife, a bowl of water, and a writing instrument.

Three of the four chimpanzees tested in this way required no more than general adaptation to the test format before responding correctly. Their ability to place the knife between the intact and severed apple, the water between the dry and wet sponge, and the pencil between the unmarked and pencil-marked paper showed that they correctly identified the instrument needed to change each object from its initial to its terminal state. Simple as this outcome is, it can be given a stronger interpretation than may first meet the eye. The visual sequences are infinitely ambiguous: each can be coded in indefinitely many ways, such as *red-blank-red, one-blank-two, round-blank-flat, large-blank-small.*

Not only the test items but also the three alternatives are subject to indeterminately many codings. "Knife," for instance, need not be read as knife (instrument that cuts) but can be coded as sharp, metal, long, shiny, and so on, and the same holds for the other alternatives. However, the subjects evidently did not code the sequences or alternatives in these ways, since they consistently chose alternatives compatible with only one coding, namely, how do you change the object from the intact to the terminal stage? With what instrument do you produce the change? Because the subjects read the sequences in a specific and consistent way—finding the same question in each of the sequences—I infer that they have a schema, a structure that assigns an interpretation to an otherwise infinitely ambiguous sequence.

The apes' ability to respond in this fashion was by no means limited to familiar object-implement pairs. They performed equally well not only on pairs they had never experienced, but even on pairs that were anomalous or nonsensical, such as apples that had been written on, sponges that had been cut, and writing paper that had been dunked in water.

It is also noteworthy that the visual sequences were by no

means iconic representations of the actions tested. Cutting, wetting, and marking are analog processes in which an agent brings about a continuous change in an object. In cutting, for example, an agent applies a knife to an apple, exerting pressure until the apple divides. The test items did not portray the gradual division of the apple, but presented only the digital highlights of the analog process, and did not present the agent at all. Nevertheless, the chimpanzees evidently recognized the test sequences as representations of the actions. If the tests had failed we might then have considered using motion pictures or other iconic forms of representation; but the animals succeeded despite the abstract form of the representation. Thus, chimpanzees not only have a schema for cause-effect relations, but they have one that can be activated by noniconic representations.

Because these tests dealt only with the physical domain, they leave open the question of whether or not the chimpanzee can recognize cause-effect relations in the psychological or social domain. The lack of appropriate stimuli has prevented us from making such tests, yet it is easy enough to describe the form such tests would take. For example, in one test, the three pictures would consist of Elizabeth begging food from Peony, a blank frame, and Elizabeth and Peony playing, hugging, and engaging in mutual grooming. The alternatives would include: (1) Peony ignoring Elizabeth's request, (2) Peony sharing with Elizabeth, (3) Elizabeth stealing Peony's food, and so on. Of these alternatives, only Peony sharing with Elizabeth would be compatible with the harmonious outcome in frame 3, and the chimpanzee's appropriate choice in this and comparable tests would indicate that it could recognize representations of social as well as of physical actions. Notice, incidentally, that the test is designed so that selection of the missing frame can not be based simply on knowledge of physical action. If in frame 3 both animals were shown to be eating, one could conclude on physical grounds alone that Peony must have shared with Elizabeth. But since neither animal is shown eating, the content of the second frame can only be inferred from the social character of the behavior in the third frame.

Let us assume for the sake of discussion that the apes can pass the social tests as they have passed the physical ones, which may not be too risky an assumption given the evident social intelligence of the chimpanzee. If the ape can recognize representations of both physical and social actions, perhaps it can take the next step and recognize higher order structures that are composed of physical and social actions. Physical and social acts are the building blocks of stories, novels, tales, and the like. Indeed, all narrative prose is formed by appropriately combining physical and social acts. If a species can recognize the basic elements of which stories are formed, perhaps it can also recognize stories themselves.

The individual's ability to recognize a picture story can be revealingly tested with verbal procedures, such as those Walter Kintsch, his students, and I are now using with 3- and 4-year-old children; but it can also be tested in at least some degree with nonverbal procedures. First, the animal can be given story books, of appropriate simplicity, in some of which the pictures are in appropriate order and in others of which they are out of order. A preference for books with appropriate order would be suggestive. Second, the animal can be given serial learning tasks requiring that he learn to arrange, say, five pictures in a designated order. In some cases the designated order is the normal order in which the pictures would occur in a story book, and in other cases it is not. If serial learning is sensitive to the sequence of the story, so that the animal learns the former faster than the latter, this too can be taken as evidence of the ability to comprehend picture stories. Comprehension of this kind is important, since it would indicate that the animal can not only divide his experience into causal units, but can use still higher order schemata to organize the causal units.

Accessibility to Information and Circumstantial Evidence

One might do a still weaker test, not to prove causal inference, but to produce circumstantial evidence hinting at the merest possibility of causal inference. I propose this approach as an antidote to any approach which, like behaviorism, is unbalanced in its eagerness to avoid false positives, that is, so intent on its quest for an antiseptic position that it commits one false negative after another. Is it not possible to get at what's what, as my old teacher Herbert Feigl used to call it, without ricocheting wildly from nothing but to something more? Often it does not seem so.

A hint of a capacity for causal inference might be obtained from a test of this kind, which is thus far hypothetical. We know that even nonprimates can learn on an observational basis, although exactly what they learn, merely a motivational change or something more cognitive, is not yet resolved. Let us do the experiment with rats, since they are sufficiently low in the hierarchy for the question to be of interest. We give rats two scenes to observe, and see which of them is more influential. In the first, the rats watch a model rat push a marble off the edge of a table; the marble falls to a dish below, after which food appears in a cup. In the second scene, the rats watch a model rat push the same marble off the edge of the table; but now the marble rises to the ceiling, after which food appears in the cup.

Suppose the rats shown the first scene are more likely to imitate the behavior of the model (and we carry out those controls necessary to eliminate competing hypotheses concerned with novelty and the like). For species at this level of intelligence, this general kind of circumstantial evidence may be the strongest we can get that the species has any access to the knowledge or information that is stored in it. (Certainly we do not expect rats to produce conditional sentences, or to pass even any version of the visual causality tests described earlier, no matter how simple they may be made.) Even though rats do not leap wildly when faced with a small gap, or jump short for a large one, but behave sensibly in the world, they may have no access to the information underlying their sensible performance. And the failure may not lie in the form in which the information is stored, but simply in its accessibility—a factor about which we know too little.

I showed in a sentence, simpler than but logically equivalent to Chomsky's first case (see Chapter 1), that Sarah pluralized not on the basis of physical features but on the basis of the meaning of the sentence. The same capacity is employed when the animal makes a judgment about the equivalence of two sentences: it is responding not to strings of verbal elements in terms of their physical properties but in terms of what they mean.* These are all examples of the animal's representational capacity, its ability to process the pieces of plastic not at the level of their physical properties, but at the level of their meaning.

* Editor's note: Such an ability is what Chomsky has previously defined as "structure dependence." Premack is asserting here that chimpanzees possess the ability to perform structure-dependent operations. The point appears to be controversial, however, as Scott Atran points out in the discussion that follows. (See also the exchange between Putnam and Chomsky in Part II.)

Discussion

Bateson It seems to me that we should pay close attention to the latter part of Premack's material. What seems to me outstanding in the whole story is what he referred to at one point as a time lag. He keeps saying that an ape can learn this or that, but obviously, the experiments have a sequential structure to them which is in itself a learning sequence. This is, I think, very important. This is the best data I have ever heard in support of the fact of *progress in learning*, learning how to learn.

Premack I'm not a great believer in the word "learning," and I am rather more in favor of Fodor's argument (see Chapter 6). I think that the main thing human training is doing here for the chimpanzee is disclosing capacities that are present. The human intervention is a very modest contribution; we are setting the stage in such a way that the animal's existing intelligence can be expressed. I do believe that there is such a thing as learning how to learn, which of course is also found in species a great deal lower than the chimpanzee. But the point I was really trying to make is about the progression from being able to look at a sequence like an apple, a knife, and a cut apple, and judging that sequence relative to one's previous performance: this already presupposes the very critical psychological capacity of being able to recognize representations of one's own behavior. I don't know how far down the evolutionary ladder that capacity might be found, but I will hazard a guess that it might be strictly a primate phenomenon.

Bateson The thing I'm trying to get across is that to recognize representations is one thing—and these play-repetitions in one sense carry the notion of recognizing representations. On the other hand, to be able to answer a question about representations is much more than that.

Godelier Let's return to the first part of Premack's discussion; he shows that there is symbolization, and that it is an active process leading to the capacity of representing the form of one's own behavior. Here is my question: the chimpanzee appears to be capable of symbolization, of organizing his experience, of representing his own scheme of behavior, but it seems that he cannot transform the rules generating his behaviors, that is, the rules of his social relationships. Piaget was saying that the function of symbolization—therefore evocation—appeared in the course of the second year of childhood, and he attempts to connect this with sensorimotor practice as a creative practice, and so on. Now, it seems to me that these two examples, the one presented by Premack on the function of symbolization, and the other one on conservation presented by Piaget, show us that the symbolic function is, from a certain point of view, already programmed. But what is programmed, then, is the potential capacity to transform—for example, for us, the human species—social relationships, that is, rules of behavior, institutions, which is a much deeper question than that of language. In this case, both the limited formal syntax of the chimpanzee and ours, which is much more complex, would be aspects of the capacity for a species to transform or not to transform the rules of its games, and thus to create any new social relationships, whatever they might be, or to act on anything whatsoever. I would like to ask Changeux a question concerning this problem: can we, with a perspective of the evolution of species and of the formation of the human central nervous system, give an account of the massive capacity to create social relationships, and also to create the languages that are necessary to transform and represent these relationships? At one fell swoop, the question is asked concerning, on the one hand, the capacities of syntaxes and the possibilities of transformation, and on the other, the nervous system and its evolution, in which the differentiation of the species is seen. It is a question that permits one to introduce the function of symbolization, genetically programmed. At the same time, however, it is not merely the function of symbolization, it is the capacity for a species to transform the conditions of its existence. From this point, the problem is to know whether the capacity to transform these conditions is programmed with the differentiation of nervous systems and the central nervous system that Changeux spoke about (see Chapter 8).

Personally, then, I would stand on Chomsky's side in regard to the programming of capacities, but it would not only be a problem of specificity of language for man, it would be the problem dealing with the aptitude for our human species to transform its conditions of existence and the interplay of its behavior.

Premack   The experiment that would maximize the likelihood of that outcome has simply not been done. I was also asked whether the animal accepts passively the inputs that the world gives it, or whether there are situations in which it operates on those inputs and transforms them. That question is also present in the cases in which the animal, having been given a picture of a chimpanzee's face with a hat on, takes the puzzle and does not merely reconstruct it so as to produce a chimpanzee's face, but rather operates on it in a way that produces an equivalence between the input and the given material. I consider this as a weak example of the fact of not merely accepting the input of the world passively, but rather operating on this input. This is admittedly very limited, but nonetheless it shows that the disposition to produce equivalence is involved in self-description, in images. Incidentally, this is what is involved when a husband returns from a trip and, while riding home with his wife, tells her what he did, and she tells him what she did; both of these conversations appear to be expressions of interest by the husband and wife in each other, but I consider them as examples of replay, for which language is nearly the perfect instrument. I would very much like to understand why we have this deeply rooted disposition to produce equivalences between one experience and another in a somewhat modified form. Now, I think we already see a weak instance of that in the chimpanzee when he transforms the face, operates on it, so as to make it more like the image that he had before.

Papert Let me mention first an experiment that was carried out recently by Stambak, Sinclair, and others relevant to the idea of schemas in Piaget's sense.[1] It consists of giving human babies a collection of objects, such as a glass, a box, or a small stick, and watching what they do with them. The interesting observation was that during certain periods, perhaps as long as a month, the child would become highly occupied with one activity belonging to a very small set. For example, for a while the child might get very involved with putting things into his mouth. Then after a while the child would turn away from that and get interested in another kind of activity, such as putting sticks into containers. I will use the word "frame" for the data structures that handle each situation (think of it as case grammars if you like): each frame has places for entities, its cases, for example a container, a thing to be put in, and an action; there is the in-frame (the container), the on-frame, and so on.

It does seem to be clear that a small vocabulary of very basic schemata of this sort either develops early in the child or is innate. Now, it seems to me that people who want to find the innate mechanisms behind language and of conceptual manipulations would do well to look at these things rather than at complex, specially linguistic phenomena such as the specified subject condition.

Now, I would like to look at the situation of apple, knife, cut apple. To describe that as a "frame," let's say that it includes three cases: the initial state, the final state, and the trajectory or an instrument. I think this is a better way to look at it than to think of it as knowledge about causality; or rather, let's say that the knowledge about causality would come later and would be coded in terms of the prior coding of real situations according to schemata of that sort. The first question to ask is whether syntactic properties of the schemata have been pursued. An example comes from the suggestion that chimpanzees aren't very good at word order; now, are they good at object order in the representation of the schemata? For example, does the chimpanzee care whether the cut apple is on the left and the whole apple is on the right?

Premack I regard a schema as a structure that is responsible for the interpretation, the reading that is given to these items, so that they do not end up being interpreted in the many arbitrary ways in which an apple, a blank, an apple can be read. They are read in a specific way which it is necessary to assume to account for the consistency of the results. This is what I mean by schema, and I presume it is very much like what Piaget means by schema: a structure imposing an interpretation on a set of items that would otherwise be susceptible to an infinite number of interpretations.

In regard to the question of order, we have excellent evidence that the chimpanzee can respond to the order of the items in the visual sequence. To establish this, we first acquainted Sarah with actions the reverse of those on which she had been tested. *Cut, wet,* and *mark* were the actions on which she had been tested; we therefore acquainted her with *join* (patch together with tape), *dry,* and *erase.* Next we taught her that the visual sequences had to be read left to right. We did this by training her on sequences consisting of the same elements in the opposite order. For instance, we gave her the sequence: *blank paper ? marked paper;* and the opposite: *marked paper ? blank paper.* Her alternatives in both cases were the following: pencil, eraser, and cup of water. You can see that for the first case the answer is pencil (it will convert blank paper to marked paper); whereas for the second case, the answer is eraser (it will convert marked paper into blank paper). We trained Sarah on a limited number of such cases—cases that required her to pay attention to order—and then tested her on sixty new cases. She was correct on forty of the sixty cases; with three alternatives, this is highly significant (P < .001).

Papert It seems that there is a small vocabulary of a few very important discrete schemata that play a crucial role in the structuring of the child's environment.

Atran As far as I can see, there is no compelling evidence to indicate that such schemata, which are common to the child and chimpanzee, could constitute the basis for the construction of human language. Even the correlation by analogy is extremely weak, since the examples given simply suggest that a "schema" does little more than present items in succession and restrict the possibility of "reading them off," or representing them in an infinite number of ways. To look for analogical "equivalents" of grammatical rules in the behavior or the representation of causal behavior that may be exhibited by children or chimpanzees is likely to be a waste of time.

I think that these remarks also apply to cases of "formal equivalence" of the kind mentioned here by Premack. For example, as evidence of "structure-dependent" rules in chimpanzee "language," Premack cites the following experiment: Given markers for the simple declarative, "apple is fruit," Sarah is taught to pluralize with these markers: "apple"; "banana"; "is"; "plural article of"; and "fruit." Premack goes on to say: "For from the training we had given her, she could have learned either of two rules, only one of which was correct. She could have learned to use a physical feature comparable to the physical feature in Chomsky's example, namely, applying a plural particle whenever there are two words to the left of 'is.' Or she could have induced a rule based not on a physical feature but on a grammatical one, namely, applying a plural particle when the subject is plural." Now, Premack says that this is a formal logical equivalent of Chomsky's rule for question formation, where the animal is pluralizing not on the basis of physical features but rather on the basis of the meaning of the sentence, that is, the internal representation of the string of words. But this seems to me to be an unwarranted generalization of a principle of syntax for human language.

First, the rule of question formation in human language

does not invariably depend upon any understanding of meaning. Second, the notion of structure dependence is not simply meant to reflect the fact that there is some relation between elements other than simple perceptual successions, but also that rules of syntax operate on abstract representations of a certain kind, namely, noun phrases, verb phrases, and so forth.

Within the theory of grammar it is widely recognized that the meaning of a sentence is based on the meaning of its parts and the manner of their combination; however, this does not mean that the nature of semantics is the same as that of syntax with respect to the rules operating on representations of phenomena in these two domains. Even the notion of meaning appears to be trivialized when applied to chimpanzees since many, if not all, of the semantic features of language can only be defined with respect to the notion of a sentence, just as rules of structure dependence can only be defined in terms of noun phrases and the like.

The use of metaphors for sentences and noun phrases does not help matters at all. Only insofar as some principle is fully and coherently integrated into a well-formed theoretical system, the whole of which can be tested with respect to a significant range of phenomena, does it become a principle of any scientific interest. To take any such principle in isolation and "demonstrate" its presence in some other cognitive domain or in some other species, whether in spontaneous behavior or through conditioning, coaxing or evoking, is to demonstrate nothing at all.

Premack   This whole argument confuses theory with evidence. As theoretical proposals, Atran's statements are unobjectionable. But he has no proof for any of them, and indeed does not bother with matters of proof. To begin with, his distinction between syntax and semantics avoids the painful fact that it is seldom possible to find actual language performance that realizes the distinction—that gives evidence of syntactic competence while perfectly excluding the role of semantics. So, to my example of Sarah's pluralization, it is easy enough to say that this had nothing to do with syntax, it is purely semantics. I wonder how many of Chomsky's examples would escape a similar objection—for example, how many questions do human speakers form that are independent of meaning?

Second, the notion of meaning is not trivialized when applied to the ape. On the contrary, at least some ape concepts are reminiscent of our own, specifically with respect to their abstractness. For example, the terms "color of," "shape of," and "wash," as they appeared in the ape sentences "red color of apple," "round shape of ball," and "Mary wash orange," were used abstractly by Sarah as they are by us. She applied them not only to the training exemplars but to countless new cases. Indeed, she exceeded the usual transfer criterion, for she not only applied these predicates to new cases but used at least one of them to generate a new word. The instruction "brown color of chocolate" was used successfully with Sarah to generate the new word "brown"—showing that she can use the predicate productively, that is, to generate new instances of itself.

This is not to say that there is no difference between human and ape words. But Atran's account does not point us in the right direction. I suspect that the difference between the two species may be contained in the answer to this question: what defines a word in the chimpanzee and the human mind? Oversimplifying greatly, I suggest the following: in the ape, a word is defined by an image or sensory representation; whereas in man, a word is defined by other words. I can offer circumstantial evidence now, but actually proving this claim is another matter.

Bischof   My question comes back to the problem of teaching. There is a correspondence between the teaching on the part of the parents and the desire to be taught on the part of the child, and as far as I know, there is a specific age in the development of the human child (I think around age 2) which is called the "age of what's that" by developmental psychologists, when children very eagerly try to find out the names of things. Interestingly, a little bit later there is another age called the "why age," when children inquire about causal relations. Of course, it is obvious that there is nothing like a spontaneous "why age" or "age of what's that" in chimpanzees. Have you ever encountered any instances in which your chimpanzees asked you questions?

Premack   The only thing I can say in that regard is that despite the resolute way in which I followed a checklist of what I suppose to be basic elements in language and forced the animal to carry out a lesson built exclusively around the topic of my interest, so that it had available only those things that I deliberately made available to it, the animal would decide otherwise in the middle of my beautiful lesson and would run off with the plastic words to the middle of the floor, where it was most difficult to reach. It would then ask itself the questions of the lesson as well as others, and it would answer them, for the most part, correctly. Indeed, on those occasions the animal's performance level was very close to 100 percent, whereas when the animal was answering my questions the performance level was about 85 percent. Similarly, Elizabeth, another trainee who was very active but by no means the equal of some of our other apes, was given a lesson in which she had to describe what the trainer was doing (the trainer carries out simple acts and the ape has to describe them), and there too she was about 85 percent correct. But often, while waiting for the next test during which the trainer carries out an act, the animal performed the act and then described it spontaneously, which we didn't ask her to do, and in these cases she was 100 percent correct.

Finally, one can ask whether the animal has at least the idea of the word, the idea that things can be named. You can do the following experiment with even the least capable of the animals: you include in the set of words a potential word, that is, a piece of plastic which is demonstrably a potential word in the sense that it has all the properties of the class, but it has never been used as a word. You also use an item which is familiar but which has never been named; even the stupidest animal rapidly constructs the sentence, "Give X [the name of the animal] this new piece of plastic." In other words, the animal requests the unnamed item with the so far unused piece of plastic. Thus the chimpanzees recognize that the potential word, which has not yet been so employed, is the appropriate thing to use in requesting the desired item, which is however not yet named. There are more elegant ways of doing that, but people often prefer the nonelegant way.

Wilden   Something that emerged from your data is the question of negation and the various different types or levels of negation. Obviously, what one would expect is a crossing of boundaries between the two domains, between the chimpanzee communication system and the human communication system. My question has to do with how the chimpanzee manages to use negation.

Premack   If the animal is asked what the relationship is between A and B, and if the word "different" is deliberately removed from its available lexicon, the animal will answer "no same," so it can, with proper training, carry out acts of negation.

Wilden   That is one form of negation, not the only form.

Premack   It is a form of negation, and not a trivial one. There is also an aversion to the negative; you find the same thing in retarded children. Normally, if you wanted to teach, for instance, the concept of "name of" or "color of" or "shape of," or any predicate of that kind, by contrasting the positive with the negative case, you would introduce "color of" by contrasting it with "not color of." But there are occasions when you cannot do that, when the animal rejects negative forms, in which case you are required to train him with "name of" or "color of" in relation to an already known affirmative predicate. Thus you contrast "name of" with "color of" rather than "color of" with "not color of." As I said, sometimes in retarded or autistic children to whom these procedures are applied, the rejection of the negative form is so pervasive that you can only work on the negative for a short period, and then henceforth you introduce the names of new predicates only by contrasting all positive forms.

Even though Premack, by his exhaustive analysis of the chimpanzee's cognitive universe, opens the way to a third position between Piaget and Chomsky, one of his sentences betrays his basically innatist attitude. In replying to Bateson (on learning to learn) he says: "I'm not a great believer in the word 'learning,' and I am rather more in favor of Fodor's argument. I think that the main thing that human training is doing here for the chimpanzee is disclosing capacities that are present." The zone of convergence between Premack and Piaget has to be found elsewhere: in the general (that is, nonlinguistic or prelinguistic) capacities that are common to higher primates and to man. According to Premack, representational capacity and the complex trait he calls accessibility of knowledge are detectable both in man and in the chimpanzee, and language can develop on the basis of such capacities (if suitable brain structures are present). However, Premack considers these cognitive capacities to be innate, in contrast to Piaget. In his "Afterthoughts," Piaget will comment further on Premack's views concerning the innatist hypothesis and the possible sources of "necessity" in cognitive development.

In the next chapter, the floor is given to Norbert Bischof, an ethologist of the Lorenzian school. In his paper and in the course of his discussion with Piaget, further relevant problems concerning interspecies comparison are brought out.

CHAPTER TEN

Phylogenesis and Cognition

In a previous editorial comment (see Chapter 1) I drew the reader's attention to the convergent attacks that the participants have launched, each from his particular position, against empiricism and behaviorism. Piaget jokingly calls empiricism his preferred dummy target (tête de Turc), a cherished adversary in a philosophical battle, out of which most of his central ideas have arisen. Premack, following the views of Feigl, argues convincingly against behaviorism. Bischof, attaining a felicitous synthesis between Konrad Lorenz and Feigl, expounds here a concise and convincing theory of knowledge based on phylogenesis and likewise concludes with a refutation of behaviorism. We are witnessing here more than a confrontation between different theories of language or theories of learning—it is a confrontation between theories of knowledge, taking the term in the somewhat lofty and slightly deterring meaning it was imbued with in the nineteenth century by German philosophers (Erkenntnistheorie). "What is reality?" and "What is truth?" are, at least since the fifth century B.C., two of the archetypal questions of a "perennial" philosophy whose very legitimacy has been questioned again and again in recent times. It is one of the characteristics of the present debate, and of the intellectual epoch to which it belongs, that such "eternal" questions are now rejuvenated and approached from different angles than that of "pure" or professional philosophy. Piaget, a child psychologist, and Lorenz, an ethologist, attempt to meet at face value precisely such questions. Bischof, quoting (and, it can be said, refining) the evolutionary theory of knowl-

231

edge developed by Lorenz, responds to some of Piaget's critiques of Lorenz as expressed in his introductory paper (see Chapter 1). The faults attributed to Lorenz by Piaget are substantially the following: (1) to have based his theory of knowledge on Kant without attaining the level of (in Piaget's terms) a "dynamic Kantism"; (2) to have held that the "categories of thinking" are not only "static" (that is, always identical to those present in the adult mind), but specific to man; (3) to have ascribed their origin to a species-specific genetic heredity; and (4) to have explained their character of "necessity" in terms of their innateness.

For Piaget, as we have seen in the preceding chapters, necessity is logically and factually independent of innateness. Moreover, he is disturbed by the Lorenzian concept of "innate working hypotheses" as being both necessary (detectable in all human beings) and efficient (that is, adequate in representing reality). Lorenz, and with him many of those who have developed an evolutionary sensitivity in dealing with the problem of human knowledge, conceives of the match and mismatch between internal representations and external reality as the outcome of a long selective process. Through random mutations and selections, only those cognitive structures have been maintained that allow for an adequate representation of the outside world; all the others (rather, all the neuronal structures on which they were based) have been eliminated. This line of argument also appears in Karl Popper's later work under the label of the "amoeba to Einstein" principle.* The unmistakable flavor of Darwinism embedded in these theories is unsavory to Piaget.

Bischof presents here a detailed rejoinder to Piaget's arguments. The coherent picture he presents of the "realist" approach to knowledge, pioneered by Lorenz, is in a way the outcome of a philosophical syncretism between Darwin and Kant. It offers a persuasive answer to the question that Bertrand Russell formulated some thirty years ago: "How comes it that human beings, whose contacts with the world are brief and personal and limited, are nevertheless able to know as much as they know?"

---

* See K. Popper, "The Rationality of Scientific Revolutions," in *Problems of Scientific Revolutions: Progress and Obstacles to Progress in the Sciences,* ed. R. Harre (Oxford: Clarendon Press, 1975).

Remarks on Lorenz and Piaget: How Can "Working Hypotheses" Be "Necessary"?

Norbert Bischof

In his paper, Piaget argues against the viewpoint of Konrad Lorenz, who holds that the categories of thinking have developed in the process of phylogenetic adaptation of the human species to its environment. Logically enough, Lorenz calls these categories "innate working hypotheses" of the human cognitive system. Piaget, on his side, feels that the contingent and provisionary status of a "working hypothesis," born out of the haphazard guesswork of mutation, contradicts the "necessary" character of our cognitive structures.

I would like to argue in favor of the Lorenzian view. In particular, I intend to point out that the notions of "working hypothesis" and "necessity," as used by Lorenz and Piaget, respectively, are not at all contradictory.

AN EPISTEMOLOGICAL ARGUMENT

Lorenz proceeds from an epistemological viewpoint which is shared by most other ethologists (and also, for instance, by Gestalt psychologists and logical empiricists such as Feigl) and which has been labeled "critical realism."* The basic assumptions of critical realism are the following:

1. There is a structured reality, the so-called "objective world," the structure of which remains the same whether or not there are organisms who perceive it correctly, or perceive it at all.

2. Organisms form a special subset of this "objective world." They are characterized by the fact that their behavior can be interpreted as "adaptive" in the sense of optimizing their chances of survival.

3. This adaptiveness defines a mapping relation: for every possible behavior of an organism, a set of environmental situations in which this behavior would be optimally adaptive can be

---

* Editor's note: The debate between Putnam, Chomsky, and Fodor in Part II brings further clarification of the issue of "critical realism." Putnam is considered to be one of the most authoritative exponents of this school of thought.

233

assumed to exist. Thus it can be stated that the behavior of an organism contains "information" about the features of the environment. This information refers to the intersection of all possible situations in which the given behavior would be optimally adaptive.

4. The concept of information is, in this context, not confined to the mere syntactic meaning that it has in information theory. Rather, it can be interpreted *semantically:* we can speak of "true" or "false" information depending on whether a behavior is in fact adapted to the *existing* situation or not. This should be elucidated by a brief example. There is a set of involuntary eye movements that are controlled by the vestibular organ, so-called "vestibular eye reflexes." Among other possibilities, the human eye may, in a given situation, perform a steady rotation in the horizontal plane; in other situations, the eyeballs may be tilted to a given angle around their sagittal axes. If a human organism is subject to a lateral linear acceleration, the eyes will perform a reactive movement. However, this movement does not consist of a lateral drift, which would allow the person to keep track of the environment passing by, but rather consists of a steady tilt around the optical axis. This response would only be adaptive in the context of a lateral body tilt; in this case it would help to maintain the stability of the retinal image. Thus we can describe the situation in terms of the organism having "misinterpreted" the lateral linear movement as a steady body tilt (actually, the lateral acceleration has interfered with the pull of gravity to yield a deflection of the otoliths that is equivalent to and indistinguishable from a lateral body tilt). In this case, the "information" contained in the eye movement about the spatial situation of the body is *false:* to be adaptive, the behavior would require a situation that does not exist in reality.

5. The subject of the experiment just described is not aware of his (involuntary) eye movements. But if he is asked about his subjective experience, he will indeed report the sensation of being laterally tilted. In other words, subjective experience corresponds to the "information" that the external observer assigns to the responses of the organism. Critical realism, now, generally postulates that our subjective experience (or our "phenomenal world") can be understood as the "information" contained in the totality of our behavioral states of readiness; that is, every subject's phenomenal world stands in a mapping relation to objective reality, corresponding to it more or less exactly, but by no means identical with it.

In everyday life, we do not make this distinction. To my naive understanding, there is no other mysterious world beyond the world of my immediate experience: the object that emits light waves to my eyes, and the object that accordingly appears in front of my eyes, are taken to be one and the same, located in one and the same space. This everyday viewpoint is called "naive realism"; we get along with it very well outside our laboratories (due to the fact that the mapping apparatus is so ingenious that it makes only a very few, minute errors). But even as scientists, we have to be very careful not to relapse into the naive view when the theoretical situation actually demands a more critical position.

The critical-realistic dichotomy between objective world and subjective world is indispensable as soon as we want to deal theoretically with the concept of "false information," as for example, in the case of an optical illusion, or any kind of cognitive error. In addition, the naive subject engaged in the struggles of everyday life has a vital interest in the veridicality of his cognitive structures. Far from being a mere issue of academic epistemology, success in the attempt to subjectively map objective reality in an adequate way does in fact determine the chances of survival. So what the subject vitally needs are cues in his phenomenal world that tell him when there is good reason to assume that the cognitive representation is correct.

At this juncture I will make a brief excursion into the psychology of thinking.

An Argument Borrowed from Cognitive Psychology

I would like to present the thesis that man's quest for knowledge has a structure that is similar, in principle, to that of a natural drive.

Ethologists usually distinguish two main phases in a drive process, called "appetency" and "consummation." These can be distinguished in the following ways:

1. Appetency (for example, searching for food) is accompanied by a state of tension. In consummation (for example, eating), this tension is more or less suddenly reduced. This reduction is felt to be pleasurable.

2. During evolution, appetency behavior becomes more and more complex, variable, and sophisticated, whereas consummation behavior remains comparably primitive, inflexible, and unmodifiable by experience.

3. Every natural drive can be expected to have a biological meaning, that is, to produce with sufficient certainty an *effect*

which directly establishes a selective advantage. However, in spite of its importance, this effect only seldom plays a role in our subjective experience; the fact of whether or not the effect occurs touches our passions less than might be expected. The reason for this failure is that it would be too difficult for our perceptual apparatus to ascertain the effect directly. Therefore, at first we hold fast to an earlier, more accessible link of the causal chain, which is the consummation. Thus the consummation is the *experienced* goal of appetency behavior, even though it does not constitute the *biological* goal. The latter—namely, the "effect" mentioned above—is only a sequel of consummation.

Thus, for example, in pairing behavior it is not the process of fertilization itself which is experienced as consummation, but rather certain events which are accessory to the transport of semen from the male to the female organism, that is, events preparatory to fertilization and, indeed, not necessarily entailing fertilization.

We note, therefore, as a matter of principle, that a successful consummatory experience, however tension-reducing it may be, *never necessarily* entails the naturally intended effect. Our emotions, however, do not know this, and it is only toward consummation that we feel driven, and in which we come to rest. Everything beyond consummation is, at best, a matter for ethics.

Perhaps the parallelism with cognitive behavior will already have become clear from the foregoing. Indeed, the analogy is striking if we allow for the "act" of cognition occurring internally rather than in the realm of observable behavior.

With cognitive activity, too, we find a more or less complex appetency—a state of tension in which the solution for the problem is sought by trying out various strategies, by applying past experience, and by engaging in productive thinking. Eventually, if we are lucky, this tension is released all of a sudden in a consummatory experience. This consummatory situation has been investigated mainly in Gestalt psychology. It was called the "aha-experience" by Karl Bühler—the sudden emergence of a meaning that justifies itself by an unquestionable, cogent *evidentness*.

This experience is accompanied, and in fact caused, by a characteristic change in the cognitive structures at issue. In terms of Gestalt psychology, unsolved problems have the character of "defective structures": they are structures with apparently missing parts, or with parts that contradict each other. Generally speaking, problems are structures in disequilibrium.

During the process of productive thinking, we observe sudden spurts of equilibration. It is these sudden gains of equilibrium and harmony that are emotionally reflected by the "aha-experience."

So much for the consummatory situation. The effect, however, which normally is coupled with this consummation, and to which this consummation owes its biological existence—this effect is the *truth* of the cognition: "truth" in the critical-realist sense of optimal adaptation of the cognitive structures to objective reality.

In this sense, we can say that whereas truth is the objective effect of thinking, the experience of evidentness is its subjective goal. Evidentness, as we have seen, grows out of structural equilibrium, harmony, and order, which ultimately are aesthetic rather than epistemological categories. But according to how our cognitive system is constructed, beauty seems to be taken as a guide to truth. Nature appears to share the confidence expressed in the medieval formula *verum et pulchrum convertuntur*—the confidence that "true" and "beautiful" are interchangeable, synonymous concepts, both reaching, in cases of verbal insufficiency, toward the same Inexpressible.

The only problem is that this formula hides a naive realism, that is, a realism that confuses correlation with identity. Consummation is only correlated with the effect, but cannot assure it: the experience of evidentness *guarantees* truth just as little as the experience of orgasm guarantees fertilization. Otherwise, the whole business of "verification" would not be necessary in science.

CONSEQUENCES FOR THE LORENZIAN CONCEPT OF "WORKING HYPOTHESIS"

I will now outline the consequences of the previous argumentation for an evaluation of Piaget's criticism of Lorenz's views. To begin with, when we use concepts like "working hypothesis" and "necessity," we ought to make clear whether we are arguing on the level of subjective or objective reality. Generally, when we speak of a "working hypothesis," we have *both* levels in mind. Objectively, a working hypothesis is characterized by a somewhat loose correspondence with reality. Subjectively, it presents itself as a tentative, not cogent, form of noncommittal guesswork.

This subjective connotation is strictly excluded in the Lorenzian line of reasoning. As far as the subjective level is concerned, Lorenz would fully agree with Piaget as to the cogent, necessary character of the inherited categories of reason. All he wants to state is that these categories are more than simply a means of *organizing* experience (what Kant had implied)— that in fact they also have a *representative* function, in that they tell something about the structure of the thing-in-itself. On the other hand, Lorenz also wants to say that these categories, however evident, necessary, and unfailing they may appear, are nevertheless only a phylogenetic *attempt* to reach the asymptote of truth.

If we now turn to the concept of "necessity" as used by Piaget, it seems equally clear that it can only be meant to denote the *subjective* appearance of the products of thinking. The term "necessity" is obviously referring to what I have called the "cogent evidentness" of a solution that has come to be a "good Gestalt." In fact, Piaget explicitly derives "necessity" out of processes of equilibration—and we have seen earlier that, in deed, the establishment of cognitive equilibrium entails the *experience* of evidentness. If, however, equilibration processes were interpreted as producing "necessity" in the *objective* sense of being "necessarily *true*," it would be hard to see on the basis of which epistemological principles (other than naive realism) this correspondence should be established.

Since Lorenz uses the term "working hypothesis" in a strictly objective sense, whereas Piaget's notion of "necessity" must be understood to refer strictly to a subjective state of affairs, it follows that the two concepts are unable to contradict each other in a logical sense. They could only be seen as contradictory if one failed to distinguish between the subjective and objective levels; this, however, would amount to a naive realist position.

The Problem of Logical and Mathematical Necessity

It could be argued by Piaget that the above considerations miss the point he wanted to make. He could state that, when speaking about "necessity," he was not referring to mere subjective *cogentness*, nor did he mean objective truth in a realist sense; rather, what he actually had in mind was logical *validity*. A proposition like "$2 + 2 = 4$" is, indeed, not a "working hypothesis" in any sense of the term. It is worth mentioning that Lorenz, in the paper referred to by Piaget, has already dealt at length with exactly this problem. He says:

> Nothing that our brain can think has absolute a priori validity . .
> not even mathematics with all its laws. The laws of mathematics
> are but an organ for the quantification of external things, and what

is more, an organ exceedingly important for man's life . . . which thus has amply proved itself biologically, as have all the other "necessary" structures of thought. Of course, "pure" mathematics . . . is, as a theory of the internal laws of this miraculous organ of quantification, of an importance that can be hardly overestimated. But this does not justify us in making it absolute. Counting the mathematical number affects reality in approximately the same manner as do a dredging-machine and its shovels. Regarded statistically . . . each shovel dredges up roughly the same amount but actually not even two can ever have exactly the same content. The pure mathematical equation is a tautology . . . Two shovels of my machine are absolutely equal to each other because strictly speaking it is the same shovel each time, namely the number one. But only the empty sentence always has this validity. Two shovels filled with something or other are never equal to each other, the number one applied to a real object will never find its equal in the whole universe.[1]

I doubt, though, whether Piaget would be content with this explanation. However tautological mathematics may be, it is certainly not trivial in a psychological sense. Solving a mathematical problem is a genuine act of productive thinking—a kind of highly complex interaction of the "dredging machine" with itself, an interaction not covered by Lorenz's model.

Mathematical reasoning is an activity of the brain, just like any form of empirical problem solving. Thus the initial Piagetian question persists: how could a contingent and basically defective creature of random mutation and selection ever reach a state to produce things like a mathematical equation, which is necessarily true because it is *ideal?* In fact, this is just the old Cartesian riddle of how we can possibly perceive, through a mathematician's sloppy drawing on a blackboard, the ideal triangle with an angular sum of exactly (and necessarily) 180 degrees.

If, then, our categories of thinking would just reflect the state of perfection of our genetically acquired brain hardware, our mathematical thinking would, according to this line of argument, never reach the ideal state of conceiving "$2 + 2 = 4$," but rather would be confined to something like "$2 + 2 \cong 3.98$."

However, this argument implies a very concrete notion of isomorphism between mental structures and brain structures. Indeed, if a perceived or imagined triangle were nothing else but a kind of photographic mapping of a triangle constructed out of visual cortex potentials, it would admittedly be hard to understand how it could come to have ideal properties—even after an infinite duration of phylogenesis! Gestalt theorists were caught in precisely this kind of argumentation when they postulated the existence of "field forces" in the brain to account for the regularities of mental gestalt.

Blind alleys of this kind can be avoided only if one gives up, once and for all, expecting subjective phenomena to be "facsimiles" of brain processes. It is not the *configuration,* but the *meaning* of a neural message that can be understood to be directly represented in one's consciousness; the term "meaning" (or as Lorenz prefers to say, "information") refers to the environmental features that would have to be presupposed to render the behavioral effects of this neural message optimally adaptive.

Interestingly, this notion implies a complementary relation between the *limitations* of behavior and the degree of *regularity* of the assigned meaning.

If there were a method to ask Jerome Lettvin's frogs about the shape of flies,[2] they would probably agree that all flies are ideally round—simply because their sensory system does not allow any behavioral differentiation with respect to the orientation of the fly. Higher organisms whose sensorimotor equipment enables them to, say, predict the direction in which the fly is most likely to make its next move, have to pay for this increased competence with some loss of perfect symmetry in their representations of the world.

Viewed from this angle, the Platonic world of pure ideas, which to our intuition reveals itself behind the distorted shadow-world of empirical things, is far from being an asymptote that could never be reached by a cognitive apparatus tinkered up by blind mutation and lame selection. On the contrary, our ability to conceive of ideal forms and relations is a heritage of ancient, primitive stages of our cognitive phylogenesis.

It is in this realm of ideal forms that we experience logical necessity. A syllogism like "All X are U; Y is X; so Y is U" is necessarily valid only for a mind that is capable of understanding the *idea* of areas nested in such a way as to successively enclose each other. Only the ideal character of this conceptual image supplies the intuition of the nonexceptionable validity, that is, the necessity, of the above syllogism.

To summarize: whoever intends to question the phylogenetic origin, and hence the "hypothetical" character, of the basic categories of thinking, can certainly not do so on grounds of their being "necessary" in the sense of evident, cogent, ideal, and perfect. Of course, this leaves entirely aside the question of whether, in general, the conception of a phylogenesis by way of random mutation plus survival of the fittest is a good model. As things stand, it is certainly the only legitimate model available; but we ought to be aware that it does not explain the reality of consciousness. Selection, it is true, enables us to introduce the concept of adaptiveness into the description of organisms, hence to assign "meanings" to brain processes, meanings that can then be taken as descriptions of conscious contents. But this is a purely *formal* procedure, a "manner of speaking" *(façon de parler)*, a way of organizing our knowledge. Consciousness, however, is more than a mere formal construct—at least to the owner of the brain in question. This *reality* of consciousness, which was only neglected but never validly refuted by behaviorism, ought to remind us of the preliminary character of our present understanding of nature.

Comments

Jean Piaget

I find it difficult to reply to Bischof; his discussion is so rich and so subtle that I would have to reread it very closely to respond in detail to what he says.* First of all, I would like to say that unfortunately (and I regret it), I have not read much of Konrad Lorenz. On the other hand, I have known him very well, having been with him and Inhelder in a study group of developmental psychobiology at the World Health Organization for four consecutive years, where we both realized that it was only at the end of the fourth year that we were beginning to understand each other. During the fourth year, Lorenz suddenly said to me: "You are not an empiricist—and I thought you were!" This is to show how little we understood each other. I answered him: "I am completely opposed to empiricism, and I thought it was you who were the empiricist"; he then replied: "Not at all, I am a disciple of my old colleague from Königsberg, that is, of Kant, and I am trying to translate his categories in biological terms under the form of innateness."

In the passage that Bischof criticizes in my paper, I was not

---

* Editor's note: See Piaget's "Afterthoughts" (Chapter 13).

trying to discuss the problem of innateness to which I referred when talking about Chomsky; I simply wanted to point out that Lorenz, to whom I had asked the question, in the case where the Kantian categories would be innate, of whether he thought they consisted of general or simply specific heredity, answered me that he was thinking of specific heredity, which was therefore capable of varying from one species to another. It is in this perspective that I understood the notion of "innate working hypothesis." In my paper, I praised him for his prudence, that is, for not considering the innateness of Kantian categories as being a universal characteristic. Therefore I said to Lorenz (and still continue to believe): "You retain from Kant above all the idea of preconditioning—that which conditions experience —and I totally agree with this anti-empiricism, but you sacrifice necessity insofar as this necessity would only be species-specific. For my part, I insist on a necessity which is logical in kind and which—needless to say—cannot result from the closing of systems. From this point of view, equilibration is the construction of ultimately closed structures, that is to say, of structures that are self-composed and autonomous, like a group in the mathematical sense." In other words, I praised Lorenz for his prudence in regard to the Kantian categories, but at the same time, I felt that his preconditioning delimitation seemed secondary, and, for my part, I question this preconditioning in the sense of innateness of structures, but I retain the concept of necessity in the sense that I have just discussed. Of course, if there had been a more detailed discussion of Lorenz in my paper, I would have made other reservations, in particular, that of explaining the adaptation of knowledge simply by selection and by the advantages that a more or less adequate knowledge provides to the species. I think that if this is true in regard to elementary practical knowledge (that is, search for food, search for a favorable place for a bird's nest, and so on), I absolutely do not see, as soon as we are dealing with human knowledge, how selection can explain to us the advantage obtained by the human species, for example, that of inventing imaginary numbers under the form of the square root of a negative number. For me, what is difficult to understand in the neo-Darwinian concept of instincts as conceived by Lorenz is the correspondence between the hereditary formation of morphogenesis and that of behaviors. For behavior goes beyond the bounds of the soma and presupposes all kinds of anticipations in relation to the external environment. If I had discussed this problem in his neo-Darwinism more closely with Lorenz, I would have mentioned the example of the pagurians, which for me is very illustrative. Pagurians are the victims of random mutation in the sense that they have a soft abdomen, but at the same time a specific hereditary behavior appears, consisting of finding refuge in the shells of gastropods; thus we have, on the one hand, an unfavorable mutation concerning the survival of the species, and then, on the other hand, a behavior that remedies and compensates, and brings back a normal situation. Now, it is doubtful in this case that there would be two formations of the same nature, and thus both due to random mutations to be placed on the same level. This is the direction I would have taken in discussing things with Lorenz, but I repeat that, in regard to what Bischof said, I simply cited this interpretation of the innate working hypothesis as praise for the prudence of Lorenz in not immediately confusing the innate and the universal.

Piaget's more detailed rejoinder to Bischof will appear in Chapter 13. In this brief reply to Bischof that we have just read, which Piaget gave during the debate, there is a passage that helps to understand Piaget's conception of necessity: "I insist on a necessity which is logical in kind and which—needless to say—cannot result from the closing of systems. From this point of view, equilibration is the construction of ultimately closed structures, that is to say, of structures that are self-composed and autonomous, like a group in the mathematical sense." The terms "ultimately closed," "self-composed," and "autonomous" seem to hold the key to necessity as conceived by Piaget. What he appears to suggest is a "locking" process, similar to the "order-from-noise" process, followed by the combinatorial closure of the system after the pieces have reassembled themselves. These, presumably, are the mechanisms that ensure both novelty and necessity in Piaget's model. This dilemma (necessity versus unpredictable fluctuation, actualization of a predetermined pathway versus order from noise) has already come closest to its final solution (a solution that will be provided by empirical evidence) in Changeux's paper and in the discussion immediately following it (see Chapter 8).

As far as this debate is concerned, we will get no clearer picture from Piaget of the origins of necessity. Many of his books, however, deal with this problem. Passing mention should be made of the role that Bischof attributes to "equilibration" and "reequilibration" when describing the biological agent of conceptual novelty (the "aha-experience"). Here, indeed, the overlap with Piaget is evident.

CHAPTER ELEVEN

Cognition and the Semiotic Function

*Dan Sperber, a cognitive anthropologist whose original ap-
proach to symbolism is quite in tune with Chomsky's generative linguistics,* has already questioned the meaning of "the
symbolic or semiotic function" (see Chapter 7). His critique of
semiology is developed here, and his underlying innatist hypothesis explicitly stated. Basically, Sperber argues that anything can become a symbol. He feels that there is no closed
and definable class of entities (percepts, strings of phonemes,
external objects, and so forth) that can be characterized by the
common property of being symbols, actual or potential. All
percepts, concepts, and relations can be processed both as descriptions and as symbols. There is no such thing as a "grammar of symbolism," Sperber argues, because the set of phenomena susceptible to being interpreted in the symbolic mode is
neither numerable nor rule-bound. "Input conditions" (conditions d'entrée) are the only valuable criteria for ascribing a
phenomenon to the symbolic world of a given individual or a
given culture, or both. Which specific input conditions are
criterial here and now is something to be discovered empirically by careful study of the "mental setup" (dispositif mental)
associated with symbolic processing and of the innate dispositions that influence the selection of data, mapped onto suitable
(symbolic) patterns and charged with adequate resonances
(cognitive, emotional, or both). Sperber pairs each conceptual
representation with the corresponding perceptual representa-*

---

* See D. Sperber, *Rethinking Symbolism* (Cambridge, 1975).

244

tion in three distinct, but compatible, modes: the semantic mode, the encyclopedic or descriptive mode, and the symbolic mode. The same percept can be associated with three corresponding representations, but this does not mean that the three processing mechanisms merge. In other words, Sperber rejects the "current thesis" that semantic and symbolic representations are both subsumed under one "deciphering" mode (decodification), called the semiotic function. There is a specific, inborn capacity for symbolism. The symbolic mode of representation also develops in the course of ontogenesis; its inner workings are untaught and cannot be accounted for in terms of "general intelligence." Sperber anticipates that cognitive anthropologists, once freed from their relativist prejudice, will contribute significantly to the unraveling of the problem of the innate bases of human knowledge. The domain of symbolic representations, showing both species-specific inborn capacities and, at the same time, a variety of culture-dependent contents, is of unique interest. We are faced, says Sperber, with another "major mental activity" distinct from language, but equally relevant to the inner workings of conceptual thought.

In the ensuing discussion, Sperber's positions are challenged by Piaget and Papert. They contend that what seems at first to be "untaught" is actually the result of indirect teaching.

Remarks on the Lack of Positive Contributions from Anthropologists to the Problem of Innateness

Dan Sperber

Unfortunately, present-day anthropology does not have much of a contribution to make to this debate; I will therefore limit what I have to say to a few rather simple remarks.

Up to now, the major contribution of anthropology to the problem of innateness has been negative: it has supplied glaring counterexamples to ethnocentric innatist hypotheses that attributed a natural character to Western values and institutions and made of the customs and manners of our life-style the characteristics of accomplished manhood. Anthropologists, in refuting this naive naturalism, arrived at the conviction that *all* innatist hypotheses are naive and henceforth treated them with nothing but scorn. They stopped taking part in a debate whose futility they thought—over-hastily—they had demonstrated.

Today, however, the research and arguments of generative linguists carry such weight that it is hardly reasonable any longer to deny that language can have strong innate bases. Anti-innatist anthropologists would probably concede this point, inasmuch as it does not concern them directly, but they would argue, nonetheless, that precisely because *Homo sapiens* is genetically equipped with the foundations of language, no other innate basis is necessary to explain the learning of culture. Language and the general intelligence that accompanies it probably constitute a powerful enough instrument to account for all the rest of the learning process; that is, linguistic relativism is being abandoned in order to provide more safeguards for cultural relativism. It is this abandonment which stands out clearly among contemporary anthropologists, and which I would like to criticize here.

Those who favor the "linguistic innatism plus cultural relativism" theory have two types of arguments at their disposal. First, all of the encyclopedic knowledge capable of being learned can be explained and therefore verbally taught; therefore, a child who understands his language would not need anything else in order to understand his culture. Second, the aptitude for symbolic interpretation, which is an essential aspect of culture, would be dependent on a semiological system analogous to that of language, and any child who knew how to speak could by that very fact make use of structures that would allow him to symbolize. Language would therefore intervene in cultural learning in two ways: directly, as an instrument for the transmission of encyclopedic knowledge, and indirectly, as a model of symbolic setups. I would like to demonstrate briefly that these two hypotheses lose their plausibility when they are confronted with the facts for which they are supposed to account, and that this position of withdrawal, which seems to tempt the cultural relativists, cannot be defended.

First of all, even if in principle the propositional contents of cultural knowledge could be transmitted verbally by explicit and complete teaching, this is not exactly how things happen. Direct instruction plays only a partial—even a minimal—role in the learning process; and each human being knows much more than what he has been taught. To give only one example, every human being living in society knows how to recognize, understand, and appreciate, within the limits of his culture, an open repertory of witticisms. Now, not only are adults' instructions on grasping witticisms very vague, but in addition, a witticism is really recognized as such only by a person who does not need to see others laughing in order to find it humorous himself, and is appreciated only by a person who did not need any explanation of it in the first place. If example and instruction do play a role in the learning of wit, they would in any case be unable to teach it without an aptitude having been previously developed by the individual. As a rule, even if the learning process relies heavily on heard utterances, it does not simply consist of recording the propositional content of these utterances; consequently one could not assert that acquired knowledge is deducible from heard utterances through the sole operations of a general intelligence deprived of innate specializations. The truth of the matter is that we do not know anything about this, and it would be wrong to exclude innatist hypotheses a priori (just as it would be wrong, of course, to give them preference a priori).

The second hypothesis, which states that symbolic activity uses mechanisms analogous to those of language, poses a more interesting problem, first because it is very commonly accepted, not only among anthropologists but also among psychologists, philosophers, and so forth; second, because it can be completely disproved; and third, because disproving it reveals the possibility of innate mental mechanisms of a new type.

A conceptual representation can be associated in three ways with the perceptual representation from which it originates. First, in the particular case in which perceptual representation consists of the phonetic representation of a sentence, a semantic representation is associated with it through grammar. Second, all perceptual representation can be described by an encyclopedic representation. Third, a perceptual representation can evoke a symbolic representation, which is neither a meaning determined by the grammar of the language nor a description of the percept.

Obviously, semantic, encyclopedic, and symbolic representations are not incompatible and can be associated with the same percept. For example, if Paul says to Marie "I love you," Marie associates with the perceived sound a semantic representation of the sentence, an encyclopedic representation such as "Paul has declared his love," and finally, a symbolic representation which depends on her own feelings. Likewise, a religious sermon has the meaning of its uttered sentences; it is described as a behavior of the preacher; and it elicits in the faithful an awe toward their own sins.

The thesis most generally accepted, either implicitly or explicitly, is that this tripartite representation of concepts is only apparent and that it is in fact subsumed by a bipartite one: semantic and symbolic representations together would depend on one semiotic function and would bear on signs, utterances, or symbols which the mind would decipher, in contrast to other objects of perception which the mind would be content to describe. If this semiological conception were exact, it would give an initial plausibility to the conception according to which symbolic activity is patterned on linguistic activity and does not presuppose any distinct innate aptitude.

This conception, however, is wrong, as I have attempted to demonstrate in detail elsewhere.[1] I will present here only a single argument against the semiological conception, but this argument alone will be sufficient to invalidate it and has direct consequences for the problem of innate mental equipment.

Either the semiological conception is without any precise empirical significance, and in this case there is no reason to discuss it (a point of view that was defended earlier by Chomsky [see Chapter 7]), or it must assert that there exists a grammar of symbolism comparable to that of language. A grammar is an apparatus that enumerates (in the mathematical sense of the term) the sentences of a language. In this respect, a grammar differs from other mental apparatuses in which the set of parts that constitutes them cannot be enumerated. For example, no one could conceive of making a grammar out of possible visual stimuli; these stimuli are generally limited by input conditions (such as wavelength and intensity) and cannot be enumerated. The question, therefore, is to know whether the set of phenomena susceptible of being symbolically interpreted is enumerable and dependent on a grammar, or whether it can be defined only by input conditions. Once the question is expressed in these terms, the answer is obvious: under certain conditions, every object of thought can elicit a symbolic evocation; thus the set of symbolic phenomena is not enumerable and can be defined only by input conditions. Consequently, the mental apparatus that underlies symbolic activity is of a completely different type from that which underlies linguistic activity. Every semiological conception, whether that of the anthropologists or that of Piaget, which attributes structures of the same type to both language and symbolism is therefore erroneous. The so-called semiotic function does not exist. The problem of learning symbolism remains untouched.

This refutation suggests a few speculative remarks. If the semiological conception had been correct, it would have immediately answered the two basic questions of every theory of symbolism: (1) Under what conditions is a phenomenon symbolically interpreted? (2) What is the link between the symbolic phenomenon and its interpretation? Indeed, if symbolism had a grammar, all the objects created by that grammar would be symbolically interpreted, and the grammar itself would define the link between the object and its interpretation. But since there is no grammar of symbolism, these two basic questions remain unanswered. Two other types of answers can also be discarded quickly. First, symbolic activity is not the object of explicit and exhaustive instructions, and therefore the range and the mechanism of interpretation of symbolism are not determined by teaching. Second, it is not clear what rational considerations (of adaptation, for example) would constrain all human beings to make of certain percepts the point of departure for a symbolic evocation; it would therefore be arbitrary to assert that the symbolic apparatus is the mere product of general intelligence. On the contrary, it seems conceivable that the better we understand the mechanisms of symbolic selection and interpretation, the more we will come to believe that the organism that developed them was equipped to do so from the outset. Now, this hypothetical innate aptitude is doubly interesting, on the one hand because it concerns a major mental activity (in contrast, for example, to minor innate mechanisms connected with the identification of colors or the recognition of faces), and on the other hand, because this aptitude is of a type completely different from the aptitude for language, even though it intervenes, like language itself, at the level of conceptual thought.

If anthropology is ultimately to contribute in a positive way to the study of the genetic foundations of knowledge, it will be at the level of conceptual thought, where the experimental method has obvious limits, especially in the area of symbolism where cultural variations are the most enlightening. Such a contribution will be possible only if anti-innatism and semiologism are abandoned.

Discussion

Papert   I would like to say something about Sperber's reference to abilities that appear in a child without having been *taught*. It is wrong to identify *teaching* with a standard situation in which a teacher stands in front of a class or a mother interacts with her child. There are much more indirect ways in which society transmits knowledge to its young. For instance, we see many examples of one-to-one correspondence in our social life. The system of monogamy teaches many things; among them is a precursor of arithmetic, that is, the idea of one-to-one correspondence. Is it not plausible that social forms are selected for this kind of function by some evolutionary process?

Sperber   One must distinguish between explicit, direct instruction, which in itself can account for the learning process, and objects of reflection, which can suggest to the subject a systematic development only if this object is equipped to do so. An organism that constructed the one-to-one relationship from observing monogamy would not owe his learning to any kind of "teaching" per se, but rather to his own faculties.

Papert   Part of the function of teaching is giving models, and this might amount to saying: "Look, this aspect of the world is important; think about it, internalize it as a model for use later." Chomsky says, and so does the whole artificial intelligence tradition, that a very difficult problem concerning the learning process is the question of why, among the many routes that the learner could take, he chooses some and not others. I think that there are many explanations, some involving things of the sort Piaget would call "equilibration," among other factors; others having to do with the fact that society has ways of attracting the learner's attention by labeling certain things as important. Whether or not there is such guidance can play a fundamental role in determining whether something is learnable or not.

Let's suppose you wanted to teach children, among others, that a thing like "the man who was here yesterday" should be treated as an object in itself in some sense. One way you might do that would be to go around saying "the man who was here yesterday" outside the context of putting it in a whole sentence. Doing this could build up a particular structure that would play a role in learning to perceive structures in general. The real point I want to make is this: I don't know of any study that makes a serious attempt to survey the multitude of possible indirect modalities of teaching that might exist within a given society, and unless we do make such an attempt, we are on extremely poor grounds to make any responsible statements.

Chomsky   There are very good reasons why there is no such study, and that goes along with what Papert was saying, which I think is wrong. Papert said that the real problem (and here I agree with him) is to find out why learning takes one path rather than another; he then said that there are many explanations for this, but I don't agree with that. I know of only one explanation for it, namely, *the assumption about the built-in conditions limiting the possible output;* if there were indeed many other explanations, many proposals that would have consequences we could test, we could then make a survey of those many explanations as Papert suggests. But before that survey is undertaken, it is necessary that something exist to be surveyed. Until a proposal or a set of proposals are advanced that have empirical consequences that we can investigate, it is simply not true to say that there are many explanations.

I am not saying that for any physical event that takes place, there aren't infinitely many conceivable things that may have caused it. One can't survey all the infinite number of possible causes. What one does try to do is to develop scientific theories that have consequences and then possibly compare them. In cases where there is a set of alternative theories, a survey can compare them, but when there isn't a set of alternative theories you can't do anything.

Premack   Let me say that Chomsky has taken the problem and put it back where it belongs in terms of the subject of this conference, namely in language, but I think that the problem of how a student ever learns anything is a mystery that goes beyond language. In trying to teach even the simplest thing, you are not teaching one thing but an infinite number of things. You will see exactly what things you may be teaching, and how many of them the subject may learn before ultimately learning the one thing on which you have focused, if you take the trouble to enumerate even some of the things that have played a part in your training program. Suppose you try to teach an animal one-to-one relations between pieces of plastic and different fruits, and the animal is exceedingly slow to learn that in the beginning. You say, incorrectly as it turns out, that it has not learned anything because it continues to respond in a random way with respect to which word goes with which referent. Ultimately, you notice that there are other relations you may also be teaching: class properties of words, class properties of referents, operators appropriate to words, operators appropriate to referents. There is also the possibility that before learning any one-to-one relations, the subject learns a superordinate relation, so to speak —that any member of the word class can be used to obtain any member of the referent class—and he learns this even though it is incorrect. The subject may learn all that before learning that only a specific word gives him a specific referent. If you consider the months that are required to do this, you will find that in fact, before the subject learns that a particular word is required to obtain a particular object, he does learn all of the above, and doubtless much more that has evaded us. That the student learns the precise thing that the teacher has in mind (among the indeterminate number that his teaching may also be seen to provide as relevant examples) is a mystery that I think we should spend more time pondering.

Fodor　Anybody who understands the first step in a theory of nondemonstrative inference (of which learning is clearly a special case) knows that you don't have such inferences *unless you put prior constraints on the class of properties that can be projected.* By now, this is just a banal remark in the philosophy of science; everybody has understood this for many years. So the only possible argument about nativism is an argument about strictness. What are the nature and the extent of the constraints? The fact that there must be some is demonstrable on logical grounds.

Premack　Let me correct the impression that I have accused anthropology of being irrelevant or trivial either in a technical or a nontechnical sense. I was simply trying to say that the anthropologist announces with great insight a problem of which we are all a victim and then leaves us with no solution. If the anthropologist disappoints me, it is only because, following his extremely elegant formulation of the problem, he has nothing more elegant to offer as a solution than to say, "Don't get discouraged; try, try again," which is what we all do anyway.

The pedagogical problem consists of putting together the two things that we have discussed. The question of whether monogamous marriage can furnish an example for one-to-one correspondence is only half the problem; the other half is that it can in principle be an example for infinitely many things. Except in cases where there are schemata or devices that assure a particular reading or interpretation of the example, there is not likely to be a specific or dependable outcome. Let me just mention some elegant and simple evidence given by Levine in support of the view that for learning to take place, the hypothesis must be in the learner's head.[1] Levine uses a situation that is so simple that one can ascertain immediately what hypotheses the subject is using. From the subject's behavior regarding choice over a series of trials, one can say whether he is entertaining color, shape, size, and so on. The data show that despite a perfect conjunction of stimulus-response and reward, if the hypothesis is not in the subject's head, no learning takes place. Moreover, as Fodor can testify, studies on verbal conditioning show that it does not take place unless a co-extensive hypothesis about what is being considered is already known to the subject. Levine's work shows this in a very conclusive way.

The discussion is focused around two crucial issues, which proceed from the earlier chapters and continue into the remaining ones. The first is the problem of demarcation between a structured input, suitable material for a "constructive" action mediated by learning, and a simple triggering, humbly serviceable to the unfolding of a genetic program. The second issue, related to the first, concerns the nature of the a priori constraints acting on the pathways of knowledge. Constructivism invokes external structures and an a posteriori necessity in order to explain how the cognitive subject can learn at all, and why such learning always leads where it is expected to. Innatism first attempts to demonstrate that the supposed specific external structures have no structure worthy of the name, then to jeopardize the very notion of learning. Monod's and Fodor's argument (see Chapter 5) that if any input will elicit the proper output, then one cannot speak of "learning" but rather of a triggering mechanism, is endorsed here by Sperber in the domain of symbolism.

As far as the first issue is concerned, no further substantial clarification will emerge in Part I. The reader interested in a more detailed analysis of the anti-innatist argument is referred to Part II, where Putnam shows that there is more to the "general intelligence" thesis than has emerged heretofore. The second issue, which Chomsky has defined here as "the assumption about the built-in conditions limiting the possible output," takes a new orientation in the next chapter, where a consistent theory of induction, developed by Carl Hempel and Nelson Goodman in terms of a priori constraints on "projectible predicates," is summarized by Chomsky and Fodor. Explicitly or implicitly, a sort of challenge has been seen in the preceding chapters; in fact, the problem of innate (or at any rate a priori) constraints on possible cognitive output has appeared recurrently in this debate. Fodor's presentation in Chapter 6, Chomsky's remarks in the preceding chapters, Bischof's account of inborn working hypotheses, and Sperber's advocacy of innate cognitive dispositions all bear on this issue. In the following chapter Chomsky and Fodor expound in some detail the historical origins of a theory of induction to which they both adhere and the reasons why this philosophical issue has often been so controversial, with metaphysical, ideological, and even political overtones. A whole section of Chomsky's book **Reflections on Language** is devoted to a thorough analysis of the inductivist theories of knowledge.* In what follows, the ideological concomitants of inductivism are examined by Chomsky in response to a challenge made during the discussion by the anthropologist Thomas de Zengotita.

---

* N. Chomsky, *Reflections on Language* (New York: Pantheon, 1975).

CHAPTER TWELVE

The Inductivist Fallacy

The discussion reported in this chapter, which has been abridged for the reasons I have explained in the Preface, is the natural sequel to Chapter 6 and the basis of many of the arguments that will keep rebounding between Putnam, Chomsky, and Fodor in Part II.

As a first approximation, I will point out the three major problems that emerge from this discussion. In order of presentation, they are as follows: (1) the nature (and the plausible origins) of the lawful regularities projected a priori by the subject onto sets of relevant empirical data; (2) the failure of "Locke's program" and its impact on modern psychology; and (3) the scientific and extrascientific (religious, ideological, political) rationales for rejecting innatist hypotheses. Since the discursive unfolding of these topics is preceded by only a brief summary—a recapitulation rather than a full presentation— the general reader may benefit from a few preliminary specifications, both historical and circumstantial. The easiest way of access is presumably to be found in the critique of induction, originally framed by Hume and then elaborated by modern philosophers of science such as Karl Popper, Carl G. Hempel, Herbert Feigl, and Nelson Goodman.

Induction is, since Aristotle, the philosophical legitimization of the otherwise innocent procedure through which expectations on future events are dictated by the results of past experience. From the empirically ascertained fact that "All swans observed up to this moment are white," the "reasonable" inference can be made that "All swans (observed or as yet *unobserved) are white." Such an inference, as Chomsky and Fodor keep reminding us, is nondemonstrative; that is, it is held valid only until it is refuted by the next counterexample (the discovery of a black swan). This procedure is totally unproblematic in everyday life and, as Chomsky points out in the discussion, in the experimental sciences. What is instead problematic, and to a high degree at that, is to justify induction purely on logical grounds. Hume was the first to give up such hopes, and by reducing inductive inference merely to a "custom or habit," he provoked, in Bertrand Russell's scathing terms, "the bankruptcy of eighteenth-century reasonableness."* Hume's critique of induction did not impede the practice of induction which, logicians notwithstanding, goes successfully on today as it always has, but rather the quest for rules of induction. In a classic paper published in 1945, Carl Hempel puts the problem back where it belongs: "Generally speaking, such rules would enable us to infer, from a given set of data, that hypothesis or generalization which accounts best for all the particular data in the given set. But this construal of the problem involves a misconception: while the process of invention by which scientific discoveries are made is as a rule psychologically guided and stimulated by antecedent knowledge of specific facts, its results are not logically determined by them; the way in which scientific hypotheses or theories are discovered cannot be mirrored in a set of general rules of inductive inference." This "misconception" (or this fallacy, to use a more current linguistic terminology), as Hempel specifies, leads to a number of crucial, though unwarranted, assumptions: "An adequate rule of induction would have to provide . . . mechanically applicable criteria determining unambiguously, and without any reliance on the inventiveness or additional scientific knowledge of its user, all those new abstract concepts which need to be created for the formulation of the theory that will account for the given evidence. Clearly, this requirement cannot be satisfied by any set of rules, however ingeniously devised; there can be no general rules of induction in the above sense; the demand for them rests on a confusion of logical and psychological issues."†*

Therefore, the proper place for an "inductive logic" is, so to

* B. Russell, *History of Western Philosophy* (London: Allen and Unwin, 1961), p. 645.

† Carl G. Hempel, "Science and the Logic of Confirmation," *Mind* 54:1–26, 97–121, 1945; reprinted in C. G. Hempel, *Aspects of Scientific Explanation* (New York: Free Press, Collier-Macmillan, 1965), pp. 5, 6.

speak, sandwiched between the psychology of scientific crea-
tivity and the establishment of general "rules of acceptance"
for (sufficiently) confirmed hypotheses. These rules, "roughly
speaking, would state how well a given hypothesis has to be
confirmed by the accepted observation reports to be scien-
tifically acceptable itself." Whether these rules can be construed
on "pragmatic" or on "purely logical" grounds is considered by
Hempel "an open question."

Returning now to our debate, it can be said that much of
what is being discussed in this chapter, as well as in Chapter 6
and in Part II, precisely concerns the psychology of scientific
inventiveness. The processes implicit in Fodor's "language of
thought" and Piaget's "psychogenesis of knowledge" are just
those processes that Hempel wants to differentiate from induc-
tive logic proper once and for all. Since the issue has often been
confused and misconceived, it is not surprising that an entire
section of this debate is devoted to the inductivist fallacy.
It will be seen that fundamental disagreements subsist between
Chomsky and Fodor on one side and Papert and Bateson on
the other concerning such a neat partition between psychology,
inductive logic, and pragmatic rules of acceptance.

The statement of the "paradox," which opens the discussion,
represents a particular aspect of the inductivist fallacy: it con-
cerns the a priori definition of what is "relevant evidence"
with respect to a given hypothesis, implying also the a priori
availability to the subject of criteria for selecting that *hypoth-*
esis as opposed to the (infinite) others that are equally com-
patible with the data. Hempel's formulation is as follows:
"In the discussion of scientific method, the concept of relevant
evidence plays an important part. And while certain inductivist
accounts of scientific procedure seem to assume that relevant
evidence, or relevant data, can be collected in the context of an
enquiry prior to the formulation of any hypothesis, it should
be clear upon brief reflection that relevance is a relative concept; *experiential data can be said to be relevant or irrelevant*
only with respect to a given hypothesis; and it is the hypothesis
which determines what kind of data or evidence are relevant
for it. Indeed, *an empirical finding is relevant for a hypothesis*
if and only if it constitutes either favorable or unfavorable
evidence for it; in other words, if it either confirms or discon-
firms the hypothesis. Thus, a precise definition of relevance
presupposes an analysis of confirmation and disconfirmation."[*]

* Ibid. (Emphasis added.)

In the course of the discussion, this evident fact is constantly referred to as a "tautology." In Part II, Putnam contests the legitimacy of such a label, to which Chomsky replies that "tautology" is not to be taken here in its strict sense of "circular definition," but rather in the loose colloquial meaning of "evident truth" (as Hempel says, "it should be clear upon brief reflection"). The tautology in question is, to put it as simply as possible, that no knowledge is possible unless concepts and hypotheses are already "in the mind" before anything is observed at all. Granting this, it appears equally straightforward to postulate that the source of concepts and hypotheses is innate. Chomsky and Fodor assume this further step to be so self-evident that it is not even worth a discussion. They also state that the reason why so many thinkers, including Nelson Goodman and Willard Quine, have avoided this inevitable conclusion is to be found in the realm of ideology rather than in that of pure philosophy. The last part of this chapter, therefore, deals with the ideological shortcomings of innatist and environmentalist hypotheses.

The acceptance of the "tautology," according to Fodor, cannot alone display the full power of an alternative program in psychology and linguistics unless it is reinforced, on independent grounds, by the acknowledgment that Locke's program has failed. In Fodor's words, "The notion that most human concepts are decomposable into a small stock of simple concepts—let's say, a truth function of sensory primitives—has been exploded by two centuries of philosophical and psychological investigation. In my opinion, the failure of the empiricist program of reduction is probably the most important result of those two hundred years in the area of cognition."

Locke's program was founded on a negative heuristic rejecting all notion of "innate principles in the mind" and on a positive heuristic laying the foundations of all human knowledge only on "sensation" and "reflection." To quote him: "All those sublime thoughts, which tower above the clouds, and reach as high as heaven itself, take their rise and footing here: in all that great extent wherein the mind wanders, in those remote speculations it may seem to be elevated with, it stirs not one jot beyond those ideas which sense or reflection have offered for its contemplation."*

Locke can be considered as the founder of the "order-from-

* John Locke, *An Essay Concerning Human Understanding* (New York: Dutton, 1971), vol. 1, book II, chap. 1, sec. 24, p. 89.

*noise" program (see the Introduction) in the domain of psy-
chology. The present chapter constitutes, therefore, a further
example of how alternative research programs, once they have
set forth their basic presuppositions, confront both their negative and their positive heuristics. However, it would be premature to formulate a conclusive judgment on these matters before reading Part II, where several crucial arguments of
heuristic importance are developed. In a sense, the present
discussion is still only a general introduction.*

Statement of the Paradox

Noam Chomsky and Jerry Fodor

Chomsky   In the history of modern philosophy there is a vast
literature dealing with a few very simple points about the impossibility of induction, like the whole debate about the Goodman paradox.[1] Once you understand the paradox, it is obvious that *you have to have a set of prejudices in advance for
induction to take place;* but that doesn't change the fact that
there is a vast literature in which people have tried to show
that is not true.

Fodor   Let me state briefly how Hempel described the paradox
about thirty years ago, since it is a very easy way of seeing it.[2]
He described it in terms of induction, but if you think about
it, it is exactly the same for learning. Hempel says: suppose
you have a set of observations on the values of two variables
across some range of circumstances. These observations can
be represented as a set of points in a two-dimensional Cartesian coordinate system. Once plotted, the points can be fit
by a curve that represents an induction about the hypothetical relationship between the two variables. The problem of
induction, in this situation, is the problem of deciding which
curve to choose. This choice is underdetermined by the data.
For any finite set of data points, there will be an infinite set
of curves, all of which fit the data equally well. Imagine, for
example, a set of points arrayed in a perfectly straight line. In
this case, one would surely want to choose a linear curve to
represent the relationship. But the data do not force this
choice. For in addition to the linear solution, there is an
infinite set of sinusoidal curves, each of which fits the points

as well as the straight line. These sine waves vary freely in amplitude but have a fixed period, chosen so that every one travels through each of the observation points. Given this set of alternatives, we are obviously in need of some principle that will select the straight line and block the sine waves.

What does it mean to say that we have to block them? It means that *before* we look at the data we have to have the possible curves ordered in terms of preference, so that given just these data we choose the straight line, given slightly anomalous data we choose the closest approximation to a straight line, and so on. You can call that simplicity, or an a priori ordering of the functions, or nativism. This leads to the same point as before: *you can't carry out an induction, it is a logical impossibility to make a nondemonstrative inference without having an a priori ordering of hypotheses.* This general point about nativism is so self-evident that it is superfluous to discuss it; the only question is, how specific are the innate constraints?

Chomsky The specific question concerning predicates was a variant of the one pointed out by Nelson Goodman. His particular interpretation of it seemed very paradoxical to many people and gave rise to a huge debate. What it comes down to essentially is this: Suppose you want to carry out the most trivial sort of induction from "I have seen so many emeralds in a sequence that are green" to "All emeralds are green," a most elementary case of induction. He points out that there could be a predicate, which he calls "grue," which has for us the following meaning (but which to a person who speaks that language just means "grue"): "looked at before this precise instant, whatever today's date is, and green" or "looked at after this instant, whatever today's date is, and blue." The predicate "grue" has been verified 100 percent so far: every emerald looked at is green, and a person who speaks the language in which "grue" is the simplest predicate will simply assume that the next emerald looked at is "grue," that is, to us, green. Therefore, depending on which predicate you pick, you can predict that the next emerald is either green or blue in our language, and in the other language either "grue" or "bleen." You can escape this particular example by imposing some restriction that tells you to choose "green" rather than "grue" (one can think of millions of such restrictions), but then you have a kind of algorithm for immediately creating the next counterexample. The net effect of the infinite series of counterexamples you can develop by this algorithm is that *you must in some sense have the whole set of predicates from the beginning.* This is an elementary fact, but that doesn't change the fact that there is a vast literature, which is of very little interest (or none at all) to scientists, but which has an enormous interest for those concerned with the nature of induction.

I think that many other theories exist, but they are not theories about the question we are discussing. For example, let's assume some developmental theory of human learning which says that when a child is 3 years old he can do this class of things, and when he is 5 years old he can do some other class of things; I think that this is a perfectly substantive, fascinating, and important theory, but it is not a theory about the topic we are discussing.

I think Fodor was right when he said that the whole question of nativism is beside the point, in that the general thesis is so obviously true that it is even not worth discussing. The question that we ought to ask is, what are the innate factors that make things happen the way they do? One of these innate factors may be that there exists, for some reason that we would like very much to understand, a maturational process that brings it about that when a child has reached age 3, something in his brain has happened that enables him to do certain things. Perhaps it is even true, for reasons built into the genes, that having reached that stage, he will only get to the next stage if certain complex phenomena appear in his environment. This theory is possible, but it has nothing to do with nativism because it is just going to add to the mass of material that we are going to attribute to the genes, since that is the only place where there is going to be an explanation. In this sense, I think that the whole issue of innatism is really beside the point, and the only reason anybody discusses it is, to my view, because of the three or four centuries of illusion that has been maintained about the issue.*

Discussion

De Zengotita Could one say that if nativism is beside the point, that depends in the final analysis on the evidence of this tautology?

* Editor's note: Further clarifications on the inductivist fallacy are to be found in Part II.

Chomsky   What is important is not just to see that something is a "tautology," but also *to see its import.* The import of the "tautology" is that there isn't any point in looking for a general theory of learning. What one should do is to look at the complexities of the system of development and the relationship with the environment, the complexity of the environment, and so on. I think that what Papert was talking about is very important (see Chapter 11): I think he is right when he says that just to present evidence isn't enough; you can sit a child in front of a television set, for example, and run well-formed sentences in front of him, and I'm sure he is not going to learn a thing. So that means that simply having the evidence presented to you is not enough for learning. Suppose that I tried to teach something to Premack's chimpanzee, Sarah; I'm sure that I could give her all the evidence—an apple, a triangle—and she wouldn't learn anything because I am not doing whatever is necessary to get the system to function. I don't know how to do this; he does. We must discover what is necessary to get the system to function; then, if we are interested in going a step further, we will ask what there is in that organism (obviously genetically determined, because there is nothing else) that brings it about that in presenting the evidence as I did, I didn't do what was necessary to make the system function.

The controversy about nativism is not worth pursuing because as soon as we understand anything, we know where to make the next move. We will then make contact with the biologists, and that is especially important because they must want to know what it is that they are supposed to explain. Consequently, what we can do is to state some conditions concerning what they will have to explain.

Bateson   From the fact of the tautology, as I understand it, you should know the next step: for instance, the chimpanzee has learned to put the eyeglasses on the green; the next step is to know all the multitude of things that the chimpanzee learned from the fact of putting the glasses on the green, and this is now no longer innate but is part of the context of the next learning, and we don't know how these things fit together.

Chomsky   Right, but suppose now we went ahead and found out what was involved in his making the next step, and then we ask, what is the origin of that thing X that is involved in it? You answer, trivially, that it is genetic determination, and you keep doing it at every point where you get an answer, because there aren't any other possibilities.

Premack I simply want to say that in my opinion, the real issue has to do with the elements—not with their origin, but with the nature of the elements which, when properly combined, account for acts of intelligence of all different kinds: judgments of synonymy, the distinction between synthetic and analytical sentences, the ability to recognize representations of oneself, and so forth. Of what psychological material are these acts composed? When do they emerge? What are the experiential factors that affect them? To look for their origin is a waste of time.

Chomsky I agree with Premack to a certain extent. The substantive scientific question for most of us, at least for me, is to answer precisely the question he raised. As I understand it, his question is, what are the universals of language? What are the necessary properties of language that hold, not only by accident, by virtue of the fact that the existing languages are what they are? That is a hard question to answer, but it is possible to proceed to answer it. At that point a move is made which I don't think has any alternatives to it, and which I hardly even regard as an inference. If I assert that certain properties are the necessary properties of language, it follows at once, if you accept what we have been calling "the tautology," and its consequences, that these properties are rooted in the genes. Unless you are a mystic, you can't believe otherwise. Then the next question arises: are we going to try to give an explanation for that? This depends on the state of biology; I would love to have an explanation, and I suppose that biologists would just as much. They would like to know what their investigation of neuronal networks is supposed to be doing. To make biology capable of taking the next step, it is necessary to describe these properties of the organism, and here I think that there is not and cannot be any controversy, any debate, between the biologists, the linguists, and the developmental psychologists once they understand the nature of what they are doing. I don't at all deny the importance of what they are doing; I simply think that it has often been totally misdescribed, and once their work is described properly it can then contribute to the joint enterprise just like all other research.

Bateson As I understand it, we are trying to account for a given component of the description of an organism, whether it is a behavioral component or the color of the skin. Let's say, for example, that my skin is of a certain color. Now, is this trait determined genetically or not? And how is the question going to be handled? We all know that the color of that skin will change if it is exposed to the sun. We now have another descriptive statement about the organism: that this change happens. And this descriptive statement is to be related to the genome or to the environment. We observe the fact that *Homo sapiens* apparently has the genetic capacity to become brown in the sun. We now ask the next question: can *Homo sapiens learn* to get brown in the sun? This is conceivable. One might practice tanning in the sun. Suppose that you get an answer to the metaquestion; what we are dealing with is the problem of logical levels. It is not a question of nativism versus non-nativism; it is a question of *what is the logical level where contribution of the genotype is located?* The genotype could furnish the capacity to learn something or the capacity to learn about learning something. Whatever the level, a component of the phenomenon will always lead us as far as the genotype.

Chomsky What Bateson says is entirely true, but it is really irrelevant to what I just said. Premack, I, and others, I hope, agree that the first step is to try to find out *what is essential to a given organism.* Our first guess may be wrong: we may look at everybody around the table and think that what is essential to this organism is to have white skin. Then someone could object and point out that if a person stays out in the sun for two or three hours, he won't have white skin any more. Then we say that white skin was not essential, and so our first idea was wrong. What is essential to the organism is that under one condition it has a white skin and under another condition it has a red skin. We will consider this to be essential in the organism, and then we will see if it is right or wrong—wrong in this case for other obvious reasons. We then do more experiments, and finally we find something that we tentatively think is essential to the organism. All of Bateson's questions had to do with the first step, but once this first step is made we no longer ask the question of origin because there are no alternatives, unless we are mystics; the only possibility is genetics, and that is why no one bothers to ask these other questions. It is possible that we are wrong, that we didn't do enough experiments, but that simply means that we are doing science and not mathematics. It is always possible to commit an error; we know that perfectly well. Let's stop talking about it. It is part of the nature of research that our assumptions may be proved false, but nevertheless, the logic of the inquiry is clear. Once we have satisfied ourselves to a degree X that a certain characteristic is essential to the organism, we no longer ask about its origin, because we know the general answer to that question. That's why nobody asks: Do people learn to have a heart? It could be true, but nobody asks the question because they are satisfied that this is essential to the organism.

Papert   It is relevant to recall my example of the genome of the perceptron (see Chapter 3). This determines in the most direct sense that the decision-making process be limited to linear combinations of local properties. But what about its ability to count? Do we expect to find descriptions of number in the design plans for the machine, or in its genetic code if it were a living creature? Surely not. At any rate, you'll find nothing there that directly resembles number. And investigators (in the hypothetical situation of an empirical science of living perceptrons) could get into some very sterile disputes and fruitless research if they thought they had to find a representation of number or a mechanism for generating hypotheses about number. In fact, the perceptron's ability in numerosity is an emergent one, emergent from quite different properties. It really is an amazing fact, and it required a great mathematician like Euler to discover that numbers could be computed by making local observations on blobs without having any idea of whether two nonadjacent observations concerned the same blob. The underlying fact is that the algebraic sum of all the curvatures along the circumference of a blob, whatever its shape, must be 2π. So if one finds 6π worth of curvature in a world made up of blobs (that is, surfaces of arbitrary shape but with no holes), we can be sure that there are three objects. This is remarkably counterintuitive, but nevertheless true.

Chomsky   What you have to do is to say that there is a certain property, whatever property it might be, that this device can be demonstrated to have. Having done that, we can now go back to the central issue, which is very clear in this case. You are not dealing with the question that we have been discussing. We are discussing the question of how we go from observing what an organism does to discovering its essential properties and then ultimately making an inference about its genes. You are considering a totally different question, a case where in effect you know the genes; that's given in advance. You know the initial structure of the device. Given this knowledge, you can then through deep mathematical theorems say something about . . .

Papert That's not the point. Suppose we don't know anything about the genes and can only observe the organism's behavior. Someone can then add up the genes and do the experiment with numbers and say: it must have some more genes, go and look for them, because it must have a gene for number. He has based his contention that it must have a gene for number on (1) the observation that the machine can recognize numbers and (2) the fact that he cannot conceive of a process (nor could anyone, before Euler) by which this ability could derive from other, already known genetic properties. So he postulates extra genes and sends the biologist down the garden path looking for nonexistent things.

Chomsky That is relevant, but your analysis now fails for another reason. It just illustrates the truism that I emphasized before, namely, that nondemonstrative arguments may turn out to be wrong. It is certainly true that a nondemonstrative argument may turn out to be wrong; that is in the nature of nondemonstrative reasoning, by definition. If we conclude by scientific inference that this organism must have the following 83 genes (because that is the only way we have of explaining the fact that it does so and so) somebody else may come along, since the argument is nondemonstrative, and say: This is all well and good, but I can show exactly how the same result can be obtained with only 32 of those 83 genes. We can never be sure that this is not true because we are engaged in nondemonstrative inference . . . I don't understand why these trivialities are part of the discussion.

Bateson Because it is in the nature of that tautology.

Papert Let's discuss it anyway, since you admit that most of the world hasn't accepted your tautology.

Chomsky Isn't it true that nondemonstrative inference may lead to incorrect conclusions?

Papert Of course . . . I would like to ask Fodor a question. He says that you can't find a predicate unless it is already there. In this case, was the predicate there? Was it there or not?

Fodor I wouldn't have noticed it, unless I were as clever a mathematician as Euler.

Chomsky That doesn't change the fact that it was there.

Fodor Given a hypothesis about the innate structure of the organism, it is clear that there will be quantities of interesting questions about what a device with this structure could do; and these are fundamentally mathematical questions. If you have a mathematical proof, for example, that a certain device couldn't do a certain thing, and elsewhere an experimental proof that a certain organism *can* do that thing, that is a very important result, because we can now limit the possible models for the organism. Everybody has understood this, at least since Locke—including Locke. He had a rather powerful conception of what the innate structure of an organism was: it was a combinatorial algebra of a fundamentally Boolean kind plus a sensorium. We now have a whole mass of results, which are not formal but are nevertheless highly persuasive and which suggest that an organism with *that* sort of innate structure could not acquire such workaday concepts as *buy and sell, automobile, typewriter,* and so on. But we *do* have those concepts, which suggests that our innate endowment can't be what Locke supposed it was. That is what scientific investigation in this area is like. You make hypotheses about what the expressive capacities of the device are; you ask whether a device with these expressive capacities could do such and such a thing; you compare that device with an organism by experimental procedures. That is what scientific method is like in this area.

Papert I have a comment to make about Fodor's presentation and about his book, *The Language of Thought,* which spells out his position in more detail.[1] Consider the set of predicates that I know at this moment; now suppose you see me learn what seems to be a new one. Fodor wants to deny its newness; he wants to say that it was already there, in a certain sense. But there are two senses, and I think that Fodor shifts between them. One sense says literally that the predicate was already there; the other sense simply allows the new predicate to be defined in terms of old ones. But in the second case, we are satisfied with saying that a predicate cannot come out of nothing.

Fodor The argument doesn't say that; the claim about indefinability is made on *independent grounds,* which lead back to the failure of Locke's project.

Chomsky Fodor is not denying that the set of available predicates may have interconnections that allow some of them to be defined in terms of the others. That's a matter of discovering the structure of the set of predicates.

Papert   A real developmental psychologist, or somebody who really wants to make a machine that functions well, must recognize the tautology that you can't start from nothing. But it makes all the difference in the world whether we start with a small number of elements or whether we have to assume some very complicated things like the specified subject condition and the existence of number. That is really the issue between you and Piaget: not whether something has to be there from the beginning, but rather *how much* and what kind of something.

Chomsky   Exactly, but as I said before, that is a noble enterprise and I would like to see some results from it, but it is not going to bear on the general issue of nativism.

Papert   That is still a mystery to me, like the question about why everybody doesn't accept Chomsky's tautology. I would like to ask Fodor why he wrote a book that was so difficult that I had to spend many hours deciphering it, if all he wanted to say was the tautology that you can't build from nothing?

Fodor   I wrote it for three reasons. The first is that despite this triviality, at least the triviality that Papert mentioned, it seems to me that developmental literature includes doctrines that are taken very seriously (including notably Piaget's views) which fly in the face of this tautology. Piaget's system, as far as I can see, requires a passage between stages that couldn't occur: the development of structurally richer logics out of poorer ones. The second reason is that the auxiliary hypothesis that is required to construct a serious argument (as opposed to just a tautology) is the failure of Locke's program. I consider that the notion that most human concepts are decomposable into a small stock of simple concepts—let's say, a truth function of sensory primitives—has been exploded by two centuries of philosophical and psychological investigation. In my opinion, the failure of the empiricist program of reduction is probably *the most important result of those two hundred years in the area of cognition.* The third point is that the argument cited by Papert is not the one I gave. The argument I gave was this: models of learning have invariably been *models of hypothesis formation and confirmation.* The implications of this are much stronger, as I keep saying, than the *potential* availability of a stock of predicates. It presupposes the actual *exploitation* of the defining predicate as part of the learning procedure, as I tried to demonstrate earlier (see Chapter 6). So the reason that I pursued my line of argument, despite the fact that I find it embarrassingly trivial, in the way Papert puts it, is that (1) I didn't put it the way he puts it; I presented something much stronger, and (2) it seems to me to have ramifications of a very great importance, so great, as a matter of fact, that when you put these three reasons together, I am inclined to think that the argument has to be wrong, that *a nativism pushed to that point becomes unsupportable, that something important must have been left aside.* What I think it shows is really not so much an a priori argument for nativism as that *there must be some notion of learning that is so incredibly different from the one we have imagined* that we don't even know what it would be like as things now stand. This was, by the way, what I said at the beginning of my talk.

Bateson   May I point out to Fodor a problem that has intrigued me all during this debate? We imagine an initial state S_0 which is essentially a stock of predicates, propositions, injunctions, and so forth. The thing that I don't know from the way people have been talking is whether that stock is imagined to be essentially a tautologically coherent body so that the premises agree with each other to make a structure of some kind, or whether it contains incoherences, inconsistencies, perhaps contradictions, and so on.

Fodor   What I do know is this: on the one hand, the elementary states have to be the sort of things that can be true or false, because they are going to form the premises of inferences. On the other hand, they have to have the capacity to generate an infinite set of hypotheses, because there is an infinite number of things one can learn. That, plus a general view that Kant was somehow right, is about all I know and all I even suspect about the general structure of this device.

I think, moreover, that methodologically speaking, to put things as ambitiously as Kant did—"Let's get a general picture of this device straight off"—is probably hopeless. I think the best procedure is exactly the reverse strategy: *let's find a small domain that has as little rapport as possible with the rest and try to study it as a sort of protomodel of what is going on.* After all, this device is quite probably the most complicated system in the universe, and it seems to me that anybody who asks himself what the general structure of this system is like is just doomed to fail. It is possible that certain aspects of this system can be isolated, that is, that they are specific to, say, language. Perhaps the examination of very restricted properties of that form of behavior will lead us to ask what the set of axioms must look like for *that* case, and assuming that we have a model for that case, perhaps we can go on to other things. The reason that I think it is so important for Chomsky to be right about the innate specificity of language, or at least about the innate specificity of *some* interesting psychological subdomain, is that if there is nothing that can be studied in a truly independent way, then I doubt that we are going to find anything out; the problem will become too difficult.

Chomsky Just one brief remark: Why has the illusion of the existence of other possibilities been harbored so long, and why is it still harbored? I don't know the correct answer, but I want to point out one possible answer that has to be obvious, at least to anybody who knows any mathematics. A mathematician can have some very obvious assumptions, but nevertheless the consequences of those assumptions can be very hard to discover; that is what mathematics is all about. I think that in a sense we have a situation which is not unlike that, even though we are not dealing with mathematics. There are assumptions which everybody will agree to when they look at them. But along the way, if inference leads to some result they don't like, they back out, which I think is unfortunate. Sometimes consequences of assumptions that we ought to accept are not easy to accept (there is a psychological compulsion to withdraw), but that doesn't mean that we shouldn't accept them.

De Zengotita Can you describe what you would consider to be a psychological compulsion?

Chomsky I think there is a long tradition, which certainly goes back to scholasticism and then becomes intermingled with empiricist currents, that would have us believe that the human mind is empty, a *tabula rasa*. Nobody will agree explicitly with that any more, but some people find it hard to stray very far from that assumption. Secondly—and this is pure speculation on my part, I have no evidence whatsoever—the belief that the human mind is empty provides a justification for all sorts of authoritarian systems. If the human mind is empty, any method of molding minds is legitimate, and you see this worked out in extreme forms, as with Skinner, for example.

This can end up in a kind of design for fascism originating from the assumption that after all, the human mind is empty . . . so that we, the good architects, will fix it up so that the environment is right and everybody will live happily ever after. Intellectuals are often prone to this sort of thing, because they see themselves as the ones who are going to do the molding of minds.

Again speculating, I will mention a very curious inversion of ancient religious beliefs: it is a very ancient religious doctrine that the human soul is out of bounds; you cannot investigate the human soul, that's the domain of the priest. Science may deal with other things, but not the human soul. Why people hold that view, I don't know, but some certainly hold it very strongly. In my view a very curious thing happened around the seventeenth or eighteenth century, namely, that under the pretext of trying to overcome that belief, people found a new way of formulating it, which was to say: we are not going to study the human soul by the methods of the natural sciences, we are going to study it by purely a priori methods, that is, we are just going to insist that the human mind is empty, or that it has this or that set of properties, and then we are going to investigate these properties. This is the case with associationist psychology, for example, which doesn't have even the appearance of a science. A scientific approach will say: here is what the mind achieves; here is what I will have to postulate to explain that. Associationist psychologists took the opposite approach. They say: here is what the mind is, and I am going to investigate the consequences of that assumption *ad infinitum,* without determining whether whatever I find actually resembles what the mind achieves. You can pursue a study like that forever; you can always find more consequences of those inadequate assumptions, and nothing stops you from going on indefinitely. What is interesting is that this was presented as if it were a scientific approach, but of course, it is precisely the antithesis of science. It is a purely dogmatic approach that starts with a priori, unchallengeable assumptions about the nature of the mind and then goes on to draw out consequences from these assumptions, never paying any attention to the question of whether the assumptions happen to be the right ones. In my view, this is a kind of inversion—and I don't know of any other historical examples—of traditional religious dogma disguised in the name of science. People no longer say that the soul cannot be studied; rather they say implicitly that it cannot be studied by the methods of natural science. I think that there must be very powerful reasons why people find it extremely difficult to accept the conclusions that follow from very simple observations. There are some very striking examples. Take, for instance, the "grue" paradox that I mentioned; the person who devised it and developed it in a classic book was Nelson Goodman, who is perhaps the most extreme environmentalist who ever lived. He seems to think that everything is learned; the way I read what he says is that any attribution of innate structure to the mind is false—there cannot be such an innate structure. If I interpret his views correctly, he believes that if you were to visit a primitive tribe and to present one group with photographs of people and another group with reproductions of Kandinsky abstractions, then the training period to get them to recognize that the photographs are photographs of people and the Kandinsky abstractions are representations of people would be approximately the same, because there is no built-in system of representation that determines that photographs have some special relation to the things photographed. He has argued things of that sort. Now, it is striking from the point of view of the sociology of science that the very person who gave fundamental arguments that demolish this view should nevertheless uphold it in a certain sense. Another important example is Quine, who is probably the leading philosopher in America, if not in the world. He has taken views on this subject at opposite extremes almost in successive paragraphs. He says at some points that there cannot be anything beyond conditioning, though he agrees with Fodor's basic point that you have to have a quality space fixed for conditioning to take place. He has sometimes said that all that is learned is conditioned, and at other times he has said that it is inconceivable that what you know is the result of conditioning. I think he just contradicts himself. I think one ought to explain all of this by the indirect arguments I suggested; I don't see any other rational explanation.

Papert It is certain that there are powerful irrational motivations for both sides of the nativist controversy. Intellectuals have a vested interest in believing in the existence of natively superior brain power, so they are subject to powerful forces opposing the idea that their minds are constructed. If we think we are intelligent, we prefer to think that we are intelligent by nature; we prefer to believe that the intelligence is a property of our essential selves. Thus, elitism and associated authoritarian and fascist positions are drawn to support nativism. On the other hand, as Chomsky says, fascists have an interest in believing that the masses are pliable, and not at all determined by their genes; thus the political aspects of the controversy are no less confused, and no more explanatory, than the scientific arguments. Moreover, Chomsky's theory is only plausible if one uses a very particular criterion of rigor which is highly demanding for the justification of all statements except the assertion of innateness.

Chomsky   I agree with what Papert just said, but I would like to point out that there is a fundamental asymmetry. The question was asked, *Why, in the face of overwhelming evidence to the contrary, do people still maintain a certain position?* And I suggested some answers. Papert, on the other hand, is asking why, given overwhelming evidence *in favor* of their position, people maintain a certain position. And there may even be irrational answers to this question.

Papert   But what is "overwhelming evidence" for what is already in the eye of the observer? It is perfectly symmetrical as I see it.

Chomsky   Then you have to tell me where the argument from the "tautology" to the conclusion breaks down.

Papert   From the tautology to which conclusion? From the tautology to the conclusion that there must be *something* innate, that there must be *some* structure that determines, nobody would deny. But the existence of those *particular* things depends at best on whether or not one accepts what I call the Chomsky principle 17 . . .

Chomsky   The argument that *specific* things have to be attributed to the mind is of course nondemonstrative, and therefore it would be totally unfair for me to ask you where the argument breaks down. Of course, we all know where it breaks down; it is not a deductive argument. But I will ask you another question: in the face of the fact that this is the only theory in existence so far to explain a certain category of facts, why do you persist in saying that it can't be right?

Papert   Because, as inconceivable as it might seem to you, it doesn't seem to me to be the only theory that exists.

Chomsky   It is not "certainly" true; these are all hypotheses. I will repeat again that they are conjectures, scientific hypotheses, and if you want to know my feeling, I'm sure that they are false. I cannot believe that any detailed hypothesis that I can propose today, or that anybody else can propose, is likely to be true.

The debate proper concludes on this note of modesty. The rest of the book is composed of papers written on the debate and after the debate. At the time of our meeting, Chomsky's book Reflections on Language *was in press. It is my feeling that the last part of the present exchange between Papert and Chomsky on the "ideology" of innatism and environmentalism becomes much clearer in the light of two passages from* Reflections on Language, *where the problem is analyzed with unprecedented clarity and exhaustiveness.*

> The doctrine that the human mind is initially unstructured and plastic and that human nature is entirely a social product has often been associated with progressive and even revolutionary social thinking, while speculations with regard to human instinct have often had a conservative and pessimistic cast. One can easily see why reformers and revolutionaries should become radical environmentalists, and there is no doubt that concepts of immutable human nature can be and have been employed to erect barriers against social change and to defend established privilege.
>
> But a deeper look will show that the concept of the "empty organism," plastic and unstructured, apart from being false, also serves naturally as the support for the most reactionary social doctrines. If people are, in fact, malleable and plastic beings with no essential psychological nature, then why should they not be controlled and coerced by those who claim authority, special knowledge, and a unique insight into what is best for those less enlightened? Empiricist doctrine can easily be molded into an ideology for the vanguard party that claims authority to lead the masses to a society that will be governed by the "red bureaucracy" of which Bakunin warned. And just as easily for the liberal technocrats or corporate managers who monopolize "vital decision-making" in the institutions of state capitalist democracy, beating the people with the people's stick, in Bakunin's trenchant phrase . . .
>
> It is reasonable to suppose that just as intrinsic structures of mind underlie the development of cognitive structures, so a "species character" provides the framework for the growth of moral consciousness, cultural achievement, and even participation in a free and just community. It is, to be sure, a great intellectual leap from observations on the basis for cognitive development to particular conclusions on the laws of our nature and the conditions for their fulfillment; say, to the conclusion that human needs and capacities will find their fullest expression in a society of free and creative producers, working in a system of free association in which "social

bonds" will replace "all fetters in human society." There is an important intellectual tradition that stakes out some interesting claims in this regard. While this tradition draws from the empiricist commitment to progress and enlightenment, I think it finds still deeper roots in rationalist efforts to establish a theory of human freedom. To investigate, deepen, and if possible substantiate the ideas developed in this tradition by the methods of science is a fundamental task for libertarian social theory. Whether further investigation will reveal problems that can be addressed or mysteries that will confound us, only the future can tell . . .*

* N. Chomsky, *Reflections on Language* (New York: Pantheon, 1975), pp. 132–134.

CHAPTER THIRTEEN

Afterthoughts and Clarifications

Steering a Way between Constructivism and Innatism

Stephen Toulmin

The difference of views between Piaget and Chomsky, concisely expressed in the papers for this meeting—with Piaget claiming that "the functioning of intelligence alone is hereditary" and Chomsky arguing *per contra* that "human language" is a "mental organ" having an innate structure as specific as that of the eye or the heart—is so extreme that participants may be tempted simply to choose up sides, for or against innatism and constructivism respectively. This would (in my view) be a barren confrontation: rather, I shall argue, we should consider seriously the possibility that *both* views are unacceptable, as they stand, so that we should be looking for an account of the development of mental abilities that steers a way between these extremes.

My reasons are partly epistemological, partly biological. First, as to the epistemological considerations: both writers equate the "logical structures" of our systems of representation (grammatical, mathematical, and so on) with the "empirical structures" of the supposed mental counterparts of these representations, in a way that raises grave and difficult issues which they do not adequately deal with. (This is the burden of my paper, written with Carol Feldman, entitled *"Logic and the Theory of Mind."*)[1] It would surely be safer to avoid speaking of the internal relations within, for example, one of Piaget's cognitive "stages" or a child's preliminary grasp of indicative sentences as being "logically necessary" or as exemplifying the child's "theory" about the grammar of the utterances it has heard to date, except in cases where there has been some explicit "internalization" of the relevant formal system—as when the child learns abstract geometry in a scholastic context, or when the adult learns how to form the ten possible verbs from the Arabic triliteral root in approaching Arabic as a foreign language of unfamiliar type. Elsewhere, one may seriously question whether phrases like "mental structure" and "the child's grammar" do not confuse more than they help our discussion.

Secondly, in regard to the biological and other empirical reasons for taking a middle way: both writers seem to me to play fast and loose with the available evidence, such as it is. Piaget's claim quoted above is far too sweeping in one direction. Many species with complex neural networks are known to display highly specific perceptual/cognitive responses and skills that are evidently "hereditary": how, then, can one so confidently declare that the human species is exempt—that "innate cognitive structures do not exist in man"? (I suspect that Piaget is confused on this point by thinking of "cognitive structures" as meaning only "logically necessary structures"; see the first argument above.) On the contrary, there is growing evidence *for* the existence of "preprogramming" in the neonate's perceptual/cognitive equipment, as in Bower's work on the reactions of the newborn to simulated "physical objects."[2]

Chomsky's arguments, on the other hand, are too sweeping in the opposite direction. In his introductory paper, as elsewhere, he is unmoved by considerations from evolutionary theory: "Little is known concerning evolutionary development, but from ignorance, it is impossible to draw any conclusions" (see Chapter 1). Yet there are some very real problems in regard to reconciling his theories of the human "language capacity" with general biology, including evolutionary theory, which cannot be dismissed in this manner: for example, the saltatory character of the initial appearance of that "capacity" in early man.[3] Certainly, as against Piaget's claim, we must suppose that the ability to learn language depends on the human infant's possessing some quite specific "capacities" that are "innate" in the sense of being "wired into the central nervous system"; there is, of course, independent neurological evidence of such "innate" capacities. But the particular capacities Chomsky attributes to the child appear *far too* specific to be plausible, quite aside from the difficulty of conceiving what sort of neurological counterparts they might have.

There are many other points one might touch on, but I confine myself here to the central issue.*

Afterthoughts

Jean Piaget

In his concluding remarks, Changeux said that a compromise between Chomsky's innatism and my own constructivist point of view was possible, and I have already expressed my pleasure at this possibility during the symposium. Since then, his inspiring inaugural lecture at the Collège de France has been made public, and I have learned a great deal from it.[1] For me, the essential point made by Changeux is the following: against Chomsky's and Fodor's positions, where "interaction with the external world . . . [is] limited to triggering preestablished programs," Changeux opposes a "functional epigenesis" which "permits an economy of genes." This is due to the fact that "the activity introduces an extra order into the developing network"; "the genetic envelope offers a hazily outlined network, and the activity defines its angles" (see Chapter 8).

I cannot help but be pleased to hear this assertion from this eminent biologist, all the more because he concludes that through learning the organism "becomes receptive to those combinations of signs that it also knows how to produce." This brings me back to an idea that I was unable to explain clearly during our discussions: insofar as a behavior implies a programming that oversteps the bounds of the soma and that is well adapted to the external environment, there are only two solutions: that of chance followed by selections, the classic but unacceptable explanation for the formation of cognitive structures, such as logico-mathematical structures; or the solution of a combinatorial structure, but composed of elements indirectly influenced by the environment. Now, without going back to the Lamarckian notion of a direct action by the environment

---

* Editor's note: These remarks were circulated among the participants in September 1975. Toulmin terminated his short text by suggesting that the discussion not be "restricted to those two possibilities only" (that is, Piaget's constructivism and Chomsky's innatism). Part II of this book and Appendixes B and C can be considered as an implementation of Toulmin's proposal.

on the genome, today more and more authors recognize, under the name of "genetic assimilation" (Waddington), "Baldwin effect," or "phenocopy," the possibility of the replacement of a phenotype by a genotype of the same form. For my part, I see in this the effect of a selection performed by the internal and epigenetic environment, when this environment has been modified on some point by an acquired phenotype and where this disequilibrium has brought about a sensitization of the regulatory genes (which is not at all the case for every phenotype). There is thus no need to bring in any "message" from the soma to the genome, but only a simple perturbation bringing about semi-random variations upon which internal selection is exerted, whence the readjustments simulating a fixation of the phenotype—whereas what really happens is a "replacement" of the phenotype through a reconstitution arising from inside the organism itself.

This is, of course, only speculation, but even though I respectfully bow to the simplicity of the neo-Darwinian explanation when it deals with changes in the color of a butterfly, I ask recognition of the role of speculation that occurs in the generalization of this model to the case of behavior. There the model becomes simply implausible, as soon as one thinks of the many mysterious processes that are biologically comparable, such as the refinement of some specialized instincts or the incredible adaptation of human mathematics to the smallest details of physical reality elucidated by contemporary techniques. I believe, therefore, that speculation is useful in opposing other speculations, since the awareness of new problems can arise from their opposition; moreover, in areas in which neither observation nor experimentation is possible any longer, such as the historical development of behaviors, a critical awareness of the problems should not be neglected. Chomsky probably believes that he has simplified his position by sending back to the biologists the question of the innateness of his "fixed nucleus"; but I, for one, think that this simplification is perhaps only apparent, since many nonethological biologists (and sometimes the ethological ones as well) find it difficult to understand that behavior raises many other kinds of questions besides just those of the pervasive influence of genes, or of their mutations and recombinations. One must therefore hail Changeux as an exceptional author in this respect. I regret not having known his position when I wrote a small work currently in print which remains, unfortunately, purely speculative.[2] I defend in it the following idea which, if it were to gain support, would effectively reverse today's fashionable trend toward innatism: for me, behavior conceived not à la Lamarck as a product of external "circumstances," but as the expression of a constant need for overtaking (extension of the environment and increase of the organism's powers) would constitute in fact the principal moving force of evolution. A very critical biologist friend of mine, alarmed by my audacity, nevertheless returned the manuscript to me with the following comment: "Stimulating and perhaps even true." I am not asking for anything more, and if I tell this little story, it is to point out that if epistemic constructivism is true for man, such constructivism appears to me as having to begin at the level of animal behavior; in other words, if it is valid in relation to its intrinsic reasons (a minimum of "preformations" and a maximum of self-organization), it must remain valid throughout the whole range of life forms.

In conclusion, and to come back to what Changeux calls a "compromise" between Chomsky and myself, I do not see in this compromise anything greatly different from what I have always maintained; for, if I do not believe in the existence of innate cognitive structures within intelligence, it goes without saying that I regard its functioning as implying hereditary nervous mechanisms, such as the Boolean network that McCulloch and Pitts discovered in neuronal activities.[3] All I am maintaining, and the theses of Changeux seem to give me that right, is that from this innate functioning, new arrangements, this time constructed step by step by the subject, are required in order to elaborate preoperative and then logical structures, including in particular those of sensorimotor intelligence which lead to Chomsky's "fixed nucleus." It does not seem, therefore, that one has to give up a great deal in order to refute (as I do) a massive innatism which merely mirrors, and does not transcend, naive environmentalism.

This leads me to Toulmin's considerations on autoregulation, which appears to him insufficient to explain the progress of cognitive structures. However, he did not understand me correctly when he credited me with a "homeostatic" model, which I agree appears totally insufficient. I only refer to a type of generalized epigenetic "homeorhesis,"[4] and I believe the experimental evidence speaks in favor of a progressive passage from regulation to autoregulation (with "feedforward," and so on) and from there to the self-organization that characterizes the operative stages and the formation of balanced structures. At this level, self-organization even prolongs itself in many cases into autoprogramming; the general process is therefore that of an "accretive" *(majorante)* equilibration, which I have analyzed in detail in a recent book.[5]

As for the role of culture in the education of the individual, one would have to be very naive not to take it into consideration, but the psychological problem is to establish how culture acts: it gives rise to an active assimilation and uses the same structures and instruments as the adaptation (practical and cognitive, which are one) to every reality.

In regard to the mechanisms that are common to the history of science and the psychogenesis of cognitive functions, I am currently writing a book on this subject in close collaboration with Rolando Garcia, a physicist and a historian of science, and we have both been struck by the generality of some of these mechanisms. I will mention only one of them, that of an abstraction which I call "reflective abstraction" because it proceeds not from objects but from the operations of the subject. The theory of "categories" and morphisms, for example, was extracted from MacLane and Eilenberg from the establishment of those correspondence systems that the Bourbaki group utilized, instrumentally and without any systematization, in the construction of their structures. Now, in its elementary form reflective abstraction is precisely one of the instruments of self-organization by means of which the child constructs his operative structures, and it even intervenes in the explanation of physical facts when transitivity, recursion, commutativity, or distributivity are attributed to the relationships between objects when empirical abstraction based on observables does not suffice for this understanding. But in order to convince my excellent colleague Toulmin, it would be necessary to look very closely at the psychological facts upon which I am trying, with more or less success, to establish my epistemology. I will return to this point when commenting on Premack.

Another point on which I cannot agree with Toulmin, along with most biologists (with the exception of Paul Weiss and Changeux), has to do with how lightly behavioral and cognitive adaptations are explained by selection, as if selection constituted a kind of organizing power that could transform any kind of haphazard or random variations into adapted behavior. There are two types of adaptation that have to be distinguished: (1) survival-adaptation, which favors the rate of multiplication and the preservation of the species by the screening of useful and noxious variations, both having occurred prior to this screening and independent of it; and (2) adequacy-adaptation, which implies a teleonomy in relation to the environment (for example, birds' nests embody the three conditions of shelter against predators, solidity, and above-threshold temperature). Now, it is this teleonomy that has to be explained because, if it also constitutes by itself a favorable factor toward survival, it could no longer result from a mere sorting; otherwise thousands of generations of swallows, for example, would have had to be sacrificed before chance produced their highly refined nests. In regard to logico-mathematical structures inherent to intelligence, and among others to the linguistic "fixed nucleus" that Chomsky believes to be innate, I wonder what the stages of their genetic formation would be if one were to stay within the framework of neo-Darwinian selection. This is why Paul Weiss rightly considers the necessity of attributing to behavior an organization by "systems" with their "global dynamics,"[6] although he is the first one to admit that the mechanism remains to be found, and this is why Changeux invokes a "functional epigenesis." For my part, I retain, of course, the idea of selection, but as far as specialized instincts or the beginnings of intelligence are concerned, I would conceive of a selection by the internal and epigenetic environment, insofar as it has been modified by phenotypic activities which, in the case of behavior, presuppose much more than an internal teleonomy since they deal with actions performed *on* the environment, leading to new systems of regulations, still endogenous but with a finality external to the soma.

As for Premack, I was greatly impressed by his beautiful presentation. In contrast to Toulmin and so many Anglo-Saxon authors, he understands what I mean by "structures" and gives beautiful and new examples relating to causality in the chimpanzee during tool using, analogous to that which is observed in the young child (12 to 18 months) at the end of my six sensorimotor stages. Now, it goes without saying that in the chimpanzee, a structure corresponds to the definition that I always give: it is the system of what a subject "can do" and not of what he says of it or thinks about it. Thus the causal structure utilized by the chimpanzee exists not only in Premack's brain, but also in the very actions of his engaging subjects. I am therefore asking Toulmin and the other critics of the theory of structures to extend me the same tolerance: these structures exist in what the children I study "do" and not only in the semiformalizations that I make of them. But the beautiful discoveries of Premack go still further with his analyses of the "language" acquired and understood by the chimpanzee, for one finds in these observations, in a much more spectacular form, the cognitive structures that I have considered to be the constituents of a sensorimotor logic: coordinations and interlocking of schemes, with subordination of empirical abstractions to reflective abstractions taken from these same coordinations.

Rereading Bischof's subtle and interesting paper, I understand better the points of agreement and disagreement between Lorenz and myself. I, for one, have always maintained that the surprising adaptation of mathematics to physical reality was not (or not only) due to the actions that the organism and the subject carry out on objects external to them, but to an endogenous source; that is to say, since the organism is itself also a physicochemical object, its actions and reactions are from the outset transparently dependent on the physical universe because, through its very inner structure, the organism participates in and obeys the laws of this universe. But even if I am completely in favor of an endogenous origin of logico-mathematical structures, this does not at all mean that they are innate in their successive states, for the following reason: the formation and the development of knowledge are not accomplished according to a linear course or progression, but proceed level by level with necessary reconstructions at each new level. Now, these reconstructions offer a remarkable twofold character of an enlargement or an enrichment of the previous structures (since we are now dealing with a new level possessing more powerful instruments, as for example representation in regard to sensorimotor action) and, at the same time, a deeper implantation in the direction of endogenous sources, by virtue of the mechanisms of reflective abstraction. The endogenous origin of knowledge is therefore the point on which I agree with Lorenz, but for me a divergence seems to remain in regard to the necessity of substituting for innateness a mechanism of continual reconstructions and of constructions broadened by autoregulation or self-organization (this, let me repeat, is in rather close convergence with von Foerster's theses, which I was not acquainted with at the time of our symposium).

As for critical realism, which Bischof analyzes so well, and the characteristics of optimal (but never complete) adaptation of knowledge, and so on, I think that I generally agree with Bischof's considerations, with the exception of perhaps one important point. Bischof, if I understand him correctly, thinks as I do that the object is never completely attained; it remains a limit, and he speaks in this regard of an asymptotic progression. But the problem is to know whether this limit allows for convergence or divergence. I believe that the progression is divergent in the sense that the object is transformed as knowledge closes in. Now, this makes me differ even more from the "naive realism" to which Bischof fears that the utilization of mechanisms of equilibration might lead me.

In regard to Putnam's reflections on conservation and reflective abstraction,* there is complete disagreement between us, and this disagreement is based on facts of which, in my opinion, Putnam seems to have insufficient knowledge. It is wrong to believe that these processes imply language; the proof of this is that around the age of 9 to 10 months, an infant arrives at an understanding, after a long and very instructive construction, of the permanence of objects that have been hidden behind screens. This precocious "conservation" is therefore much anterior to language and requires reflective abstractions from coordinations of actions (which are most unlikely to consist of an empirical generalization, but of a simply extensional one), since there exists, as I have mentioned previously, a whole sensorimotor logic, with coordinations of order, interlockings, intersection, correspondences, and so on, and on the spatial plane, construction of a "group of displacements" as Poincaré already believed. To call all of these "metaphors" simply reveals an incomplete analysis of the experimental facts.

Having now arrived at the point of drawing my own conclusion from our debates on innatism, what strikes me the most is the absence of symmetry between the Chomsky-Fodor position and my own. For them, everything happens as if the interpretation of cognitive mechanisms were a question of all-or-none: radical innatism or behaviorist empiricism. I have, on the contrary, the obligation, in the line of constructivism, to take into account all the factors that come into play—innateness of the points of departure, endogenous character of logical and mathematical constructions, requirements of experimentation for the knowledge of objects—but also the necessity, in order to attain the observables, to assimilate them into frameworks that are again endogenous, and so on. I have no ambition at all to decide between all or none, but only the candor of wanting to differentiate the situations and to consider myself a winner at every level.

* Editor's note: See Part II of this volume.

PART II

Comments on the Debate

CHAPTER FOURTEEN

What Is Innate and Why: Comments on the Debate

Hilary Putnam

I can say in a nutshell what I think about Chomsky and Piaget; neither has good arguments, but there is almost certainly something to what each one says. In this paper I am first going to say why the arguments are not good, and then discuss the more important question of why there is something right to what they say.

I shall begin with Chomsky's arguments. When one reads Chomsky, one is struck by a sense of great intellectual power; one knows one is encountering an extraordinary mind. And this is as much a matter of the spell of his powerful personality as it is of his obvious intellectual virtues: originality; scorn for the faddish and the superficial; willingness to revive (and the ability to revive) positions (such as the "doctrine of innate ideas") that had seemed passé; concern with topics, such as the structure of the human mind, that are of central and perennial importance. Yet I want to claim that his individual arguments are *not good*. I will examine only one example here, but I claim that a similar examination could be carried out on any of the arguments he has offered at this conference, with similar results.

The argument concerns "the process of formation of simple yes-or-no questions in English." In his introductory paper (see Chapter 1), Chomsky considers "such declarative-question pairs" as:

(1) The man is here.—Is the man here?
The man will leave.—Will the man leave?

And he considers two hypotheses "put forth to account for this infinite class of pairs" (of course, H_1 has never been "put forth" by anyone, nor would any sane person put it forth):

H_1: process the declarative from beginning to end (left to right), word by word, until reaching the first occurrence of the words *is, will*, etc.; transpose this occurrence to the beginning (left), forming the associated interrogative.

H_2: same as H_1, but select the first occurrence of *is, will*, etc., following the first noun phrase of the declarative.

Chomsky then writes:

Let us refer to H_1 as a "structure-independent rule" and H_2 as a "structure-dependent rule." Thus, H_1 requires analysis of the declarative into just a sequence of words, whereas H_2 requires an analysis into successive words and also abstract phrases such as "noun phrase." The phrases are "abstract" in that their boundaries and labeling are not in general physically marked in any way; rather, they are mental constructions.

A scientist observing English speakers, given such data as (1), would naturally select hypothesis H_1 over the far more complex hypothesis H_2, which postulates abstract mental processing of a nontrivial sort beyond H_1. Similarly, given such data as (1) it is reasonable to assume that an "unstructured" child would assume that H_1 is valid. In fact, as we know, it is not, and H_2 is (more nearly) correct. Thus consider the data of (2):

(2) The man who is here is tall.—Is the man who is here tall?
The man who is tall will leave.—Will the man who is tall leave?

These data are predicted by H_2 and refute H_1, which would predict rather the interrogatives (3):

(3) Is the man who here is tall?
Is the man who tall will leave?

Now the question that arises is this: how does a child know that H_2 is correct (nearly), while H_1 is false? It is surely not the case that he first hits on H_1 (as a neutral scientist would) and then is forced to reject it on the basis of data such as (2).

Chomsky's conclusion from all this is the following:

Such observations suggest that it is a property of S_0—that is, of LT(H,L)—that rules (or rules of some specific category, identifiable on quite general grounds by some genetically determined mechanism) are structure-dependent. The child need not consider H_1; it is ruled out by properties of his initial mental state, S_0.

I wish to discuss this example by considering two different questions: (1) can we account for the child's selection of "structure-dependent" hypotheses and concepts in the course of language learning on the basis of general intelligence, without postulating that the preference for H_2 over H_1 is built in, or that a template of a typical human language is built in, as

Chomsky wishes us to do; and (2) can we account specifically for the preference of H_2 over H_1 without assuming that such a specific preference is built in? Before discussing these questions, however, I want to consider the vexed question, "What is a grammar?"

THE NATURE OF GRAMMARS

A grammar is some sort of system which—ideally—generates the "grammatical sentences" of a language and none of the ungrammatical ones. And a grammatical sentence is one generated by *the* grammar of the language (or by any adequate one, if one believes as Zellig Harris does that there is no such thing as *the* grammar of a language).[1] This is obviously a circular definition. But how does one break the circularity?

Chomsky suggested long ago (in "Explanatory Models in Linguistics")[2] that a child *hears* people classing sentences as "grammatical" or "ungrammatical"—not, of course, in those words, but by hearing them correct each other or the child—and that he projects a grammar as a simplest extrapolation from such data satisfying some innate constraints.

The trouble with this view is that the factual premise is clearly false. People don't object to all and only *ungrammatical* sentences. If they object at all, it is to *deviant* sentences—but they do not, when they correct each other, clearly say (in a way that a child can understand) whether the deviance was syntactic, semantic, discourse-theoretic, or whatever.

Chomsky asserts that the child is, in effect, supplied with "a list of grammatical sentences" and "a list of ungrammatical sentences" and has to extrapolate from these two lists. But this is surely false. If anything, he is supplied rather with a list of acceptable sentences and a list of sentences that are deviant-for-some-reason-or-other; a grammar of his language will generate (idealizing somewhat) all of the acceptable sentences in the first list, but unfortunately, it will not be the case that it generates none of the deviant sentences in the other list. On the contrary, the grammatical sentences will be a superset of the (finite list of) acceptable sentences, which is *not disjoint from* the (finite list of) deviant sentences.

Moreover, the second list does not have to exist at all. Chomsky has cited evidence that children can learn their first language without being corrected; and I am sure he also believes that they don't need to hear anyone else corrected either. Chomsky might reply to this by scrapping the hypothetical second list (the list of "ungrammatical," or at least, "unacceptable" sentences). He might say that the grammar of an arbitrary language is the simplest projection of any suitable finite set of acceptable sentences satisfying some set of innate constraints. This throws the whole burden of defining what a grammar is on the innate constraints. I want to suggest a different approach: one that says, in quite traditional fashion, that the grammar of a language is a property of the *language*, not a property of the brain of *Homo sapiens*.

PROPOSITIONAL CALCULUS

Let us start with a simple and well-understood example: the artificial language called "propositional calculus" with its standard interpretation. The grammar of propositional calculus can be stated in many different but equivalent ways. Here is a typical one:

(I) A propositional variable standing alone is a well-formed formula.

(II) If A and B are well-formed formulas, so are $\sim$ A, (A & B), (A v B) and (A $\supset$ B).[3]

(III) Nothing is a well-formed formula unless its being so follows from (I) and (II).

The fact that a perfectly grammatical sentence may be deviant for semantic reasons, which is a feature of natural languages, is possessed also by this simple language, since "p & $\sim$ p" (for example) is perfectly grammatical but would not be "uttered" for obvious semantic reasons.*

Now consider the "semantics" of propositional calculus as represented by the following inductive definition of *truth* in terms of *primitive truth* (truth for propositional variables, which is left undefined). The fact that primitive truth is left undefined means that this can be thought of as an *interpretation-schema*, which becomes an interpretation when joined to any definition of primitive truth.

Definition:

(i) $\sim$ A is true if and only if A is not true.

(ii) (A & B) is true if and only if A and B are both true.

(iii) (A v B) is true if and only if at least one of A, B is true.

(iv) (A $\supset$ B) is true unless A is true and B is not true.

---

* Editor's note: In ordinary language it is rendered by "p and not-p." Its interpretation is blocked by definitions (i) and (ii). This state of affairs is often described as "the principle of excluded middle."

Notice that the inductive definition of *truth* in propositional calculus parallels (in a sense which could be made precise, but which I will not attempt to make precise here) the inductive definition of *grammatical* in propositional calculus. Now, there are other ways of defining grammatical in propositional calculus with the property that corresponding to them there exist parallel inductive definitions of truth in propositional calculus. But if we limit ourselves to those that are computationally feasible (that is, the corresponding decision program is short, when written in any standard format, and the typical computation is also short), not a great many are known, and they are all extremely similar. In this sense, propositional calculus as an interpreted system possesses an *intrinsic* grammar and semantics.

Let me elaborate on this a little. If Martians exist, very likely they have hit upon propositional calculus, and it may be that when they use propositional calculus their logicians' brains employ different heuristics than our logicians' brains employ. But that does not mean that propositional calculus has a different grammar when used by a Martian and when used by a Terrestrian. The grammar is (any one of) the simplest inductive definition(s) of the set of strings in the alphabet of propositional calculus for which truth is defined—that is, the simplest inductive definition(s) with the property that there exist parallel inductive definitions of truth. Given the semantics of propositional calculus (and no information about the brains of speakers), the class of reasonable grammars is fixed by that semantics, *not* by the structure of the brains that do the processing.

It may seem that I have begged too many questions by introducing the predicate "true"; but it is not essential to my argument. Suppose we do not define "true," but rather "follows from." Any reasonably simple definition of the relation "x follows from y" in propositional calculus will have the property that it presupposes a syntactic analysis of the standard kind. In other words, checking that something is an axiom or a proof, etc., will involve checking that strings and components of strings have the forms (p & q), ~ p, (p v q), (p ⊃ q). The grammar (I), (II), (III) not only generates the set of strings over which the relation "follows from" is defined, but it generates it in a way that corresponds to properties of strings referred to in the definition of "follows from."

Coming to natural language: suppose we think of a natural language as a very complicated formalized language whose formalization is unknown. (This seems to be how Chomsky thinks of it.) Suppose we think of the speaker as a computer that, among other things, computes whether certain strings are "true," given certain inputs, or if you don't like "true," as a computer that computes whether certain sequences of strings are "proofs," or computes the "degree of confirmation" of certain strings, and so forth. The fact is that any one of these semantic, or deductive logical, or inductive logical notions will have an *inductive definition* whose clauses parallel or at least presuppose a syntactic analysis of the language.

To come right out with it: I am suggesting (1) that the declarative grammar of a language is the inductive definition of a set of strings which is the set over which semantic, deductive-logical, inductive-logical (and so on) predicates are defined;[4] (2) that it must be in such a form that the inductive definitions of these predicates can easily "parallel" it; (3) that the corresponding decision program must be as computationally feasible as is consistent with (1) and (2). If a language is thought of in this way —as a system of strings with a semantics, with a deductive logic, with an inductive logic, and so on—then it is easy to see how the grammar can be a property of the *language* and not of the speakers' *brains*.

The Nature of Language Learning

Let us consider the linguistic abilities of Washoe (the chimpanzee brought up to use a certain amount of deaf-mute sign language by Alan and Beatrice Gardner). No doubt Chomsky will point out that Washoe lacks many of the syntactic abilities that humans have, and on these grounds he would claim that it is wrong to apply the term "language" to what she has learned. But the application of this term is not what is important. What is important is the following:

1. There is a certain class of words, which I will call *nouns-for-Washoe*, which Washoe associates with (classes of) *things*. For example, Washoe associates the word "grape" (in sign language) with more-or-less stereotypical grapes, "banana" with more-or-less stereotypical bananas, and so forth.

2. There is a *frame*, _____ gives _____ (to) _____, which Washoe has acquired (for example, "Alan gives apple to Trixie").

3. She can project *new* uses of this frame. If you teach her a new word, say "date," she will figure out herself the use she is expected to make of "_____ gives *date* (to) _____."

4. She can use the word "and" to combine sentences. She can

figure out the expected use of *p and q* from the uses of p and q separately.[5]

Actually Washoe's abilities go far beyond these four capacities; but let us just consider these for now. The only plausible account of what has occurred is that Washoe has "internalized" a rule to the effect that if X is a *noun-for-Washoe,* and A, B, and C are people's names—counting Washoe (of course) as a person —then "A gives X to B" is a sentence, and a rule to the effect that if p, q are sentences so is *p and q.* And these are *structure-dependent rules* which Washoe has learned *without benefit of an innate template for language.*

Nor is this really surprising. Let us introduce a semantic predicate to describe the above tiny fragment of Washoe's "language" (where the "shudder-quotes" are inserted to avoid the accusation of question-begging), say, the predicate "corresponds to the condition that." Here are the "semantic rules" for the fragment in question:

(I) If X is a *noun-for-Washoe* and B, C are people-names, and X corresponds to things of kind K, and b, c are the people corresponding to B, C, then "B gives X (to) C" corresponds to the condition that b gives something of kind K to c.

(II) If p, q are *sentences-for-Washoe, p and q* corresponds to the condition that the condition corresponding to p and the condition corresponding to q both obtain.

Now, I submit that Washoe is not really interested in learning that certain *uninterpreted* strings of gestures have a certain *uninterpreted* property called "grammaticality." She is interested for practical reasons—reward, approval, and so forth—in learning (I) and (II). But learning (I) and (II) automatically involves learning the grammatical facts that:

(i) If B, C are people-names and X is a *noun-for-Washoe,* "B gives X (to) C" is a sentence-for-Washoe.

(ii) If p, q are sentences-for-Washoe, so is *p and q.*

For the set of sentences "generated" by the "grammar" (i), (ii) is precisely the set over which the semantic predicate—"corresponds to the condition that ____"—is defined by the inductive definition (I), (II); and the clauses (I), (II) presuppose precisely the syntactic analysis given by (i), (ii). Given that Washoe is trying to learn the *semantics* of Washoe-ese, and the syntax is only a *means* to this end, there are only two possibilities: either her intelligence will be too low to internalize "structure-dependent" rules like (I), (II), and she will fail; or her intelligence will be high enough, and as a corollary we will be able to ascribe to Washoe "implicit knowledge" of the syntactic rules (i), (ii)—not because she "knows" (I), (II) *and in addition* "knows" (i) (ii), but because having the "know-how" that constitutes implicit knowledge of (I), (II) *includes* implicit knowledge of (i), (ii).

But the same thing is true of the child. The child is not trying to learn a bunch of *syntactic* rules as a kind of crazy end-in-itself. He is learning, and he wants to learn, *semantic* rules, and these *cannot* be stated without the use of structure-dependent notions. There aren't even plausible candidates for structure-independent semantic rules. So *of course* (given that his intelligence is high enough to learn language), *of course* the child "internalizes" structure-dependent rules. And given that he must be building up an "inner representation" of abstract structural notions such as *sentence, noun, verb phrase,* and so on in learning to understand the language, the mere fact that H_2 uses such notions and H_1 does not, does *not* make H_2 so much less plausible than H_1.

Chomsky has, so to speak, "pulled a fast one" on us. He presents us with a picture of the child as being like an insanely scientistic linguist. Both are looking at language as a stream of uninterpreted noises; both are interested in an occult property of "grammaticality." From this (crazy) point of view, it is not surprising that H_1 seems infinitely "simpler" than H_2. So —Chomsky springs his carefully prepared trap—"Why doesn't the child try the simpler-but-false hypothesis H_1 *before* the correct hypothesis H_2?'

But this isn't what children (or sane linguists) are like at all. The child is in the process of trying to *understand* English. He has already tumbled (if Washoe can, so can he!) to the fact that he needs to internalize structure-dependent notions to do this. So the mere fact that H_2 *uses* such notions doesn't at all make it implausible or excessively complex. The point is that *the learning of grammar is dependent on the learning of semantics.* And there aren't even any candidates for structure-independent semantic rules (if there are, they get knocked out pretty early, even by a chimpanzee's brain).

H_1 Considered More Closely

So far I have argued that H_2 is not nearly as weird from the point of view of the intelligent brain unaided by an innate template of language as Chomsky wants to make it seem. But I haven't argued against H_1. So still the question remains, why doesn't the child try H_1?

Let us try applying to this problem the conception of grammar we just sketched (grammar as, so to speak, semantics minus the semantic predicates). H_1 will only be "tried" by the child if the child "tries" some *semantic* hypotheses that correspond to H_1. The child wants to *understand* questions, not just to "flag" them as questions. But it is plausible to assume (and Chomsky himself would assume) that understanding questions involves recovering the underlying declarative. This means that the question-transformation must have an *inverse* the child can perform. H_1 is indeed simple, but *its inverse is horribly complicated*. Moreover, *its inverse uses the full resources of the grammar*; all the notions, such as "noun phrase," that H_1 does not employ have to be employed in recovering the declarative from the output of our application of H_1. So it is no mystery that the child (or its brain) never "tries" such an unworkable semantic theory, and hence never "tries" H_1.

Incidentally, H_1 itself employs "abstract" notions, since it contains the phrase-structure concept "declarative," and applying it, if it were a rule of English, would therefore involve working with notions such as "noun phrase," since these have to be used to recognize declaratives. And some languages do have question-transformations that are as "structure-independent" as H_1 is; for example, in Hebrew one can form a question from a declarative by just prefixing *na im*. But this prefixing operation *does* have a simple inverse, namely, deleting *na im*.

I would like now to discuss Chomsky's more abstract remarks at the beginning of his paper (see Chapter 1). Let me begin with what he says about intelligence.

CHOMSKY ON GENERAL INTELLIGENCE

So far I have assumed that there is such a thing as general intelligence; that is, that whatever else our innate cognitive repertoire may include, it *must* include *multipurpose* learning strategies, heuristics, and so forth. But Chomsky appears to deny this assumption explicitly (see Chapter 1). I quote:

> More generally, for any species O and cognitive domain D that have been tentatively identified and delimited, we may, correspondingly, investigate LT(O,D), the "learning theory" for the organism O in the domain D, a property of the genetically determined initial state. Suppose, for example, that we are investigating the ability of humans to recognize and identify human faces. Assuming "face-

recognition" to constitute a legitimate cognitive domain F, we may try to specify LT(H,F), the genetically determined principles that give rise to a steady state (apparently some time after language is neurally fixed, and perhaps represented in homologous regions of the right hemisphere, as some recent work suggests). Similarly, other cognitive domains can be studied in humans and other organisms. We would hardly expect to find interesting properties common to LT (O,D) for arbitrary O,D; that is, we would hardly expect to discover that there exists something that might be called "general learning theory." As far as I know, the prospects for such a theory are no brighter than for a "growth theory," intermediate in level between cellular biology and the study of particular organs, and concerned with the principles that govern the growth of arbitrary organs for arbitrary organisms.

The key notion in this argument is the notion of a "domain." How wide is a domain? Is all of mathematics one domain? If so, what about empirical science? Or are physics, chemistry, and so on, all *different* domains?

If Chomsky admits that a domain can be as wide as empirical science (that there can be a "learning theory for empirical science"), then he has granted that something exists that may fittingly be called "general intelligence." (Chomsky might retort that only exceptionally intelligent individuals can discover new truths in empirical science, whereas everyone learns his native language. But this is an extraordinarily elitist argument: the abilities of exceptionally intelligent men must be *continuous* with those of ordinary men, after all, and the relevant mechanisms must be present at some level of functioning in all human brains.) Even if only physics, or just all of solid-state physics, or just all of the solid-state physics of crystals is one domain, the same point holds: heuristics and strategies capable of enabling us to learn new facts in these areas must be extraordinarily multipurpose (and we have presently no idea what they are). Once it is granted that such multipurpose learning strategies exist, the claim that they *cannot* account for language learning becomes highly dubious, as I argued long ago.[6] (Consider Washoe!)

On the other hand, if domains become so small that each domain can use only learning strategies that are highly specific in purpose (such as "recognizing faces," "learning a grammar"), then it becomes really a miracle that evolution endowed us with all these skills, most of which (for example, higher mathematics, nuclear physics) were not used at all until *after* the evolution of the race was complete (some 100,000-odd years ago). And the analogy with organ growth does not then hold at all: the reason there does not have to be a multipurpose learning mechanism is that there are only limited numbers of organs, whereas there are virtually unlimited numbers of "domains."

THE PROSPECTS OF GENERAL LEARNING THEORY

Chomsky feels that the "prospects" of "general learning theory" are bad. I tend to agree. I see no reason to think that the detailed functioning of the human mind will ever be transparent to the human mind.[7] But the existence of general intelligence is one question; the prospect for a revealing *description* of it is another.

Incidentally, if the innateness hypothesis is right, I am also not optimistic about the prospects for a revealing description of the innate template of language. The examples Chomsky has given us of how to go about inferring the structure of the template (such as the argument about H_1 and H_2) are such bad arguments that they cast serious doubt on the feasibility of the whole program, at least at this point in history (especially if there exist *both* general intelligence *and* an innate template).

On the other hand, we may well be able to discover interesting facts and laws about general intelligence without being able to describe it completely, or to model it by, say, a computer program. There may be progress in studying general intelligence without its being the case that we ever succeed in writing down a "general learning theory" in the sense of a mathematical model of multipurpose learning.

CHOMSKY ON EVOLUTION

Chomsky dismisses Piaget's question regarding how such a thing as an innate template for language might have evolved (see Chapter 1). But he should not dismiss it. One answer he might have given is this: primitive language first appeared as an *invention*, introduced by some extraordinary member of the species and learned by the others as Washoe learns her fragment of language. Given such a beginning of the instrument, genetic changes to enable us to use the instrument better (including the enlargement of the so-called speech center in the left lobe of normal humans) could have occurred, and would be explained, if they did occur, by natural selection. Presumably Chomsky did not give this answer because (1) he wants to deny that there exists such a thing as general intelligence, and to deny that even the simplest grammar could be internalized by general intelligence alone; and (2) he wants to deny that Washoe's performance is continuous with language learning, and to deny that it has any interest for the study of language learning. But this is surely perverse. If the first language user *already* had a complete innate template, then this could only have been a miraculous break in the evolutionary sequence, as Piaget in effect points out.

Chomsky remarks that we don't know the details of the development of the motor organs either, and this is surely true. We do postulate that they developed bit by bit. This poses difficulties, however, since there are no creatures with two thirds of a wing! But there have been impressive successes in this direction (for example, working out the evolution of the eye). We have found creatures with gliding membranes which are, in a sense, "two thirds of a wing." And we have found eyes with only rods (no cones) and eyes with only cones (no rods). Since the first draft of this paper was written, there have been exciting new suggestions in evolutionary theory.[8]

It is one thing to say that we cannot scientifically explain how certain structures were produced (and the theory of natural selection does not even claim that those structures were *probable*), and quite another to say that we now have scientific reason to postulate a large number of "mental organs" as specific as the various domains and subdomains of human knowledge. Such a mental organization would not be scientifically explicable at all; it would mean that God simply decided to produce these structures at a certain point in time because they were the ones we would need a half a million (or whatever) years later. (Although I don't doubt that God is ultimately responsible for what we are, it is bad scientific methodology to invoke Him as a *deus ex machina*. And, in any case, this is such a *messy* miracle to attribute to Him! Why should He pack our heads with a billion different "mental organs," rather than just making us smart?) On the other hand, if our language capacity did develop bit by bit, even with "jumps," a description of the first bit will almost certainly sound like a description of Washoe. But then we will have conceded that *some* internalization of linguistic rules (at least in prototype form) can be accounted for without innateness.

A BETTER ARGUMENT

But this suggests that there *is* an argument for *some* "innateness" that Chomsky might have used. Consider the phenomenon called "echo-location" in the bat. The bat emits supersonic "noises," which are reflected from the prey (or whatever—for example, a single insect), and the bat can "steer" by these sound-reflections as well as if it had sight (that is, it can avoid fine wires, catch the mosquito that is trying to avoid it, and so forth). Now, examination of the bat's brain shows that there has been a tremendous enlargement of the centers connected with hearing (they fill about seven-eighths of the bat's brain), as compared to other mammals (including, presumably, those in its evolutionary past). Clearly, a lot of the bat's echo-locating ability is *now* "innate."

Suppose Chomsky were to grant that Washoe has proto-speech, and thereby grant that general intelligence can account for *some* language learning. He could then *use evolution as an argument for (some) "innateness."* In other words, we could argue that, given the enormous value of the language ability (as central to human life as echo-location is to bat life), it is *likely* that genetic changes have occurred to make the instrument better—for example, the development of the "speech center" in the left lobe. (But caution is needed: if the left lobe is damaged early, speech *can* develop in the right lobe.) This argument is the only one I know of that makes it plausible that there is *some* innate structuring of human language that is not simply a corollary to the innate (that is, genetically predetermined) structuring of human cognition in general. But the argument is not very strong: it could be *general intelligence* that has been genetically refined bit by bit and not a hypothetical language template. Indeed, even species-specific and functionally useless aspects of all human languages could be the product of unknown but genetically predetermined aspects of the overall functioning of the human brain and not clues to the character of a language template; so the mere existence of such aspects is no evidence at all for the template hypothesis.

I think there is an answer that Chomsky can make to this objection; but I will defer it until I have discussed Piaget.

PIAGET'S "CONSTRUCTIVISM"

The view I have been putting forward—that everything Chomsky ascribes to an innate template of language, a "mental organ" specifically designed to enable us to *talk*, can, for all we know, be explained by general intelligence—agrees in broad outline with the view of Piaget. However, there seem to me to be serious conceptual difficulties with this view when it is combined with Piaget's specific account of what general intelligence is like.

Piaget supposes that human intelligence develops in stages, each stage depending on biological maturation (that is, the age of the child) and on the successful attainment of the previous stages. At a certain stage, certain concepts characteristically appear, for example, the concept of "conservation." But what is it to have such a concept as conservation?

I submit that the only coherent account presently available for having the concept of conservation is this: to have the concept is to have mastered a bit of *theory*, that is, to have acquired the characteristic uses of such expressions as "same amount," and some key *beliefs*, expressed by sentences involving such expressions, or equivalent symbolism. I don't claim that all concepts are abilities to use symbolism; an animal that *expects* the water to reach the same height when it is poured from a pot back into the glass might be said to have a minimal concept of conservation, but I claim that anything like the *full* concept of conservation involves the ability to use symbolism with the complexity of language in certain ways. (I don't claim that this is a "tautology"; rather that it is the only coherent account presently available for what full-blown concepts *are*. And I don't claim to have argued this here, but I have discussed this elsewhere;[9] and, of course, this insight is not mine but Wittgenstein's—indeed, it is the main burden of *Philosophical Investigations*.)

But if a maturational schedule *involving the development of concepts* is innate, and *concepts are essentially connected with language*,[10] then Piaget's hypothesis would seem to imply Chomsky's; "constructivism" would entail "nativism."

Of course, Piaget does not commit so crude an error. He does not suppose that the maturational *schedule* is given (that is, innate); what he takes as given is "reflective abstraction"—it is this that "precedes language" and that is supposed to take us from one "step" to the next.

But "reflection" and "abstraction" have *no literal meaning* apart from *language!* If "reflective abstraction" is not literally meant, it is either a metaphor for empiricist "generalization," which is insufficient to account for language learning and use (see below), or a metaphor for we-know-not-what.

It seems to me that Piaget should take the view that "reflective abstraction" is something *like* the use of language in the making of hypothetico-deductive inferences, as Chomsky and Fodor urge, and hence conclude that something *like* the use of language is "innate." This position would have brought him into convergence with Chomsky, instead of into an unnecessary sectarian squabble. Moreover, his own suggestion in 1958 that formal logic is the best model for human reasoning[11] is very consonant with such a position.

FODOR'S "TAUTOLOGY"

In the discussion Fodor said some things that were a little careless. I want to rectify some of these errors, not for the sake of being "picky," but because the discussion becomes hopelessly confused at the critical point if we let them stand.

First a quibble: Fodor and Chomsky are simply wrong when they say that it is a "tautology" that we can't learn anything, unless some innate "prejudices" are "built in" (see Chapter 12). It is not *logically* impossible that our heads should be as empty as the Tin Woodman's and we should still talk, love, and so on; it would just be an extreme example of a *causal anomaly* if it ever happened that a creature with no internal structure did these things. I don't doubt for one moment that our dispositions *do* have a causal explanation, and of course the functional organization of our brains is where one might look for a causal explanation (although I myself think that we won't be able to describe this in very much detail in the foreseeable future).[12] But this still is not a tautology.

Second, it is true that we can't learn how to learn unless we have some prior learning-dispositions: we have to have some dispositions to learn that are not themselves learned, on pain of infinite regress (however, the impossibility of an infinite regress in the real world is hardly a tautology!); but that does not mean that it is *logically necessary* (a "tautology") that the unlearned dispositions be innate. We might *(logically possibly)* acquire a new *unlearned* disposition every five minutes for no cause at all, for example, or for some cause that does not count as a form of "learning." There just aren't any significant tautologies in this area.

The reason this is not *just* a quibble is this: once we pare down Fodor's and Chomsky's big "tautology" to something like this: *as a matter of fact* (not logic!), *no learning without some laws of learning,* we see that no one, least of all the empiricists, has ever denied it. Chomsky's and Fodor's claim that there is a big, mysterious tautology that no one appreciated until Nelson Goodman and that everyone they dislike fails to appreciate is mere rhetoric (see Chapter 12).

FODOR AND CHOMSKY ON THE PERCEPTRON

In the discussion (see Chapter 12) Papert described the perceptron as a simple device for measuring "three-blobness" (or any other property that depends on certain kinds of *local* properties of figures); that is, a device that can be programmed to print "yes" if three blobs are exhibited on its screen (or a pattern with whatever property P of the requisite kind is exhibited) and "no" if the number of blobs is not three. Fodor insisted (with Chomsky agreeing) that this device "has the predicate 'three blobs.'" On the same reasoning, he would have to say that the thermometer "has the predicate 70°," that the speedometer "has the predicate 60 mph," and so on. Far from showing that the model of language processing is the only model now viable for "general intelligence" (which is what he wished to show), all Fodor was doing was showing that he (and Chomsky) can stretch *their* terms to fit *whatever facts they please* in just the way they accuse Skinner of stretching his terms.

If I may use the term "tautology" now: that every system capable of learning (or, apparently, even of measurement) has predicates is something Fodor has *turned into* a tautology! But on the customary meaning of "have (the use of) a predicate," it is just *false*.

The "Inductron" and the "Carnaptron"

Consider the following device, which I will call the "inductron." The device consists of a standard digital computer that is programmed to (1) tell (in the manner of the perceptron) whether or not there are 3 blobs on a certain screen; (2) tell whether the blobs are all white; (3) increase the total stored in a certain address (call it "address 1") by 1 each time the answer to both questions is "yes"; (4) change the 0 stored in a certain address (call it "address 2") to a 1 if the answer to the first question is "yes" and the answer to the second question is "no," and leave the 1 stored in address 2 unchanged thereafter; (5) print out "whenever the number of blobs is 3 they are all white" if the count in address 1 ever passes 100 and the number stored in address 2 is 0; (6) print out "sometimes the number of blobs is 3 but they are not all white" and stop if the number in address 2 is ever 1. Addresses 1 and 2 are both supposed to contain 0 at the start.

I take it that the inductron is a trivial realization of a simple associationist model of learning (simpler than any associationist has ever postulated, of course). It is capable of making one, and only one, "induction"; it can "induct" that all 3-blob-groups are white provided that N is greater than or equal to 100, and the generalization has not been falsified (here N is the number of "positive instances").

Now consider the following second device, which I will call the "carnaptron." The carnaptron is a computer coupled to a pattern-recognition program which enables it to "accept" certain "observation sentences" in simple first order language under appropriate circumstances (they could be the sorts of circumstances the perceptron can detect). "Accept" just means that these sentences are stored in a special file. The carnaptron operates by computing the *degree of confirmation* (in the sense of Carnap's "c*") for whatever sentence the operator inquires about, and prints out "this sentence is probable to the degree . . . ," where . . . is the value it computes for c*. (The "evidence" *e* used in the computation is just the set of sentences in the file, of course.)

I take it that it is *minimally* appropriate to describe the carnaptron as "having" a language, since it makes use of an inductively defined computation program whose definition is over precisely the set of sentences of something we call a language.[13] Similarly, a "hypothetico-deductive machine" might carry out eliminative inductions, given a "simplicity ordering" of hypotheses in the same language in the manner suggested in my paper in the Carnap Volume.[14]

I take it that what Chomsky and Fodor are really arguing—and I find this very plausible—is that the inductron is a terrible model for either general intelligence or language learning (and not just because we only gave it 1 generalization class instead of 100 or 10,000), and that the only plausible hypothesis is that our minds have (at least *in part*, I would add) a structure more like the carnaptron or the hypothetico-deductivetron.[15] But the mistake of saying that the perceptron "has predicates" *blurs* this point instead of sharpening it. For if the perceptron "has predicates," then even the inductron is a "hypothetico-deductive" machine (with a trivial "simplicity ordering" consisting of one "hypothesis" and a caution parameter set at N = 100). But then, the contrast—Locke *or* Kant, associationism *or* built-in linguistic computation—is lost. If all is water, why should I hand you a towel? (The towel is water too.)

FODOR'S ARGUMENT FOR THE INNATENESS OF ALL CONCEPTS

My aim in the remainder of this paper is to develop a modest a priori argument for the Fodor-Chomsky view that something *like* a language-processing capacity must be innate. But if Fodor's argument in *The Language of Thought* (summarized in Chapter 6 of this volume) were acceptable, *my* work would be all done. So I must first explain why I reject Fodor's argument.

Fodor's argument has two parts. First, he contends that the

only model we have presently available for the brain is the a·
purpose digital computer. He contends, moreover, that such
computer, if it "learns" at all, must have an innate "program"
for making generalizations in its built-in computer language.
(Here he goes too fast—this is precisely what I think we need
an *argument* for.) Second, he concludes that every predicate that
a brain could learn to use must have a *translation* into the computer language of that brain. So no "new" concepts can be acquired: all concepts are innate!

I want to examine this second part of the argument, which is
fallacious even if the first part is granted. Fodor's reasoning is
as follows: Learning the meaning of a predicate is inferring what
the semantic properties of that predicate are, that is, concluding
(inductively) to some such generalization as:

(A) For every x, P is true of x if and only if Q (x).

But if (A) is in brain language, so is Q. (P need not be; P is mentioned, not used in (A). But Q is *used*, not mentioned.) And if
(A) is correct, Q is coextensive with P, and is so by virtue of
what P *means* (otherwise (A) is not a correct semantic characterization of the meaning of P). So Q is *synonymous* with P;
P is not a *new* concept, because there is a predicate (namely, Q)
in "brain language" that is synonymous with it. But P is an
arbitrary predicate the brain can learn to understand—so no
new concepts can be learned!

What is wrong with this argument is clear. The assumption
is as strong as what Fodor wishes to prove. So all we have to do
is show how it could be false, even given Fodor's general outlook, and nothing is left but a simple case of begging the question.

First a point of terminology: Every computer does have a built-
in "computer language," but *not* a language that contains quantifiers (that is, the words "all" and "some," or synonyms thereof).
Let me explain.

A digital computer is a device that stores its own program
and that consults its own program in the course of a computation. It is not at all necessary that the brain be a digital computer
in *this* sense. The brain does not, after all, have to be repro-
grammed as an all-purpose digital computer does. (One might
reply that learning is "reprogramming"; but Fodor is talking
about the program *for* learning, not about what is learned, and
this program might be stored as the brain's *structure*, not as a
code.) Waiving this objection: the program that a digital computer stores consists of "instructions" such as "add the two

numbers in address 12" and "go back to step 6"—none of which use the word "all." So generalization (A) *cannot ever be stated* in "machine language," even if the computer's program is a program for making inductive inferences in some formalized language (for example, if the program is that of the hypothetico-deductive machine mentioned earlier). Moreover, machine language does not contain (nor can one introduce into it by definition) such notions as "tree," "cow," "jumps," "spontaneous," "pert," and so on—it only contains such notions as "add," "subtract," "0," "1," "put result in address 17," "go back to instruction so-and-so," and "print out contents of address blah-blah."

Let us suppose, however (what needs to be proved) that our brain is a hypothetico-deductive machine, and that it carries out inference in a formalized language ILL (for Inductive Logic Language) according to some program for eliminative induction. And let us suppose that Fodor is not really talking about the brain's *machine language* when he postulates his "language of thought," but about ILL. Even if so strong an assumption is conceded, his argument still does not work.

To see why it does not work, let us recall that when the speaker has finally mastered the predicate P, on Fodor's model, he is supposed to have acquired a new "subroutine." Even if this subroutine is described initially in ILL or in some special "programming language," or both, it has to have a translation into machine language that the brain's "compiler" can work out, or the brain won't "execute" this subroutine. Let S be the description of the subroutine in question *in machine language;* then even if we grant that the brain learns P by making an induction, it need not be an induction with the conclusion (A). It would suffice that the brain instead conclude:

(B) I will be doing OK with P if subroutine S is employed.

And *this* can be stated in ILL provided ILL has the concept "doing OK with an item," and ILL contains machine language. But this does *not* require ILL to contain (synonyms for) "face," "cow," "jumps," "spontaneous," "pert," and so on. Fodor's argument has failed.

Fodor's reply to Papert (see Chapter 12) suggests that he would claim that the machine language description of how to use, say, "tree" *is* (a form of) the predicate *tree.* But this is simply an extension of use designed to make his thesis an uninteresting "tautology."

Of course, the predicate "doing OK with P" may arouse suspicion. But it should not. The "machine" (the brain) doesn't have to understand this predicate as linguists and philosophers would! The generalization (B) is simply a signal to the machine to add subroutine S to its repertoire of subroutines. (We should keep in mind Dennett's caution that talk of "machine language" is dangerous because we are tempted to confuse *our* abilities with the formalism in question with the machine's abilities.)

ARE OUR BRAINS HYPOTHETICO-DEDUCTIVE MACHINES?

There is, if I am right, no possibility of proving that "all concepts are innate."[16] But what of the more modest claim that the only presently available model for the functional organization of our brains (or of the aspect thereof that explains learning) is the hypothetico-deductive machine?

Here, too, one has to avoid a number of bad arguments. The associationist is *not* making the mistake Fodor and Chomsky accuse him of making—denying innate structure (laws of learning) altogether—and, as we have seen, having innate generalization classes *is not* the same thing as having innate predicates. Nor is it an argument that the associationist has to postulate a vast number of innate generalization classes. Our functional organization developed over millions of years, we know not how (as Chomsky correctly observes). Why should it have a *short* description? Nor is it an argument that the associationist cannot spell out his hypothesis in any detail; the attempt of inductive logicians from Bacon (who was "no mere empiric," to quote his own phrase) to Carnap and after to spell out how hypothetico-deductive inferences are made in any detail has also failed. And as I have already remarked, Chomsky's view that *there is no program* for general-purpose learning—that what is innate are specific answer schemata to specific questions —cannot possibly be right.

Thus Fodor's argument for the hypothetico-deductive model —that no other model is presently available—suffers from two shortcomings. Another model *is* presently available (associationism); and *neither* model is worked out in testable detail. Nevertheless, I feel that Chomsky and Fodor are right: that the hypothetico-deductive machine (or, perhaps, a *collection* of such machines) is the best model. What I am going to do is try to defend this.

I am not, however, going to claim that I can produce a "knockdown" argument where Chomsky failed. I have already expressed my admiration for Chomsky's mental powers; and if there were a knockdown argument in this area, very likely he would have produced it. What I think I can offer is an indication of why the hypothetico-deductive model seems today more plausible, a priori more *right,* than the associationist model.

The associationist model can accommodate any number of independent first-level inductions (of very complicated kinds: the "law of reinforcement" can be much more sophisticated than the simple "caution parameter" model I called the inductron). What it seems unable to accommodate *without becoming indistinguishable from the inductive logical model* is higher-level inductions—what Reichenbach called "cross-inductions."[17]

A simple example of a cross-induction is this: We make a number of independent first-level inductions, for example to such conclusions as "night follows day," "water boils when (sufficiently) heated," "all swans are white," "all crows are black," "lead never turns to gold"; then, looking at one *type* of these inductions—namely, inductions of the form "all *birds* of such and such a species are such and such a color"—we discover that (based on past experience) inductions of this *type* are unreliable, because very often color (of birds) varies geographically (for example, there are black swans in Australia but not in Europe). So we *weight* such inductions in the future with a weight that reflects our estimate of their reliability (in this case, that it is not very high).

There seems to be no doubt that cross-inductions of many kinds do take place, and even cross-inductions about cross-inductions—"higher-type" inductions. (Carnap recognizes this —in his late work—under the name of "analogy.")

If indeed, as Bayes seems to have thought, the so-called "prior probability distribution" we use in statistical inferences is itself the product of experience, the learning process involved can hardly be anything but cross-induction.

As soon as we try to complicate the associationist model to allow cross-inductions, however, it begins to change character. Not only do we need higher-type generalization classes (classes of classes, classes of pairs of classes, and so on) but we need some way of symbolizing classes, inductions, and so forth. For, although one can program a device to recognize a property *in a thing* (for example, "square") and to respond whenever that property is presented, we cannot program it to recognize an induction unless that induction is somehow *represented.* A program for making the simple cross-induction that Reichenbach described ("going from bird species to color is unreliable, even when the number of 'positive instances' is large") involves, as far as one can presently see, keeping a record of all inductions made; segregating those that are about bird species/color (say, by classifying the record in a suitable way); segregating those that have proved bad; and making a calculation. But isn't this like using a rudimentary *language?* It isn't that we are just doing what the perceptron did: accepting in one state and rejecting in another;[18] we are recording what we do and making complicated transformations on our record.

Keeping a record of past inductions (cases in which we have concluded that "all A's are B's") involves having some uniform way of representing "all"—hence, something like a quantifier in one's "language of thought." And assigning "weights" to inductions is not going to be useful unless those weights eventually influence our *behavior*. The only models presently available for using higher-level probabilities in decision theory are, respectively, the Bayesian model (higher-level probabilities are used as "prior probability distributions") and the eliminative induction model (which uses a rank ordering of hypotheses instead of a numerical scheme). Both of these models require considerable syntactic transformation of the representations of hypotheses and data. And if deductions are to be interwoven with inductions in thought—and Piaget himself has suggested that *formal logic* is the best model for deductive reasoning—even more transformations of a "linguistic" kind will be involved. In short, a complicated associationism can account for a practically infinite number of *independent* first-level inductions. What it cannot account for (or has not even sketched a way of accounting for) is the making, and even more, the employing of higher-level inductions, and the interweaving of deductions and inductions.[19] Perhaps the latter only appears *after* language is learned; but I myself doubt if *any* model for general-purpose learning is going to succeed without something like cross-induction, and something like deductive reasoning.[20] It is amusing to note that if the associationist denies the need for cross-induction, his model will look very much like Chomsky's: independent generalization classes predesigned to everything we are supposed to learn are very much like so many specific "mental organs." Perhaps Chomsky is an associationist after all!

In conclusion, let me say that both Chomsky and Piaget have, in my opinion, made an enormous contribution in shifting the center of our attention in psychology away from the forms of learning curves (which is not to say that these are unworthy of study) and onto the *mechanisms* of learning. Perhaps Piaget is more clear that this is what the problem is than Chomsky; but

Chomsky and especially Fodor are more clear about the quasi-syntactic character of mental processing (insofar as we have present models for it at all) than Piaget. I would only add that Fodor's hypothesis of a "language of thought"—a brain symbolism *analogous* to language—is not, however, the same as Chomsky's hypothesis of a "mental organ" for *speaking;* it even makes the latter hypothesis totally unnecessary.

CHAPTER FIFTEEN

Discussion of Putnam's Comments

Noam Chomsky

Putnam's discussion of what he calls "the innateness hypothesis" extends an earlier critical analysis of his to which he refers.[1] The earlier criticism, I believe, is based on a series of specific errors and a mistaken conception of the problem at hand. I have discussed all of this in detail elsewhere[2] and will not recapitulate here. Putnam's current "Comments" (see Chapter 14) contain some new arguments, all of them, I believe, erroneous. I will not review them all, but will concentrate on those that are directed specifically to my paper in this volume.

According to Putnam, I advocate the "innateness hypothesis" as he formulates it, and I (and Fodor) attribute to "associationists"—the adversary—the mistake of "denying innate structure (*laws* of learning) altogether." The second of these claims is utterly false. I have repeatedly, consistently, and clearly insisted that all rational approaches to the problems of learning, including "associationism" and many others that I discuss, attribute innate structure to the organism.[3] I am sure that the same is true of Fodor.[4] The question is not whether innate structure is a prerequisite for learning, but rather what it is. Furthermore, the literature is clear and explicit about this point.

For just this reason I have never used the phrase "the innateness hypothesis" in putting forth my views, nor am I committed to any particular version of whatever Putnam has in mind in using this phrase (which, to my knowledge, is his and his alone) as a point of doctrine. As a general principle, I am committed only to the "open-mindedness hypothesis" with regard to the genetically determined initial state for language learning (call it S_0^L), and I am committed to particular explanatory hypotheses about S_0^L to the extent that they seem credible and empirically supported. In my contribution to this volume, I outlined one possible research strategy for determining the nature of S_0^L and sketched a number of properties that it seems reasonable to attribute to S_0^L, pursuing this strategy. Putnam investigates one of these examples, namely, the "structure-dependent" property of syntactic rules, arguing that the point is not well established. He contends that this particular property derives from "general intelligence." If indeed Putnam could characterize "general intelligence" or "multipurpose learning strategies" in some manner, and indicate, however vaguely, how the structure-dependent property of syntactic rules follows from the assumption that innate structure is as characterized, I would be happy to consider the hypothesis that this property should be attributed to "general intelligence" rather than to S_0^L, as I presently suppose to be the case. Nothing will follow, obviously, about the other properties that I argue can plausibly be attributed to S_0^L. Furthermore, if it can be shown that all properties of S_0^L can be attributed to "general intelligence," once this mysterious notion is somehow clarified, I will cheerfully agree that there are no special properties of the language faculty. But Putnam offers not even the vaguest and most imprecise hints as to the nature of the "general intelligence" or "multipurpose learning strategies" that he believes to exist. Therefore, his claim that some particular property of S_0^L can be explained in terms of these notions cannot be assessed.[5] It has the form of an empirical hypothesis, but not the content of one. Furthermore, his specific arguments with regard to the single example he discusses are all based on errors of fact or reasoning. Therefore, I see no reason to qualify the tentative suggestions in my paper with regard to structure dependence.

Putnam considers my two hypotheses H_1 and H_2, advanced to explain the formation of yes-or-no questions in English. He observes that the structure-independent rule H_1 would not be put forth by any "sane person," which is quite true, but merely constitutes part of the problem to be solved. The question is: Why? The answer that I suggest is that the general principles of transformational grammar belong to S_0^L, as part of a schematism that characterizes "possible human languages." It can easily be shown that H_2 can be directly formulated as a transformational rule in accordance with these principles, whereas H_1 cannot. In other words, the property "main verb" or "first occurrence of *is* (etc.) following the first noun phrase" is easily expressed in this particular theory, whereas the property "first occurrence of *is* (etc.)" cannot be expressed without a vast enrichment of theory (technically, it requires quantifiers in structural descriptions of transformations, whereas the former property does not). It follows, then, that a language learner equipped with the principles of transformational grammar as part of S_0^L will formulate H_2 rather than H_1 on the basis of data consistent with both. These principles are not, of course, invented ad hoc for this example; there is independent evidence to support them. Therefore, we have a plausible explanation for the fact that children automatically make the correct "induction" to a hypothesis which on general grounds would be regarded as more complex. Similarly, "sane persons," who also have an intuitive, pretheoretical grasp of the nature of language, will not put forth H_1, despite its great simplicity as compared with H_2. On the other hand, a Martian scientist, not equipped with the principles of transformational grammar as a schematism for human language, would have no hesitation in putting forth H_1. He would not be "insane," but merely "nonhuman"; that is, he lacks S_0^L.

Putnam offers several arguments to the contrary, which I will consider in turn. The first has to do with the data available for language learning. I have argued that we can, under an appropriate idealization, think of the language learner as being supplied with a sample of well-formed sentences and (perhaps) a sample of ill-formed sentences—namely, corrections of the learner's mistakes. No doubt much more information is available, and may be necessary for language learning, although little is known about this matter. Nothing that Putnam says in this connection has the slightest bearing on my (rather innocuous) proposal, as it has actually been formulated. Thus his "false premise" that people object to all and only ungrammatical sentences is one that I have never proposed, and his discussion of deviance is compatible with my views on this subject, as expressed since the mid-1950s. Therefore, I will not comment further on these remarks, which have no relevance to the issue at hand or, as far as I can see, to my expressed views on language learning.

Putnam objects to my conclusion that "the whole burden of defining what a grammar is [falls] on the innate constraints," arguing rather that the grammar of a language is a property of the "language." I find it difficult to make much sense of this part of his discussion, which seems to me quite confused. Before considering his "different approach," consider what he rejects. Is he proposing that only part of the burden of defining what a grammar is falls on the innate constraints? If so, which part? Which part of the burden falls elsewhere, why, and in what manner? No answer is suggested; therefore it is not clear that, and if so how, he is objecting to my conclusion. Note that he could hardly be claiming that none of the burden falls on the innate constraints, that is, that there are no innate constraints on what is a possible grammar, hence a possible human language. Thus even if language is constrained only by Putnam's "general intelligence," it follows that the burden of defining what a language is falls on the innate constraints, and hence the burden of "defining what a grammar is" falls on the innate constraints, if grammar is, as he claims, a property of "language." Thus to begin with, it is quite unclear to what view Putnam believes he is objecting.

In fact, Putnam's counterproposal suggests that he has something different in mind, and that his objection is just misstated. His counterproposal is that "the grammar of a language is a property of the *language*, not a property of the brain of *Homo sapiens*." But this formulation refers to the grammar of a particular language, say English, not to the innate constraints on possible languages and grammars. Apparently, Putnam is confusing the grammars of particular languages (the topic of his counterproposal) with "universal grammar," his notion of "what a grammar is" (the topic of his objection). Let us turn now to his counterproposal, as he formulates it.

The two counterposed views, then, are these: (1) my view, that grammars are represented in the brains of mature speakers, that languages are determined by these grammars, and that speakers of language can communicate to the extent that the languages characterized by the grammars in their brains are alike; (2) Putnam's view, that grammars are not represented in the brains of speakers but are properties of "languages."

It is difficult to compare these views, because Putnam's seems to me barely intelligible and, insofar as it is clear, inconsistent with other positions that he maintains. Let us put aside the fact that such notions as "the English language" are not linguistically definable, but are rather sociopolitical in nature. Consider now Putnam's "different approach." Note first that Putnam agrees, of course, that language is neurally represented (namely, in "the speech center in the left lobe," or the right lobe under early injury; see his "better argument"). It follows, then, that my language is a property of my brain. But Putnam claims that the grammar is a property of this language. Therefore, it is also a property of my brain, contrary to what Putnam asserts. If, as

Putnam claims, grammars *are not* properties of brains but *are* properties of languages, then it follows that neither languages nor grammars are "properties of the brain of *Homo sapiens,*" which is to say that my knowledge of English (and ability to use English) is not a property of my brain and is not represented in my brain, in the "speech center" or anywhere else. But this is surely not Putnam's view. One might take a different tack and argue that grammar is just an artifact of some sort, but that is not Putnam's approach; he is, it seems, a "realist" as far as grammar is concerned.

One can, perhaps, choose to think of propositional calculus (Putnam's example) as a "mathematical object" with whatever kind of existence we attribute to such "objects," but that has nothing to do with the empirical problem of determining the properties of natural systems such as some human language, as represented (I assume) in the brains of individuals in their mature state, or the problem of determining the properties of S_0^L, whatever these may be. Putnam gives no explanation of his alternative and allegedly "traditional" approach. I doubt that a coherent account is possible as a real alternative to the approach he wants to reject, which takes grammar to be a property of a brain and the "definition" of grammar to belong, in effect, to the theory of S_0^L. I see no need to comment further on Putnam's remarks about propositional calculus, except to note that even these are not free from error.[6]

Putnam proposes that the "declarative grammar of a language is the inductive definition of a set of strings which is the set over which semantic, deductive-logical, inductive-logical (and so on) predicates are defined" and that it must facilitate these definitions, be computationally feasible, etc. Let us grant all of this, for the sake of discussion, putting aside an ample literature that is concerned with the alleged "parallel" between semantic and syntactic properties of natural language.[7] From Putnam's suggestion, nothing follows about grammars being a property of "language" rather than "the speakers' brains," contrary to what Putnam asserts, without argument. The suggestion is entirely compatible with the view that grammars are represented in the brain, and represented in such a way that semantic (etc.) predicates have definitions whose clauses "parallel . . . syntactic analysis" (though I think there are adequate grounds to suspect that the latter conclusion is incorrect—an empirical question, which I cannot consider here).

Putnam next turns to Washoe, arguing that she has developed structure-dependent rules. His discussion, however, is vitiated by an equivocation with respect to the notion "structure-dependent." Note that both of my hypotheses, H_1 and H_2, present rules that apply to a sentence, deforming its internal structure in some way (to be precise, the rules apply to the abstract structures underlying sentences, but we may put this refinement aside). Both the structure-independent rule H_1 and the structure-dependent rule H_2 make use of the concepts "sentence," "word," "first," and others; they differ in that H_2 requires in addition an analysis of the sentence into abstract phrases. A rule that does not modify the internal structure of a sentence is neither structure-dependent nor structure-independent. For example, a phrase structure rule, part of a phrase structure grammar in the technical sense of the term, is neither structure-dependent nor structure-independent.

The rule for conjunction that Putnam discusses in his Washoe comments takes two sentences p and q and combines them to form p & q; in the framework of my discussion, it is a phrase structure rule rather than a transformational rule. It is neither structure-dependent nor structure-independent in my sense of these terms, since it does not require an internal analysis of the sentences to which it applies as a sequence of words *or* as a system of phrases. The rule does nothing to the internal structure of the sentences, and thus lies outside the bounds of the present discussion altogether.

Notice that in discussing question formation, I counterposed a structure-dependent and a structure-independent hypothesis, H_2 and H_1, respectively, and raised the question of why one is selected over the other on evidence compatible with both. In discussing conjunction, Putnam does not put forth competing hypotheses. The reason is that neither the notion "structure-dependent" nor the notion "structure-independent" applies in this case. There is no "structure-independent" counterpart to his rule, because it is neither structure-dependent nor structure-independent. Thus even if we were to grant that Washoe has learned her rule, and can form p & q (in principle) for arbitrary sentences p, q, nothing at all follows with regard to structure dependence or the choice between H_1 and H_2. The other Washoe examples also fall outside the domain of our discussion. They have nothing to do with structure dependence or structure independence; they illustrate substitution of items in a fixed frame. There is, to my knowledge, no evidence that chimpanzees use structure-dependent (or structure-independent) rules, in the sense of my discussion. Clearly, Putnam's account involves no rules of either sort. Therefore, we can put aside the discussion of Washoe, which has no more relevance to the problem under consideration than the discussion of propositional calculus. Both concern a kind of syntax to which the concepts under discussion do not even apply (in the case of propositional calculus, context-free phrase structure grammar; in the case of Washoe, an extremely limited finite-state grammar, perhaps even without any cycles). The same is true of Putnam's Hebrew example, which involves a nontransformational phrase structure rule like the rule introducing an abstract question marker in many treatments of English grammar.

Putnam later argues that my H_1 is itself structure-dependent, again equivocating on the term. I did not patent the terms and Putnam is free to use them as he likes, but in my usage, the rule is plainly not structure-dependent.

It is not clear why Putnam introduced propositional calculus and Washoe into the discussion of structure dependence. Perhaps his argument is that since the child (like Washoe, allegedly) can learn the rule for conjunction, and since this rule is "structure-dependent" (in Putnam's sense, though not mine), then the child will, by some kind of induction, choose the structure-dependent H_2 over the structure-independent H_1. I hesitate to suggest that this is Putnam's implicit argument (there is no explicit argument), since it would be inconsistent with his assertion that both H_1 and H_2 are structure-dependent (in his sense); if this is so, then either could have been posited by "induction," so the original problem remains. Or perhaps Putnam means to suggest that the concept of "structure dependence" in his sense is a notion of "general intelligence" (since Washoe allegedly has it). But that is of no help to his argument, since Washoe also undoubtedly has the notion "before" in time and probably "first," so that these too, by the argument, form part of general intelligence. We are still faced with the problem of why the child selects H_2 over H_1, which "general intelligence" makes available (since it involves only the notions "before" or "first," applying to word sequences). Similarly, if both hypotheses are (as Putnam alleges) "structure-dependent" (in his sense), then we are still left with the original problem: Why is H_2 selected?

Whether or not Putnam has something like this in mind, in case anyone else might be misled into supposing that there is an argument here based on some kind of "induction," let me add a few remarks. Imagine some new concept of "structure dependence" (call it SD*) under which the rule of conjunction and H_2 are structure-dependent (have the property SD*) but not H_1. Suppose further that the child learns the rule of conjunction and others like it which have the property SD*. Can we then account for his choice of H₂, which has the property SD*, over H₁, which does not? Only if we suppose that the predicate SD* is "available" as a projectable predicate for induction. But that is to beg the very question at issue. That is, we can now ask why the child carries out an induction with the predicate SD* instead of another, equally good predicate SI*, which holds of the rule of conjunction and H₁, but not H₂ (for example, consider the property of being a rule that does not deform a sentence in accordance with its internal phrase structure). In short, this pseudo-argument requires that the predicate SD* but not SI* be available for "induction" (learning). The question then arises: why SD* but not SI*? But that is just a variant of our original problem—we have just another variant of the familiar Goodman paradox, except that in this case we cannot even tell which is "grue," SD* or SI*, since neither seems a reasonable choice as a "projectable" predicate.

Putnam next turns to H₁ and H₂ directly, presenting his first real argument that the child "of course" uses structure-dependent rules. He argues that this follows from the fact that the child wants to learn "semantic rules" which cannot be stated without structure-dependent notions. Let us assume, for the sake of argument, that the semantic rules are structure-dependent. Does this explain why the child selects H₂ over H₁? Obviously not. Suppose that in fact English used the structure-independent rule H₁ to form yes-or-no questions. This would pose no problem at all for the formulation of the appropriate semantic rule. The rule for yes-or-no questions merely requires that these be distinguished from declaratives; they can be distinguished by H₁, by H₂, by painting them green, by standing on one's head while saying them, or in any other way, as far as the semantic rule is concerned. The rule asks: Is the corresponding declarative true or false? (Actually, the matter is more complex, but in no way that bears on this discussion.) We will turn in a moment to the matter of finding the "corresponding declarative." But Putnam offers no argument at all to support his claim that H₂ facilitates statement of the relevant semantic rule in a way that H₁ does not. Furthermore, there is no such argument, as the semantics makes clear. I should add that it is very common in discussions of language learning to appeal to "semantics" or "pragmatics" when problems arise. It is often not appreciated just what is at stake. Putnam's argument, which is completely without force, is a clear example of this unfortunate tendency.

Putnam argues that the child must use abstract phrase structure to understand the language, and that therefore H_2 is natural. He fails to add that the child also uses the notions "word" and "first" (presupposed by both H_1 and H_2) to understand the language; thus H_1 is no less "natural," in this regard. We then face again our original question: Why does the child use H_2, which employs analysis into phrases in addition to the notions presupposed in H_1? Putnam's argument is neutral with respect to this question, and therefore goes the way of the preceding ones.

Putnam next claims that (A) *"the learning of grammar is dependent on the learning of semantics."* He offers (A) as an apparent paraphrase of his earlier assertion that the grammar must provide for the definition of semantic predicates, but it is certainly no paraphrase of this assertion. Elsewhere, Putnam has been quite clear about the distinction and has indeed advanced a very different and more plausible thesis.[8] Indeed, it is not easy to reconcile (A) with Putnam's earlier observation that the inductive definitions of semantic notions "parallel or at least presuppose a syntactic analysis of the language." If the definitions of the semantic notions presuppose a syntactic analysis (that is, a formal grammar that assigns phrase structure, determines well-formedness, and so on), then how can the learning of this grammar be "dependent on" a (prior?) learning of semantics?[9] But putting this question aside, suppose that (A) is true, in some sense that remains to be explained. Does anything follow concerning H_1 and H_2? Not as far as Putnam has argued or shown. The semantics of yes-or-no questions prefers neither H_1 nor H_2.

Putnam next argues that H_2 is preferable to H_1 because its "inverse" is simple, whereas the inverse of H_1 is "horribly complicated." He does not explain why he believes that this is so. As far as I can see, it is not; the inverses are very similar. In each case, the inverse operation requires that we find the position from which *is* (etc.) has been moved—a position immediately before the predicate. Given H_1, we seek the first such position (and if someone wanted to argue that the inverse of H_1 is in fact simpler, he might note that our search is facilitated by the presence of the word *who* [etc.] in this case). Given H_2, we will seek the "main" position, using the full phrase structure analysis. One can think of various algorithms, none of which, as far as I can see, differentiates between H_1 and H_2. Since Putnam offers no argument, I have to leave it at that.

Note, incidentally, that even if the inverse algorithm must be "structure-dependent," that has no bearing on the choice between H_1 and H_2, that is, on the question of whether it is the first occurrence of *is* (etc.) or the "main" occurrence that is proposed. We cannot argue that because (by assumption) the inverse is structure-dependent, then so is the rule. In fact, even if one were to put forth this illegitimate argument, it would not bear on the essential point. We could then rephrase our original query, asking why it is that the occurrence of *is* after the main noun phrase is moved, rather than the first occurrence after a noun phrase (that is, the leftmost occurrence in "The man who is here is tall").

To allay any lingering confusion about this matter, consider the three relevant question forms:

(I)   Is — the man here?
(II) Is — the man who is here tall?
(III) Is — the man who here is tall?

Both Putnam and I are assuming that the language learner is presented with many examples such as (I), and formulates either H_1 or H_2 to account for them. The facts of (II) and (III) show that H_2 was correct. To apply the inverse algorithm in (I), (II), and (III), the child must be able to detect where *is* is missing in the form to the right of — in these expressions. The question has never been studied, but it seems likely that at the stage of language acquisition when children can freely form sentences such as (II) (using H_2), they would have no difficulty in determining where *is* is missing in any of the forms to the right of — in (I), (II), and (III). Indeed, I would not be surprised to learn that they can solve the problem more easily for (III) than for (II). But ability to solve this problem is all that is required for the inverse algorithm to operate. Therefore, Putnam's unargued assertion that the inverse operation for H_1 is "horribly complicated" as compared with the inverse for H_2 seems far from the mark. If in fact it is easier to solve the problem for (III) than for (II), we would have an additional puzzle for the Martian observer, who might have taken this as further support for the obvious hypothesis that H_1 is to be preferred.

These comments exhaust Putnam's arguments concerning structure dependence. As far as I can see, none of them have any force. My conclusions, therefore, remain as stated in the paper that appears in this volume (see Chapter 1).

Next, Putnam turns to the question of "general intelligence," beginning with the following assertion:

(IV) "So far I have assumed that there is such a thing as general intelligence," including "*multipurpose* learning strategies, heuristics, and so forth."

Actually, (IV) is a rather misleading assertion. All that Putnam has so far assumed is that S_0^L, whatever it may be, contains only the general mechanisms for learning. Recall that he gives no hint as to what these are. To invoke an unspecified "general intelligence" or unspecified "multipurpose learning strategies" is no more illuminating than his reference, at one point, to divine intervention. We have no way of knowing what, if anything, Putnam has assumed. The point is worth stressing, since it illustrates a common fallacy in discussions of this sort. The use of words such as "general intelligence" does not constitute an empirical assumption unless these notions are somehow clarified. As matters now stand, very little is asserted by (IV).

Putnam claims that his "multipurpose learning strategies" enable us to learn and create physics. He seems to feel that I should also grant something of the sort, since I insist, naturally, that these achievements are possible. But I am not committed to an empty claim. If Putnam tells us what these "multipurpose learning strategies" are, even in the most vague and informal way, I will be glad to join him in inquiring as to their efficacy in accounting for our learning of physics, etc. In the absence of any proposal, I have nothing to say about the problem. Nor does Putnam, it is crucial to emphasize.

There are, in fact, striking and obvious differences between language learning and the learning (or discovery) of physics. In the first case, a rich and complex system of rules and principles is attained in a uniform way, rapidly, effortlessly, on the basis of limited and rather degenerate evidence. In the second case, we are forced to proceed on the basis of consciously articulated principles subjected to careful verification with the intervention of individual insight and often genius. It is clear enough that the cognitive domains in question are quite different. Humans are designed to learn language, which is nothing other than what their minds construct when placed in appropriate conditions; they are not designed in anything like the same way to learn physics. Gross observations suffice to suggest that very different principles of "learning" are involved.

As for the proper delimitation of cognitive domains and their nature, I have nothing to add here to earlier discussion, at the Royaumont conference and elsewhere.[10] Where a rich and intricate system of belief and knowledge is rapidly attained in a uniform way on the basis of limited and degenerate evidence, it makes sense to suppose that some "mental organ" with special design is involved, and to try to determine the nature and properties of this "organ" and the cognitive domain related to it, as well as its relations to other systems that form part of the general structure of mind. Progress in delimiting these domains and determining their nature may come through studies analogous to those I have discussed in the case of language, or perhaps in other ways. Putnam asserts that the number of domains is "virtually unlimited" and that the strategies we use "must be extraordinarily multipurpose," although he adds that "we have presently no idea what they are." I know no more about these strategies than Putnam does, or about the delimitation of domains, or about their number or specific character. As far as I can see, we differ here only in that I am disinclined to put forth what appear superficially to be empirical hypotheses where, as we both admit, we have "no idea" as to what the facts may be. I would urge that Putnam too should adopt the "open-mindedness hypothesis" and refrain from putting forth assertions such as (IV) and others that appear in that section of his "Comments."

Putnam argues that if there are such cognitive domains as "learning a grammar," "recognizing faces," and others that are "so small" and have such "highly specific-purpose" learning strategies, then "it becomes really a miracle that evolution endowed us with all these skills," since most of them (for example, mathematics) weren't used until after the evolution of the race was complete. I see no miracle here. Consider the human ability to handle fairly deep properties of the number system. I suppose that this ability is genetically determined for humans, though it is hard to imagine that it contributed to differential reproduction. But we need not suppose that this is a miracle, if true. These skills may well have arisen as a concomitant of structural properties of the brain that developed for other reasons. Suppose that there was selection for bigger brains, more cortical surface, hemispheric specialization for analytic processing, or many other structural properties that can be imagined. The brain that evolved might well have all sorts of special properties that are not individually selected; there would be no miracle in this, but only the normal workings of evolution. We have no idea, at present, how physical laws apply when 10^{10} neurons are placed in an object the size of a basketball, under the special conditions that arose during human evolution. It might be that they apply in such a way to afford the brains that evolved (under selection for size, particular kinds of complexity, etc.) the ability to deal with properties of the number system, continuity, abstract geometrical space, certain parts of natural science, and so on. There are innumerable problems here, but

I see no need to appeal to miracles. Nor do the problems that arise seem qualitatively different from familiar problems in accounting for the evolution of physical structures in organisms.

Putnam's further remarks about evolution seem to me mystifying. He feels that I have "dismissed" Piaget's concerns about evolution, but that is quite false. Rather, I remarked that the structures I have been led to postulate for S_0^L, though "biologically unexplained," are not, as Piaget asserts, "biologically inexplicable." Furthermore, I see no specific problem that arises in this connection beyond those that are familiar (if often mysterious) in the case of physical organs. Putnam's further discussion seems to indicate that he agrees. Therefore, I assume that he has somehow misunderstood what I said about this matter.

In my earlier discussion of Putnam's criticisms of the "innateness hypothesis" (see note 2), I noted that his views about evolution seemed to me very curious. Thus in the paper to which he refers,[11] Putnam asserts that *"invoking 'innateness' only postpones the problem of learning; it does not solve it."* This is a very odd principle, one that would never be put forth in connection with the development of physical organs. If, in fact, the general properties of binocular vision or the fact that we grow arms instead of wings is genetically determined, then it would be senseless to say that "invoking 'innateness' only postpones the problem of the learning of binocular vision or the learning of arms rather than wings." There is no such problem to be "solved." True, a problem remains, but it is not the problem of learning; it is the problem of explaining the origin and development of structures that are innate. I see no reason to take a different approach when we study higher mental faculties. If, indeed, certain properties of language are genetically determined, then "invoking 'innateness' " does not "postpone the problem of learning" with regard to these properties, but rather is the proper move, since there is no "problem of learning" in these respects. Putnam seems to believe otherwise, but I have no idea why.

I will not comment on Putnam's "better argument," except to observe that it does not bear even in a remote way on the questions that I discussed and that seem to me to be the interesting ones, namely, what is the nature of S_0^L, how does it relate to other faculties of mind or to "general intelligence" (whatever it may be), and so on.

Putnam summarizes the view that he has been putting forward as follows: "Everything Chomsky ascribes to an innate template of language, a 'mental organ' specifically designed to enable us to *talk,* can, for all we know, be explained by general intelligence." And he suggests that this conclusion agrees "in broad outline" with Piaget's views. At the level of vagueness at which he discusses the problem, I would not disagree, once his specific arguments are dismissed as fallacious. Thus I agree that "for all we know" some notion of "general intelligence" about which we have "no idea" might explain everything I have ascribed to S_0^L. Similarly, there would be little point in debating the claim that "for all we know" some mysterious force, as to the character of which we have "no idea," might explain everything that physicists try to explain in terms of their complex constructions. Thus, contrary to what Putnam believes, I would not deny his contention. We differ only in that I dismiss it, whereas in contrast he seems to think the contention is important—why, I do not know.

There is much to say about Putnam's discussion of Piaget, but I will not go into the matter here. One point deserves mention, however. Putnam feels that Piaget's approach converges with mine in that the notion of "reflective abstraction" relates to the use of language in inference. At the risk of seeming ungracious, I must demur. My uneasiness with "reflective abstraction" is not that it is placed "apart from language" (as Putnam asserts), but rather that I do not know what the phrase means, to what processes it refers, or what are its principles, any more than I know what Putnam has in mind when he speaks of "general intelligence," "multipurpose learning strategies," and the like. Hence it is impossible for me to take a position on the potential convergence that Putnam perceives.

Putnam argues that Fodor and I misused the term "tautology." He fails to note that the term did not appear in any presented paper, but was introduced in the informal discussion (by whom, I do not recall)* and was then used by all participants not in the technical sense of "logical truth" but in the informal sense of "obvious truth." Since one cannot speak with warning-quotes, this may not be explicit in the transcript, but it surely is obvious enough from the context. Since Putnam agrees that the contention at issue is an obvious truth, there is no disagreement here.

Putnam's further discussion of induction, learning, inference, and so forth deserves comment, but this is not the place to expand on the matter. I see no arguments here that bear

---

* Editor's note: By de Zengotita and Bateson.

even remotely on any position that I was maintaining or even offering as a speculation.

Putnam concludes his paper with the claim that Fodor's hypothesis of a "language of thought" makes my hypothesis concerning a " 'mental organ' for *speaking* . . . totally unnecessary." He offers no hint of an argument in support of this contention. He would be right if the "language of thought" had, in general, the properties of S_0^L. But it is exactly this question that Putnam has failed to address, once errors in argument and incorrect statements of fact are eliminated. I do not state categorically that the thesis is false; only that no argument to support it has been offered by Putnam or anyone else, to my knowledge, whereas there are empirical (though, obviously, nondemonstrative) arguments to the effect that S_0^L has certain properties for which there are no known significant analogues elsewhere. Furthermore, there are real and generally unappreciated difficulties in the thesis that intelligence is "undifferentiated."[12] Perhaps the reason why we can offer no specific analogues elsewhere to the properties postulated for S_0^L is that we just do not know enough about other aspects of cognition, or perhaps postulation of these properties is incorrect. Or perhaps the reason is, as I suspect, that the "mental organ" of language really has special properties, hardly a surprising conclusion, though of course far from a necessary truth.

Perhaps I may conclude with a personal remark. My old friend Hilary Putnam and I have been debating these issues for quite a few years. He begins his discussion here with some kind remarks, for which I am grateful. He even goes so far as to say that if I am unable to provide arguments for what he calls "the innateness hypothesis," then probably no case can be made for it. As noted, I do not feel that he has established any of his points; rather, it seems to me that my arguments stand, as given, with just the qualifications and strictures given. But let me return the compliment. Putnam has remarkable intellectual gifts and an awesome command of many fields of knowledge. Furthermore, more than any other philosopher to my knowledge, he has concerned himself with the problem to which his present comments are addressed, seeking to establish that "general intelligence" or "multipurpose learning strategies" suffice to account for the specific workings of language. I feel that to date, he has not made a case for his contentions, and indeed, has not even succeeded in making clear what these contentions are. Perhaps, then, we may conclude . . .

CHAPTER SIXTEEN

Reply to Putnam

Jerry Fodor

Not many of Putnam's criticisms seem to me to require extended discussion; and many of those that do have been covered in Chomsky's reply (see Chapter 15). I shall therefore restrict myself almost exclusively to those of Putnam's remarks that concern things I said at this conference and in my book *Language of Thought*.[1]

PUTNAM ON "FODOR'S TAUTOLOGY"

Professor Putnam thoughtfully reminds me (and Chomsky) that it is "not *logically* impossible that our heads should be as empty as the Tin Woodman's and we should still talk, love, and so on"; it was "a little careless" of me to suggest the contrary. It would have been if I had. In fact, "tautology" is not a term that appears in my formal presentation, nor did I introduce it into the discussion, nor did I suggest (ever or anywhere) that "no one appreciated until Nelson Goodman" that there can be "no learning without some laws of learning." (What I *did* suggest is that the demonstration that there is no induction without an a priori delimitation of the field of *projectible predicates* is owing to Goodman and has profound implications for theories of learning. This remark, which has nothing to do with the existence or otherwise of laws of learning, is one I continue to endorse.) Finally, the sense of "tautology" at issue in the discussion was, of course, *not* "truth of logic," but rather "obvious truth, self-evident truth . . . etc." Putnam denies that his strictures on "tautology" are "just a quibble," but they'll do until a real one comes along.

PUTNAM ON FODOR AND CHOMSKY ON THE PERCEPTRON

1. Putnam suggests that if I say that the perceptron "has the predicate P" when the device learns to distinguish between instances of P and instances of non-P, then I would have to say that "the thermometer 'has the predicate 70°,' that the speedometer 'has the predicate 60 mph,' and so on." Putnam gives no arguments *at all* for this (I should have thought) rather unself-evident claim, so we don't know why he believes it or even which such hypotheticals he takes to be true. For example: are *all* machines such that if I say they have predicates then I have to say that thermometers do? I don't know and Putnam isn't talking.

Suffice it that to block the inference from perceptrons to thermometers we need only find some (reasonably relevant) property that perceptrons have but thermometers (and so on) do not. This is easy to do since (as Putnam appears to notice one paragraph down) perceptrons are (but thermometers and speedometers are not) *learning* devices. And the claim that "every system capable of learning . . . has predicates" is not (oh dear) a tautology in either the strict or the loose sense; it is part of a theory of the computational operations underlying learning: namely, that such operations involve projecting and confirming hypotheses. (I assume that the enthymemic premise "no hypotheses without predicates" *is,* if not tautological, anyhow patent.)

2. Putnam offers a challenge: if the perceptron has predicates, why does the "inductron" (a device programmed *only* to converge upon printing out "yes" if presented with three white blobs and queried whether all the blobs are white) *not* have predicates? What Putnam seems to have in mind is a slippery-slope argument, a form of dialectic that I should have thought philosophers had by now learned to distrust. ("If a small oak tree is an oak tree, why isn't an acorn an oak tree? But if nothing is an oak tree unless an acorn is, then nothing is an oak tree.") Here, in any event, is *one* reason for not saying that the "inductron" has predicates: if we did, we should not be able to say *which* predicate it has. When the inductron says "yes," is it saying "yes, there are three white blobs" or "yes, my receptors are stimulated in a certain way" or "yes, there are three white blobs and you just typed in 'are all the blobs white' " or "yes, I'm now typing out 'yes' "? Since all these descriptions (and indefinitely many others) are coextensive for the device that Putnam describes, we have no reason for choosing one or

the other as deploying the predicate that the device "has." The notion of having a predicate makes sense, in short, only for a device that "has" access to a sufficiently rich set of computational options. Predicates come in systems. It is quite true that I can't say *when* a system becomes sufficiently rich to be plausibly thought of as a language. I also can't say when an acorn turns into an oak.

But suppose that, in fact, one's theory of language *does* somehow require one to say that the inductron is a (limiting) case of a device that "has predicates." It is hard to see just why one is supposed to be embarrassed, as long as the theory doesn't *also* require that the thermometer and the speedometer do have them. Putnam provides only the rhetorical answer that if "even the inductron is a 'hypothetico-deductive' machine . . . then the contrast—. . . associationism *or* built-in linguistic computation —is lost." But this suggests that Putnam has lost track of the discussion. What Chomsky and I have been arguing is precisely that the issue is *not* associationism versus innateness; all theories of learning are ipso facto nativist about *something* (that being the point we took to be [loosely] tautological). This issue is, rather, domain-specific nativism versus the assumption that only general learning principles are innate. I fail to see why the question whether inductrons have predicates affects *that* distinction *at all*. (It is, I think, a general point about Putnam's remarks that issues about computation and internal representation have been run together with issues about nativism in a way that helps with neither. I will return to this point further on.)

Putnam on Fodor on the Innateness of All Concepts   Putnam (mis)construes an argument that I gave in *Language of Thought*. I'll work with his version first and then come back to how he got it wrong and why that matters.

> Fodor's reasoning is as follows: Learning the meaning of a predicate is inferring what the semantic properties of that predicate are, that is, concluding (inductively) to some such generalization as:
>
> (A) For every x, P is true of x if and only if Q (x).
>
> But if (A) is in brain language, so is Q. (P need not be; P is mentioned, not used in (A). But Q is *used*, not mentioned.) And if (A) is correct, Q is coextensive with P, and is so by virtue of what P *means* (otherwise (A) is not a correct semantic characterization of the meaning of P). So Q is *synonymous* with P; P is not a *new* concept, because there is a predicate (namely, Q) in "brain language"

that is synonymous with it. But P is an *arbitrary* predicate the brain can learn to understand—so no new concepts can be learned!

Putnam has an analysis of what's wrong with this argument: "The assumption is as strong as what Fodor wishes to prove. So all we have to do is show how it could be false . . . and nothing is left but a simple case of begging the question." Now, I suppose that Putnam is being a little careless here, for it is not easy to see how an argument *could* be valid unless its "assumptions" were (at least) as strong as its conclusion. What Putnam must mean to say is that the assumptions are as *tendentious* as the conclusion. But that is surely just false, since the (operative) assumptions are that learning a predicate is learning its meaning, and that language learning is (inter alia) the projection and confirmation of hypotheses. And there is a tradition of making just such assumptions which goes back for literally hundreds of years in philosophy, and which is, to all intents and purposes, simply unquestioned in contemporary cognitive psychology. Indeed, what is puzzling about the argument (if anything is) is exactly that it requires only these fairly banal assumptions to arrive at the wildly paradoxical conclusion that all concepts are innate. (I assume that it's part of the philosopher's job to reveal the paradoxical lurking in the prima facie untendentious—and then to make it go away.)

Now, what can Putnam offer to replace these trouble-making assumptions? Putnam does a very odd thing at this point. Instead of following the doctrine about language learning proposed in such of his papers as "The Meaning of 'Meaning' " (to which doctrine we shall presently return), he suggests that "even if we grant that the brain learns P by making an induction, it need not be an induction with the conclusion (A). It would suffice that the brain instead conclude: (B) I will be doing OK with P if subroutine S is employed." Putnam does not tell us what sort of subroutine S is, and he is thunderously silent on where such subroutines come from, but he remarks (correctly) that S will have to be specifiable in machine language if the machine is to be able to execute it. We may add (as Putnam rather astonishingly does not) that if learning to execute the subroutine S is to be identifiable with learning P, then the machine (brain, etc.) must not only conclude, but conclude *truly*, that it is "doing OK" with P if it uses S. (There is, after all, a distinction between having a predicate and merely believing that you do.) Well, then, what might be the subroutine vis-à-vis P such that, when you have learned to execute *that* subroutine, your belief that you are doing OK with P is *true?* The classic suggestion is, of course, that you must have a procedure for sorting things that do and don't satisfy P by reference to whether they exhibit some property Q. And now if we add that the fact that the possession of Q determines the satisfaction of P is supposed to be a consequence of the meaning of P, what we have is just (A) all over again. In effect, my (A) is a version of Putnam's (B). It is, moreover, the standard version of (B); and Putnam neither suggests how we are to avoid the paradoxes that arise from taking (B) on construal (A), nor proposes a version of (B) that provides an alternative to (A).

Putnam seems to sense this sort of reply in the offing, because in his comments on my exchanges with Papert, he says that I might claim "that the machine language description of how to use, say, 'tree' *is* (a form of) the predicate *tree*. But this is simply an extension of use designed to make his [my] thesis an uninteresting 'tautology.' " It doesn't, however, seem to be an extension of use at all. Putnam has, in effect, endorsed the view that what we learn when we learn "tree" is a set of procedures for using the word. It was, after all, Wittgenstein (and not I) who suggested that the best candidate for meaning is rules-of-use. And Putnam is surely aware of a long philosophical tradition that identifies such rules with (one or another form of) operational *definition* of a term. (This tradition is, by the way, enthusiastically endorsed by the "procedural semanticists" whose work was at issue in the discussion between Papert and me that Putnam adverts to.)

I think, however, that what Putnam must really have in mind is something quite different from what this argument suggests—something that has very little to do with all this business about "subroutines." I think what he really has in mind is that we should abandon (the classic form of) the proposal that to learn a word is to learn what it means; that is, he wants to distinguish between *learning P* and *learning the meaning of P* and to argue that the latter is *not* necessary for the former (not, at least, if the meaning of P determines logically necessary and sufficient conditions for P's applying). This move, of course, really *is* tendentious, but Putnam argues for it in "The Meaning of 'Meaning' " and, though I think his arguments there do not, in the long run, persuade, I won't try to deal with them here. For present purposes, my point is just that, on *this* account, not any old subroutine S will do vis-à-vis P. We require a very special kind of subroutine associated with "tree" such that something might satisfy the subroutine and fail, for all that, to *be* a tree. Of course, if one can show *that* then one *has* shown that (A) fails; hence that no argument that rests on (A) would prove that the meaning of "tree" is innate.

The trouble is, however, that on this view the meaning of "tree" isn't *learned* either. Indeed, on this view it is quite possible that nobody now knows, or ever will know, the meaning of "tree" (in the traditional sense of, roughly, the essential conditions for being a tree). For, whether something is a tree depends (so the story goes) *not* on its having the properties we learned to associate with "tree" (in particular, it is not determined by the outcome of executing subroutine S) but rather on whether it has those properties that "the progress of science" will (or may) come to tell us that trees must have. And, of course, learning *those* properties (the ones which, as it were, give the *real* meaning of "tree") isn't part of learning "tree."

This is where it becomes important that Putnam has misrepresented the argument I gave in *Language of Thought*. What I did there was *not* to endorse (A) (the principle which, on our present reading, Putnam has brought under attack) but simply to run it as an example of what you would be committed to if you were to hold that to learn a word is to learn its (for example, operational) definition. But, as I pointed out (ad nauseam and with explicit reference to Putnam's views),[2] weaker assumptions than (A) might be made about what is learned when one learns P; and, given the structure of my argument, those weaker assumptions about what is learned will comport with correspondingly weaker conclusions about what is innate. What I endorsed was, in short, an argument scheme: you tell me what you think is learned (when P is learned), and I'll tell you what you must be assuming to be innately available to the learning device. You say: "meanings are learned," and I'll show you that you must assume that meanings are innate; you say: "subroutines are learned," and I'll show you that you must assume that subroutines are innate; in effect, you tell me what sense of "concept" you have in mind when you speak of "concept learning," and I'll show you that you must take concepts *in that sense* to be innate. I don't think there is anything in Putnam's remarks that undermines this strategy; I can't find anything in Putnam's remarks that even bears on it.

Putnam on Associationism

Putnam thinks that associationism offers an alternative to the hypothetico-deductive model. If, however, what Putnam means by the hypothetico-deductive model is that learning is hypothesis testing, then he must have a very crude form of associationism in mind. For, all the "mediational" models of learning by association *explicitly* require a notion of internal representation and require it, indeed, precisely in order to provide the computational domain for induction. Perhaps what Putnam is thinking of is (not Hume, Locke, Berkeley, Titchner, Wundt, Hebb, Mill, Osgood, Hull, Jenkins, Tolman, and so on, but) a specifically Skinnerian associationism that defines learning over classes of overt stimuli and responses rather than over internal representations. But does Putnam *really* think that learning consists of altering the probability function from Ss to Rs? Do we really have to go through all that *again*?

PUTNAM ON THE LIMITS OF ASSOCIATIONISM

Putnam offers the suggestion that the one thing that associationism *can't* cope with is cross-inductions. For cross-inductions we need "some way of symbolizing classes, inductions, and so forth. For, although one can program a device to recognize a property *in a thing* . . . we cannot program it to recognize an induction unless that induction is somehow *represented*." It will be noted that the question, here and in the preceding section, isn't any longer "What is innate?" but rather "What psychological processes require mediation by internal representations?" The suggestion seems to be that we should resort to internal representation when the property attributed by a belief isn't actually "in a thing."

One sympathizes with what is behind this suggestion; a rather similar line of argument is contemplated in *Language of Thought*.[3] A *very* rough way of making the point would be like this. If I believe a thing is red, then *redness* has to come in *somewhere*. If the thing *is* red (if the property is "in the thing"), then *that's* where the redness comes in; otherwise, the redness must come in in the way I *represent* the thing. It comes in as a property-I-represent-the-thing-as-having.

If, however, this *is* the sort of point that Putnam is making, then we will need a notion of representation long before we get to cross-inductions. We will need it (for example) to account for beliefs about the future, beliefs about the past, beliefs about what is not perceptually present, modal beliefs, and (N.B.) *false* beliefs. (Suppose I believe that Putnam is Marie of Rumania. This is not a matter of my recognizing a property "in an object," for Putnam *isn't* Marie of Rumania, nor is anybody else. But it is, however, presumably a matter of my representing Putnam in a certain way.)

Suppose, however, that Putnam is right and it is only when we consider the phenomenon of cross-induction that we are forced to attribute internal representations to organisms. It would hardly follow that organisms don't employ internal representations in *other* psychological processes (for example, in the formation of *first*-order inductive beliefs), which, if Putnam *were* right, *could* be explained without attributing internal representations (namely, by appeal to "association"—or something). That is, Putnam seems to have confused the question "What psychological phenomena force the theorist to acknowledge internal representations?" (a *purely* epistemological question) with "What psychological phenomena actually involve internal representations?" (a question about how the world is). A parallel fallacy might go: "Since it is only when we notice phenomena like solubility that we are forced to postulate the molecular nature of matter, it is only soluble materials that are made of molecules." Even if, in short, it were only in respect to cross-induction that we *knew* associationism *had* to be false, that would be no reason for believing it not to be false in the other cases too—quite the contrary.

PUTNAM ON WHAT FODOR HAS RENDERED OTIOSE

Putnam says that "Fodor's hypothesis of a 'language of thought' . . . is not . . . the same as Chomsky's hypothesis of a 'mental organ' for *speaking;* it even makes the latter hypothesis totally unnecessary." I don't understand *what* Putnam could have in mind here. Perhaps he has confused the question of whether cognitive processes (for example, language learning) presuppose a medium of representation with the question of whether such processes presuppose (unlearned) information couched *in that medium.* As far as I can see, Chomsky's thesis (which, for purposes of discussion, let's take to be that General Linguistic Theory is innate) entails mine on the principle: no (innate) information without (innate) representation. On the other hand, there could be an innate medium of representation without there being innate information about (for example) natural languages (or, I suppose, anything else). I remarked earlier that a tendency not to distinguish between issues about innateness and issues about internal representation is pretty general in Putnam's paper: it may be that this is just a case of it. Alternatively, it may be that Putnam has confused issues about the innateness of *concepts* with issues about the innateness of *beliefs*, the thesis that GLT (General Linguistic Theory) is innate being primarily a claim about the latter while the thesis that LOT (Language of Thought) is innate is primarily a claim about the former. Nor should I wish to suggest that these alternatives are exclusive, since it may be that Putnam is confused about all of them at once.

PUTNAM ON GOD AND MAN

Putnam says: "I don't doubt that God is ultimately responsible for what we are . . . [but] this is such a *messy* miracle to attribute to Him! Why should He pack our heads with a billion different 'mental organs,' rather than just making us smart?" This is, however, a bad argument even on what appears to be the operative assumption: that God's aesthetic principles are indistinguishable from Putnam's. To see how bad it is, try applying it to any *other* species. Why didn't God make the spider *smart* instead of merely teaching it to eat flies and spin webs? Why endow the robin and the stickleback with a parochial talent for building nests instead of "general intelligence" and a bent for architecture? And what a messy miracle the bee's dance comes to. Clever gods would make clever bees, which could then invent navigation and the telephone in the fullness of time. Sloppy old God! Better consult a philosopher the next time 'round!

The point is, of course, that in all other species cognitive capacities are molded by selection pressures as Darwin taught us to expect. A truly *general* intelligence (a cognitive capacity fit to discover just *any* truths there are) would be a biological anomaly and an evolutionary enigma. Perhaps that is not what Putnam thinks we've got. Since he tells us nothing about what general intelligence is, we have no way of knowing.

The reasonable assumption, in any event, is that human beings have an ethology, just as other species do; that the morphology of our cognitive capacities reflects our specific (in both senses) modes of adaptation. Of course, we are in some respects uniquely badly situated to elucidate its structure (to carry through [what I take to be] the Kantian program). *From in here* it looks as though we're fit to think whatever thoughts there are to think (compare "a billion different mental organs"). It *would*, of course, precisely because we *are* in here. But there is surely good reason to suppose that this is hubris bred of an epistemological illusion. No doubt spiders think that webs exhaust the options.

We know more than spiders do; we can (and should) bear the biological precedents in mind. These precedents suggest that we must seem to angels the way that other species seem to us: organisms whose intelligence is shaped by their history and is therefore fragmentary, task-oriented, and domain-specific. I'll bet that's what the angels say when they are doing anthropology. Assuming that the angels bother.

CHAPTER SEVENTEEN

Comments on Chomsky's and Fodor's Replies

Hilary Putnam

COMMENT ON CHOMSKY'S REPLY

1. The reply by Chomsky asserts that the notion of general intelligence is hopelessly vague (as opposed to such notions as "the genetically determined initial state responsible for language learning," "universal grammar," and "the language faculty"). In fact, it is not vague at all. By "general intelligence" I mean the heuristics the brain uses for learning the answers to questions for which the answer (or an answer schema) is not genetically built in in the way in which Chomsky thinks a schema for the grammar of a human language is built in. Such heuristics certainly exist—subjective probability metrics over well-formed formulas in a suitable language are one mathematical model; the "trial and error" procedures for extrapolating functions from finite amounts of data studied by a number of workers in artificial intelligence are another. That such models are not realistic does not mean that the ability they model is vague; we know what preference is, although our mathematical model of preference is certainly idealized and oversimplified. The notion of a faculty for *learning* is not a metaphysical notion. (Nor is it, as Fodor charges, the notion of a mysterious faculty for discovering whatever truths there are to be discovered—indeed, theorems on what inductive machines *cannot* learn form a considerable part of the literature.)

2. Much of Chomsky's reply to me rests on the mistaken assumption that anyone who denies that grammars describe *properties of the brain* is committed to denying that they are rep-

resented in the brain. This is a non sequitur. I deny that the grammar of propositional calculus is a description of properties of my brain; but I do not deny that, if I learn propositional calculus, some representation of that grammar (probably not the one I should use in writing a logic book) will be formed by my brain. The geography of the White Mountains is represented in my brain; but the geography of the White Mountains is not a description *of* my brain.

3. Chomsky also suggests that I may be confusing the grammar of a specific language (English, or propositional calculus) with "universal grammar"—the theory of the genetically determined normal form for all grammars learnable by human beings. This begs the point at issue, which is whether there *is* such a thing as "universal grammar" at all.

Of course, our constitution limits and determines what languages we can learn and what sports we can learn. Chomsky does not believe in a science called "universal sport" because he doubtless thinks that many different constraints, coming from many different aspects of our makeup and operating in different ways, determine what sports we can learn. Hence there is no reason to think that a normal form for what sports we can learn is necessary or possible. He believes that the constraints that determine what languages we can learn are, to quote a term he used in the *Russell Lectures*,[1] "language-specific"—which is why he thinks such a science as "universal grammar" is possible. After twenty years of vigorously espousing this point of view in print and in conversation, it is a little unfair of Chomsky to say that he is only advocating the "Open-mindedness hypothesis" with respect to our genetic makeup. Who could be against open-mindedness?

4. Chomsky admits that not all our abilities need be task-specific and specifically selected for by natural selection (unlike Fodor, who compares us to the beavers). In connection with mathematics, he speaks of "analytic processing" ("analytic processing" is apparently all right, although "general intelligence" is taboo), and says that our abilities in this area "may well have arisen as a concomitant of structural properties of the brain that developed for other reasons." I agree emphatically. That is just what I think. But if this is true of mathematical ability, it could be true of linguistic ability as well.

5. Finally, I must say something about two of the technical points Chomsky raises.[2]

a. I regret if what I wrote left the mistaken impression that chimpanzees cannot learn that sentences have internal structure (beyond substitution in fixed frames); they certainly can. In particular, the structure-dependent semantic rule that a sentence of the form "the N Vs" is true just in case the object corresponding to "the N" has the property corresponding to "Vs" is clearly acquired by chimpanzees; and the alternative explanation Chomsky puts forward, that they learn "substitution in fixed frames," is refuted by a great deal of data.

b. The inverse of H_1 requires trying all possible positions for the moved "is," "does," etc.—at least I know of no other algorithm, and Chomsky suggests none. The inverse of H_2 requires only *locating the main break;* and, at least for phrase structure grammars, there are elegant algorithms for doing this without such a search, algorithms that were discovered by the Polish logicians many years ago.

COMMENT ON FODOR'S REPLY

1. Fodor's book *The Language of Thought* defends two theses:
   a. That the brain is analogous to a computing machine which carries out symbolic reasoning in a formalized language (call it "mentalese").

   (If this is true, then it is not surprising that natural language might appear to have an innate grammar; the grammar of natural language could be expected to be—in some respects though not in all [since "mentalese" is not a spoken language, but only a medium of computation]—the grammar of "mentalese." But "mentalese" evolved before language; doubtless chimpanzee brains compute in a primitive form of "mentalese." So the "mentalese" hypothesis renders hopeless the task of sorting out which "innate" features of natural language reflect the structure of mentalese and which are "language-specific"—at least until we have a description of "mentalese.")

   b. Fodor also argues for the thesis—he himself regards it as shocking—that *all concepts are innate.*

   In my paper I argued that (a) is probably true, although not for the reasons Fodor gives, and that (b) is just a mistake. Since I discussed *both* (a) and (b), I was discussing—not "confusing"—*both* "issues about representation" and "issues about nativism."

2. Sometimes Fodor uses the word "representation" so that it seems to be a tautology that, if I believe something is red, then my brain contains a representation of the predicate *red;* and at other times he speaks as if the thesis that belief involves

representations is a discovery made by "cognitive psychology." If it is a tautology that belief involves representations, then the thesis that our brain contains representations of predicates is compatible with our being *inductrons;* it has no bearing on the substantive thesis (a), that the brain computes in a medium with such devices as quantifiers and truth functions. On the other hand, while "cognitive psychologists" may talk somewhat as Fodor does, the mere existence of a philosophically loaded manner of speaking does not impress me greatly. Fodor asks plaintively whether the view that we are inductrons (or Skinner's form of that view) has to be gone over *again.* I claim that the stock arguments against that view only show that the view has difficulties; they do not yet show that any other view has fewer difficulties, or give good reasons for accepting any specific alternative to Skinnerian behaviorism.

3. The previous remark should make it clear why I reject the easy argument that Fodor offers me—that of course cross-induction involves representations because it involves beliefs. If we are inductrons, then we do make associations and we "represent" them in the sense of keeping some record of associations made. But, since there are no cross-inductions, the record does not have to be *uniform*—"All A's are B's" may be recorded in different ways in the case of different association pairs A, B. In other words, even if we do think of the inductron as having predicates (and I am glad that Fodor agrees with me that it does not) it does not have *quantifiers.* My argument in the paper is that a device that makes *cross-inductions* and elementary deductions needs a record with the *formal structure* of a quantificational language. "All A's are B's" must have a representation some recoverable feature of which represents the logical form "All ____ are ____."

4. Fodor writes: "Suppose, however, that Putnam is right and it is only when we consider the phenomenon of cross-induction that we are forced to attribute internal representations to organisms. It would hardly follow that organisms don't employ internal representations in other processes (for example, in the formation of *first*-order inductive beliefs), which, if Putnam *were* right, *could* be explained without attributing internal representations . . ." Here Fodor "runs through open doors," as the Germans say. Of course, we employ "mentalese" in the formation of first-order inductive beliefs if we employ it at all. The question is, how do we *know* that we employ "mentalese" at all?

Fodor writes: "Putnam seems to have confused the question 'What psychological phenomena force the theorist to acknowledge internal representations?' (a *purely* epistemological question) with 'What psychological phenomena actually involve internal representations?' (a question about how the world is)." Fodor does not quote any words of mine that confuse these two questions, or that take the view that "mentalese" is only used in cross-inductions, because no such words occurred in my paper.

5. The theory of meaning I have advanced proposes that knowing the meaning of a word (for example, "gold"), in the sense of *understanding* the word—not to be confused with knowing a normal form *description* of the meaning of the word—is a matter of (1) acquiring the various dispositions that make up a normal use of the word (this would be a matter of internalizing suitable subroutines, in a computer model); and (2) being connected to things in the extension of the word by causal chains of the right sort. This second element—the causal/referential element—is *not* a matter of one's psychological state in the sense of brain state. Thus one's brain state does not, in this view, determine whether a speaker means "gold" when he uses a word W. One has to see not only if his *use* (his subroutine) resembles sufficiently English speakers' use of the word "gold," but also *if the stuff in question is gold.* On this theory, *concepts are not in the head.* In Wittgenstein's words, "If God had looked into our minds, He would not have been able to see there what we were speaking of."

My reply to Fodor's "argument" that all concepts are innate will go through on *any* account on which there is a referential element as well as a "use" element in meaning. But Fodor's argument would be incorrect even if "use" were *all* there was to meaning. For a subroutine is a *description of the employment* of a concept; not the concept (the predicate) itself. If use were meaning, Fodor's argument would show that "mentalese" contains devices for *representing the employment of all predicates;* not that "mentalese" already contains all predicates.

6. Finally, on the word "tautology": I thought, and still think, that the claim that there is a big, mysterious "tautology" that all the opponents of "nativism" (or "domain-specific" innateness) flout, somewhat spoiled the informal discussion. The fact that no such "tautology" is cited by either Fodor or Chomsky in their replies to me confirms my belief that the alleged "tau-

tology" simply doesn't exist. That it might be "no learning without laws of learning" was only a suggestion by me, not a quotation I imputed to Fodor or Chomsky, and I cheerfully withdraw the suggestion, since Fodor has now said what the "tautology" is supposed to be: "The demonstration [*sic!*] that there is no induction without an a priori delimitation of the field of *projectible predicates* is owing to Goodman and has profound implications for theories of learning." Three remarks on this, and I am done:

a. Goodman does not think that the distinction between projectible and nonprojectible predicates is a priori.

b. It isn't even *true* that "there is no induction without . . ." Any inductive logic at all presupposes that some hypotheses are better confirmed than others in some situations, but the ordering is not necessarily an order based on the *predicates* that occur in the hypotheses, let alone on a dichotomous division of predicates into "projectible and "nonprojectible." What Fodor is now claiming to be "demonstrated" is something that no inductive logician, least of all Goodman, believes.

c. Both Chomsky and Fodor say that by "tautology" they only meant "obvious." Alas! In the words of Georg Kreisel, "It isn't obvious what's obvious."

CHAPTER EIGHTEEN

Psychology and Psycholinguistics: The Impact of Chomsky and Piaget

Jacques Mehler

At the root of Chomsky's innovative impact on linguistics lie his philosophy of science and his epistemological approach to behavior, both of which are revolutionary. In regard to methodology, Chomsky claimed that linguistic intuitions were no less respectable than the taxonomic data in use up until the 1960s. He maintained that intuitions must be considered as data when they are reproducible, stable, and representative of our knowledge of language.[1] The fact that they are not measurable presents no problem; in its absurdity, operationalism would have virtually rendered impossible the advent of theoretical physics and the progress of the natural sciences, if its stipulations had been taken into strict account. Along the same lines, Chomsky developed another major idea in the 1960s. The behaviorists claim to describe behavior by utilizing only concepts referring to behavior itself.[2] Chomsky clearly demonstrated that in order to arrive at a correct formulation of language, it was necessary to employ abstract underlying entities deriving their justification from reasons internal to the grammar, hence from their function in the grammar itself. The justification of these entities would become a matter of their operational relevance within the grammatical system. This conception is so well accepted in our day that it is difficult to imagine that it could have been otherwise in the recent past. As a matter of fact, the positivists had already led linguists like Bloomfield and psycholinguists like Osgood or Mowrer to overstep their methodological constraints and to carry out implicitly what Chomsky subsequently proclaimed explicitly. Hull is perhaps the most flagrant example of this move.

Piaget, on the other hand, strongly advocated the necessity of utilizing the *clinical method*. Like Chomsky, he spent a large part of his life working in a climate dominated by logical positivism. It would not have been surprising if Piaget had led the Geneva school to employ the reigning methods of behaviorism; we must therefore recognize the foresight which led him from the very outset to ban such methods while trying to impose his own clinical method. Essential to this method is the fact that exchanges between the experimenter and the child being tested are nonnormative and nondirective. The investigator, with the aid of objects that vary from test to test, tries to evaluate the mental stage or the level of development at a given stage which characterizes the child being tested. This evaluation is done in a manner analogous to that which a clinician employs for determining whether a patient has a certain disease. The clinician does not generally pinpoint a syndrome by means of a single symptom; he establishes his diagnosis by considering several symptoms and the dynamics of their development. Likewise, a psychologist employing the clinical method must not, according to Piaget, content himself with the observation of one single conduct to assess which stage a child is in. Thus a chance error would not lead to false conclusions, since the psychologist tries to evaluate the child's stage from the sum total of responses and opinions expressed by the child on a given problem, this sum total of data permitting him to infer the state of equilibrium that characterizes the child's stage of development. By this method, one would always give credence to what children say over what they do.

Psychology has lived through numerous tensions and conflicts resulting from the ambiguous relationship that psychologists have with empirical data. Over the centuries, the precursors of psychology elaborated theories and proffered hypotheses on psychological functioning without trying to base them on data and observations; the advent of experimental psychology upset this state of affairs by disputing all attempts to understand and explain psychological reality while disregarding observation and experimental data. It is precisely from this reversal and from the utilization of more rigorous methods that experimental psychologists thought they might be able to bring psychology closer to the other natural sciences.

Pre-Wundtian psychology had not been able to solve the contradictions born of theory without evidence, while the most episodic and arbitrary introspections often found a respectful audience among psychologists. On the other hand, experimental psychology directed exclusively toward the collection of data without a theoretical organization did not result in an accrued knowledge of psychological mechanisms either. Therefore, many psychologists sought in Chomsky or Piaget a solution enabling them to surmount the many obstacles which they had thus far encountered.

The perspective of the Chomskian model has often been poorly understood by psychologists in search of a theory of language use. Transformational grammar is a theory that deals with the inherent knowledge of the speaker, and not with the procedures, mechanisms, and heuristic devices involved in sentence recognition or the production of linguistic utterances. Unfortunately, the great interest shown by psychologists in psycholinguistics might cause some confusion among those who do not understand that the linguistic domain does not deal with the characteristic properties of speakers. Linguistics is based on intuitions; nevertheless, even though these intuitions are used to characterize the properties of language, they do not provide direct insight into the regularities of language, which must be theoretically reconstructed by means of formal rules and procedures. For theoreticians like Katz,[3] linguistics deals with a Platonic object while the psychology of language tries to account for the processes of comprehension and production of language. It seems self-evident that those rules that are necessary to the description of a subject (that is, formal linguistics) are not necessarily related to what is observable at the time of the comprehension or production of statements. It is not my intention to review and judge the highly controversial domain often known as the "psychological reality" of grammar. This question has recently become the subject of increasing and, in my opinion, very satisfactory analysis.[4] From a general point of view, some philosophers accuse Chomsky of psychologizing in his contributions to linguistics. Although this criticism may be partially valid, the positive aspect of Chomsky's position is that he has inspired psychologists to work in his framework, and so it is *their* contributions that should be evaluated.

A psycholinguistic school that included experimental psychologists was quickly grafted onto the movement of generative grammar. In the same way, developmental psychologists have rallied to the school of the genetic epistemologists. Among the latter group, a large number believed in the virtues of general intelligence for explaining systems as specialized as language, giving rise to a discipline that studies the origins of intelligence by utilizing the notions derived from artificial intelligence, a discipline represented in this volume by Papert and Cellérier and equally defended by Putnam.

Thus, even if Piaget and Chomsky elaborated theories which, at first, did not deal directly with psychology, they contributed to the development of axes that are currently the most in vogue and the most dynamic in my area, namely, developmental psychology and psycholinguistics. For this reason, it is very important to take into account the contribution made by these schools to psychology.

Initially, the goal of psycholinguistics was to demonstrate that generative grammars must correspond to a psychological reality. It was thought that grammar had to "represent" the cognitive processes employed in the recognition of sentences. Developmental psychology, on the other hand, was largely devoted to investigating the derivational sequence of cognitive, perceptive, and linguistic structures starting from the regularity of actions of the subject, making the fewest possible hypotheses about the initial state.

In the past few years, psycholinguistics has been influenced by two major trends. On the one hand, it has generally been conceded that the speech mechanisms are autonomous in relation to grammar, with grammar remaining, nevertheless, a theory by which the speaker understands the structure of sentences once they have been ideally recognized. On the other hand, psycholinguistics has been subjected to the assaults of cognitive and developmental psychologists. These psychologists claim that it is impossible to discover the manner in which linguistic regularities are utilized without making the best use of the temporal and sequential correlations of utterances, and that it is difficult to give an adequate theoretical description of linguistic performance without referring to parameters brought into play by speech production and conversation. This trend is actively developing. Some researchers are giving increasing attention to the procedures that the speaker employs at the moment when he behaves like a grammarian. Thus one is concerned with the pursuit of the mechanisms responsible for intuitions on which the speaker bases his linguistic conceptions.

Psycholinguistics has therefore recently undergone some major transformations, which have made it very different from what it was in the 1960s. The trend that allows the idea that speech mechanisms are autonomous in relation to grammar seems to prevail. This shift has enlarged the role granted to cognitive processes during the recognition of utterances. It is assumed that the language user is actively engaged in a process of comprehension, which is pursued by generating hypotheses and using strategies that rely on syntactic regularities and sequences of utterances. It is clearly apparent that certain context-dependent pragmatic and conversational aspects intervene notably in the recognition of utterances. Conversely, it is not certain that the paradigm instituted by the transformationalists can be harnessed to accommodate these changes. At present, it would appear that this paradigm holds up well enough, even if one notes all the increasing number of provisos. It is hardly possible to propose a model of linguistic performance without making reference to cognitive capacities in general. For the model of linguistic competence, it would seem possible to propose a set of rules, putting completely aside the psychological or encyclopedic[5] properties of the speakers.

From the beginning of his career, Chomsky relied on notions involving language acquisition in order to put constraints on the structure of generative grammar. Specifically, he defined a language acquisition device (LAD) which would eventually derive the grammar of the language from a restricted corpus alone. But some investigators voiced criticisms aimed at proving that the LAD cannot (even under ideal circumstances) live up to the task for which Chomsky had proposed it. The majority of these criticisms question the validity of the formal and specifically linguistic conception peculiar to the LAD, and doubt that it is possible to conceive of a process of language acquisition that is independent of the development of other cognitive capacities.[6] On the other hand, for most developmental psycholinguists, the formulation of the LAD is still sensible, at least in its spirit if not in the letter. This step allows for the postulation of a device by which the speaker comes to utilize an efficient grammar of his language while having at his disposal only the experience of a restricted corpus. In effect, the LAD would be the nucleus from which language could become the characteristic instrument of mankind. Nonetheless, it is fair to admit that, although we stand by this belief, we are often embarrassed by a certain paradox. One generally accepts that a grammar based on the formal principles characteristic of transformational grammars alone does not seem able to account for phenomena of acceptability or interpretation; it is also necessary to appeal to notions concerning the world in which these sentences are supposed to function.

It is equally true that the only knowledge one can logically acquire has a complexity that is not superior to that of the structure with which the learning subject is initially provided (as Fodor has shown). It is necessary, all the same, to observe that this problem is less crucial for linguistics than for psycholinguistics. If the formal rules describe a syntax and if this syntax is interpreted on the basis of dictionaries and more or less sophisticated sources of knowledge, the main point of the model does not change. In contrast, if one demonstrates that the LAD cannot function outside of a cognitive context and acquisition in general, then a large part of the advantages initially attributed to the model of transformational grammars disappears. For this reason, some psycholinguists and linguists hope to be able to resolve the impasse with the help of a model possessing properties equivalent to those of the LAD. This model could function as a guide to the interaction between subject and environment, thus ensuring a supplementary experience for the comprehension of the functioning of the natural languages. To understand the manner in which the natural languages operate, beyond the common interests of Piaget and Chomsky, it is absolutely essential to consider language acquisition. One can understand it either as an autonomous process or, conversely, as a process inseparable from the development of intelligence.

For the Geneva school, the choices have been clear for a long time. Thus, Sinclair says that "Piaget considers that language is not a sufficient condition for acquiring intellectual operations."[7] She claims to have validated empirically the Piagetian point of view, according to which language would be not the source but the consequence of logic. But Sinclair's experiments do not seem absolutely conclusive. She discovered, on the basis of tests, major differences in the linguistic proficiency of two groups of children, one of which showed conservation of quantity and the other did not. She then subjected the less advanced children to lexical training and ascertained that their linguistic progress had not had the slightest influence on their logical thought. In 1970, Piaget concluded that the intellectual operations promoted linguistic progress without the inverse being true. Along with many other authors, including Fodor, Bever, and Garrett, I would like to emphasize that Sinclair's conclusions do not follow necessarily from her results. One could very well imagine that the development of logical thought and that of language acquisition proceed along autonomous paths; this view would be entirely compatible with Sinclair's experiments, if not her conclusions. But if the arguments advanced by the psychologists of the Geneva school can be rejected, still the question of the role of intelligence in language acquisition remains. A convinced Chomskian like Bever affirms that "certain universal structural properties of language could manifest general constraints on knowledge rather than innate structures particular to language."[8] As for the question of specificity, it seems premature to claim to give a definitive response. Still, it is necessary to point out that the hypothesis of a linguistic specificity constitutes the basis on which the discipline of psycholinguistics is organized.

Returning to developmental psychology, it is clear that genetic epistemology rests on an impressive amount of empirical data. The stages are predictable; the data concerning conservation, inclusion of class, transitivity, and so on, are highly reliable. Nevertheless, problems persist and are situated elsewhere. Thus, the status of base concepts often remains vague; the notion of conservation, for example, became an almost universal instrument of measure, and practically all developmental psychologists considered it to be an instrument enabling the evaluation of the stage of cognitive development reached by a child. The results obtained from the child to prove conservation are supposed to indicate if the child has achieved the structure of the grouping or *groupement* (the *groupement* being itself one of the most important theoretical notions of the Piagetian system). As a matter of fact, in *La Psychologie de l'enfant*, Piaget writes: "Concrete operations therefore make the transition between action and more general logical structures, implying a combinatorial ability and a 'group' structure coordinating the two forms of reversibility . . . The nature of these structures, which we will call '*groupements*,' is constituted by progressive sequences, including constructions of direct operations (for example, a class A combined with its complement A' gives a total class B; then $B + B' = C$, etc.), inverse operations ($B - A' = A$), identical operations ($+A - A = 0$), tautological operations ($A + A = A$), and partially associative operations: $(A + A') + B' = A + (A' + B')$ but $(A + A) - A \neq A + (A - A)$."[9]

However, recently some investigators independently held that the theory of groupings seemed to present contradictions and indeterminacies so that it could no longer serve as a theoretical framework in the study of the development of intelligence. If this framework is abandoned, notions like conservation, permanency, and so on, no longer seem utilizable, at least under the same conditions. Moreover, Osherson showed that the Piagetian idea according to which conservation was the result of three primitive components—*inversion, identity,* and *compensation*—poses a problem, since these three components apply equally well to conditions of conservation and to conditions of nonconservation.[10] It is, for example, impossible to know a priori that a covariance is the consequence of an exact compensation. In Piagetian theory, the status of conservation was never very clear, and in particular the manner in which conservation and the identity of invariance would be acquired is nowhere made explicit. Apart from vague notions of lags *(décalage),* the theory says practically nothing on the subject. Now, I do not see why a child would know a priori that weight in invariant in relation to transformations of shape whereas area is not,[11] or that lateral displacement of mass leaves weight invariant when displacement of the same from the tenth floor to the first floor results in a weight variation. Bryant showed that the empirical basis of constructivism was not as solid as it seemed, and that much of the data on which it was based could be usefully interpreted within a different framework.[12] Similarly, Bever and I have discovered, in a series of experiments, the existence of precocious performances in very young children confronted with tasks similar to those utilized by Piaget for testing conservation.[13] The precocious performances became disorganized during a certain number of months or even years, up to the time when a performance similar to that described by Piaget appears in the ages indicated by him. Since then, Bower has reproduced these experiments and obtained precocious success in proofs bearing on conservation, and has drawn conclusions akin to ours.[14]

Without going into the experimental or theoretical details of positions that have evolved in reaction to the genetic psychology of Piaget, one can argue that the face of developmental psychology is in the process of profound change, as is shown, indeed, by the rise of the study of the psychology of the newborn.

For a large number of developmental psychologists, this domain presented little of interest. Young children were supposed to have only limited dealings with their environment, and their acquisitions were thought to be still very weak. Piaget had been once attracted by the study of very young children, but he then rapidly found older children more instructive. This tendency was reversed in the course of the 1960s, with serious studies performed on newborns around one month old. At present, infants are studied earlier and earlier, and certain experiments could be conducted on infants the very day of their birth. After a few years of these studies, one can already make certain claims.

One can no longer argue that the human infant is a *tabula rasa* without innate dispositions, curiosity, and capabilities. In fact, the very young child seems capable of certain complex and unexpected sensorimotor coordinations.[15] Moreover, the infant seems to possess a certain body schema permitting him to imitate the gestures of the adults with whom he interacts.[16] His capacities for distinguishing colors,[17] certain forms, and distances[18] are very sophisticated. In the domain of hearing, his ability to orient toward a sound source is no longer in doubt,[19] and his capacity to make judgments on the temporal properties of certain acoustic stimuli is beginning to be understood better.[20] It also appears that the linguistic capacity of the newborn human is relatively important; it would seem, in fact, that he is endowed with a device that processes linguistic sounds in a fairly determined manner; however, it remains uncertain, for the moment, whether this device is specific to language or not.

Certain properties of the cognitive apparatus seem rather well developed in the newborn. One could argue on the basis of reasonably convincing data, although they are not totally unassailable, that the notions of causality, object permanency,[21] spatiotemporal continuity, and sensory construction[22] are, among many others, propensities inherent to the cognitive apparatus of the newborn. In fact, the experiments mentioned are controversial and may receive parallel interpretations. But it seems that one can no longer maintain that the individual merely undergoes a structuring of his cognitive apparatus without contributing to the structure in an active way. On the contrary, for the past decade, a number of psychologists have been marvelling at the extraordinary capacities of newborns.

The findings described pose many problems, without bringing a solution to the Piagetian position. The innate can no longer be repudiated or dealt with in a superficial manner without being integrated into the theory that one is elaborating. The indifference that the Piagetians show with regard to the innate makes the theoretical terms they employ appear more and more metaphorical. These terms cannot account for certain observations (although they were themselves conceived from observations). For example, it would seem that conservation, object permanency, inclusion of classes, and so forth, could be better explained in frameworks different from those proposed by Piaget. One can verify that certain observations which contributed most to creating the force of the Piagetian system are precisely those which are currently the most disputed.

Piaget's findings will certainly endure for a long time to come and will have to be taken into account in every developmental theory that strives to consider development and acquisition dynamically. I personally understand the Piagetian theory as a series of static models which are progressively and hierarchically linked to each other as children attain the age of a, b, . . . n, (n + 1) years. But this theory never accounts for what makes a child pass from one stage to the next.

As became evident in this debate, Chomsky and Piaget share certain opinions and positions, even if in a general sense their points of view are fundamentally divergent. Thus, their opposition to the behaviorists would appear to bring together their systems, just as their differences on innatism separate them. But it is doubtless important to consider these aspects in detail.

One of the most important results that emerged from the confrontation between Piaget and Chomsky at Royaumont was their convergent rejection of positivism and empiricism.* Both constantly reiterated that empiricism is a cramped vision, one that is false with regard to learning in that it considers organisms as entirely passive. In this case, the environment could then be described as the independent variable, while the behavior of a subject under study would be the dependent variable. For Piaget, this empirical conception is too limited. The process of immersion in an environment and of interaction with it can be conceived as a process by which the developing organism will assimilate fragments of the environmental structure while accommodating its own schemas in the process of assimilation. Piaget demonstrates forcefully that the pair *assimilation/accommodation* cannot be separated: there can no more be accommodation without assimilation than assimilation without accommodation. It is chiefly because of this point of view that Piaget has always been very critical of the errors of associationists. He was thus able to say: "The fundamental relationship that constitutes all knowledge is not, therefore, a mere 'association' between objects, for this notion neglects the active role of the subject, but rather the 'assimilation' of objects to the schemes of that subject" (see Chapter 1). There can be no doubt, then, that Piaget is an antiempiricist; so much so that

---

* Editor's note: See Piaget's declarations in Chapter 1 and the arguments presented by Chomsky and Fodor in Chapters 1 and 6; see also the editorial comment at the end of Chapter 1.

certain psychologists considered his position to be a sort of neo-Kantism. But, as we shall see later, this judgment is a gross approximation, for Piaget feels that constructivism presents a dialectical solution halfway between empiricism and innatism.

The positions of Chomsky are even more violently anti-empiricist in the sense that he adheres almost unreservedly to innatist views. This stand in favor of the innate permits him to enter into a very polemical argumentation against the behaviorists. In his celebrated review of Skinner's *Verbal Behavior*,[23] he showed down to the smallest detail why positivism and empiricism seemed to him false as philosophical positions, indefensible as psychological positions, and totally unacceptable as theories of natural science. He demonstrated in this regard that the notions embodied in the stimulus-response (S-R) chain were defined circularly and were useless, even from a purely descriptive standpoint. By formal demonstration, he showed that by virtue of their low complexity, the rules of the S-R type could not account for many human capacities such as language, the solution of complex problems, and so on. Chomsky also asserted that our theoretical conceptions could not advance without our taking a position precisely counter to the positions of the empiricists, which is to say that he rejected the idea that a theory must be constituted only of observables and, more specifically, denied that all acquisition must be attributed to the action of the environment on the subject in the process of learning. In fact, Chomsky challenged all models of learning that depend only on induction.

This convergence of Piaget and Chomsky on strongly anti-empiricist positions could be one of the reasons for their great influence on modern cognitive psychology; it would even explain why a certain number of psycholinguists could alternately adopt positions closer to one or the other of the two theories. Many others have tried to borrow a maximum from both theories at once. However, it is in no way evident that any such mixture is possible. The antiempiricism of these two theoreticians takes place within very different theoretical frameworks. Piaget says, for example, that "an epistemology consonant with the data of psychogenesis could neither be empiricist nor preformationist, but could consist only of a constructivism, with a continual elaboration of new operations and structures" (Chapter 1). Chomsky, for his part, feels that "a genetically determined language faculty, one component of the human mind, specifies a certain class of 'humanly accessible grammars.' The child acquires one of the grammars . . . on the basis of the limited evidence available to him" (Chapter 1). As these two quotes show, sharing the same enemy never obliged anyone to share the same crusade. The differences between Piaget and Chomsky concerning empiricism are very profound, and to understand their significance, we must go further in our thematic comparison of their positions.

In regard to innatism, it seems that Piaget's position evolved over the course of the Royaumont confrontation, since he started out in his first presentation with a total rejection of preformationism and ended up with a rather cautious acceptance of the concept of a fixed nucleus. And so, in Chapter 1 of this volume, he says: ". . . nor do any a priori or innate cognitive structures exist in man"; then he specifies in Chapter 2: "I also agree with him [Chomsky] on the fact that this rational origin of language presupposes the existence of a fixed nucleus necessary to the elaboration of all languages . . . why, then, is there a disagreement on the question of the innateness of the fixed nucleus?"; and finally, he says later in the same chapter: "The real question is: what has been their formation process? And, in the case of innateness [of a fixed nucleus], what is the biological mode of formation of that innateness?"

In his introductory paper, Chomsky postulated the existence of a fixed nucleus which he calls universal grammar. The question of knowing to what extent such a universal grammar is grounded upon general innate structures that overdetermine it (let us say, principles of self-regulation, cognitive dispositions, or even principles of action), is, up to a certain point, an empirical question. For Chomsky, the fundamental question lies in evaluating, on the basis of linguistic universals that one could empirically isolate, which universal grammars will eventually be obtained.

The positions of Chomsky and Piaget fall respectively into the camps of the innatists and the contemporary "empiricists." The empiricist philosophies do, after all, accept an innate fixed nucleus, but as Osherson and Wasow have pointed out,[24] the divisions of the two schools bear principally on the question of the specificity of this fixed nucleus for different dispositions, such as language, reasoning, or mathematics, for example. The modern "empiricists" would like to try to derive all of the specific dispositions from very general nonspecific procedures, on the basis of which one could conceive the stepwise descent of language, logic, and learning from general intelligence. In contrast, the innatists try to show that each of these dispositions finds its origin only if specific innate dispositions are provided.

In this sense, the final position of Piaget at Royaumont represents a manifestation of the "empiricist" position. Once the existence of a fixed nucleus is acknowledged, the contrast between the paradigms is even more remarkable. For Piaget, accounting for the stability of the fixed nucleus in terms of self-regulating mechanisms becomes the first goal of epistemology, whereas for Chomsky, the fundamental issue is precisely the specificity of the fixed nucleus and not the manner in which its fixity has been attained. According to Chomsky, unless this specificity is acknowledged, there will be no progress whatsoever in our understanding of human thought. Piaget feels that "a science gives itself, on the contrary, a limited subject and only begins to qualify as a scientific discipline with the success of one such delimitation,"[25] and the goal that he himself has assigned to his inquiry seems to him perfectly legitimate.

This would almost suggest that the disparity between Piaget and Chomsky is to be found at the level of their respective self-assigned goals. Chomsky attempts to characterize a specific nucleus on the basis of a subject's knowledge of natural languages; the results of this exploration should in turn lead to an understanding of what makes this nucleus possible. Whereas, for Piaget, the principles of development always have first priority. And so, even if the existence of a fixed nucleus could be demonstrated to him, nothing would be different because his next question would immediately be: how did it become fixed in the first place? It is necessary to remark that if Piaget's position seems praiseworthy, it is not at all evident that his project can actually be implemented.

APPENDIX A

Guy Cellérier elegantly states (see Chapter 2) that Piaget has been having for a long time a "private gentleman's disagreement" with Darwin. A notion that appears crucial to Piaget's advocacy of constructivism is that of "phenocopy," as discussed in his "Introductory Remarks (see Chapter 2) and in his recent book, Le Comportement moteur de l'évolution,* which appeared after the meeting. In his "Afterthoughts" (see Chapter 13) Piaget gives a clearer picture of the meaning he attaches to the term "phenocopy," a word that during the debate had appeared to the biologists as "metaphorical" (to quote Danchin). The dissatisfaction that the biologists had felt with the Piagetian drift of an otherwise precise genetic concept is in fact brought out, though only briefly, by the debate between Jacob and Piaget and by Changeux's remarks (see Chapter 2). Piaget's subsequent clarification did not settle the question, however, and we felt that the book should leave room for a rejoinder to the argument on phenocopy. Antoine Danchin, a molecular biologist of neo-Darwinist persuasion, has therefore been entrusted with this task, in order to have the problem adequately analyzed from both sides.*

---

* Jean Piaget, Le Comportement moteur de l'évolution (Paris: Gallimard, 1976).

A Critical Note on the Use of the Term "Phenocopy"

Antoine Danchin

Insofar as confusion still seems to persist in the use of some terms, I believe it necessary, in speaking of Piaget's metaphorical treatment of the concept of "phenocopy," to review the definitive and explanatory contribution of molecular biology to this concept in order to avoid any future misunderstandings.

Actually the whole opposition that characterized the biology of the Stalinist period between Lysenko and the proponents of Mendelian neo-Darwinism is involved here. Indeed, in Lysenko's view the phenotype can exercise a considerable influence on the genotype, for "in natural selection . . . heredity, variability, and capacity of survival (autoregulation) of organisms are always included," and this autoregulation ". . . an elective faculty of organisms, organs, and cells, is the result of the historical adaptation of earlier generations to the conditions of their external environment . . . Thus, change in the nature of a living organism is due to change in the type of assimilation, in the type of metabolism. External conditions, once absorbed and assimilated by the living organism, are no longer external but internal conditions; they become, in other words, elements of the living organism, and require for their growth and development both food and the conditions of the external environment such as they were in the past. The living organism is, in a way, composed of elements of the external environment that it has assimilated."[1] One could continue Lysenko's argument against the innate nucleus of the "Morganists"* by calling on the necessity of equilibration in living organisms. Let us mention at this point that Piaget's description of the evolution of a Limnea (see Chapter 2) is strictly parallel to that of Lysenko for wheat.[2] Now, this whole attitude is the result of a profound ignorance of the role of chance and variability at the level of the genome, where it produces families of variations capable of interacting differently with the external environment.

Let us return, for example, to the notion of phenocopy used in a metaphorical fashion by Piaget (see Chapters 1, 2, and 13)

* Editor's note: A derogatory term used by Lysenko to designate geneticists (of whom T. H. Morgan was one of the most famous representatives).

356

and offered as a reference leading to an analogy with the constructivist hypothesis. Although it may have been possible, before the existence of molecular biology, to believe in an "instructive" or "creative" principle that would explain the determination of traits in a living organism, producing an adaptive phenocopy (similar to Lamarck's notion of the inheritability of acquired characters), this point of view is today merely an episode in the history of ideas.

Let us be more precise. Until about 1940, what genetics had mostly accomplished was to enable us to define the existence of a fixed heredity preserved in complex chromosomal matter. Most geneticists had therefore realized that the influence of the environment exerts itself only in the expression of the genome and not in its identity: *mutations occur before the selective event.* A latent controversy persisted, imbued with a certain interpretation—which was inexact, moreover—concerning Lamarck's ideas on this effective and stochastic preexistence of mutations. Following the particularly simple and conclusive experiments of Luria and Delbrück,[3] which proved this absolute influence of chance, observations were eventually substantiated by the discovery of the *material* carrier of heredity.

Around this time, in fact, the relationship between genetics and biological chemistry became more precise: Morgan, Ephrussi, Beadle, and Tatum arrived at the simplified conclusion of the central correspondence "one gene/one protein."[4] The relationship between the individual and its environment became clearer, and the distinction between genotype and phenotype acquired precision; the discovery of the structure of DNA enabled research scientists to provide a material support to the principal characteristic that crystallized around the genotype, namely, the *genetic program.*

This central concept—the abstraction of all observable data linked to the genotype—was to have only a limited usefulness as long as this abstraction did not permit researchers to find a direct relationship with phenotypic expression. It is in fact this lack of relationship that led Lysenko—because he observed an enormous phenotypic variability in plants (sensitivity to cold, practice of vernalization)—to reject completely the concept of genes.

The discovery of the concrete basis for genes, and especially the clarification of mechanisms regulating genetic expressions (in particular those that bear on the stepwise processing of hereditary information from the sequences of DNA nucleotides to the proteins) was to give meaning to the concept of a genetic program, for these regulations introduce *relationships of order* between the various elements of information contained in the genes. These order relations are then revealed during the temporal expression of the genetic program. They can lead therefore, in the case of a given program, to a plethora of particular *outcomes*, because the number of possible combinations rapidly becomes enormous. Since the discoveries of Jacob and Monod,[5] it is clear that the genes corresponding to the regulatory functions will be responsible for phenotypic variability, especially for the apparently ideal adaptation of a living organism to its environment, and more generally for all the genotype-bound manifestations as they unfold in time.

Thus we are led to consider three particular characteristics that allow for the representation of living beings: a *program*, which summarizes the hereditary constraints and is, in fact, the abstract notion underlying the definition of all individuals in a given class (species); an *initial state* of the system,[6] which represents the context in which the program must express itself at the time of the individual's birth; and a *particular outcome or concretization* of each program, which coincides with individual development. The set of all concretizations constitutes the *genetic envelope* and allows the essential characteristics of the program to be obtained by induction. Theoretically, a structured set equivalent to the aforementioned one could be reconstructed by providing the program, the initial state, and the totality of the events of the external environment, producing any interaction whatever with the individual.

The very definition of a species, at that, corresponds to the intersection of a particular family of individual concretizations; it is thus only a global and therefore precarious approximation, insofar as the program may not have been grasped to the full extent of its implications (if the individuals in question, say, were part of an environment having exceptional characteristics). Thus some species have been confused with others because, in a given environment, individuals looked remarkably similar, and it is only after observing a particular variability of one class of individuals in relation to another that one can draw the line between such classes. Let us note, moreover, that this consideration easily supplies an explicative model of some aspects of the evolution of species: a family of regulator genes, for example, in an unusual and highly specialized environment for that species, allows for the production of a "phenocopy" that is rather distinct from the usual parental phenotype (an anaerobic environment, for example, for individuals generally accustomed to an aerobic life, but who have the option of becoming anaerobic). In such cases, after many generations, one often finds: (1) *an invariant type whose phenotype always mirrors the stable phenocopy,* as well as (2) the original type whose descendants revert to their standard expression as soon as they return to the usual environment. This fact often led to the belief that one had demonstrated an instructive effect of the environment which led in some way to making acquired traits hereditary, *whereas in fact one was witnessing a simple degeneration of the initial type which had lost the regulatory aptitudes that allowed it to change its phenotype according to the environment and had only retained one aspect.* This aspect is that which is adapted to the specialized environment in which a collection of individuals happened to be located as they moved about randomly. This loss could take place without damage only because the environment in question remained constant long enough; there was no selection of the fittest in any general sense, but only a preservation of all those individuals who could manage to carry on in such a peculiar external environment, including those who, through the randomness of mutations, had lost one of the adaptive properties of the original species.

The general regulatory patterns affecting the expression of one's genetic endowment, such as they have been known for a few years, are probably sufficient to describe a very large number—if not all—of the properties of individual phenotypes *without allowing the intervention of even the least instructive notion on the part of the environment.* The adaptive properties seem to arise simply from the fact that at every moment the program supplies a possible choice among various interactions (due to various molecular movements and fluctuations of form and position) and also from the fact that the laws of thermodynamics lead to the selection of the most stable, hence of the most durable, options which, through appropriate amplifying mechanisms, yield suitable counterparts in the overall structure and functioning of the individual. Thus the environment makes a systematic selection of individual characteristics which are precisely those that best suit the environment itself, taking into account, of course, the heavy constraints of the program— a fish can live in a rather large number of aqueous environments but usually not in the air!

This brief review has, of course, considered only a very simple phenotype, determined by a single regulator gene, but the coordinated expression of the sum of the components in the individual phenotype is the result of a trade-off between one (or several) regulator genes and one (or several) environmental characteristics ("sum" refers here to general behavior, morphology, or metabolism). Thus, a phenocopy is in no way a construction but simply a particular realization of a given program according to a strict determinism: there is neither preformation nor acquisition, but only diachronic expression. The realization will take place at a different level depending on whether one considers individual phylogenesis, ontogenesis, or epigenesis. Since mental representation is the ultimate stage, it already represents the result of the evolution of species, the diachrony of cellular differentiation and individual development, and finally the diachrony of the epigenesis of the central nervous system.

The Genesis of Representational Space according to Piaget

René Thom

Among the theories directly inspired by mathematics, those of Piaget on the origin of representational space in the child appear particularly unconfirmed. The first thing that must be pointed out is that the problem of the psychogenesis of the concept of space cannot be dissociated from an implicit ontology. For is it possible to consider the elucidation of the origin of the concept of space without raising the fundamental question of the ontological status of space itself? One of two things: either exterior space exists as such, as the universal framework in which all reality is localized (and, in particular, man himself); or, on the contrary, space is not exterior to man. In other words, either it is, from the Kantian viewpoint, a projection of an internal structure in man, an a priori condition of all experience; or it is constructed from nonspatial elements, from elementary psychological experiences; this latter point of view has been endorsed by the philosophical school named phenomenology and also by logicians, such as Carnap and Russell, who have endeavored to reconstruct space logically by means of rules of combinations ranging over elementary events. Henri Poincaré has also presented a similar theory. It is obvious that these last theories of a subjectivist nature can formulate only with difficulty the *genetic* problem of the formation of the concept of space in the child, for it is difficult to see an a priori category being progressively constituted in the mind: either it is, or it is not. And if a synthetic mechanism—like Carnap's *Aufbau* —exists in the adult, it is not clear how one could describe the precursor mechanisms that could precede its formation in the animal, the newborn, or the young child. Therefore, it would seem at first sight that the genetic problem requires a realist theory of space. But then, the solution of the genetic problem becomes simple, almost tautological: the idea of space draws its origin from the surrounding space itself which, in a way, creates inside the space of mental activity a replica or model-system of itself. All that remains is to define the stages, the possible distortions, and, if possible, the physiological mechanisms underlying this construction of mental space from physical space.

Insofar as it can be clearly understood, Piaget seems indeed to adopt the realist thesis of an external existence of space. But like most professional psychologists who carefully preserve the autonomy of their own scientific domain, he seems to shrink from the apparent tautology that finds in physical space the origin of mental space, and he prefers to "construct" the child's space from "sensorimotor schemes" and the "activity of the subject." What are these famous "sensorimotor schemes"? Often invoked, they are nowhere described; one does not know, therefore, whether they possess a spatial structure, a geometry, a topology, and so forth, and if, for example, they possess nonspatial elements, say of an affective nature. In fact, the psychogenesis of space, according to Piaget, is conceived on the model of a logic-like construction similar to Carnap's, with the time of development playing the role of the time intervening in a logical deduction, which leads one from premises to conclusion. The hope is thus to be able to be delivered from the apparent tautology that consists of making mental space come out of physical space. It is worth a reminder, in passing, that all logicist constructions are hopelessly enmeshed in difficulties linked to the following problem: how can geometrical continuity arise from a discrete "dust" of psychological states or processes? The necessity of defining "proximal" events forces a structure on the data (companionship, memory resemblances, tolerance relationship for Poincaré) which is the pure and simple substitute for the locally Euclidian topology of space-time, which means that these constructions are in reality only disguised tautologies. Piaget admits, I suppose, that these sensorimotor schemes, as primitive as they may be, include metric elements. This is all the more difficult to deny because a 6-month-old infant is capable of grasping and putting in his mouth an exterior object placed within his reach; this is, of course, a typical metric problem which the infant resolves with great precision and efficiency. Let us recall that Piaget's main thesis is that representational space begins with the integration of the most general structure of space, that is, topological structures, and then structures associated with the projective group and ending with the Euclidian group. Psychogenesis is thus assimilated to the Erlangen program by Félix Klein. The existence of metric elements in the 6-month-old infant could not be retained against the theory since, says Piaget, one has to distinguish carefully between "representational space," which is space as it is conceived mentally, and sensorimotor space, which regulates sensory and motor activities. Strictly speaking, sensorimotor space is never defined; is it the usual Euclidian space, or if it differs from it, how does it differ? (However, one could not blame Piaget for his silence on the question, since this silence is shared by all his psychologist and physiologist colleagues.) Having said this, I feel that the very concept of representational space seems tainted with a serious ambiguity. For, ultimately, what is consciousness? What distinguishes someone who is awake from someone who sleeps? The conscious person is someone with an (internal) representation of the space that surrounds him and of the position of his body within that space. I do not understand how one could see in this local map that contains the organism anything other than "representational" space. For even if representational space is something other than this local map, at least the map is contained in it as an essential and original part associated with the body and its activities. In other words, at least in the immediate vicinity of the organism, representational space is directly and necessarily geared to the space of sensorimotor activities; there cannot be a serious discrepancy between local representational space and physical space without creating equally serious behavior disorders: mishandling, vertigo, hallucinations, delirium, and so on. In fact, the pathology of the states of consciousness, to a large degree, coalesces with the pathology of spatial representation. Of course, on the contrary, the mental representation of distant objects can suffer considerable distortion without any serious functional inconvenience. How many adults, even well-educated ones, have an accurate spatial representation of the diameter of the earth, the solar system, the galaxy? How many are able to take their bearings in poorly known surroundings? It is obvious that the precision of our spatial representation decreases very quickly with increasing distance from our organism, but that in our vicinity, representation, constantly controlled by our actions and our changes in position, can only be extremely reliable.

It is within this concept of an abstract "representational"

space, completely and artificially separated from sensorimotor and postural activities, that lies the main weakness of the Piagetian theory. The following question could also be asked: do animals, especially the higher animals, have a "representational space"? It seems very difficult to deny them an internal representation of surrounding space; and the example of migratory birds raises the question of whether this representation is not infinitely more reliable and accurate than that which is found in man.

Piaget offers two types of arguments to justify his thesis: on the one hand, experiments of blind manipulation of hidden objects show that the connectivity of objects is perceived before their metric properties; on the other hand, the drawing of children reveals, until a rather late age, a major difficulty in representing the projective, then the metric properties of objects. Experiments of the first sort are based on sensory function (or, in any case, on perception); since they have recourse to a conflict situation, one can wonder to what extent this relative priority of these rather coarse topological properties is not an artifact based on the weakening of the tactile sense in the sighted person yielding to visual activities which are infinitely more rapid and efficient. The argument that invokes the drawing of children requires a more detailed discussion.

The succession of stages in children's drawing defined by Luquet is well established (ideographic stage,[1] intellectual realism, visual realism). At the stage of intellectual realism (around the ages of 5 to 7), one often observes metric distortion in the figures, and in particular, according to Luquet, the "lean-over" *(rabattement)* phenomenon. Horizontal and vertical lines are frequently transformed into oblique ones. Can it reasonably be concluded from this, as Piaget does, that at this age children do not have a correct conception of the size of objects and of their position in space? Liliane Lurçat's experiments seem to demonstrate, in any case, that an important percentage of younger children are capable of respecting vertical and horizontal directions; the design of the experiment itself is very important here in regard to the results obtained. Without further discussion of this rather technical question, one can only agree with Lurçat when she invokes the specificity of graphic representations. Graphic space is a true space, distinct from representational space and subject to specific constraints; furthermore, let us not forget that it corresponds to a ludic function. The child knows that he represents the object with his drawing; he takes pleasure in it. The sheet of drawing paper is no longer the "representational" space, but a fragment of representational space to the second degree entirely subordinate to the object (to the subject) of the drawing. Would we dare to maintain that our caricaturists, our cartoonists have not reached the stage of visual realism under the pretext that their work very often shows a total misreading of the metric properties of the reference objects?

Rather than invoking a very hypothetical parallelism between psychogenesis and mathematical inclusion of groups, in order to explain the evolution of children's drawings, one should reconsider a basic human fact, namely, the existence of language and of the "symbolic function." Let me make myself clear: at a preverbal stage, as in animals for instance, the sequence *sensation → reflex action* requires a form of judgment: it involves, in the perceived sensation, the recognition of a biologically meaningful form (such as the image of a prey or of a predator); once the form is recognized, a reflex of capture (or escape) will be triggered. The symbolic function may be defined in man by the extension of this property of signifying to a very large number of objects (biologically neutral, in principle), thereby evoking a response which is initially motor, then only verbal. When a child is asked to draw an object A, the sequence *sight of A → graphic representation of A* requires a judgment as an intermediary, that is, the recognition of the object A as belonging to a well-defined class of objects, corresponding to a concept C(A). In other words, the child answers the command to draw A as if he were asked, what is A? He makes his drawing the graphic equivalent of the word. In the same way as the word, in the mind of the listener, provokes the unfolding of the meaning of the concept, the drawing actualizes a graphic unfolding of the concept. Now, a concept is analyzed into subconcepts; this analysis is accomplished linguistically by the process of the genitive. Thus, "the dog's tail" defines a subobject of the object dog, topologically expressed by the belonging of the domain of space occupied by the tail to that occupied by the dog. The correct handling of grammar, therefore, presupposes the perfect mastery of an implicit topology that bears on the connections, the proximities, the relationships between objects. All that which Piaget defines as topological relationships between objects is in fact only semantic relationships between concepts. And this implicit topology necessarily exists in the mind as soon as the child knows how to speak. In this respect, however, I would prefer to follow Luquet rather than Henri Wallon, who denies the existence of an "internal model" of the concept: how can we explain the repetitive, stereotyped character of children's drawings if they do not correspond to a quasi-universal mode of analyzing a concept?

The ideographic stage is preceded by an enumerative, very fleeting stage in which the child symbolizes a subconcept by a line, with all these elements being joined together in a connected figure by a horizontal bar. But very soon, using "bars" and "circles," the child is capable of representing graphically a very large number of elementary objects. If he is asked to draw a complex object, he will decompose it into "coded" elements that he can assimilate graphically and then will reconstitute the global figure by spatial aggregation of the corresponding elements, each one drawn in its local map. This aggregation is ordered more by the meaningful function of the elements in the concept than by visual perspective, which will appear much later. In other words, the visual image is only progressively abstracted from the concept, for the concept is one, whereas images and appearances are multiple. Moreover, very often an object —taken as a concept—has epigenetic gradients (such as the cephalocaudal gradient of an animal), according to which the "bodily schema" of the subject is going to be projected; the vision of the object has a tendency to prefer these major coordinates. For example, if the object possesses a symmetry plane, the object preferably will be seen according to the normal direction to this plane (which, in addition, allows a better manual grasp of the object); the passage from the stage of intellectual realism to the stage of visual realism expresses the progressive weakening of these semantic constraints on visual representation. Thus, it would be wrong to assert that children, at the stage of intellectual realism, fail to recognize the metric properties of objects. The simple necessity of expressing themselves graphically forces them to have recourse to the concept, which is their only way to dominate the object, and this semantic intermediary can disturb graphic representation. Let us take another example: if a child who is making a picture of his family draws a very small father next to an enormous mother, this does not mean that the child is incapable of comparing metrically the sizes of his parents, but rather that he feels the need to express in terms of physical predominance the relationships of psychological predominance that obtain in his family.

Most probably, the semantic space peels off by exfoliation from the sensorimotor map at the time of verbal learning. When a 3- to 4-year-old child is asked to draw an object, the first thing is for him to recognize the object, then to "propagate" this object on the blank receptor constituted by the sheet of paper. It is natural, then, for this propagation to borrow the verbal communication channel, which is, at this age, the only existing means for a concept to implant on an outside substratum. The concept is going to unfold itself on the sheet of paper just as the audible form unfolds itself in the mind of the listener when he listens to the word.

In conclusion, it is difficult not to see in the Piagetian theories a fundamental misappreciation of the conditions according to which mathematics interlocks with reality. Although Piaget has constantly claimed in his epistemology that he is not a Platonist, the identification that he suggests between the psychogenesis of space and the Erlangen program seems, in my opinion, to belong to this generalized hypostasis of mathematical idealized entities which nineteenth-century scientism had justified through the discovery of the great physical laws (Newton, Maxwell). Piaget does attribute, of course, the genesis of major mathematical structures (namely, the concept of group) to the "activity of the subject." But it is difficult to see how these structures could be constituted in a repetitive and stable fashion if they did not correspond to some innate schema or if they did not possess their own capacity for "embodiment" in the real world. Now, it must be understood that to form the mathematical structure in its entirety, the mind must deliberately disregard the real world. No one has ever counted all natural numbers. When a topological group acts in a real system, this group never acts in its entirety. In embryology or in organic physiology, for instance, groups are present, but only in outline or germlike form. In a joint like that of the elbow, for example, which connects the radius to the humerus, the totality of possible positions of one bone in relation to the other defines a relatively narrow area of the group of rotations; bony spurs (epiphyses) prohibit the continuation of movement beyond a certain limit. This is a very general situation: in every organic system, the mathematical structure is outlined, but spatial constraints prohibit its full realization. (Thus, man has realized the wheel, that is, the simulatory integral system of the group $S^1 = SO^{(2)}$, a group of rotations nowhere materialized by living beings.) There is in mathematical activity a deliberate desire to ignore reality, and even sometimes to ignore the constraints imposed by the activity's own rules. Almost all the progress made in algebra has come out of this desire to accomplish forbidden operations (negative, rational, or imaginary numbers, for example). Now, one must understand that this imaginative audacity has, as a counterpart, the ineffectiveness of the actions that realize these structures. To illustrate this by a (fictitious) example: let us suppose that an animal has at its disposal two motor reflexes designated by the letters a, b. If this animal is mathematically gifted, it will be able to symbolize the whole of its motor strategies by the words of the free monoid M(a, b) generated out of the alphabet (a, b). If these reflexes lead to actual movements of the animal, there will exist words of rather large size which, realized in terms of displacement, will make the animal leave its natural habitat and lead it to its death. It is only if the reflexes are totally inefficient that the entire algebraic structure can materialize. The demand of the indefinite formal repetition of operations is extremely unnatural; only the isolated miracle of the laws of physics has been able to convince us that this construction had a counterpart in reality. By confounding axiomatic demands, on the one hand, and basic structures of the psyche, on the other, the Piagetian theory in a sense "put up bail" for the modernist undertaking in the teaching of mathematics, with its resulting unfortunate consequences. There is no doubt, I am deeply convinced, that mathematics "informs" the world as well as our own structure, but this mathematics is not the one that we know, the one that the algebraists manufacture for us in the stubborn élan of infinite reiteration of formal operations. It is, on the contrary, in the study of the natural limitations of formalism that tomorrow's mathematics lies.

Reply to Thom

Jean Piaget

Since I have already replied to Lurçat in regard to her critique of my theories and demonstrated in detail how poorly she understood them,[1] and since I hold the same impression from my reading of Thom's comments, I can therefore be brief. I can understand that such an original worker does not have time to read the entire output of other researchers, but before criticizing them, a certain prudence is necessary. It is therefore somewhat surprising that he is able to say about my sensorimotor schemes that "if often invoked, they are nowhere described," when I have published an entire book entitled *Origins of Intelligence in Children*, which analyzes those schemes in their various aspects.[2]

In regard to the concept of space, Thom starts by offering an alternative which is precisely one I claim to have made obsolete: either a physical space outside or a construction of the subject. My answer is, on the contrary, that if mathematics is adapted to reality, it is because the subject, in his organic sources, is a physicochemical and spatial object, among others, and because, in the construction of his own cognitive structures, he starts from neurological and biological sources whose laws are those of reality. It is thus through primarily endogenous and not uniquely exogenous pathways that the space constructed by the subject fits in with the outside space; therefore, both exist without conflict and converge without merging.

As for the *a priori,* Thom has not seen that my "constructivism" detaches from it the two characteristics that Kant mistakenly thought to be joined: I retain the *necessary,* but place it at the end of the constructions; I dispute the *prerequisite,* for the organic sources constitute only the starting point of these constructions and do not contain them all in advance, by innateness. I have discussed sufficiently the problems of innateness elsewhere in this book, and repetition is unnecessary.

Another criticism which, for my part, I find rather amazing is to be reproached for the "great weakness" of having "artifically separated" representational space from sensorimotor activities; and yet my two recent works, *The Grasp of Consciousness*[3] and *Success and Understanding,*[4] take precisely the opposite position, as do, moreover, many of my preceding publications since *Play, Dreams and Imitation in Childhood.*[5]

As for the Euclidian or non-Euclidian character of sensorimotor space, Thom seems to be unaware of the work of Luneburg—which Jonckheere, at our Centre d'épistémologie, has followed up—dealing with the apparently non-Euclidian character of perceptual parallels, which I cautiously ascribe to a state of insufficient structuralization by the subject. On the contrary, it is clear that already at the sensorimotor level, positive and negative quantifications exist.

In regard to the pedagogical applications of my ideas (for which I am by no means responsible), a recent interview should reassure Thom as to my reservations and my lack of support for the axiomatic system.[6] On this last point, I think, as he does (thus there are points of agreement!) that there is still much to expect from the study of the limitations of formalism; and this is even a main argument of my constructivist epistemology.[7]

Thom's paper also includes a certain number of psychological interpretations which, at first sight, could leave the experimenter somewhat bewildered, but I will abstain from judging them since I have not read all of Thom's works. On the contrary, I want to end this rebuttal by pointing out the fact that, although it may not be apparent to Thom, I am trying to apply his theory of catastrophes in certain areas. The physicist Ascher, who is more competent than any of us in this respect, recently wrote: "In searching for what there could be in common between the works of Piaget and those of Thom, one finds at least the name of Waddington, along with the notions of epigenetic landscape, chreode, and homeorhesis." And he continues by comparing "attractors" to schemes and their "basins" to the extensions of these. But the difficulty is that an "epistemic landscape . . . is not rigid like the epigenetic landscape, but flexible according to the state of the system." The attractors are therefore modified, and "the basins can change in an even more complex manner."[8] Nonetheless, Ascher believes in possible mathematical solutions.

It is on this optimistic note that I wish to conclude my reply, for the numerous misunderstandings of which I have been the object, instead of affecting me, have rather led me to think, at the risk of being immodest, that my theses were perhaps not so common. It has even happened that some passionate contradictors have modified their opinions quite abruptly. For my part, I consider myself much closer to the constructive parts of Thom's works than Thom does to mine, and if he will stop attributing to me theses that are both trivial and contrary to my own, perhaps we can come to a point of mutual understanding.

APPENDIX C

This book would not have been complete without the inclusion of a "third" point of view, today in full emergence, that of linguistics based on the theory of catastrophes. René Thom, the author of this theory, has opened a dialogue with Piaget concerning not linguistics but rather the genesis of space in the child. We have read this very stimulating exchange between Thom and Piaget in Appendix B.

Jean Petitot is a mathematician and is interested precisely in the epistemological problem of the compatibility/incompatibility between the Chomskian innatist hypotheses, the Piagetian constructivist hypotheses, and the theory of catastrophes. Petitot, who participated in the Royaumont debate, presented there a rather technical paper dealing with Fodor's innatist theses analyzed from the viewpoint of formal logic. This part of the discussion is not included here. However, I have asked Petitot to rework and simplify his critiques of the innatist theses and his suggested alternative solutions based on René Thom's theory of catastrophes and on some aspects of case grammar. Although they are given in an appendix for the sake of space and readability, Petitot's epistemological reflections are important because they offer a true alternative, at least at the stage of a future research program, to the two prevailing positions of the debate. In a way, Petitot offers us the outline for a research program in a new type of linguistics.

371

Localist Hypothesis and Theory of Catastrophes: Note on the Debate

Jean Petitot

This paper intends to suggest how the Chomskian (neo-Kantian) hypothesis of a genetic constraint specifying within the class of formal grammars the subclass of "humanly accessible ones" depends on the methodological presuppositions of Chomskian linguistics, that is, on the *decision* whereby its proper linguistic object is determined. We know that this decision has, to a certain extent, acquired the force of evidence. However, I would like to maintain the (apparently paradoxical) hypothesis that the very force of this evidence hides *a priori* the real sense of the question of innatism, and that if the innatist hypothesis is indeed the only plausible hypothesis at the present time, we must add that it is the only plausible hypothesis compatible with the Chomskian decision. The innatist hypothesis is probably the only *intraregional* answer to the question of linguistic acquisition, but the problem is precisely that this question is not an intraregional one for linguistics but rather the demarcation of an epistemological threshold.

The Chomskian decision consists of identifying syntax as a phenomenon connected to the *automatisms* of *expressed* language. One can clearly see to what extent it determines the limits of a methodological area. Let us notice, however, that it implies a fundamental formal constraint. As Chomsky himself remarks: "The transformations *must* be applied in sequence and thus must be applied to objects *of the same type* as those they produce." This constraint is part of the Chomskian "evidence." It is *only* methodological;[1] yet it is far from being without consequences. For when one approaches the problem of acquisition, one is *naturally* led to describe this acquisition as a succession of stages leading from an initial state S_0 to a steady state S_s. Each one of these stages is a grammatical "state," and it is therefore "evident" that it is characterized by a specific set of automatisms. By regressing to the initial state S_0, one is therefore confronted with a nucleus of automatisms which are by definition *nondeducible.* If one adds that at each stage (and particularly for the steady state S_s) there exist nondeducible automatisms, one is *naturally* led to the conclusion that the original state S_0 is a genetically constrained state specifying LT(H,L), that is, "learning theory for humans in the domain language."[2] But one can see that this innatist hypothesis is nothing more than the *effect* of this "evidence" that the state S_0 is grammatical in the sense of a system of prescriptions (rules). All the examples presented by Chomsky (structure-dependent rules, bound anaphora, specified subject condition) depend on the following argument. There exist automatisms (formal universals) such that:

(1) the speaker (the child) does not make any mistake in using them;

(2) the speaker has not learned them for all that;

(3) there exists no functional privilege that allows for selecting them;

(4) they are therefore genetically constrained.

Now, if this syllogism is valid with respect to points (1) and (2), it is questionable with respect to point (3). For the established fact that there exists no *formal* criterion allowing for the *deduction* of formal universals[3] implies conclusion (4) only if one hypostatizes the real nature (unknown) of the syntactic phenomenon in the programmatic artifact of its algebraic-combinatorial description—that is, only if one admits the Chomskian "evidence." But this comes down to taking for a solicitation of truth what is in fact an option on the method.[4] Now, this method, I repeat, rests on a structural postulate of closure which, precisely because it renders the syntactic region autonomous, thereby also renders it disjoint from its own genesis.[5] Thus everything takes place as if the innatist hypothesis had as its function to implant a *radical externalization* (neurobiological and genetic) which—precisely because it is radical—allows the linguistic area to become "rooted" without mediation, without delimitation, without the effects of edges or boundaries with the areas that are "related" to it.[6]

Now, every genesis is a global phenomenon of "disentanglement" *(disintrication)* between domains (levels); there exists no intraregional description of it. One can simply say that the model-building methodologies inherent in these levels *cannot themselves be entangled,* that there exists therefore a *formal* obstruction to modellizing the genesis and it is therefore more efficient to introduce a radical externalization. The question is that of models, and from their intrinsic limitation, one cannot conclude in favor of innatism except to consider that these models are presently the only available ones (pragmatic position) or to hypostatize them (ideological position).

In short, in the final analysis the Chomskian argumentation would not have a scientific but rather a *strategic* significance. It would allow us to resolve *a priori* the aporia of language acquisition while maintaining the neo-mechanistic "myth" of language as an "organ program," to borrow one of Thom's expressions.

It remains to be seen whether there exists a method that would allow us to surmount (and therefore de-construct) the Chomskian "evidence." The question is obviously not a trivial one. Let us go back to Chomsky's conclusion (see Chapter 1): "*Our ignorance*—temporary, let us hope—*of the physical basis for mental structures compels us to keep to abstract characterization*, in this case, but there is no reason to suppose that the physical structures involved are fundamentally different in character and development from other physical organs that are better understood, though a long tradition has tacitly assumed otherwise."[7] This syllogism again mimics the previous one:

(1) one does not know (not yet) the physical bases of language;

(2) one is for this very reason constrained to formalize only the abstract structures of language on its plane of expression (externalization);

(3) formal universals are not deducible from this formal specification;

(4) therefore there exist genetic constraints.

I shall oppose to this deduction the following formulation which, although not conclusive, appears to me more rigorous:

(1) one does not know (not yet) the physical bases of language;

(2) one must nonetheless presuppose them and therefore presuppose the existence of a dynamic process underlying linguistic expression;

(3) if, in its concreteness, this process describes performance, in its abstract internal structure, it nonetheless describes competence;

(4) this process is not only unobservable, but it destroys itself while serving as the basis for linguistic expression;

(5) at variance with all procedures formalized in generative-transformational grammars, this process leaves a heterogeneous residual nucleus;

(6) it is from the structure of this heterogeneous residual nucleus that the constraints selecting the "humanly accessible" grammars must be deduced;

(7) before postulating that this nucleus is innate, one must know on what specific type of formal being it depends;

(8) what is innate is that which remains contingent in relation to the constraints that this formal being imposes.

One can see, therefore, that the question of innatism leads to a relay, to a natural mediation, namely *to the possibility of deducing from the hypothesis of the brain as a "black box" (extraregional hypothesis for linguistics) a primary nucleus of morphological constraints that are impossible to deduce directly from the (algebraic-combinatorial) formalization of the expressed automatisms.*

What prevents such a mediation from being taken into account is obviously its apparent inconsistency. There seems to exist a contradiction between the hypothesis of the "black box" itself and the possibility of deducing anything whatever of a constraining nature, all the more because this deduction can only be made *a priori* (that is, in the form of a theorem). But in fact, the "black box" does not imply that there are no processes in action, but simply that they are unobservable. Thus the definitive question is how to deduce *a priori* the nucleus S_0 from general principles that are apodictically valid for the underlying processes and from phenomenological manifestations taken as axioms.[8]

An answer (although still a very partial one) can be given, not so much with respect to formal as to *substantive* universals. For example:

(1) there exists an absolute limit to the number of actants bound together by a verb;

(2) the genitive seems to be a structurally heterogeneous case;

(3) certain ambiguities (between the prepositions "by" and "with," for example) seem to be universal.[9]

This answer rests on the catastrophic syntactic models introduced by René Thom, models which have not yet reached the linguistic audience to which they can potentially appeal. These models are deduced *a priori* (in the manner of a theorem) from apodictic principles which are linguistically acceptable only if one de-constructs the Chomskian hypothesis by taking as an axiom some phenomenological evidence that is *more primitive* than that of expressed automatisms. Therefore, these models involve, once more, a (different) hypothesis that acts as a decision on the syntactic nature of their object.

The most pertinent hypothesis seems to be the case hypothesis, and more precisely the *localist* one. In order to account for the apparent rigidity and fixity of grammatical morphologies, one must in effect introduce the hypothesis of an underlying dynamic which engenders such morphologies and regulates their stability. The problem is that case grammars

(1) have never succeeded in going beyond the triviality of their own hypothesis and have run up against the impossibility of deducing from manifest occurrences a systematic taxonomy of deep cases that were supposed to be universal;[10]

(2) have never been able to "spatialize" the deep cases (localist hypothesis) other than by utilizing a *semiotization* of space. They remain, therefore, analogical;

(3) introduce a primary heterogeneity in the syntax, since there exists an ineducible gap between case spatialization and generative resources;

(4) cannot account for predication and, in particular, for "equative" sentences.

As for "limitation" (3), it is not a limitation as such, quite the contrary. A real comprehension of the underivable nuclear constraints of the manifestation requires the establishment of a *principle of complementarity* between the formal being of primary nuclear morphologies and that of secondary morphologies described by the syntagmatic trees. The introduction of such heterogeneity allows for splitting the question of innatism into that of complementarity, on the one hand, and that of the constitution of the primary nucleus, on the other. The decisive question therefore becomes one of determining what is the *real formal being* of the deep case structures. In the framework of a description (which is true of the known case grammars), this question is replaced by that of abstract notation. It is known that Fillmore attached a great deal of importance to this and understood very well that the choice of the notation had, as a rule, decisive consequences for the functioning of the grammar. Since cases are not categories, they cannot be symbolized by labeled nodes above the noun phrase. Fillmore has moved toward a notation based on "stemmas" which is *sufficient* to block the Chomskian argument. For once a "composition plane" is introduced in place of the deep structure as an entry to the transformational cycle, indicating how the different stemmata must be embedded into each other to create the surface structure, the "automation-input-output" paradigm becomes impossible.

The solution to this difficulty involves first making a low-level attempt at transforming (in the sense of altering the formal type of the entities) the stemmata into syntagmatic trees which can be used as an entry. But this is possible only if *one has at one's disposal more than just abstract notations; one has to determine the effective formal being of the stemmata.*

As for limitation (4), it simply shows that for case grammars, "to be" is not a verb (in the sense of a singularity-bearing entity, a slot-organizing element, an element organizing case relationships). Moreover, it is the original equivocation of the verb-copula "to be" that imposes a principle of complementarity. Since the time of the Greeks (that is, the Stoics), there exists an ineducible ambiguity between the predicative approach (logical) and the case approach (scenic). One has always wanted to reduce this ambiguity whereas, on the contrary, it must be maintained *as such*.

As for limitations (1) and (2), they obviously constitute a stumbling block. *But catastrophic models precisely allow us to bypass such stumbling blocks.*

In its radicality, the localist hypothesis means essentially two things:

(1) the elementary syntactic morphologies are formally reducible *to systems of colocalized slots*. This stemmatic colocalization (reciprocal presupposition) is organized by the verb, which distributes the slots under the form of case relationships;

(2) these colocalizations (in which slots have no intrinsic identity but only an identity of locus defined by a system of thresholds) are deducible from the elementary spatiotemporal interactions existing between spatial actants: the cases are derived from original spatiotemporal situations now routinely fixed in syntactic schemes.[11]

The insuperable difficulty which the localist hypothesis has encountered until now has been the impossibility of conceiving and formulating on a *purely ideal-formal* mode the primitive concept of colocalization. This hypothesis has therefore been reduced to a semiotic spatial analogy. Now, Thom's basic result is the following: If one *defines* a system of colocalized slots separated by thresholds as a structure that is created, maintained, and regulated by the *conflict* of these slots themselves (by their reciprocal presupposition), and if one notices that this structure is necessarily a solution to the principle of existence represented by *structural stability* (apodictic evidence), one can, on this sole basis, *classify* structures. René Thom was able to demonstrate that these morphologies unfold into ideal "spaces" (called external spaces) whose dimension imposes a drastic *constraint* on their complexity. In particular, if one predicates *a priori* that this dimension is smaller than or equal to four (spatiotemporal dimension), one gets a list of archetypal "syntactic" morphologies.[12] Since in this case one is dealing with a theorem deduced on the basis of the apodictic principle of structural sta-

bility (principle of structural reason) and adjusted to the phenomenological evidence (taken as an axiom) of the syntactic
structure as a system of case relationships, one can *a priori*
identify this list of archetypes as the morphological nucleus
characteristic of the initial state S_0 as far as case universals are
concerned.

The catastrophic "modelization" allows for the reinterpreta-
tion of the localist hypothesis as a hypothesis *on the limitation
of the dimension of external spaces*. For if one plunges the
external spaces into a local spatiotemporal map, the syntactic
archetypes become identified as the elementary spatiotemporal interactions between spatial actants.[13] Thus reinterpreted,
the localist hypothesis becomes a strong and consistent hypothesis (free from any vague analogy) · which relates to
phylogenesis. During the process of hominization, the field
of perception simulating elementary spatiotemporal interactions between spatial actants would have peeled off or become "exfoliated" into a syntactic field. The archetypal morphologies would have become ritualized and, having become
rigid matrices, would have served as *schemes* for the abstract
elementary syntactic structures taken as a whole. As speculative
as it may be, this hypothesis has the advantage of being both
consistent and nontrivial, and of serving as a relay for the question of innatism. For one sees that the question does not consist
of postulating a genetic constraint for the universals that case
relationships are. These relationships are, in this instance, *deduced*. The part of innatism that it contains bears, on the one
hand, on perception (and not on language) and, on the other
hand, on exfoliation and ritualization.

The catastrophic "modelization" of the localist hypothesis
shows, therefore, that the debate between a neo-Kantism à la
Chomsky[14] and a constructivism à la Piaget remains premature
as long as no model has been constructed (however elementary
and speculative it may be) to control the dynamic process underlying the production of a sentence. Such a model has been
proposed by Thom.[15] In order to account dynamically for the
"intimate nature of the verb" (which is destroyed in the manifestation) and for the catastrophic description by archetypes
(which is still solely taxonomic), one can imagine the verb as
an oscillator retaining the undiscernible "dummy actants" represented by the case slots. When a sentence is uttered, this oscillator is "blocked" and "liberates" the dummy actants, each

one of which will select an actant (concept, substantive from the lexicon) by a catastrophe of excision.[16] More precisely: "The concept in its semantic space is joined to a region of the spatial (sensorimotor) map by a localizer-connector. This localizer is destroyed when it collides with the dummy actant, which splits itself in two: one of these partial actants issued from this catastrophe will arouse the concept and elicit the emission of the corresponding substantive; the other partial actant will excite the mental image of the spatial field, which thus becomes an attractor and elicits the apparition of a *deictic* motor field, which in turn attracts a part of the body toward this spatial region (as for example, the extremity of the forefinger), whereas the transfer from mental space to physical space simultaneously requires the emission of a demonstrative, or if the deictic gesture is repressed, of an article."

This dynamic description of the phrastic emission appeals to a connection between semantic spaces and sensorimotor maps, between representational space and motor space; thus it does not satisfy the principle of closure that animates the Chomskian decision. Still, it does not confuse itself with a Piagetian approach, since it rests on the theorem of classification of archetypal interactions. Its methodological and epistemological function is to allow us *in a natural way:*

(1) to delimit linguistics and theoretically (not only experimentally) articulate it with neighboring regions;

(2) to understand why a certain nucleus of morphological constraints is underivable from the categorical formalization of language on the plane of externalization: if the organizing center destroys itself at the time of the emission, this "external" formalization is without memory;

(3) to localize more precisely the point of impact of the innatist hypothesis: that is, the fact that the drastic limitation of case universals is underivable from external functional criteria does not imply that these are innate.

The totality of these problems becomes incomprehensible if one hypostatizes the syntactic being with the expressed automatisms.

NOTES

Introduction
Massimo Piattelli-Palmarini

1. Gerald Holton, *Thematic Origins of Scientific Thought* (Cambridge, Mass.: Harvard University Press, 1973), p. 26.

2. Ibid., p. 57.

3. Ibid., p. 28.

4. See, for example, P. G. Richmond, *An Introduction to Piaget* (London: Routledge and Kegan Paul, 1970), and J. H. Flavell, *The Developmental Psychology of Jean Piaget* (New York: Van Nostrand, 1963).

5. Jean Piaget, *Biology and Knowledge* (1967; Chicago: University of Chicago Press, 1974).

6. Ibid., p. 26.

7. Ibid.

8. Ibid., pp. 164–165.

9. Yehuda Elkana, ed., "Boltzmann's Scientific Research Program and Its Alternatives," in *The Interaction Between Science and Philosophy* (Atlantic Highlands, N.J.: Humanities Press, 1974).

10. Yehuda Elkana, *The Discovery of the Conservation of Energy* (Cambridge, Mass.: Harvard University Press, 1974), p. 128.

11. J. Lorch, "The Charisma of Crystals in Biology," in *The Interaction Between Science and Philosophy.*

12. A. Weismann, *Studies in the Theory of Descent* (London, 1882), quoted in J. Lorch, "The Charisma of Crystals in Biology," pp. 458–459.

13. E. Schroedinger, *What Is Life?* (Cambridge: Cambridge University Press, 1945).

14. Heinz von Foerster, "On Self-organizing Systems and Their Environments," in *Self-organizing Systems*, ed. M. Yovitz and S. E. Cameron (Elmsford, N.Y.: Pergamon Press, 1960).

15. A caveat must, however, be entered here: in qualifying the Chomskian philosophy of language and mind as "rational" or rationalist, we do not imply that descriptive linguistics or functionalism

or Piaget's constructivism or even behaviorism are "irrational." The program of classical rationalism is not to be seen as opposed to unreasonable alternative strategies of inquiry, but rather as opposed to environmentalism, be it in the guise of empiricism, associationism, behaviorism, or following more modern pragmatic fashions.

16. J. Lorch, "The Charisma of Crystals in Biology," p. 449.

17. Ibid.

18. M. J. Schleiden, quoted in J. Lorch, "The Charisma of Crystals in Biology," p. 452.

19. Imre Lakatos, "Falsification and the Methodology of Scientific Research Programmes," in *Criticism and the Growth of Knowledge*, ed. I. Lakatos and A. Musgrave (Cambridge: Cambridge University Press, 1970), p. 135.

20. Noam Chomsky, *Aspects of a Theory of Syntax* (Cambridge, Mass.: MIT Press, 1965), p. 53.

21. Ibid., p. 33.

22. Ibid., p. 18.

23. Ibid., p. 4.

24. See also Chomsky's *Reflections on Language* (New York: Pantheon, 1975).

25. Molecular geneticists are presently grappling with the equivalent problem of how genetic information directs its own expression through multiple self-correcting mechanisms.

26. Presented in a systematic way in his *Syntactic Structures* (The Hague: Mouton, 1957).

27. Jerry A. Fodor, *The Language of Thought* (Cambridge, Mass.: Harvard University Press, 1979), p. 27.

1. Opening the Debate
The Psychogenesis of Knowledge and Its Epistemological Significance
Jean Piaget

1. Considering the number of these additions and not only their result.

2. Let us recall that completive generalization is a constructive process essential in mathematics: for example, the transition from passages of groupoids to semigroups, then from there to monoids, then to groups, to rings, and to bodies.

3. It is true that autoregulation is in part innate, but more in terms of functioning than in terms of structures.

4. H. von Foerster, "On Self-organizing Systems and Their Environments," in *Self-organizing Systems*, ed. M. Yovitz and S. E. Cameron (Elmsford, N.Y.: Pergamon Press, 1960).

5. J. Piaget, *Adaptation vitale et psychologie de l'intelligence: Sélection organique et phénocopie* (Paris: Hermann, 1974).

6. G. Holton, *Thematic Origins of Scientific Thought* (Cambridge, Mass.: Harvard University Press, 1973), p. 102.

On Cognitive Structures and Their Development
Noam Chomsky

1. See, for example, my *Essays on Form and Interpretation* (Amsterdam: Elsevier/North Holland, 1977); or *Reflections on Language* (New York: Pantheon, 1975).

2. C. F. Feldman and S. Toulmin, "Logic and the Theory of Mind," in *Nebraska Symposium on Motivation, 1975,* ed. W. J. Arnold (Lincoln, Nebr.: University of Nebraska Press, 1977), pp. 409–476.

2. About the Fixed Nucleus and Its Innateness
Introductory Remarks
Jean Piaget

1. P. H. Mussen, ed., *Carmichael's Manual of Child Psychology* (New York: Wiley, 1970).

2. W. Wickler, "Vergleigende Verhaltensforschung und Phylogenetik," in G. Heberer, *Die Evolution der Organismen,* vol. 1 (Stuttgart: Fisher, 1967).

3. R. W. Brown, *Psycholinguistics: Selected Papers by Roger Brown* (New York: Free Press, 1970).

4. E. E. Lenneberg, *Biological Foundations of Language* (New York: Wiley, 1967); see also "On Explaining Language," *Science* 164:635–643, 1969.

5. D. McNeill, in *Sentences as Biological Systems,* ed. P. Weiss (1971), pp. 59–68.

6. J. M. Baldwin, *Dictionary of Philosophy and Psychology* (Gloucester, Mass.: Smith, 1960).

7. A. Szeminska, in J. Piaget et al., *Etudes d'épistémologie génétique,* vol. 27, *La Transmission des mouvements* (Paris: Presses Universitaires de France, 1972).

8. C. Waddington, *The Evolution of an Evolutionist* (Ithaca, N.Y.: Cornell University Press, 1975).

9. In Lake Geneva, at a depth of 900 feet, lives a small Limnea that appears to be completely different from any littoral species. As recently as a few years ago, when we were able to obtain live specimens and raise them in an aquarium, there was an immediate return to the initial type. In that particular case, we were dealing only with a phenotypic variation that recurred in each generation, with no necessity for genotypic reconstruction.

10. A. Belestrieri, D. De Martis, and O. Siciliani, eds., *Etologia e Psichiatria* (Rome: Laterza, 1974).

Discussion

1. P. Weiss, *Hierarchically Organized Systems in Theory and Practice* (New York: Hafner, 1971).

2. E. Mayr, *Animal Species and Evolution* (Cambridge, Mass.: Harvard University Press, 1963).

3. The metaphor has been analyzed with considerable acuity, in its political forms, by Garry Wills in his *Nixon Agonistes: The Crisis of the Self-Made Man* (New York: Signet, 1969).

Cognitive Strategies in Problem Solving
Guy Cellérier

1. N. Chomsky and G. Miller, "Introduction to the Formal Analysis of Natural Languages," in R. D. Luce, R. R. Bush, and E. Galanter, eds., *Handbook of Mathematical Psychology* (New York: Wiley, 1963), vol. 2, p. 276.

2. Ibid., p. 277.

3. M. Minsky, "Steps towards Artificial Intelligence," in E. A. Feigenbaum and J. Feldman, eds., *Computers and Thought* (New York: McGraw-Hill, 1963), p. 410.

3. Artificial Intelligence and General Developmental Mechanisms
The Role of Artificial Intelligence in Psychology
Seymour Papert

1. Noam Chomsky, "A Review of Skinner's *Verbal Behavior*," *Language* 35:26–28, 1959.

2. Jean Piaget and Alina Szeminska, *La Genèse du nombre chez l'enfant* (Neuchâtel: Delachaux et Niestlé, 1941).

3. Herbert Simon, *Sciences of the Artificial* (Cambridge, Mass.: MIT Press, 1970).

4. See M. Minsky, ed., *Semantic Information Processing* (Cambridge, Mass.: MIT Press, 1969); P. Winston, ed., *The Psychology of Computer Vision* (New York: McGraw-Hill, 1975); and S. Papert, *Mindstorms: Computers, Children, and Powerful Ideas* (New York: Basic Books, forthcoming).

Discussion

1. N. Chomsky, "Three Models for the Description of Language," in *I.R.E. Transactions on Information Theory*, vol. IT-2, 1956.

2. N. Chomsky, *Syntactic Structures* (The Hague: Mouton, 1957).

4. Initial States and Steady States
The Linguistic Approach
Noam Chomsky

1. P. Suppes, "Stimulus-Response Theory of Finite Automata," *Journal of Mathematical Psychology* 6:327–355, 1969.

2. T. N. Wiesel and D. H. Hubel, *Journal of Neurophysiology* 26:1003, 1963; 28:1029, 1060, 1965; *Journal of Physiology* 206:419, 1970.

5. Cognitive Schemes and Their Possible Relations to Language Acquisition
Language and Knowledge in a Constructivist Framework
Bärbel Inhelder

I thank Mrs. Annette Karmiloff-Smith for her valuable collaboration in the preparation of this paper.

1. N. Chomsky, "A Review of B. F. Skinner's *Verbal Behavior*," in *The Structure of Language: Readings in the Philosophy of Language*, ed. J. Fodor and J. Katz (Englewood Cliffs, N.J.: Prentice-Hall, 1964).

2. N. Chomsky, *Reflections on Language* (New York: Pantheon, 1975).

3. J. Piaget, "Language and Thought from the Genetic Viewpoint," in *Six Psychological Studies*, ed. D. Elkind (1966; New York: Random House, 1968).

4. R. W. Brown, *A First Language: The Early Stages* (Cambridge, Mass.: Harvard University Press, 1973), p. 200.

5. H. Sinclair, "Sensorimotor Action Patterns as a Condition for the Acquisition of Syntax," in *Language Acquisition: Models and Methods*, ed. R. Huxley and E. Ingram (New York: Academic Press, 1971).

6. J. S. Bruner, "From Communication to Language: A Psychological Perspective," *Cognition* 3:255–287, 1975.

7. Sinclair, "Sensorimotor Action Patterns," p. 126; H. Sinclair and J. P. Bronckart, "SVO—A Linguistic Universal? A Study in Developmental Psycholinguistics," *Journal of Experimental Child Psychology* 14:329–348, 1972.

8. Piaget, "Language and Thought from the Genetic Viewpoint," p. 98.

9. A. Karmiloff-Smith, "Dévelopment cognitif et acquisition de la plurifonctionnalité des déterminants," in *Genèse de la parole* (Paris: Presses Universitaires de France, 1976).

10. H. Sinclair and E. Ferreiro, "Production et répétition des phrases au mode passif," *Arch. Psychol.* 40:1–42, 1970; A. Sinclair, H. Sinclair, and O. Marcellus, "Young Children's Comprehension and Production of Passive Sentences," *Arch. Psychol.* 41:1–22, 1971.

11. E. Ferreiro, *Les Relations temporelles dans le langage de l'enfant* (Paris: Droz, 1971).

12. J. P. Bronckart, *Genèse et organisation des formes verbales chez l'enfant: de l'aspect au temps* (Brussels: Dessart and Mardaga, 1976).

13. B. Inhelder, H. Sinclair, and M. Bovet, *Apprentissage des structures de la connaissance* (Paris: Presses Universitaires de France, 1974).

14. A. Karmiloff-Smith, "The Interplay between Syntax, Semantics and Phonology in Language Acquisition Processes," in *Proceedings of the Stirling Conference on the Psychology of Language* (London: Plenum Press, 1976).

15. Sinclair, "Sensorimotor Action Patterns," p. 204.

16. R. F. Cromer, "The Development of Language and Cognition: The Cognition Hypothesis," in *New Perspectives in Child Develop-*

ment, ed. B. Foss (Harmondsworth, Middlesex: Penguin Books, 1974), pp. 184–252.

6. On the Impossibility of Acquiring "More Powerful" Structures
Fixation of Belief and Concept Acquisition
Jerry Fodor

1. The argument outlined here is given in detail in J. Fodor, *The Language of Thought* (Cambridge, Mass.: Harvard University Press, 1979).

Discussion

1. Patrick H. Winston, ed., *The Psychology of Computer Vision* (New York: McGraw-Hill, 1975).

2. Herbert A. Simon, *Sciences of the Artificial* (Cambridge, Mass.: MIT Press, 1970).

3. Gregory Bateson, *Steps to an Ecology of Mind* (New York: Chandler, 1972).

4. Anthony Wilden, "Ecology, Ideology, and Political Economy," unpublished paper, 1975.

7. Language within Cognition
Schemes of Action and Language Learning
Jean Piaget

1. I was able to observe a beginning of this symbolic function in two of my children. First, in one of my daughters: I showed her a half-opened box of matches, and while she watched I put an object in it (a thimble; I must specify that it was not something to eat, and we shall see why). The child tried to open the box to reach the object that was inside. She pulled on all sides, but nothing happened; finally she stopped, looked at the box, and opened and closed her mouth. This was the symbolization of what she had to do (since there was nothing good to eat inside). A new fact confirmed this interpretation: I repeated the experiment four years later with my son, at the same age, and he, instead of opening and closing his mouth when he did not succeed in opening the box, looked at the slit and at his hand, and then opened and closed his hand. It was, therefore, the same symbolization. This time, the hand was used instead of the mouth, but one immediately sees that it is again the representation of the goal to be reached (besides, once this evocation was over, he stuck his finger in the slit and started to pull). The two children, four years apart, resolved the problem only after this symbolic evocation.

2. The first symbolic play I observed was in one of my daughters. This child, in order to fall asleep, needed to grab the corner of a cloth, and then take her thumb and suck on it. One morning, when she was wide awake in her crib, her mother took her in her bed. The girl did not want to go back to sleep and remained sitting in bed, but she

noticed a corner of the sheet, took it in her hand, put her thumb in her mouth, and then bent her head and closed her eyes. She made believe she was asleep while smiling and without lying down. This time, she imitated herself; she imitated the whole ritual that she used every night to fall asleep. This is an example of symbolic play; several days later, there was a huge proliferation, and the symbolic play became much more complex.

Discussion

1. D. Sperber, *Rethinking Symbolism* (Cambridge: Cambridge University Press, 1975).

2. Hermine Sinclair de Zwart, *Acquisition du langage at développement de la pensée* (Paris: Dunod, 1967).

3. Carol Chomsky, *The Acquisition of Syntax in Children from 5 to 10* (Cambridge, Mass.: MIT Press, 1964).

4. P. E. Kramer, E. Koff and Z. Luria, "The Development of Competence in an Exceptional Language Structure in Older Children and Young Adults," *Child Development* 43:121–130, 1972.

5. N. Chomsky and G. Miller, "Finitary Models for Language Users," in R. D. Luce, R. R. Bush, and E. Galanter, eds., *Handbook of Mathematical Psychology*, vol. 2 (New York: Wiley, 1963).

6. A. R. Gardner and B. T. Gardner, "L'Enseignement du langage des sourds-muets à Washoe," in *L'Unité de l'Homme* (Paris: Le Seuil, 1974), pp. 32–36.

7. A. V. Glass, M. S. Gazzaniga, and D. Premack, "Artificial Language Training in Global Aphasics," *Neuropsychologia* 13:95–104, 1975.

8. G. Ettlinger, H. L. Teuber and B. Miller, "Report: The Seventeenth International Symposium of Neuropsychology," *Neuropsychologia* 13:125–134, 1975.

8. Properties of the Neuronal Network
Genetic Determinism and Epigenesis of the Neuronal Network:
Is There a Biological Compromise between Chomsky and Piaget?
Jean-Pierre Changeux

1. R. M. Yerkes, *The Dancing Mouse* (New York, Macmillan, 1907).

2. R. L. Sidman, "Contact Interaction Among Developing Mammalian Brain Cells," in *The Cell Surface in Development,* ed. A. A. Moscona (New York: Wiley, 1974), pp. 221–253.

3. S. Kaufman, in *Science* 181:310–318, 1973.

4. L. Wolpert and J. H. Lewis, in *Federation Proceedings* 34:14–20, 1975.

5. R. W. Sperry, in R. L. De Haan and H. Ursprung, *Organogenesis* (New York, Holt, Rinehart and Winston, 1965), pp. 161–186.

6. M. Jacobson, *Developmental Neurobiology* (New York: Holt, Rinehart and Winston, 1970).

7. R. Gaze, *The Formation of Nerve Connections* (New York: Academic Press, 1970).

8. S. Ramon y Cajal, *Studies on Vertebrate Neurogenesis* (Springfield, Ill.: Thomas, 1929).

9. J.-P. Changeux, P. Courrège and A. Danchin, in *Proceedings of the National Academy of Sciences, U.S.A.* 70:2976–2978, 1973.

10. F. Levinthal, E. Macagno, and C. Levinthal, in *Cold Spring Harbor Symposia on Quantitative Biology* 49:321–332, 1976.

11. Ramon y Cajal, *Vertebrate Neurogenesis*.

12. J. Mehler, "Connaître par désapprentissage," in *L'Unité de l'homme*, ed. E. Morin and M. Piatelli-Palmarini (Paris: Editions du Seuil, 1974), pp. 287–300.

13. D. H. Hubel and T. N. Wiesel, in *Proceedings of the Royal Society; Series B: Biological Sciences* 198:1–59, 1977.

14. H. B. Barlow, in *Nature* 258:199–204, 1975.

15. M. Imbert and P. Buissaret, in *Experimental Brain Research* 22:25–36, 1975.

16. H. Hyden and P. Lange, in F. O. Schmitt, *The Neurosciences, Second Study Program* (New York: Rockefeller University Press, 1970), pp. 278–289.

17. G. Ungar, in *International Review of Neurobiology* 13:223–233, 1970.

18. L. Szilard, in *Proceedings of the National Academy of Sciences, U.S.A.* 51:1092, 1964.

19. M. Kimura, in *Nature* 217:624–626, 1968; see also J. M. Thoday, in *Nature* 255:675–677, 1975.

Discussion

1. P. Weiss, *Hierarchically Organized Systems in Theory and Practice* (New York: Hafner, 1971).

2. M. Imbert and P. Buissaret, in *Experimental Brain Research* 22:25–36, 1975.

9. Interspecies Comparisons of Cognitive Abilities
Representational Capacity and Accessibility of Knowledge:
The Case of Chimpanzees
David Premack

1. See, for example, R. Hinde, *The Biological Bases of Human Social Behavior* (New York: McGraw-Hill, 1974).

2. See, for example, P. Lieberman, "The Evolution of Speech and Language," in *The Role of Speech in Language*, ed. J. F. Kavanaugh and J. E. Cutting (Cambridge, Mass.: MIT Press, 1975); and P. C. Reynolds, "Play and Evolution of Language" (Ph.D. dissertation, Yale University, 1972).

3. N. Geschwind, "The Development of the Brain and the Evolution of Language," in *Monograph Series on Language and Linguistics*, ed. C. I. J. M. Stuart (Washington, D.C.: Georgetown University Press, 1964), pp. 155–169.

4. R. K. Davenport and C. M. Rogers, "Perception of Photographs by Apes," *Behavior* 39:2–4, 1971.

5. A. Cowey and L. Weiskrantz, "Demonstration of Cross-Modal Matching in Rhesus Monkeys, *Macaca Mulatta*," *Neuropsychologia* 13:117–120, 1975.

6. P. D. Eimas and J. D. Corbit, "Selective Adaptation of Linguistic Features Detectors," *Cognitive Psychology* 4:99–109, 1973.

7. P. A. Morse and C. T. Snowden, "An Investigation of Categorical Speech Discrimination by Rhesus Monkeys," *Perception and Psychophysics* 17:9–16, 1975.

8. P. K. Kuhl and J. D. Miller, "Speech Perception by the Chinchilla: Voiced-Voiceless Distinction in Alveolar Plosive Consonants," *Science* 190:69–72, 1975; C. K. Burdick and J. C. Miller, "Speech Perception by the Chinchilla: Discrimination of Sustained /a/ and /i/," *Journal of the Acoustical Society of America* 58:415–427, 1975.

9. J. E. Cutting and B. S. Rosner, "Categories and Boundaries in Speech and Music," *Perception and Psychophysics* 16:564–570, 1974.

10. M. Lemay, "Morphological Cerebral Asymmetries of Modern Man, Fossil Man, and Non-Human Primate," in *Origins and Evolution of Language and Speech*, ed. S. R. Harnad, H. D. Steklis, and J. Lancaster (New York: New York Academy of Sciences, 1976).

11. G. Gallup, "Chimpanzees: Self-recognition," *Science* 167:86–87, 1970.

12. E. W. Menzel, "Chimpanzee Spatial Memory Organization," *Science* 182:943–945, 1973.

13. D. S. Olton and R. J. Samuelson, "Remembrance of Places Passed: Spatial Memory in Rats," *Journal of Experimental Psychology: Animal Behavior Processes* 2:97–116, 1976.

14. J. J. A. van Iersel and J. van den Assam, "Aspects of Orientation in the Digger Wasp, *Bembix Rostrats*," *Animal Behaviour [Suppl.]* 1:145–162, 1969.

15. O. L. Tinklepaugh, "Multiple Delayed Reactions with Chimpanzees and Monkeys," *Journal of Comparative Psychology* 13:207–243, 1932.

Discussion

1. M. M. Stambak and H. Sinclair, in *Bulletin du CRESAS*, no. 14, 1976.

10. Phylogenesis and Cognition

Remarks on Lorenz and Piaget: How Can "Working Hypotheses" be
"Necessary"?

Norbert Bischof

1. K. Lorenz, "Kant's Lehre vom Apriorischen im Lichte gegenwartiger Biologie," *Blätter für Deutsche Philosophie* 15:104, 1941.

2. J. Y. Lettvin, H. R. Maturana, W. S. Cullock, and W. H. Pitts, "What the Frog's Eye Tells the Frog's Brain," *Proceedings of the I.R.E.* 47:1940–1951, 1959.

11. Cognition and the Semiotic Function
Remarks on the Lack of Positive Contributions from Anthropologists to the Problem of Innateness
Dan Sperber

1. D. Sperber, *Rethinking Symbolism* (Cambridge: Cambridge University Press, 1975); see also "Rudiments de rhétorique cognitive," *Poétique* 23:389–415, 1975.

Discussion
1. M. Levine, "Hypothesis Theory and Non-learning Despite Ideal S-R Reinforcement Contingencies," *Psychological Review* 78:130–140, 1971.

12. The Inductivist Fallacy
Statement of the Paradox
Noam Chomsky and Jerry Fodor

1. Nelson Goodman, *Fact, Fiction and Forecast* (2nd ed.) (Indianapolis, Ind.: Bobbs-Merrill, 1965).
2. Carl G. Hempel, *Aspects of Scientific Explanation* (New York: Free Press, Collier-Macmillan, 1965).

Discussion

1. J. Fodor, *The Language of Thought* (Cambridge, Mass.: Harvard University Press, 1979).

13. Afterthoughts and Clarifications
Steering a Way between Constructivism and Innatism
Stephen Toulmin

1. C. F. Feldman and S. Toulmin, "Logic and the Theory of Mind," in *Nebraska Symposium on Motivation, 1975*, ed. W. J. Arnold (Lincoln, Nebr.: University of Nebraska Press, 1977), pp. 409–476.
2. T. G. R. Bower, *A Primer of Infant Development* (San Francisco: Freeman, 1977).
3. On this and other related problems, see my discussion in, for example, *Human Understanding*, sec. 7.2 (Oxford: Clarendon Press, 1972).

Afterthoughts
Jean Piaget

1. The inaugural lecture was held on January 16, 1976, at the Collège de France, Chair of Cellular Communications.
2. J. Piaget, *Le Comportement moteur de l'évolution* (Paris: Gallimard, 1976).
3. W. S. McCulloch and W. Pitts, "A Logical Calculus of the Ideas Immanent in Nervous Activity," *Bulletin of Mathematics and Biophysics* 5:113–133, 1943.

4. This expression was introduced by Waddington.

5. J. Piaget, *The Development of Thought: Equilibrium of Cognitive Structures* (1975; New York: Viking Press, 1977). See also the works of H. von Foerster on autoregulation and the self-organization of living organisms in their interactions with the environment; the epistemology of this biophysicist and cybernetician culminates in a generalized constructivism to which I consider myself very close (H. von Foerster, "On Self-organizing Systems and Their Environment," in *Self-organizing Systems*, ed. M. Yovitz and S. Cameron [London: Pergamon Press, 1960]).

6. P. Weiss, *Hierarchically Organized Systems in Theory and Practice* (New York: Hafner, 1971).

14. What Is Innate and Why: Comments on the Debate
Hilary Putnam

1. Z. S. Harris, *Methods in Structural Linguistics* (Chicago: University of Chicago Press, 1951).

2. N. Chomsky, "Explanatory Models in Linguistics," in *Logic, Methodology and Philosophy of Science*, ed. E. Nagel, P. Suppes, and A. Tarsk (Stanford, Calif.: Stanford University Press, 1962).

3. Each formula can be associated with a corresponding statement expressed in ordinary language, namely, "not-A," "A and B," "A or B," "if A, then B."

4. By "declarative grammar" I mean that part of the grammar that generates the declarative sentences of the language. The usual assumption—made also by Chomsky—is that interrogatives, imperatives, and so on are somehow derived from declaratives.

5. What I have given here is a very oversimplified account of Washoe's actual abilities. The interested reader should consult the following works: B. Gardner and R. A. Gardner, "Two-Way Communication with an Infant Chimpanzee," in *Behavior of Non-Human Primates*, ed. A. Schrier and F. Stollnitz (New York and London: Academic Press, 1971), vol. 4, pp. 117—184; B. Gardner and R. A. Gardner, "Teaching Sign Language to the Chimpanzee Washoe" (16-mm sound film), State College of Pennsylvania, Psychological Cinema Register, 1974; B. Gardner and R. A. Gardner, "Comparing the Early Utterances of Child and Chimpanzee," in *Minnesota Symposia on Child Psychology*, ed. A. Pick (Minneapolis, Minn.: University of Minnesota Press, 1974); B. Gardner and R. A. Gardner, "Evidence for Sentence Constituents in the Early Utterances of Child and Chimpanzee," *Journal of Experimental Psychology: General* 104:244–267, 1975. The last of these references bears directly on Washoe's ability to learn "structure-dependent" rules.

6. See chapter 5 of my *Mind, Language, and Reality* (Cambridge: Cambridge University Press, 1975).

7. I discuss this in my 1976 John Locke Lectures, *Meaning and the Moral Sciences* (London: Routledge and Kegan Paul, 1978).

8. For an account of some of these suggestions, I recommend Stephen Gould's *Ontogeny and Phylogeny* (Cambridge, Mass.: Harvard University Press, 1977).

9. See chapter 1 of my *Mind, Language, and Reality*.

10. It is worth noting in this connection that Piaget's research method (in all but a few experiments) consists of studying *verbal* behavior.

11. J. Piaget and B. Inhelder, *The Growth of Logical Thinking from Childhood to Adolescence* (London: Routledge and Kegan Paul, 1958).

12. This is argued in my John Locke Lectures.

13. But caution is needed! As Dennett has remarked: the machine may use something that *we* call a formalized language, but this does not mean that it has our *abilities* with the formalism in question.

14. See chapter 17 of my *Mathematics, Matter, and Method* (Cambridge: Cambridge University Press, 1975).

15. This is argued by Fodor in chapter 1 of his *Language of Thought* (Cambridge, Mass.: Harvard University Press, 1979). But I find the argument there terribly unpersuasive. In particular, there is a heavy reliance on the word "must," and a disturbing looseness with notions such as "belief" and "representation system."

16. In "The Meaning of 'Meaning' " (reprinted as chapter 12 of my *Mind, Language, and Reality*) I argue that the *use* of a predicate such as "gold"—represented in this case by the subroutine S—does not determine its *extension;* the latter is determined partly by other speakers (experts to whom the speaker in question defers) and partly by the actual nature of the objects accepted as paradigms by the experts. If this is right, then the "meaning" of such a word is not *in the head* at all. (This is probably Wittgenstein's point when he says, "If God had looked into our minds, He would not have been able to see there what we were speaking of.")

17. Hans Reichenbach, *Philosophic Foundations of Quantum Mechanics* (Berkeley: University of California Press, 1948).

18. The perceptron—or the digital computer which acts as its "brain" —also keeps a record: it writes down *numbers.* But the only "transformation" it carries out—adding up the numbers (which represent local curvatures) and dividing the sum by 6π—is one that can be carried out by any pocket calculator that has a key for "π." Although there is no *sharp* boundary between computations that count as minimal uses of a language and ones that do not, this one is surely on the wrong side!

19. Notice the need for a *uniform* notation for *all A's are B's* (if any second-level inductions are to be carried out). If we attribute to the brain the ability to "put together" *all A's are B's* and *all B's are C's* and "get" *all A's are C's*, and the ability to "put together" *all A's are B's* and *this is an A* and "get" *this is a B*, then we have attributed to this uniform notation precisely the inferential powers of a *quantifier;* that is, our model for reasoning is that of formal logic (as Piaget and Inhelder urged it should be).

20. For example, if Washoe learns structure-dependent rules (as

argued in Gardner and Gardner, "Evidence for Sentence Constituents"), then she classes together signs she has *associated with* classes of things —a second-level association. And it is hard to think of any other model for *this* learning.

15. Discussion of Putnam's Comments
Noam Chomsky

1. See H. Putnam, *Mind, Language, and Reality* (Cambridge: Cambridge University Press, 1975), chapter 5.

2. See chapters 3 and 6 of my *Language and Mind*, extended edition (New York: Harcourt-Brace-Jovanovich, 1972).

3. For a quite typical example, see chapter 1, section 8 of my *Aspects of the Theory of Syntax* (Cambridge, Mass.: MIT Press, 1965).

4. See J. A. Fodor, T. G. Bever, and M. F. Garrett, *The Psychology of Language* (New York: McGraw-Hill, 1974), pp. 436 ff.

5. We might even argue that his proposal, though nearly vacuous, can indeed be assessed, and rejected. The sole content of his proposal, as it stands, is that the properties of S_0^L are simply "general learning mechanisms," which apply freely in all cognitive domains. But there is evidence that S_0^L contains mechanisms and structures for which it is difficult to find even a vague analogue outside of language, for example, the specific principles of transformational grammar postulated to explain the structure dependence of rules (and much else). Consequently, the belief that the properties of S_0^L are in fact "general learning mechanisms" is quite implausible with regard to its minimal empirical content.

6. For example, when he asserts that "p & ~ p" is "deviant for semantic reasons," and "would not be 'uttered' for obvious semantic reasons." It is not deviant at all, and might well be "uttered" as a line in any proof by *reductio ad absurdum*.

7. See, for example, Otto Jespersen, *The Philosophy of Grammar* (London: Allen & Unwin, 1924); and for some recent discussion, my "Questions of Form and Interpretation," *Linguistic Analysis*, vol. 1, no. 1, 1975.

8. See Putnam's *Mind, Languages, and Reality*, volume 2, chapter 4.

9. Perhaps Putnam means that the learning of grammar is "dependent on" the learning of semantics in the sense that semantics provides the goal or motive for the learning of syntax. But if this is what he has in mind, the argument again fails, since as already noted, there is no problem in stating the semantics with the structure-independent rule.

10. See chapter 1 of my *Reflections on Language* (New York: Pantheon, 1975).

11. Putnam, *Mind, Language, and Reality*, chapter 5.

12. See chapters 1 and 4 of my *Reflections on Language* for some discussion.

16. Reply to Putnam
Jerry Fodor

1. J. Fodor, *The Language of Thought* (Cambridge, Mass.: Harvard University Press, 1979).
2. Ibid., p. 61.
3. Ibid, pp. 28–34.

17. Comments on Chomsky's and Fodor's Replies
Hilary Putnam

1. N. Chomsky, *Problems of Knowledge and Freedom: The Russell Lectures* (New York: Random House, 1972).
2. I would like to discuss all of his points, but I have been asked by the editor to keep this discussion short.

18. Psychology and Psycholinguistics: The Impact of Chomsky and Piaget
Jacques Mehler

1. See J. J. Katz, "Language and Other Abstract Objects: An Essay," in preparation.
2. The constructions of Hull are representative of this point of view. He set about enforcing his hypothetico-deductive model—completely abstract, in fact—by giving a behavioral name to each of his variables (habit, strength, and so on). See C. Hull, *Principles of Behavior* (New York: Appleton-Century, 1943).
3. Katz, "Language and Other Abstract Objects."
4. Z. Pylyshyn, "Competence and Performance," *Journal of Psycholinguistic Research* 2:21–50, 1973.
5. This term is used with the meaning given it by Sperber (see Chapter 11).
6. Katz, "Language and Other Abstract Objects."
7. H. Sinclair, "Language Acquisition and the Development of Thought."
8. T. G. Bever, "The Cognitive Basis for Linguistic Structures," in *Cognition and the Development of Language,* ed. J. R. Hayes (New York: Wiley, 1970).
9. J. Piaget and B. Inhelder, *La Psychologie de l'enfant* (Paris: Presses Universitaires de France, 1966), p. 78.
10. D. Osherson, personal communication.
11. The following simple and most instructive experiment can be performed by anyone on adults: using the forefingers and the thumbs of both hands, stretch a loop of string and, by adjusting the position of the four fingers, shape it into a square; then by progressively approaching each forefinger to its opposing thumb while simultaneously keeping the string well extended, form a rectangle of progressively decreasing height and progressively increasing width. The majority of

adults, if asked whether the area so delimited has varied as a consequence of the transition from the square to the rectangle, will respond that it remains constant. A certain number of them only realize their mistake, suddenly, when the experimenter reaches the limit, that is, at the moment when the whole area disappears because the experimenter stretches the string to the point where it constitutes no more than a line.

12. P. Bryant, *Perception and Understanding in Young Children* (London: Methuen, 1974).

13. J. Mehler and T. G. Bever, "Cognitive Capacity of Very Young Children," *Science* 158:141–142, 1967; "Quantification, Conservation and Nativism," *Science* 162:979–981, 1968; and J. Mehler, "Le développement des heuristiques perceptives chez le très jeune enfant," in *Neuropsychologie de la perception visuelle*, ed H. Hécaen (Paris: Masson, 1971), pp. 154–167.

14. T. G. R. Bower, in *Scientific American*, November 1976.

15. See C. Trevarthen, P. Hubley, and L. Sheeran, "Les activités innées du nourrisson," *La Recherche*, vol. 75, 1975.

16. See A. N. Meltzoff, "Imitation of Facial and Manual Gestures by Human Neonates," *Science* 198:75–78, 1977.

17. See M. Borenstein, W. Kessen, and S. Weiskopf, "The Categories of Hue in Infancy," *Science* 191:201–202, 1976.

18. See T. G. R. Bower, *A Primer of Infant Development* (San Francisco: Freeman, 1977).

19. E. Noirot, personal communication.

20. J. Bertoncini and J. Mehler, "Infant Recognition of Rhythms," in preparation.

21. See P. Mounoud and T. G. R. Bower, "Conservation of Weight in Infants," *Cognition* 3, 1:29–40, 1974–75.

22. See M. H. Bornstein, C. G. Gross, and J. C. Wolf, "Perceptual Similarity in Mirror Images in Infancy," *Cognition* 6, 2:89–116, 1978.

23. N. Chomsky, "A Review of Skinner's *Verbal Behavior*," *Language* 35:26–28, 1959.

24. D. Osherson and T. Wasow, "Task Specificity and Species Specificity in the Study of Language: A Methodological Note," *Cognition* 4:203–214, 1976.

25. J. Piaget, *Introduction à l'épistémologie génétique* (Paris: Presses Universitaires de France, 1949), vol. 1, p. 13.

Appendix A
A Critical Note on the Use of the Term "Phenocopy"
Antoine Danchin

1. T. Lysenko, *Agrobiologie* (Moscow: Editions de Moscou, 1953), pp. 171, 242, 404.

2. See also J. Piaget, *Biology and Knowledge* (1967; Chicago: University of Chicago Press, 1974).

3. S. E. Luria and Delbrück, "Mutations of Bacteria from Virus Sensitivity to Virus Resistance," *Genetics* 28:491, 1943.

4. G. S. Stent, *Molecular Genetics: An Introductory Narrative* (San Francisco: Freeman, 1971.

5. F. Jacob and J. Monod, "Genetic Regulatory Mechanisms in the Synthesis of Proteins," *Journal of Molecular Biology* 3:318, 1961.

6. This initial state can itself originate from the constraints of a strict program; individual variations then result from outstanding stochastic fluctuations, if a *small* number of components account for the initial state.

Appendix B
The Genesis of Representational Space according to Piaget
René Thom

1. The ideographic stage was, in fact, defined more precisely by Lurçat.

Reply to Thom
Jean Piaget

1. J. Piaget, *Cahiers de psychologie,* Université de Provence, 1977.

2. J. Piaget, *Origins of Intelligence in Children* (New York: International Universities Press, 1966).

3. J. Piaget, *The Grasp of Consciousness* (Cambridge, Mass.: Harvard University Press, 1976).

4. J. Piaget, *Success and Understanding* (Cambridge, Mass.: Harvard University Press, 1978).

5. J. Piaget, *Play, Dreams and Imitation in Childhood* (New York: Norton, 1962).

6. "Une heure avec Piaget," *Revue française de pédagogie*, no. 37, Oct.-Dec. 1976.

7. See J. Piaget, *Le Structuralisme,* series "Que Sais-je," no. 8 (Paris: Presses Universitaires de France, 1974).

8. See my *Epistémologie génétique et équilibration* (Neûchatel: Delachaux and Niestlé), part 3.

Appendix C
Localist Hypothesis and Theory of Catastrophes: Note on the Debate
Jean Petitot

1. This means that it is not an inherent part of the syntactic being but belongs to the formal description in terms of transformations. The formal notion of transformation requires that the input and the output (the source and the goal) be formal entities of the same type.

2. To resume Chomsky's description, if E is a sufficient corpus to know a language L, there exists an application $E \rightarrow S_s$ defining an S_s in which the grammar of L is represented. The properties of S_0 (constrained) are the properties of S_s that are not determined by E.

3. To deduce and not, of course, to describe. Formal universals are precisely described as formal rules.

4. The fault of the syllogisms produced by the Chomskian decision has been carefully noted by Fillmore with regard to the deep structures. In "The Case for Case" he asserts: "Chomsky's deep structure is an artificial level between the deep semantic structure which can be discovered empirically and the surface structure accessible to observation, a level with properties that depend more on the methodological obligations of grammarians than on the nature of human languages."

5. This disjunction is at work in all algebraic-combinatorial structural approaches; this is why there is always conflict between structure and genesis.

6. For example, the area of sensorimotor schemes or the area of symbolism.

7. Emphasis added.

8. A question of this type was resolved by von Neumann in his theorem on self-reproducing automata. In the problem of biological reproduction, the body played for a long time the role of a "black box." From this, the conclusion was drawn that the inflexibility of species was due to a cause that transcended biology. Taking as axioms the phenomenological data concerning self-reproduction of living systems, and as an apodictic principle the formal type of "finite automaton," von Neumann showed (through an *a priori* deduction) that self-reproduction requires a "genetic code"; which experience could only confirm. Curiously, Chomsky utilizes this biologically established fact as a transcendant cause of mental structures (the myth of language as organ program).

9. One may be surprised by the systematic under-evaluation of these phenomena, when they eminently show undeniable constraints (which, I repeat, does not mean indescribable) of the algebraic-combinatorial models.

10. There is, in fact, a conflict between the necessity of deducing deep cases *a priori* (since they are universals) and the methodology that gives rise to them as discriminators of sentences which, while syntactically different, have nevertheless the same syntagmatic tree. If it can be assumed that a case system cannot be formulated from surface case forms (i.e., that deep cases are of a syntactic and not a morphological nature), one is caught in the aporia of a *case interpretation* (and not of a deduction) of the deep structures.

11. At the present time, this (phylogenetic) hypothesis strikes me as being the most plausible one with respect to the genesis of basic structures.

12. One can find the list at the end of Thom's *Structural Stability and Morphogenesis: An Outline of a General Theory of Models* (Reading, Mass.: W. A. Benjamin, 1974).

13. It is for this reason that the condition that the dimension be less than four is imposed in Thom's theorem of classification.

14. To quote Chomsky, "I see no reason to doubt that . . . there are highly specific innate capacities that determine the growth of cognitive structures, some of which remain unconscious and beyond the

bounds of introspection, while others, probably quite different in kind, are explicitly articulated and put to test" (see Chapter 1).

15. See Thom's *Structural Stability and Morphogenesis*, pp. 310–315.

16. In this case again, it is only an approximation going back to Fillmore's hypothesis, namely, that in an elementary sentence there is a one-to-one correspondence between the noun phrase and the case relationship, even if the same noun phrase can be decomposed in the course of the surface projection of the stem. In particular, if several actants are joined in the same case relationship, their union is intra-case.

INDEX

"Abduction" principle, 52
Abstraction, 10; reflective and reflected, 26–28, 29, 70, 188, 281, 284, 300, 323; empirical, 27, 28
"Aha-experience," 5, 236, 237, 243
Algebraic linguistics, 103–104, 158. *See also* Mathematics
Althusser, Louis, 186
Analogy, 307
Animal Species and Evolution (Mayr), 63
Anthropology, 245–246, 249, 252, 334
Appetency behavior, 235–236
Aristopedia mutation, 191. *See also* Molecular biology
Aristotle and Aristotelian thought, 64, 75, 94, 95, 255; *antiperistasis*, 33, 34, 58
Artificial intelligence (AI), 54, 70, 87, 100, 101; MIT Laboratory of, 89; role of, in psychology (Papert's discussion of), 90–99, 250. *See also* Perceptron(s)
Artificial language, *see* Propositional calculus
Ascher, R., 370
Assimilation/accommodation, 3, 4; role of (Piaget), 24, 28–29, 31–32, 55, 58–59, 159, 163, 166, 281, 350; denial of (Chomsky), 13; "genetic," 56, 60, 63, 279; defined (by Piaget), 164–165; Lysenko on, 356

Associationism, 111, 271, 310, 327; Piaget and, 24, 55, 350; Putnam on, 302, 303, 306–308, 330–332
Atran, Scott, 221n, 227, 228; discussion by, 75, 103–105, 158, 226–227
Autoregulation theory, 3–5, 9, 16, 29–31, 57–67 *passim*, 104, 280, 283, 356

Bacon, Francis, 306
Bakunin, Mikhail, 274
Baldwin, James M., 58, 279
Barlow, H. B., 192
Bat, echo-location in, 299
Bateson, Gregory, 53, 56, 153, 230, 257, 323n; discussion by, 76–78 *passim*, 84, 222, 263–264, 266, 269
Bayesian model, 307, 308
Beadle, George W., 357
Bee, dance symbols of, 212, 215
Behavior: species-specific, 58, 242, 243; nervous system anatomy and, 187–188; adaptive, 233–234, 242–243, 281; appetency-consummation, 235–237
Behaviorism, 97, 99, 100, 241, 338; rejection of, 24, 205, 284, 351, (by Chomsky) 11, 54, 57, 96, 132, 341, 350 (by Piaget) 54, 55, 57, 96, 231, 342, 350; artificial intelligence confused with, 90–91
Belief fixation concept, *see* Fodor, Jerry A.

399